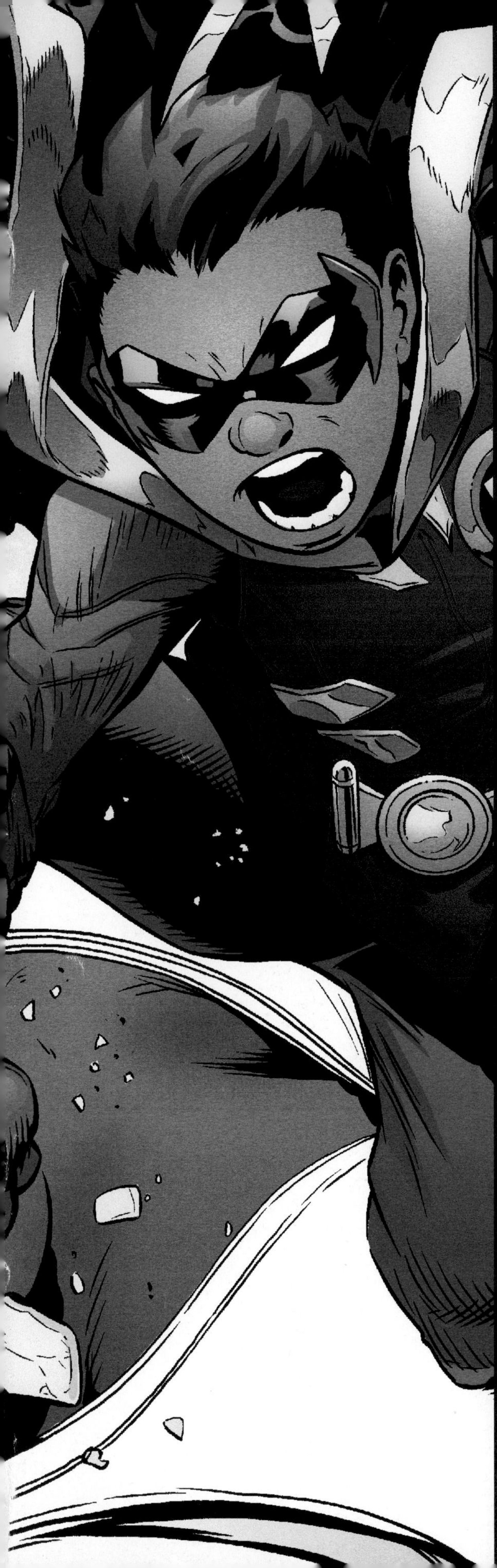

ROBIN – SON OF BATMAN

VOLUME 1

YEAR OF BLOOD

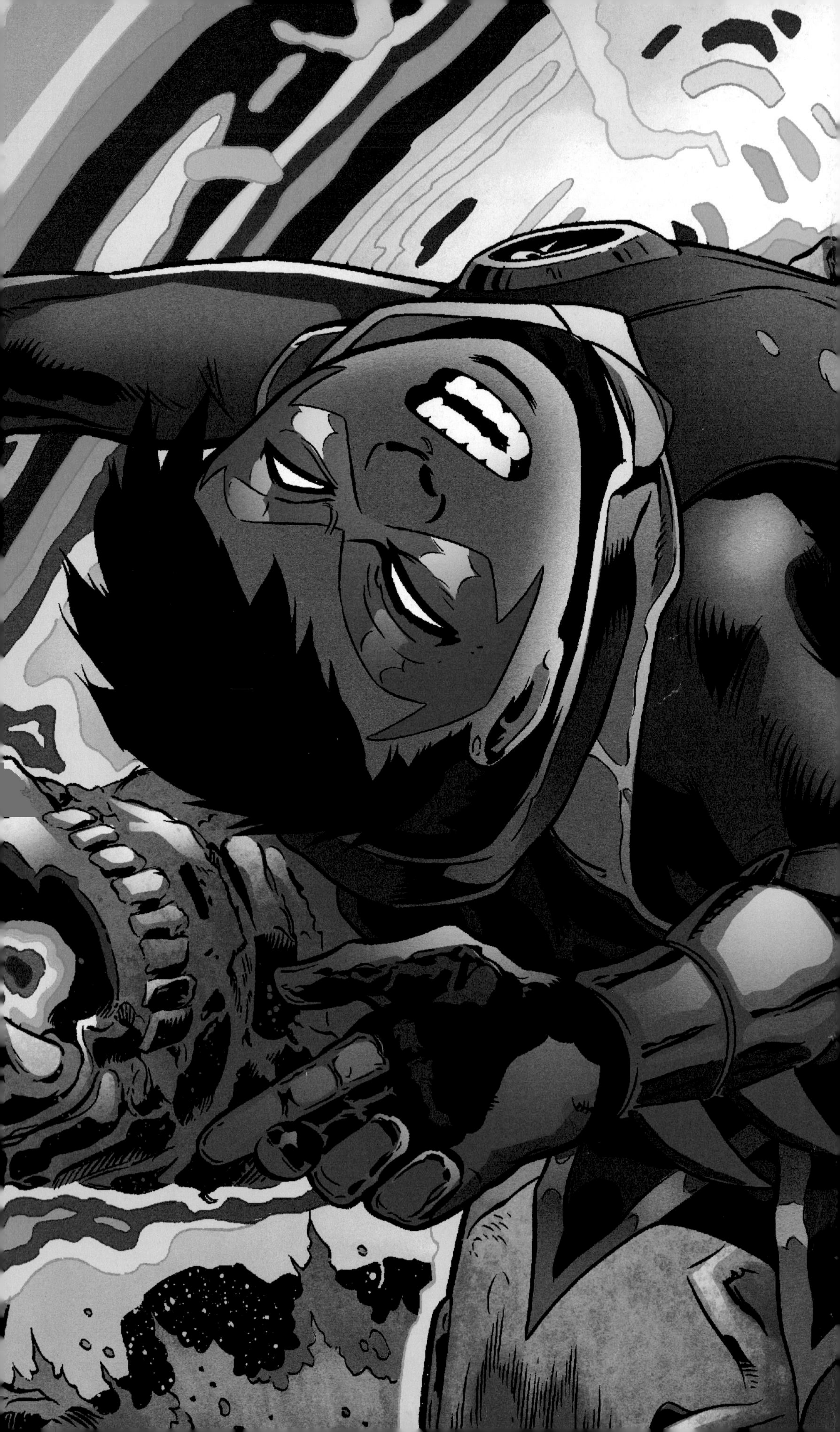

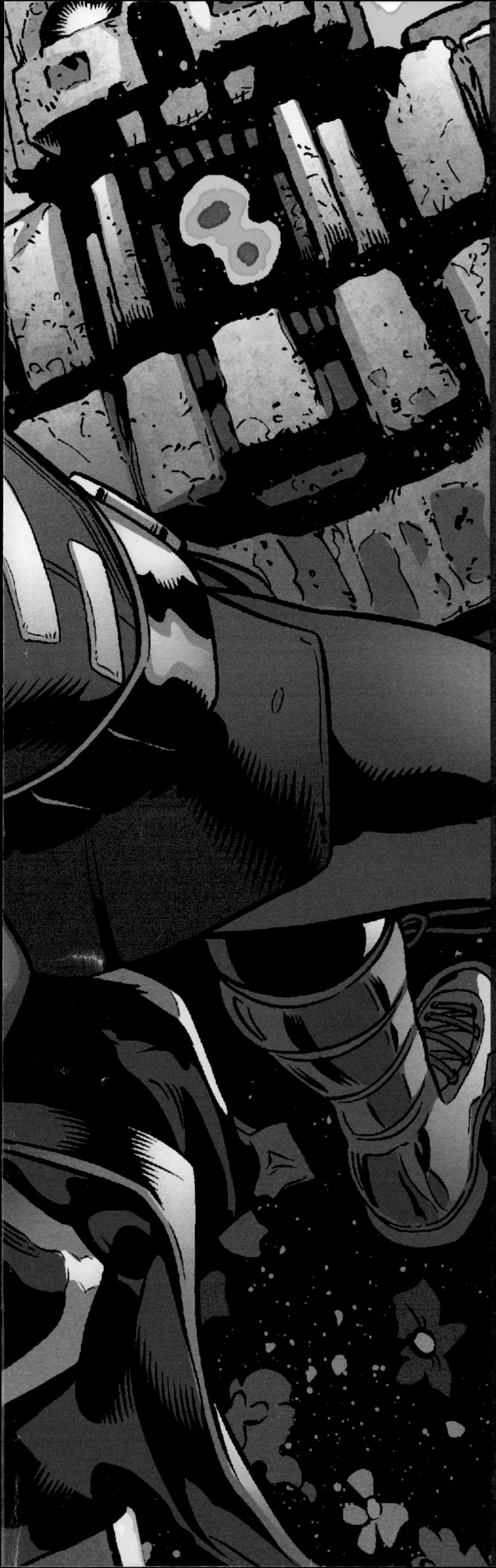

ROBIN – SON OF BATMAN

VOLUME 1
YEAR OF BLOOD

WRITTEN & PENCILLED BY
PATRICK GLEASON

INKS BY
MICK GRAY
TOM NGUYEN

COLOR BY
JOHN KALISZ
JEROMY COX

LETTERS BY
TOM NAPOLITANO
TODD KLEIN

COLLECTION COVER ARTISTS
PATRICK GLEASON,
MICK GRAY & JOHN KALISZ

BATMAN CREATED BY
BOB KANE WITH **BILL FINGER**

DEATHSTROKE CREATED BY
MARV WOLFMAN
& GEORGE PÉREZ

MARK DOYLE RACHEL GLUCKSTERN Editors – Original Series
REBECCA TAYLOR Associate Editor – Original Series
JEB WOODARD Group Editor – Collected Editions
STEVE COOK Design Director – Books
DAMIAN RYLAND Publication Design

BOB HARRAS Senior VP – Editor-in-Chief, DC Comics

DIANE NELSON President
DAN DIDIO and JIM LEE Co-Publishers
GEOFF JOHNS Chief Creative Officer
AMIT DESAI Senior VP – Marketing & Global Franchise Management
NAIRI GARDINER Senior VP – Finance
SAM ADES VP – Digital Marketing
BOBBIE CHASE VP – Talent Development
MARK CHIARELLO Senior VP – Art, Design & Collected Editions
JOHN CUNNINGHAM VP – Content Strategy
ANNE DEPIES VP – Strategy Planning & Reporting
DON FALLETTI VP – Manufacturing Operations
LAWRENCE GANEM VP – Editorial Administration & Talent Relations
ALISON GILL Senior VP – Manufacturing & Operations
HANK KANALZ Senior VP – Editorial Strategy & Administration
JAY KOGAN VP – Legal Affairs
DEREK MADDALENA Senior VP – Sales & Business Development
JACK MAHAN VP – Business Affairs
DAN MIRON VP – Sales Planning & Trade Development
NICK NAPOLITANO VP – Manufacturing Administration
CAROL ROEDER VP – Marketing
EDDIE SCANNELL VP – Mass Account & Digital Sales
COURTNEY SIMMONS Senior VP – Publicity & Communications
JIM (SKI) SOKOLOWSKI VP – Comic Book Specialty & Newsstand Sales
SANDY YI Senior VP – Global Franchise Management

ROBIN – SON OF BATMAN VOLUME 1: YEAR OF BLOOD

DC Comics, 2900 West Alameda Ave., Burbank, CA 91505
Printed by RR Donnelley, Salem, VA, USA. 2/19/16. First Printing.
ISBN: 978-1-4012-6155-9

Library of Congress Cataloging-in-Publication Data

Names: Gleason, Patrick, author. | Gray, Mick, illustrator. | Nguyen, Tom,
illustrator. | Kalisz, John, illustrator. | Napolitano, Tom, illustrator.
| Klein, Todd, illustrator.
Title: Robin, son of Batman. Volume 1, Year of blood / Patrick Gleason,
writer and penciller ; Mick Gray, Tom Nguyen, inkers ; John Kalisz,
colorist ; Tom Napolitano, Todd Klein, letterers ; Patrick Gleason, Mick
Gray & John Kalisz, collection and series covers.
Other titles: Year of blood
Description: Burbank, CA : DC Comics, [2016] | "Originally published online
as ROBIN: SON OF BATMAN SNEAK PEEK and in single magazine form as ROBIN:
SON OF BATMAN 1-6." | "Batman Created by Bob Kane with Bill Finger." |
"Deathstroke created by Marv Wolfman and George Perez."
Identifiers: LCCN 2015049453 | ISBN 9781401261559
Subjects: LCSH: Graphic novels. | Superhero comic books, strips, etc.
Classification: LCC PN6728.R576 G57 2016 | DDC 741.5/973—dc23
LC record available at http://lccn.loc.gov/2015049453

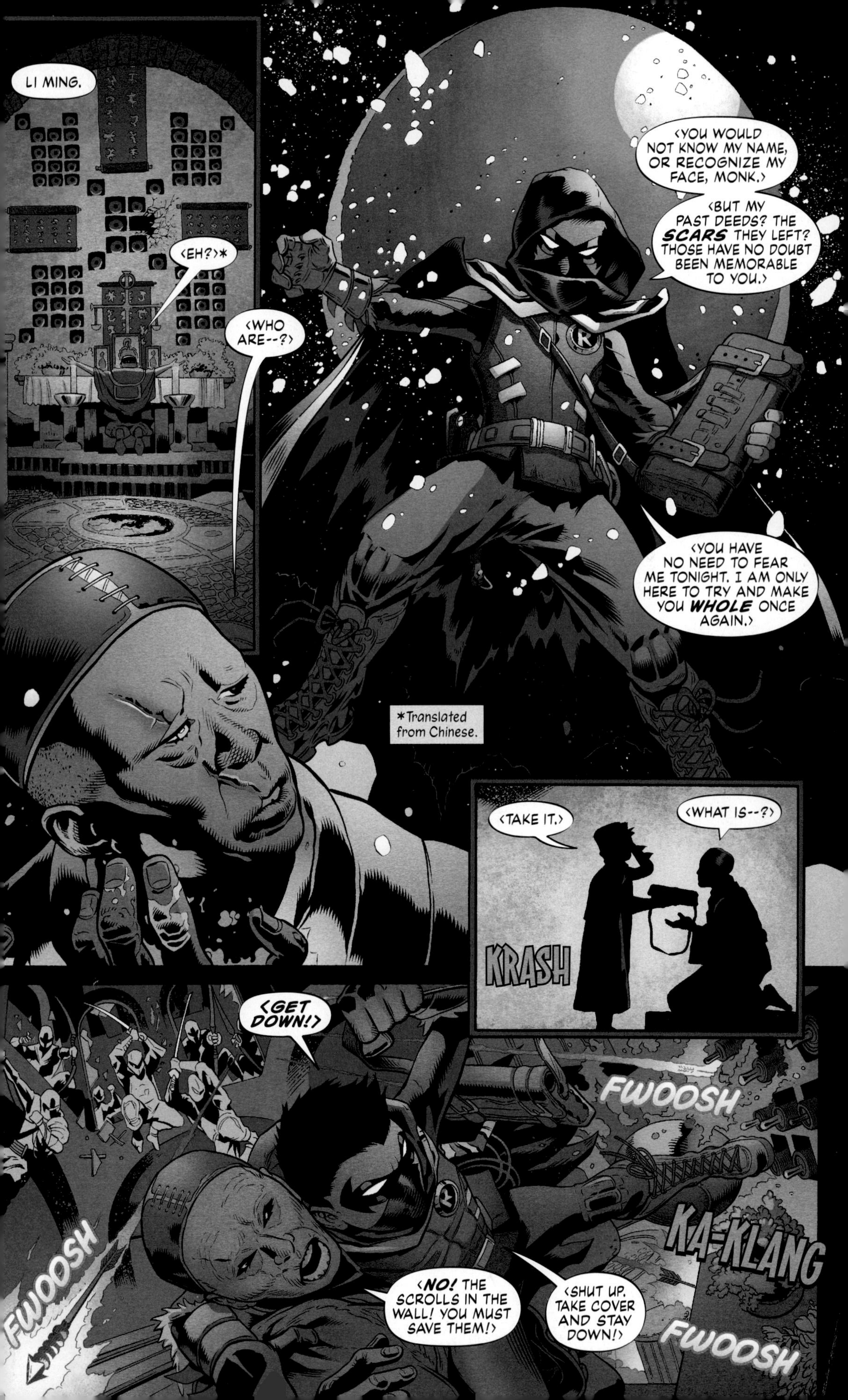
LI MING.
<YOU WOULD NOT KNOW MY NAME, OR RECOGNIZE MY FACE, MONK.>
<BUT MY PAST DEEDS? THE SCARS THEY LEFT? THOSE HAVE NO DOUBT BEEN MEMORABLE TO YOU.>
<EH?>*
<WHO ARE--?>
<YOU HAVE NO NEED TO FEAR ME TONIGHT. I AM ONLY HERE TO TRY AND MAKE YOU WHOLE ONCE AGAIN.>
*Translated from Chinese.
<TAKE IT.>
<WHAT IS--?>
KRASH
<GET DOWN!>
FWOOSH
KA-KLANG
FWOOSH
<NO! THE SCROLLS IN THE WALL! YOU MUST SAVE THEM!>
<SHUT UP. TAKE COVER AND STAY DOWN!>
FWOOSH

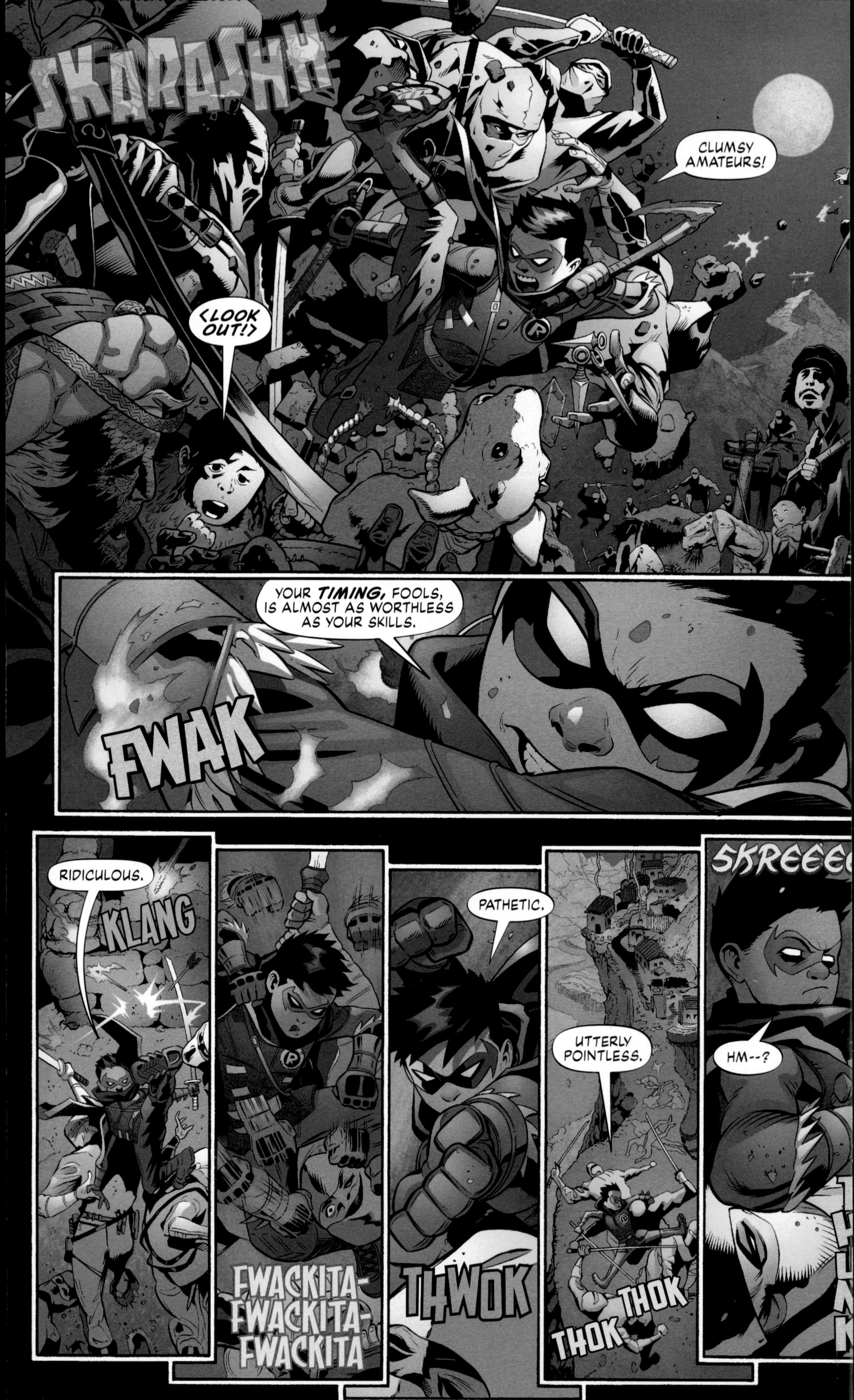
SKARASHH
CLUMSY AMATEURS!
<LOOK OUT!>
YOUR TIMING, FOOLS, IS ALMOST AS WORTHLESS AS YOUR SKILLS.
FWAK
RIDICULOUS.
KLANG
FWACKITA-FWACKITA-FWACKITA
PATHETIC.
THWOK
UTTERLY POINTLESS.
THOK THOK
SKREEE
HM--?

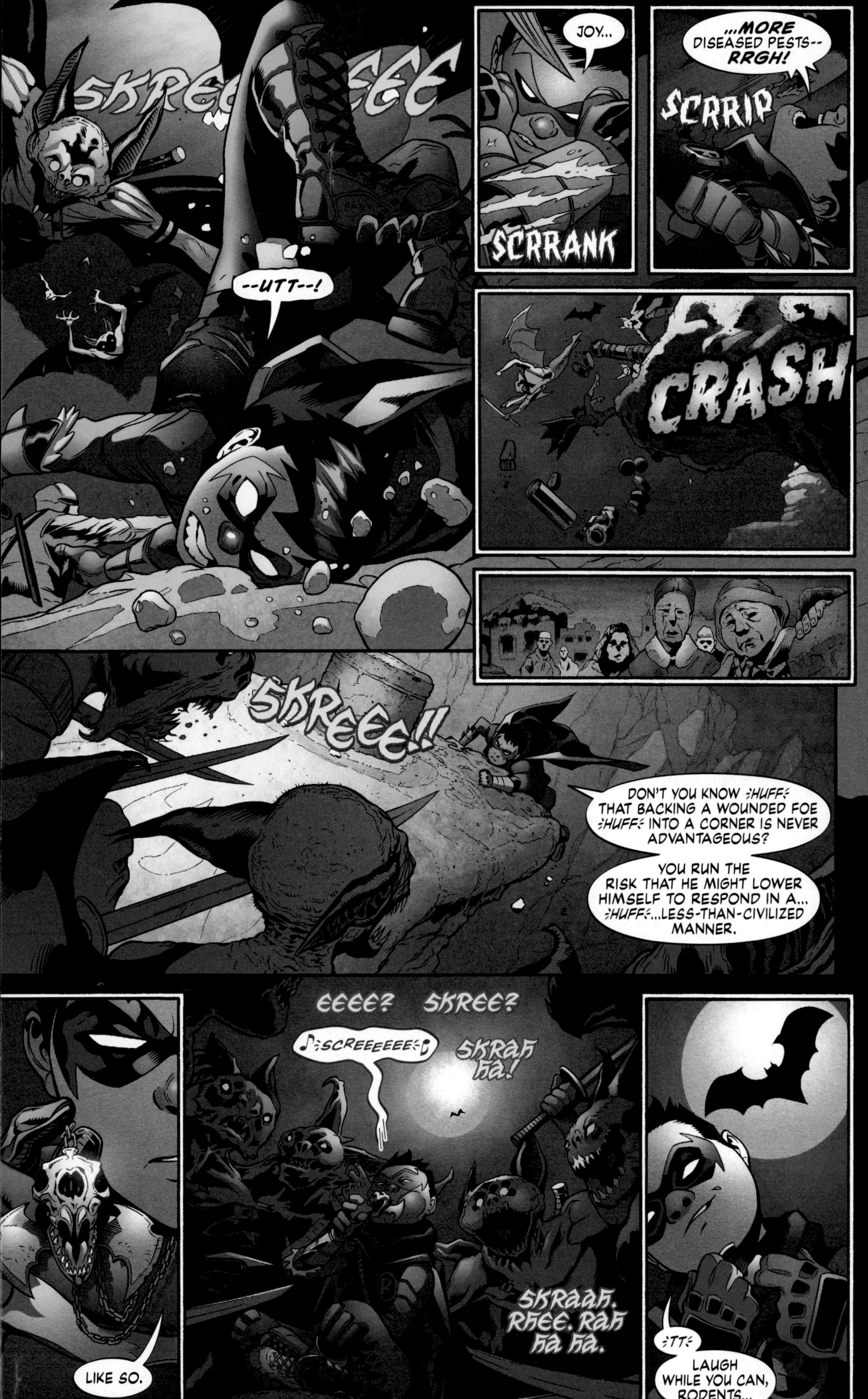
SKREEEEEE
--UTT--!
JOY...
SCRRANK
...MORE DISEASED PESTS-- RRGH!
SCRRIP
CRASH
SKREEE!!
DON'T YOU KNOW ⁏HUFF⁏ THAT BACKING A WOUNDED FOE ⁏HUFF⁏ INTO A CORNER IS NEVER ADVANTAGEOUS?
YOU RUN THE RISK THAT HE MIGHT LOWER HIMSELF TO RESPOND IN A... ⁏HUFF⁏...LESS-THAN-CIVILIZED MANNER.
LIKE SO.
EEEE? SKREE?
♪SCREEEEEEE♪
SKRAH HA!
SKRAAH. RHEE. RAH HA HA.
TT
LAUGH WHILE YOU CAN, RODENTS...

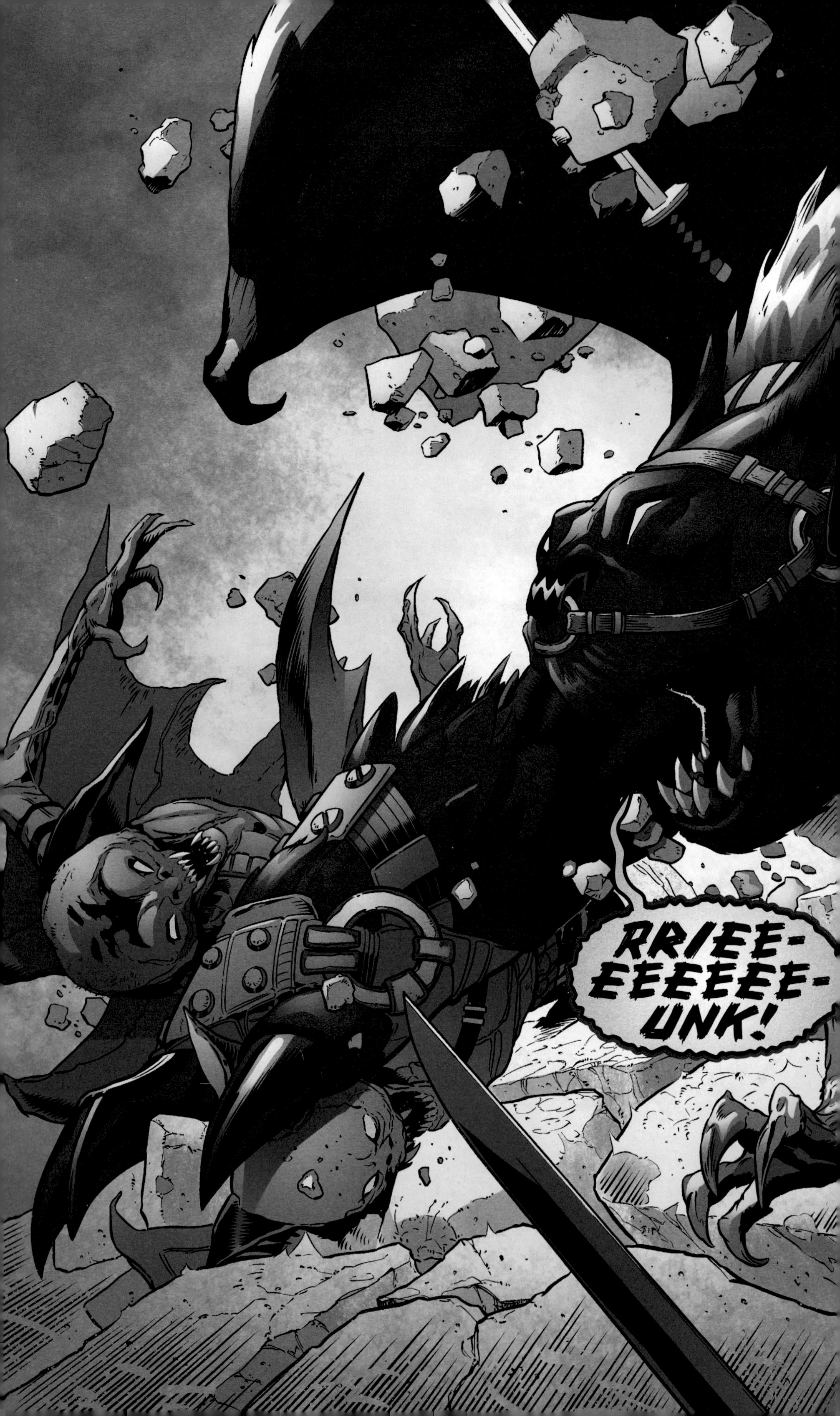
RRIEEE-EEEEEEE-UNK!

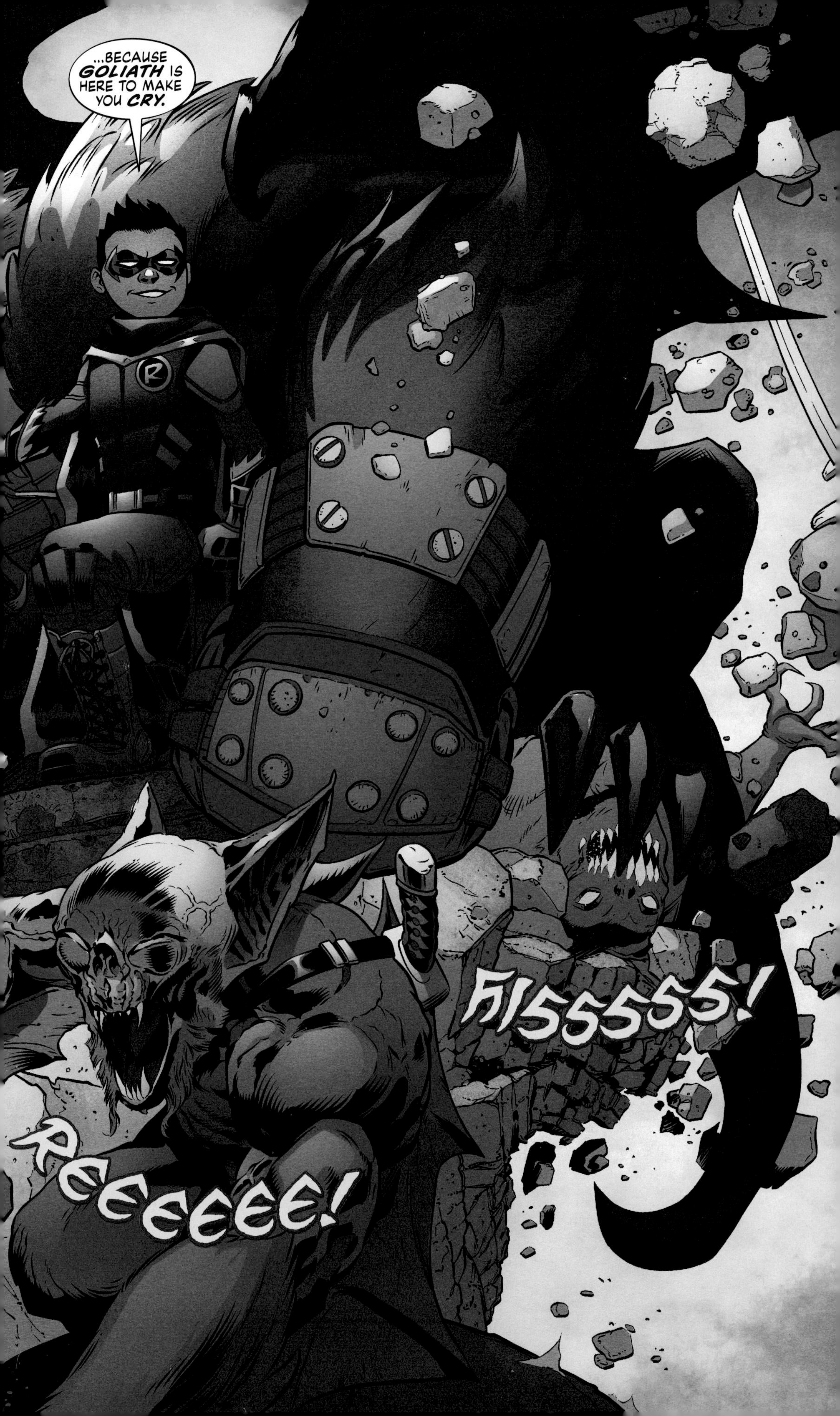
...BECAUSE GOLIATH IS HERE TO MAKE YOU CRY.
HISSSSSS!
REEEEEE!

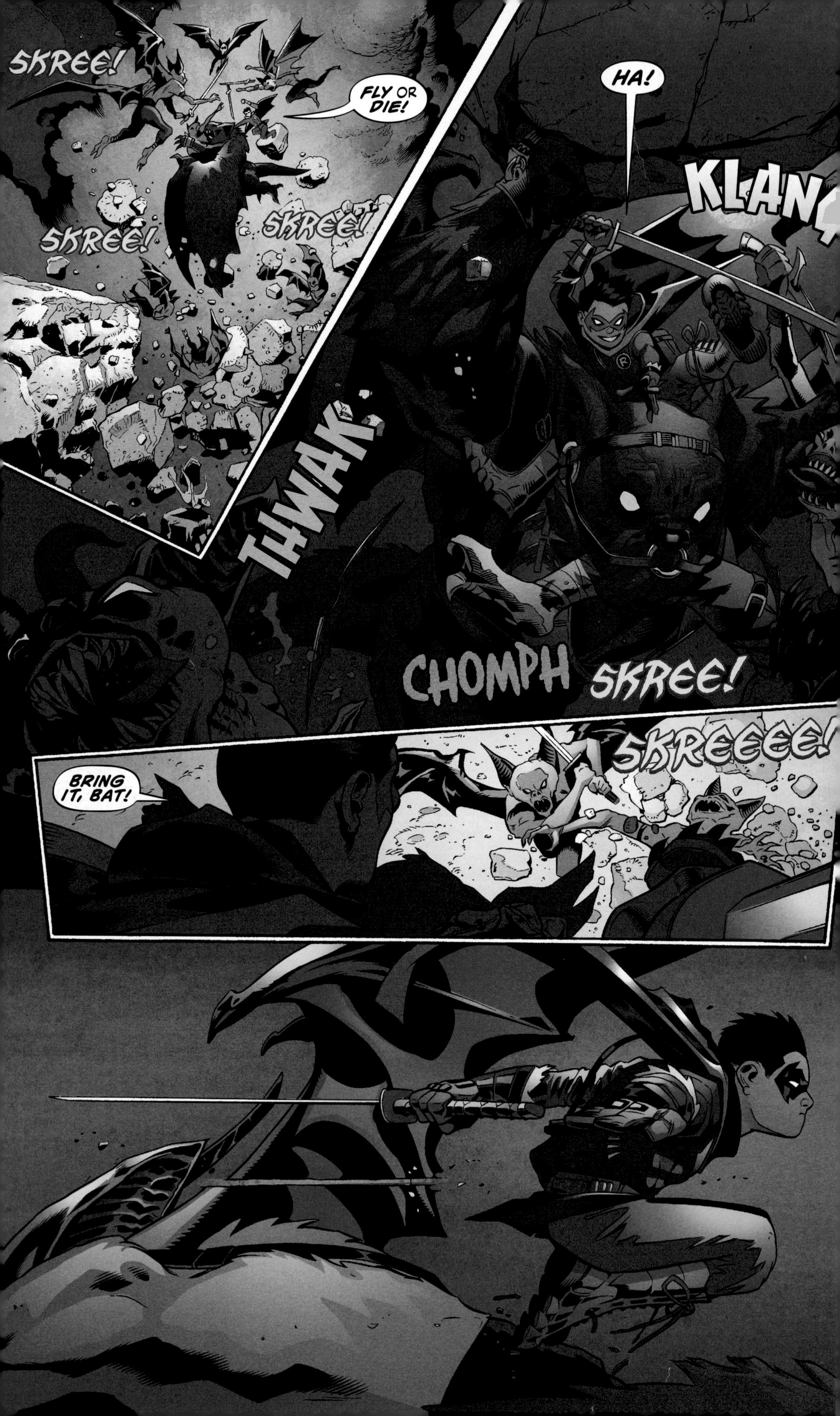
SKREE!
FLY OR DIE!
SKREE!
SKREE!
HA!
KLANG
THWAK
CHOMPH
SKREE!
SKREEEE!
BRING IT, BAT!

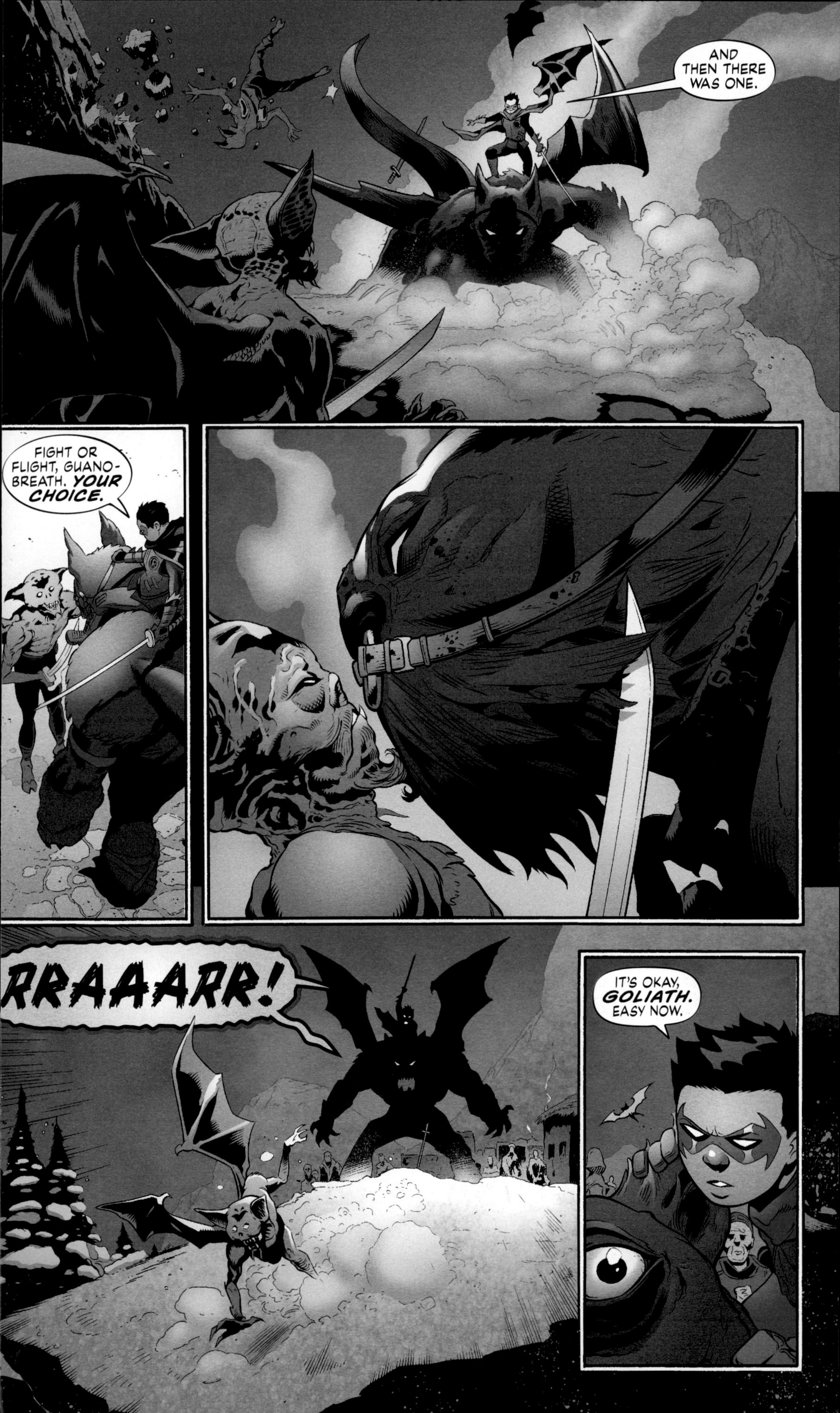
AND THEN THERE WAS ONE.
FIGHT OR FLIGHT, GUANO-BREATH. YOUR CHOICE.
RRAAARR!
IT'S OKAY, GOLIATH. EASY NOW.

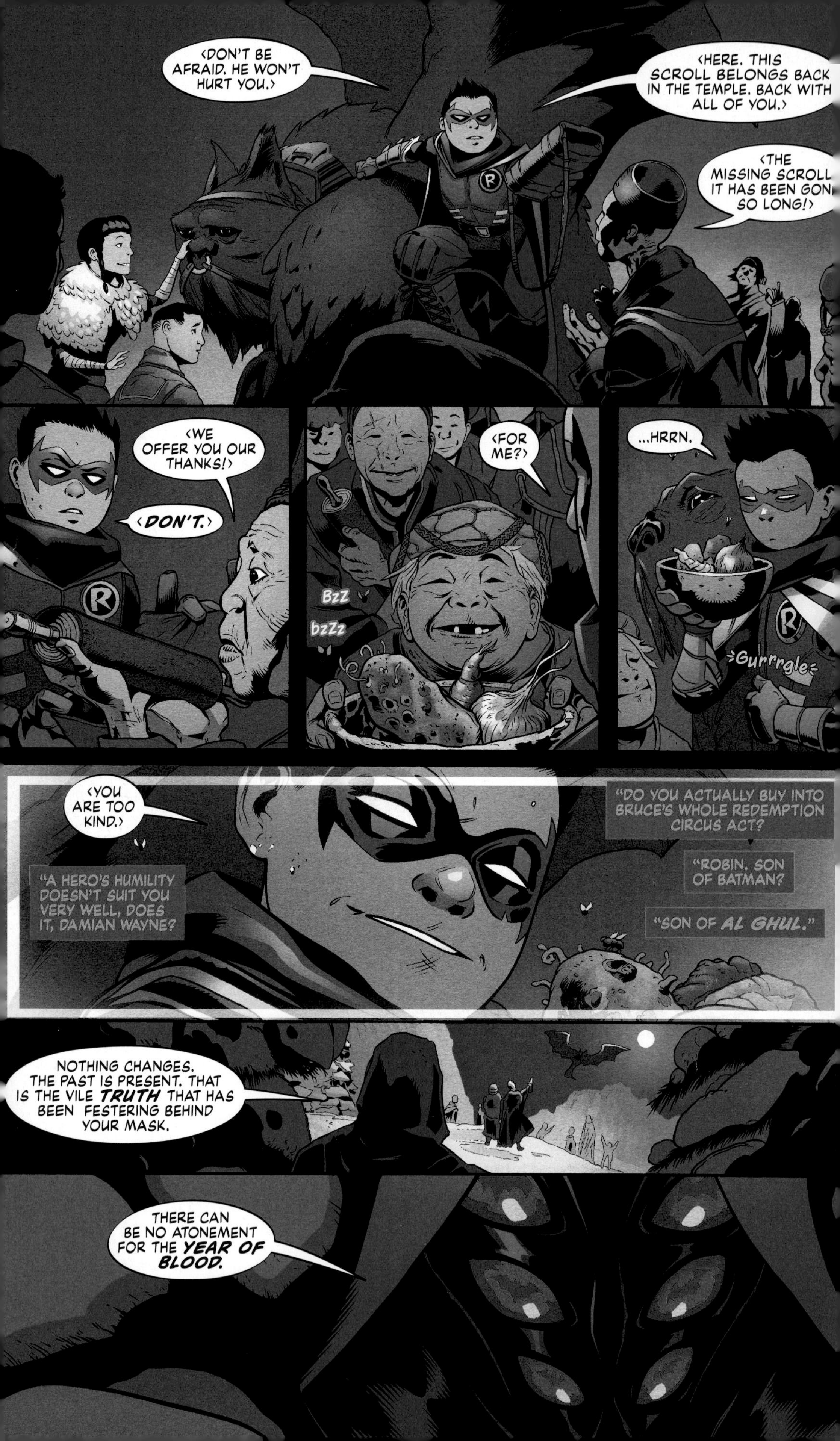
‹DON'T BE AFRAID. HE WON'T HURT YOU.›
‹HERE. THIS SCROLL BELONGS BACK IN THE TEMPLE. BACK WITH ALL OF YOU.›
‹THE MISSING SCROLL IT HAS BEEN GON SO LONG!›
‹WE OFFER YOU OUR THANKS!›
‹DON'T.›
‹FOR ME?›
BzZ
bzZz
...HRRN.
Gurrrgle
‹YOU ARE TOO KIND.›
"A HERO'S HUMILITY DOESN'T SUIT YOU VERY WELL, DOES IT, DAMIAN WAYNE?
"DO YOU ACTUALLY BUY INTO BRUCE'S WHOLE REDEMPTION CIRCUS ACT?
"ROBIN. SON OF BATMAN?
"SON OF AL GHUL."
NOTHING CHANGES. THE PAST IS PRESENT. THAT IS THE VILE TRUTH THAT HAS BEEN FESTERING BEHIND YOUR MASK.
THERE CAN BE NO ATONEMENT FOR THE YEAR OF BLOOD.

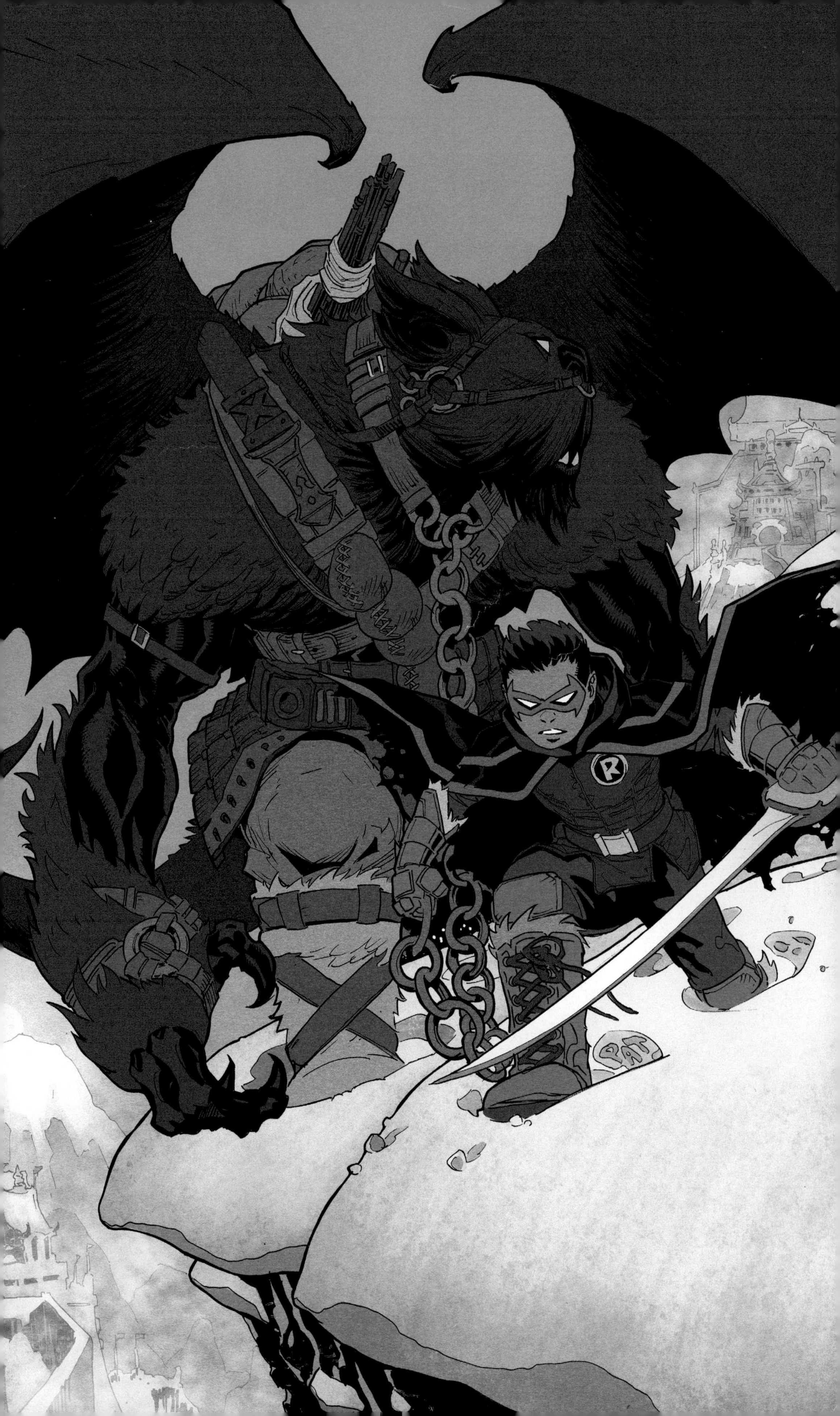
PAT

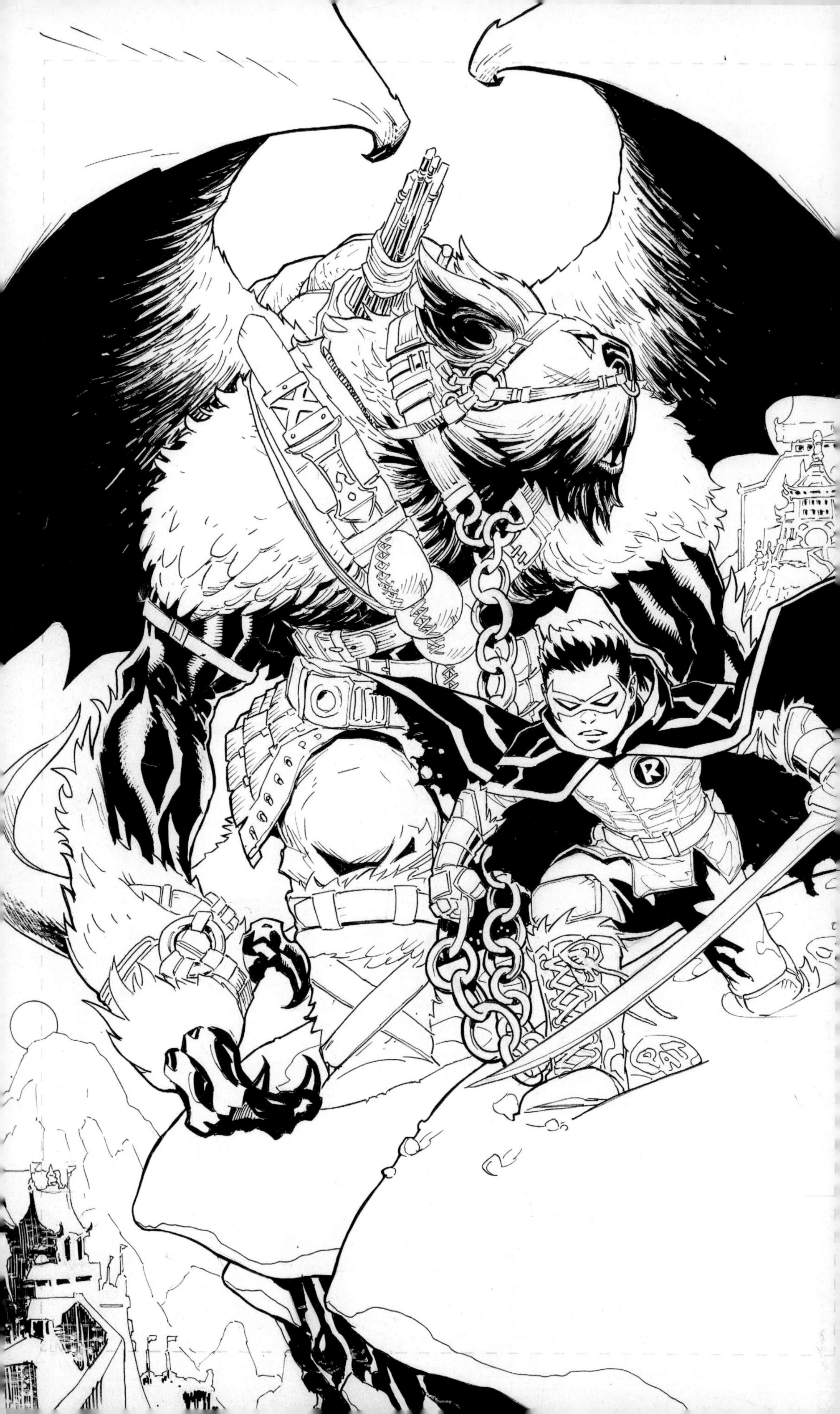

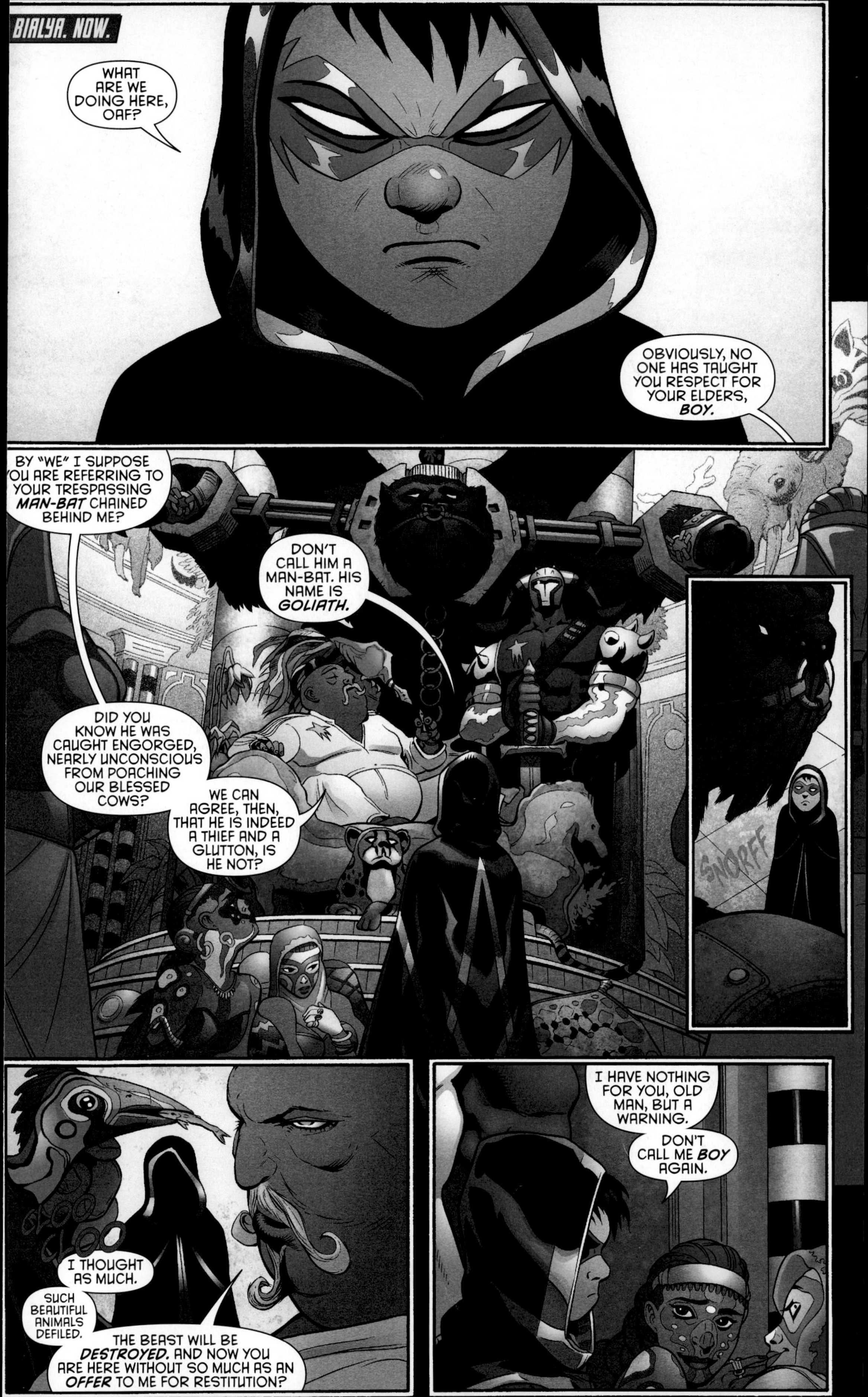
BIALYA. NOW.
WHAT ARE WE DOING HERE, OAF?
OBVIOUSLY, NO ONE HAS TAUGHT YOU RESPECT FOR YOUR ELDERS, BOY.
BY "WE" I SUPPOSE YOU ARE REFERRING TO YOUR TRESPASSING MAN-BAT CHAINED BEHIND ME?
DON'T CALL HIM A MAN-BAT. HIS NAME IS GOLIATH.
DID YOU KNOW HE WAS CAUGHT ENGORGED, NEARLY UNCONSCIOUS FROM POACHING OUR BLESSED COWS?
WE CAN AGREE, THEN, THAT HE IS INDEED A THIEF AND A GLUTTON, IS HE NOT?
SNORFF
I THOUGHT AS MUCH.
SUCH BEAUTIFUL ANIMALS DEFILED.
THE BEAST WILL BE DESTROYED. AND NOW YOU ARE HERE WITHOUT SO MUCH AS AN OFFER TO ME FOR RESTITUTION?
I HAVE NOTHING FOR YOU, OLD MAN, BUT A WARNING.
DON'T CALL ME BOY AGAIN.

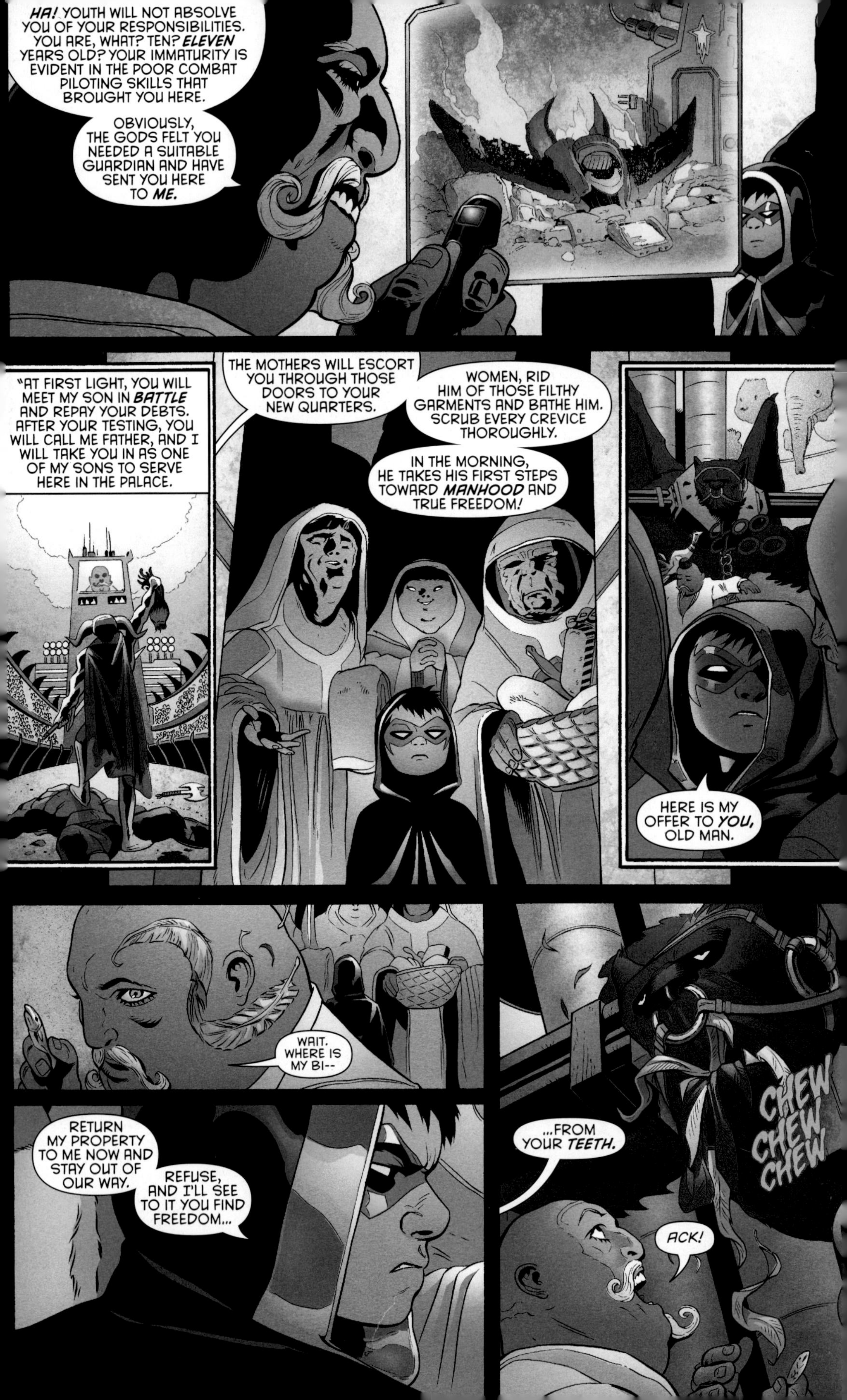
HA! YOUTH WILL NOT ABSOLVE YOU OF YOUR RESPONSIBILITIES. YOU ARE, WHAT? TEN? ELEVEN YEARS OLD? YOUR IMMATURITY IS EVIDENT IN THE POOR COMBAT PILOTING SKILLS THAT BROUGHT YOU HERE.
OBVIOUSLY, THE GODS FELT YOU NEEDED A SUITABLE GUARDIAN AND HAVE SENT YOU HERE TO ME.
"AT FIRST LIGHT, YOU WILL MEET MY SON IN BATTLE AND REPAY YOUR DEBTS. AFTER YOUR TESTING, YOU WILL CALL ME FATHER, AND I WILL TAKE YOU IN AS ONE OF MY SONS TO SERVE HERE IN THE PALACE.
THE MOTHERS WILL ESCORT YOU THROUGH THOSE DOORS TO YOUR NEW QUARTERS.
WOMEN, RID HIM OF THOSE FILTHY GARMENTS AND BATHE HIM. SCRUB EVERY CREVICE THOROUGHLY.
IN THE MORNING, HE TAKES HIS FIRST STEPS TOWARD MANHOOD AND TRUE FREEDOM!
HERE IS MY OFFER TO YOU, OLD MAN.
WAIT. WHERE IS MY BI--
RETURN MY PROPERTY TO ME NOW AND STAY OUT OF OUR WAY.
REFUSE, AND I'LL SEE TO IT YOU FIND FREEDOM...
...FROM YOUR TEETH.
CHEW CHEW CHEW
ACK!

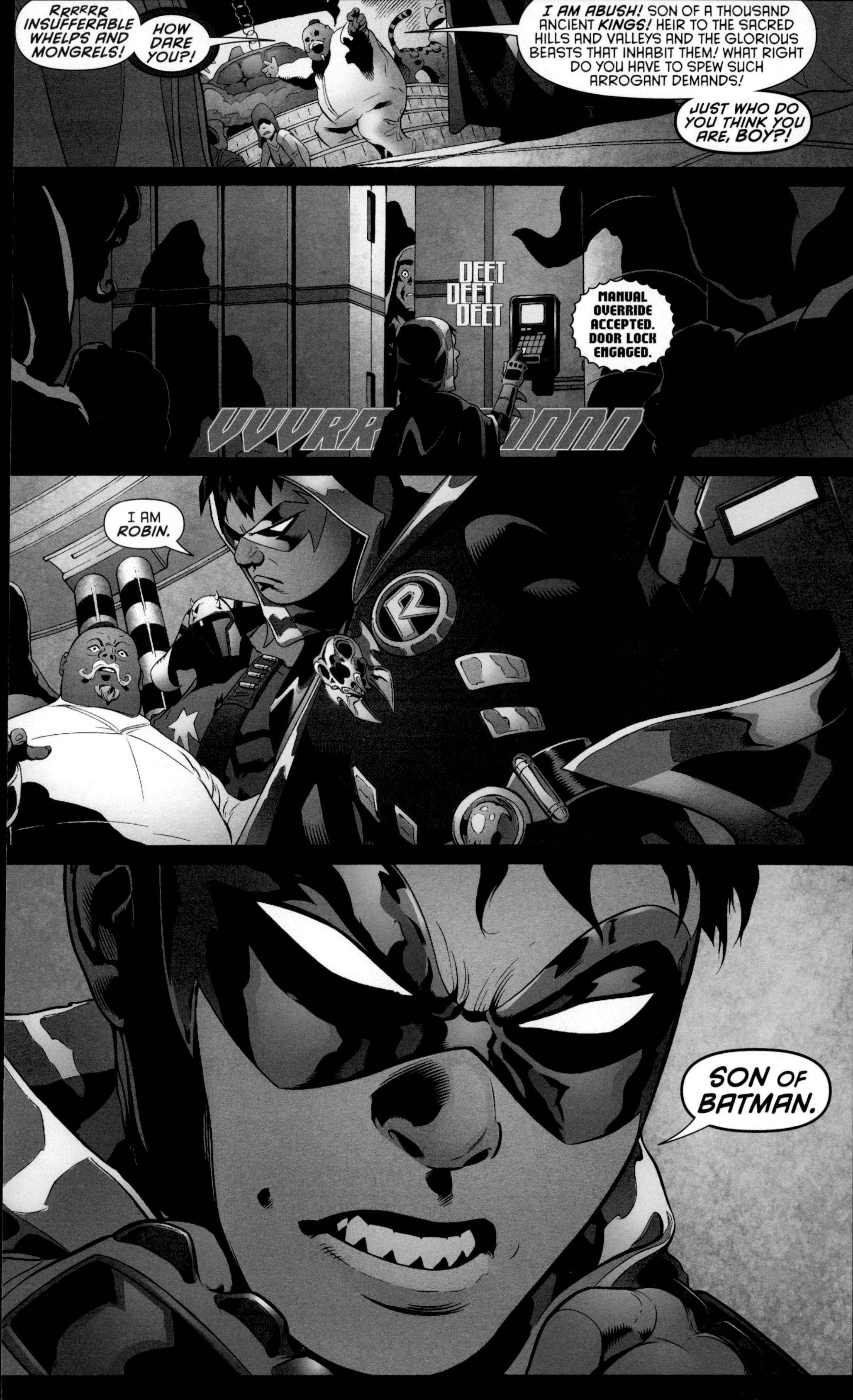
RRRRRR INSUFFERABLE WHELPS AND MONGRELS!
HOW DARE YOU?!
I AM ABUSH! SON OF A THOUSAND ANCIENT KINGS! HEIR TO THE SACRED HILLS AND VALLEYS AND THE GLORIOUS BEASTS THAT INHABIT THEM! WHAT RIGHT DO YOU HAVE TO SPEW SUCH ARROGANT DEMANDS!
JUST WHO DO YOU THINK YOU ARE, BOY?!
DEET DEET DEET
MANUAL OVERRIDE ACCEPTED. DOOR LOCK ENGAGED.
I AM ROBIN.
SON OF BATMAN.

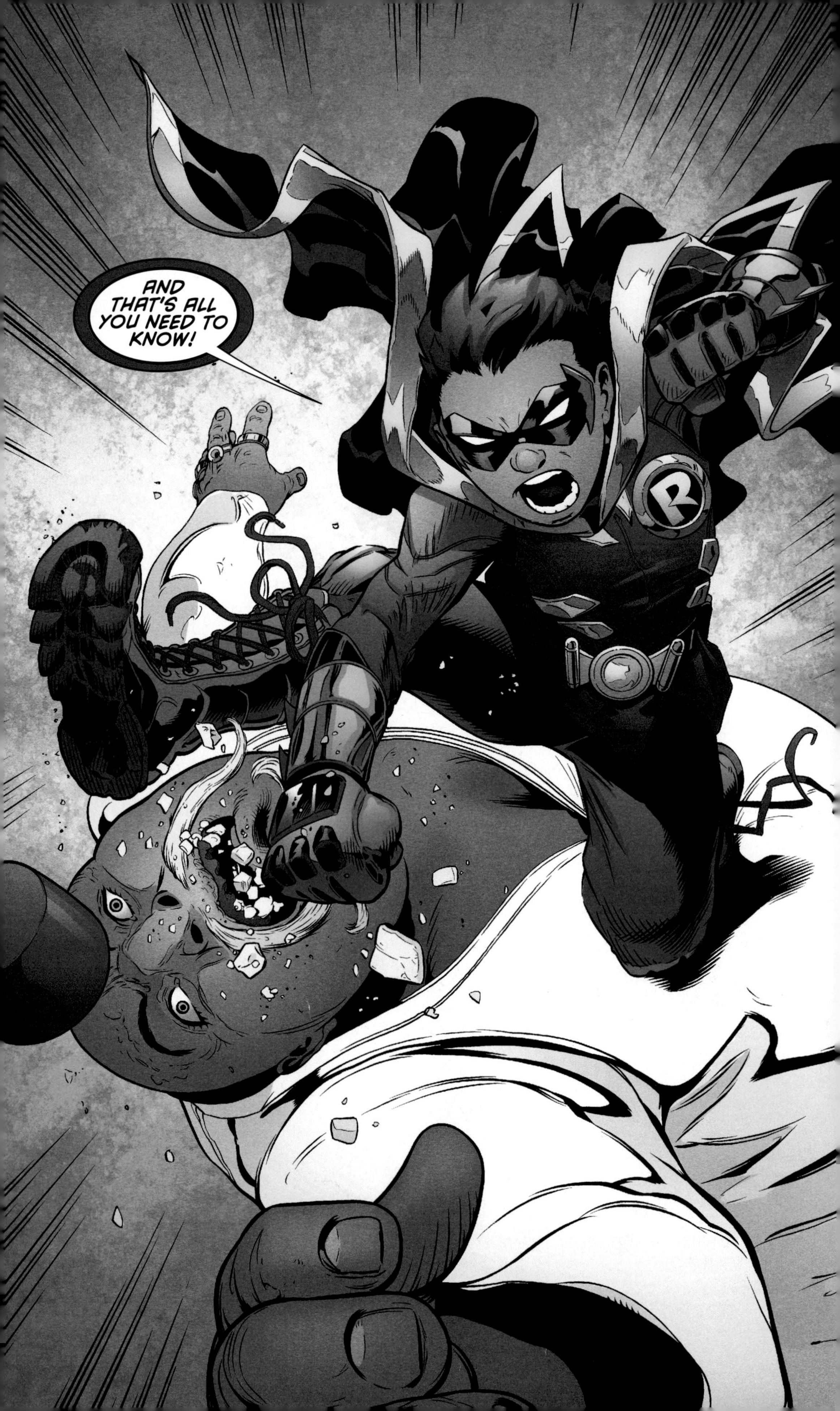
AND THAT'S ALL YOU NEED TO KNOW!

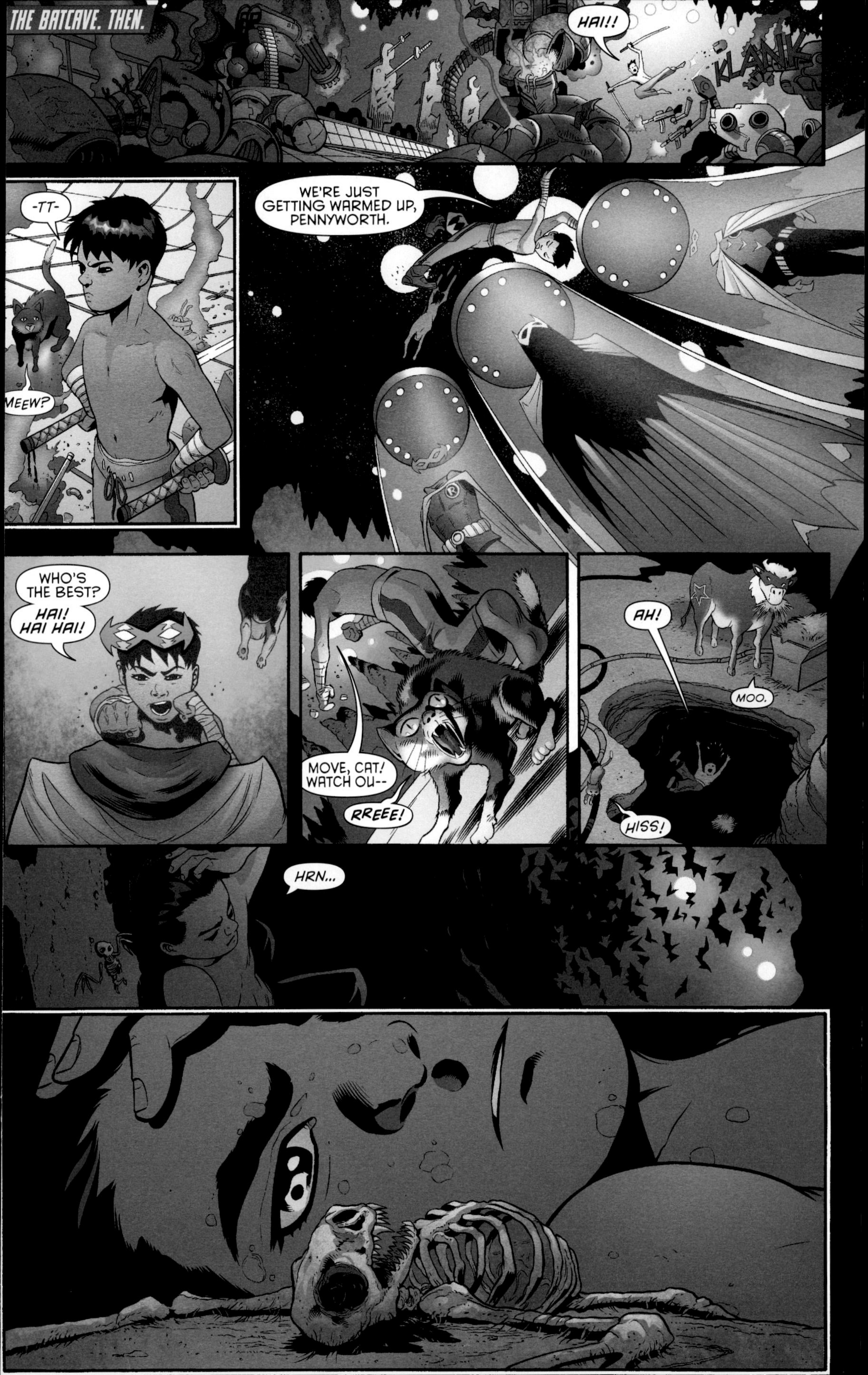
THE BATCAVE. THEN.
HAI!!
KLANK
-TT-
MEEW?
WE'RE JUST GETTING WARMED UP, PENNYWORTH.
WHO'S THE BEST?
HAI! HAI HAI!
MOVE, CAT! WATCH OU--
RREEE!
AH!
MOO.
HISS!
HRN...

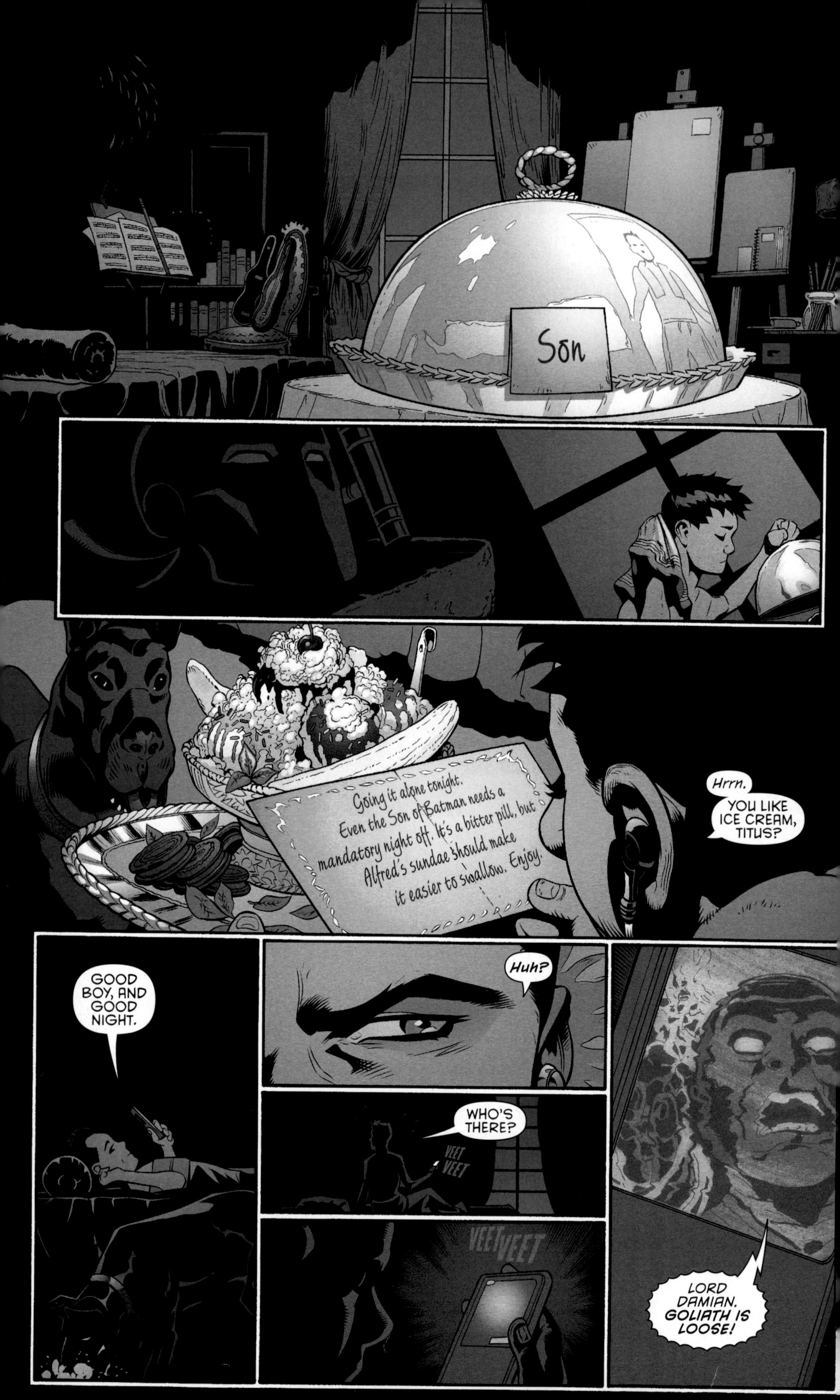
Son
Going it alone tonight. Even the Son of Batman needs a mandatory night off. It's a bitter pill, but Alfred's sundae should make it easier to swallow. Enjoy.
Hrrn.
YOU LIKE ICE CREAM, TITUS?
GOOD BOY, AND GOOD NIGHT.
Huh?
WHO'S THERE?
VEET VEET
VEET VEET
LORD DAMIAN. GOLIATH IS LOOSE!

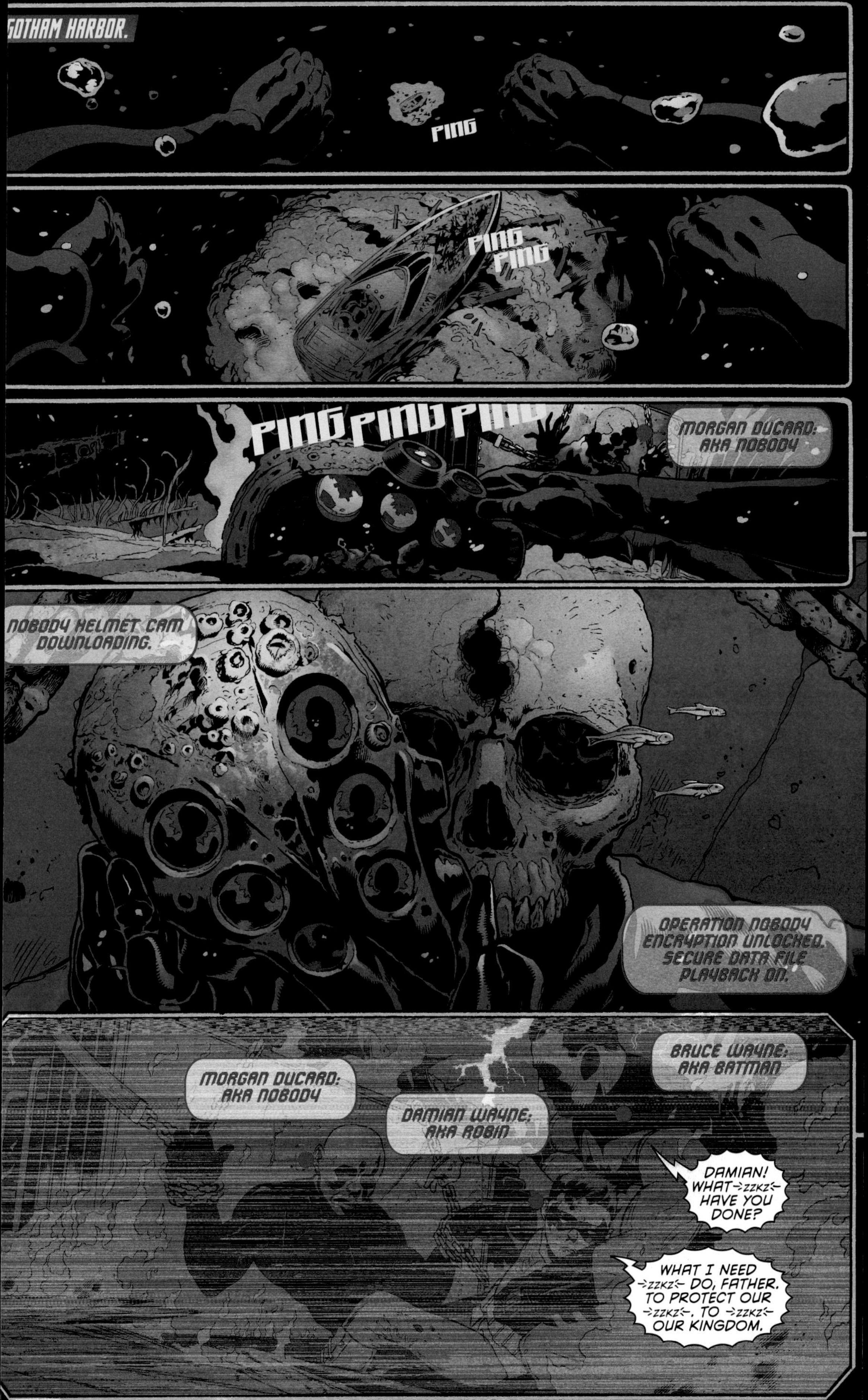
GOTHAM HARBOR.
PING
PING
PING
PING PING PING
MORGAN DUCARD: AKA NOBODY
NOBODY HELMET CAM DOWNLOADING.
OPERATION NOBODY ENCRYPTION UNLOCKED. SECURE DATA FILE PLAYBACK ON.
MORGAN DUCARD: AKA NOBODY
DAMIAN WAYNE: AKA ROBIN
BRUCE WAYNE: AKA BATMAN
DAMIAN! WHAT ~ZZKZ~ HAVE YOU DONE?
WHAT I NEED ~ZZKZ~ DO, FATHER. TO PROTECT OUR ~ZZKZ~. TO ~ZZKZ~ OUR KINGDOM.

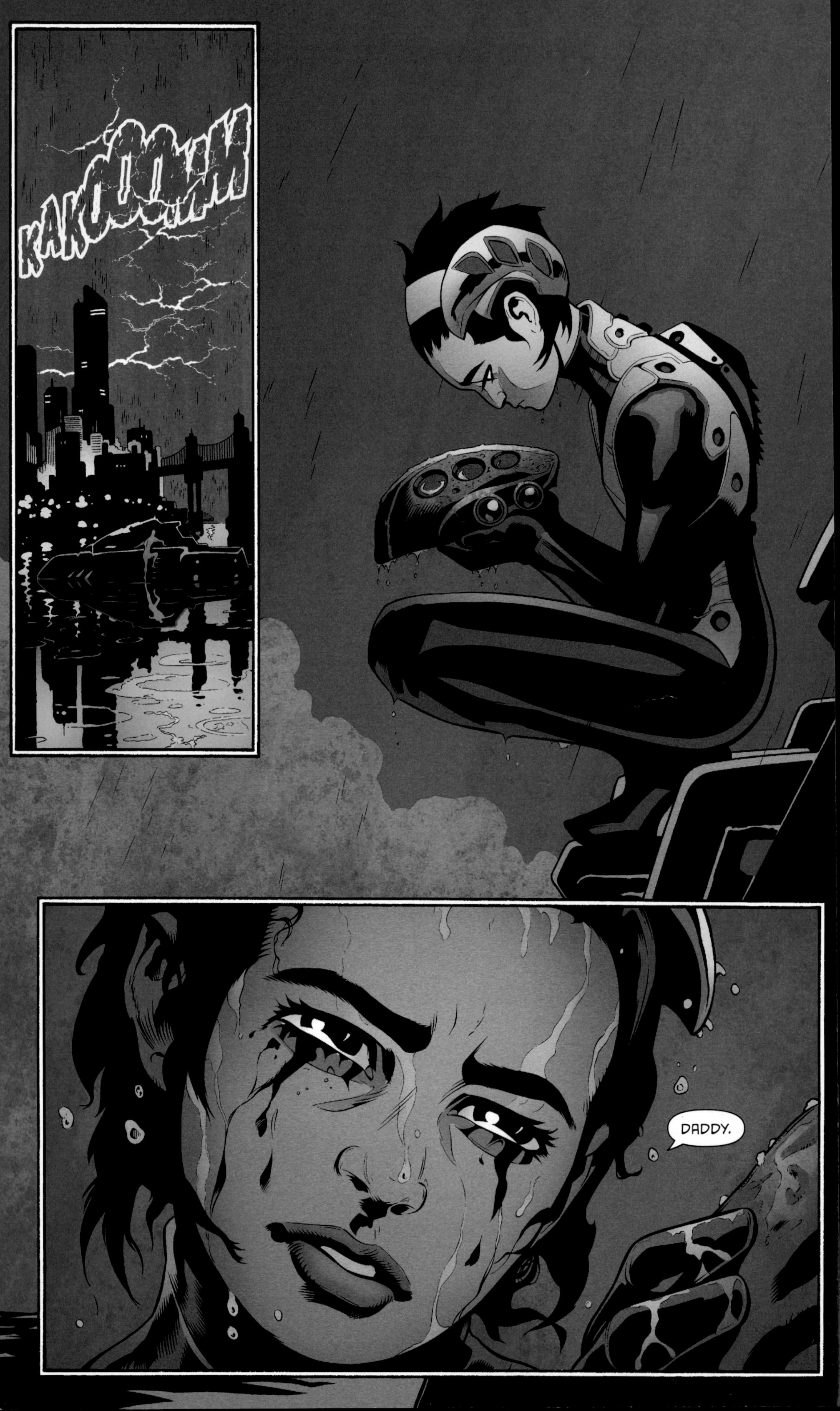
KAKOOMM
DADDY.

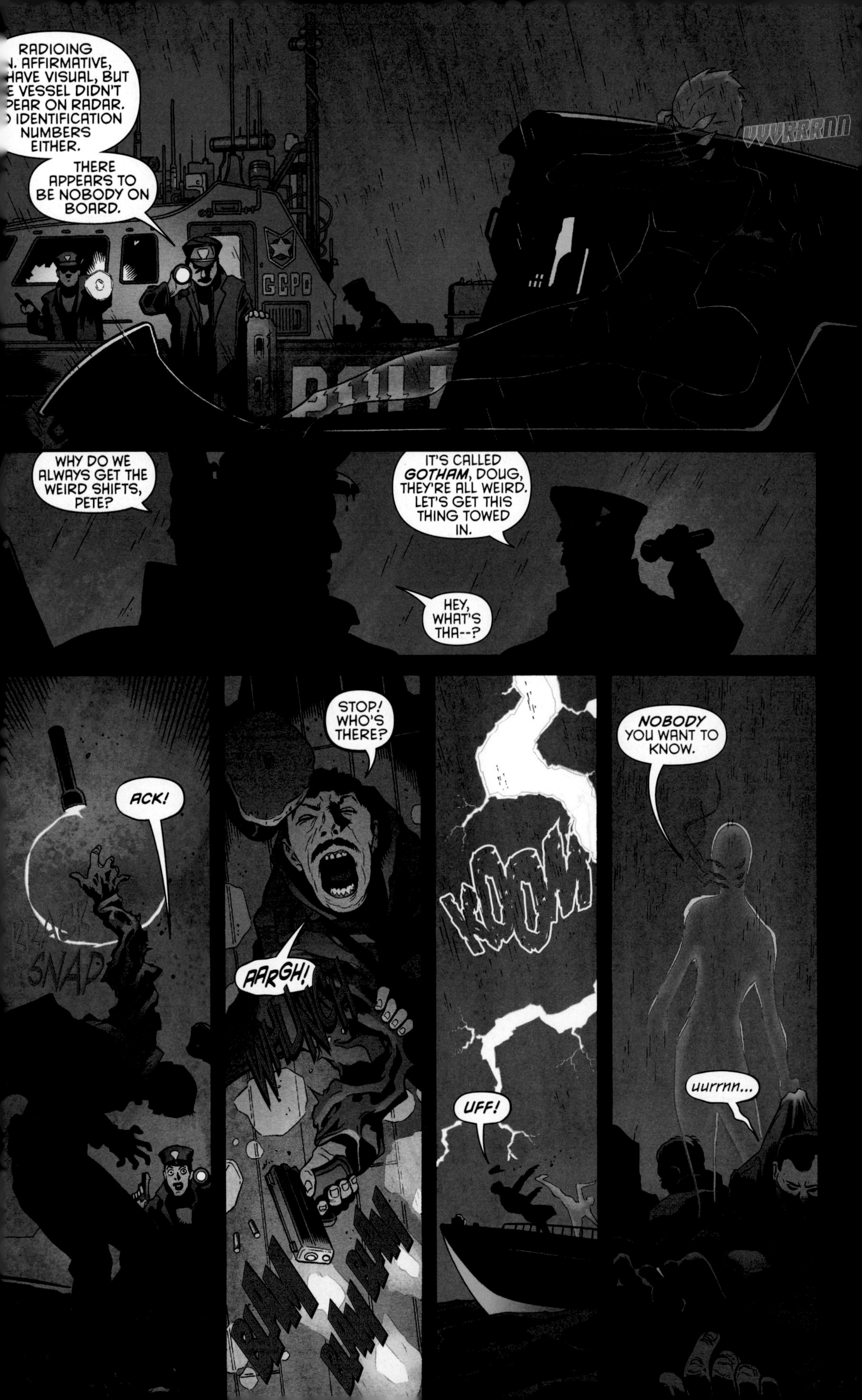
RADIOING N. AFFIRMATIVE, HAVE VISUAL, BUT E VESSEL DIDN'T PEAR ON RADAR. O IDENTIFICATION NUMBERS EITHER.
THERE APPEARS TO BE NOBODY ON BOARD.
VVVRRRNN
WHY DO WE ALWAYS GET THE WEIRD SHIFTS, PETE?
IT'S CALLED *GOTHAM*, DOUG, THEY'RE ALL WEIRD. LET'S GET THIS THING TOWED IN.
HEY, WHAT'S THA--?
ACK!
SNAP
STOP! WHO'S THERE?
AARGH!
KOOM
UFF!
NOBODY YOU WANT TO KNOW.
uurrnn...

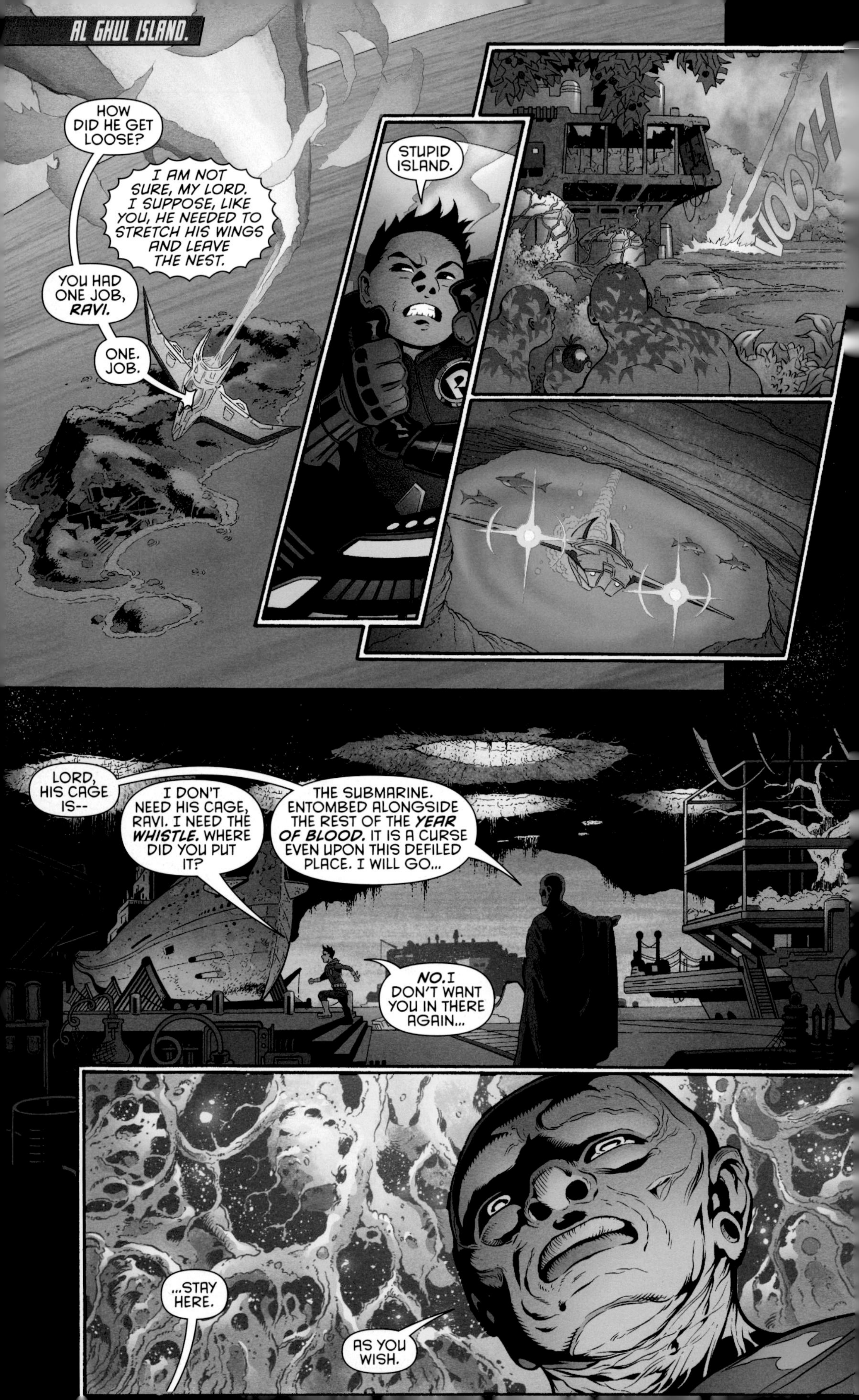
AL GHUL ISLAND.
HOW DID HE GET LOOSE?
I AM NOT SURE, MY LORD. I SUPPOSE, LIKE YOU, HE NEEDED TO STRETCH HIS WINGS AND LEAVE THE NEST.
YOU HAD ONE JOB, RAVI.
ONE. JOB.
STUPID ISLAND.
VOOSH
LORD, HIS CAGE IS--
I DON'T NEED HIS CAGE, RAVI. I NEED THE WHISTLE. WHERE DID YOU PUT IT?
THE SUBMARINE. ENTOMBED ALONGSIDE THE REST OF THE YEAR OF BLOOD. IT IS A CURSE EVEN UPON THIS DEFILED PLACE. I WILL GO...
NO. I DON'T WANT YOU IN THERE AGAIN...
...STAY HERE.
AS YOU WISH.

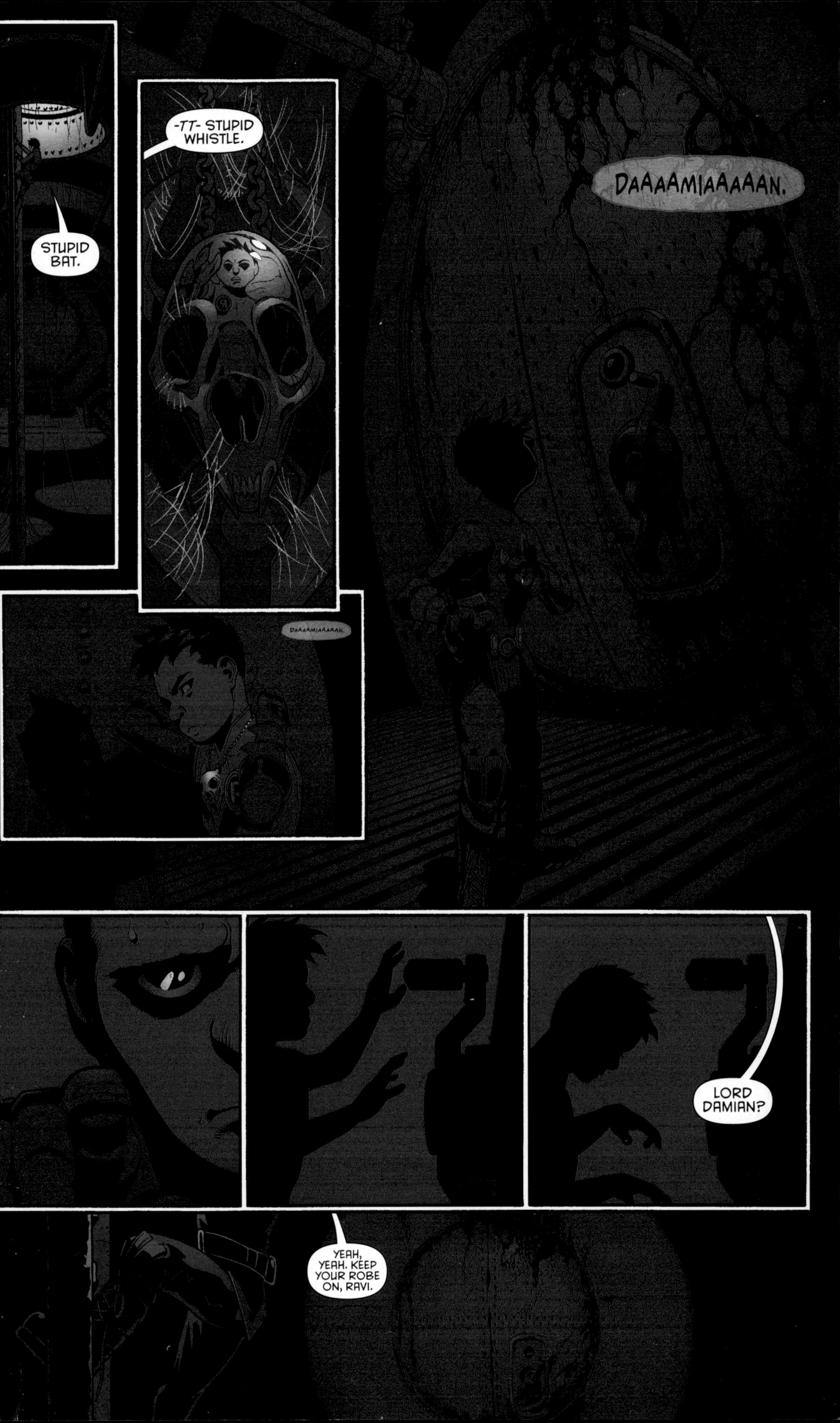
STUPID BAT.
-TT- STUPID WHISTLE.
DAAAAMIAAAAAN.
DAAAAMIAAAAAN.
LORD DAMIAN?
YEAH, YEAH. KEEP YOUR ROBE ON, RAVI.

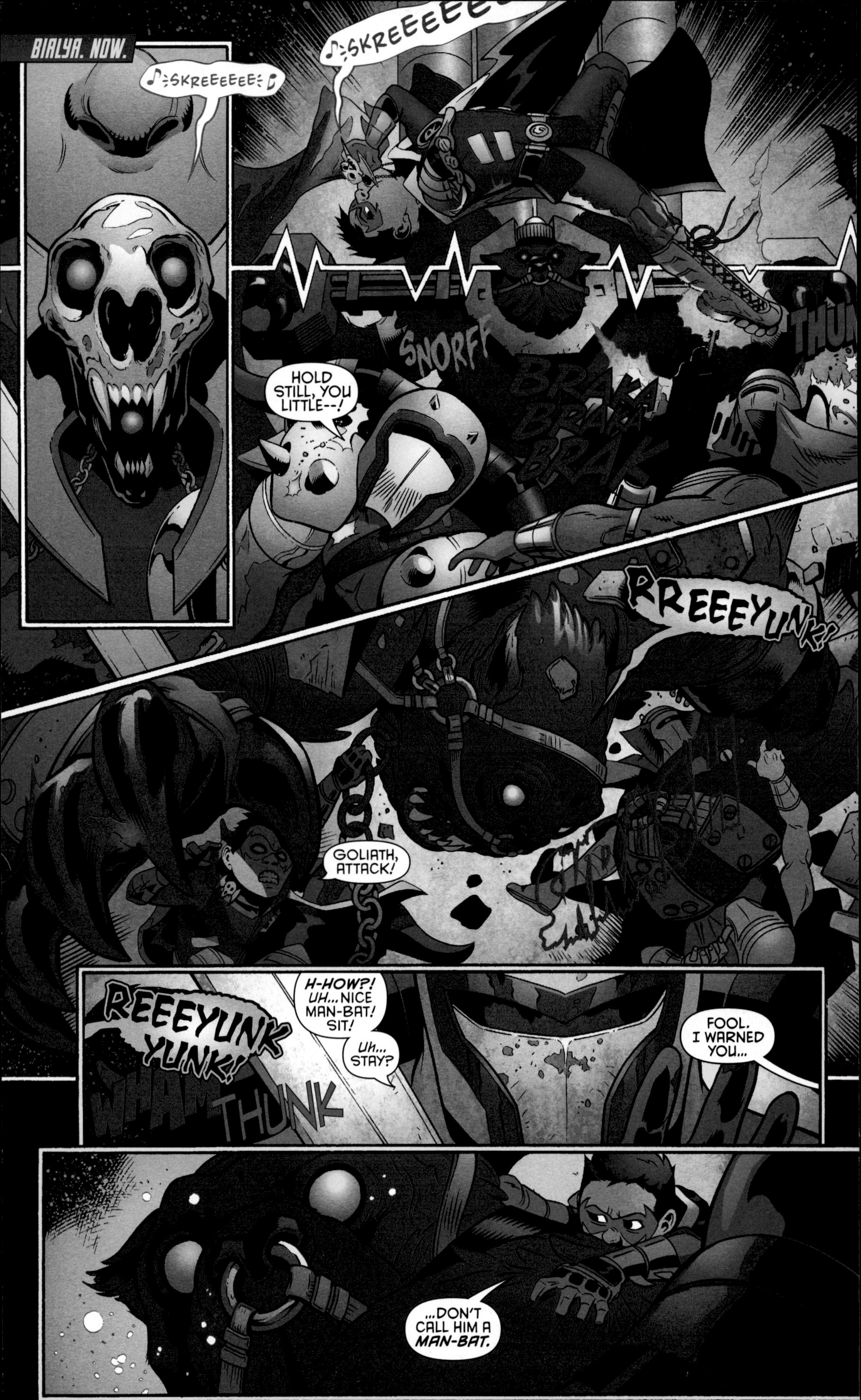
BIALYA. NOW.
SKREEEEEE
SKREEEEE
SNORFF
BRAKA BRAKA BRAK
THUNK
HOLD STILL, YOU LITTLE--!
RREEEYUNK!
GOLIATH, ATTACK!
REEEYUNK YUNK!
WHAM
THUNK
H-HOW?! UH... NICE MAN-BAT! SIT!
UH... STAY?
FOOL. I WARNED YOU...
...DON'T CALL HIM A MAN-BAT.

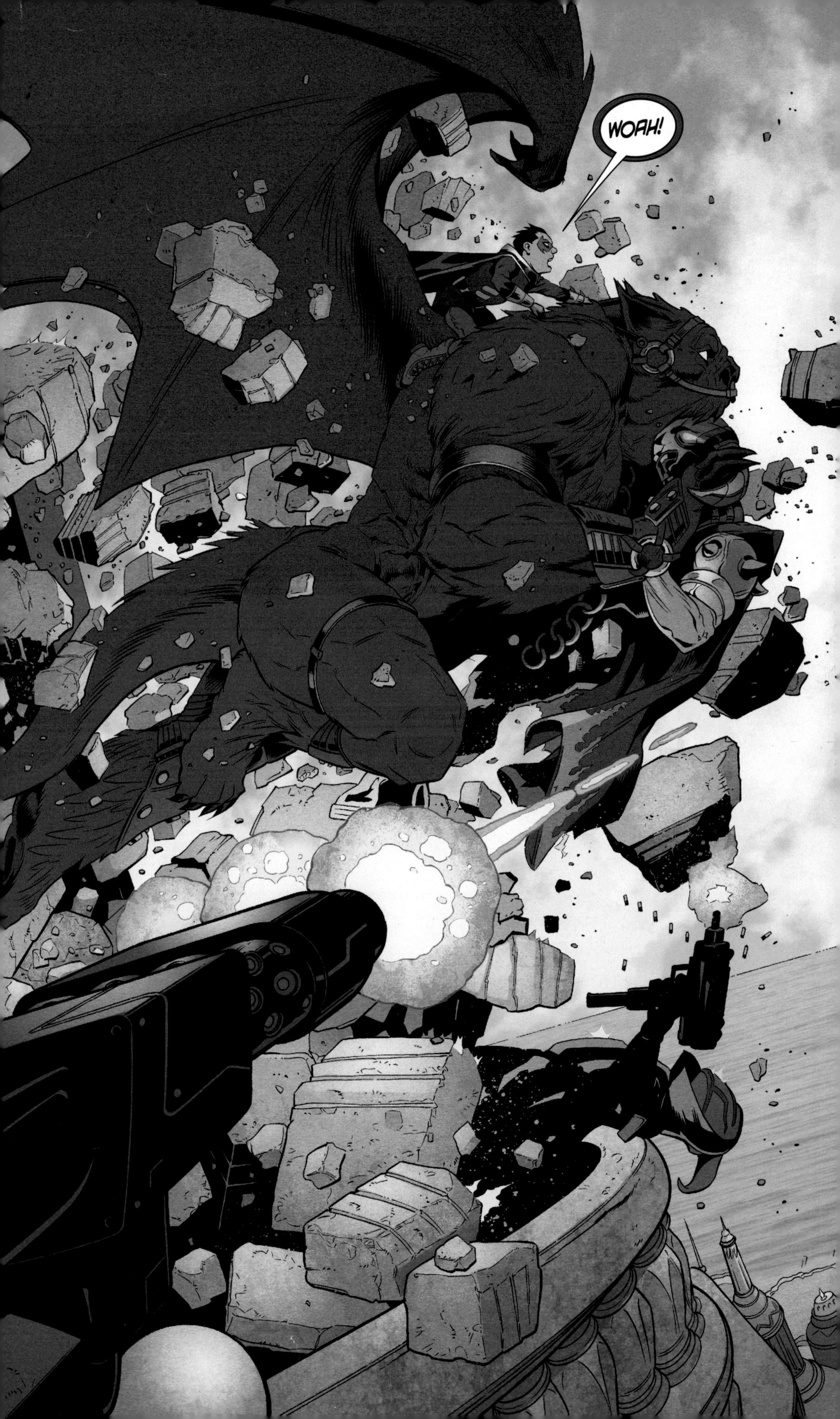
WOAH!

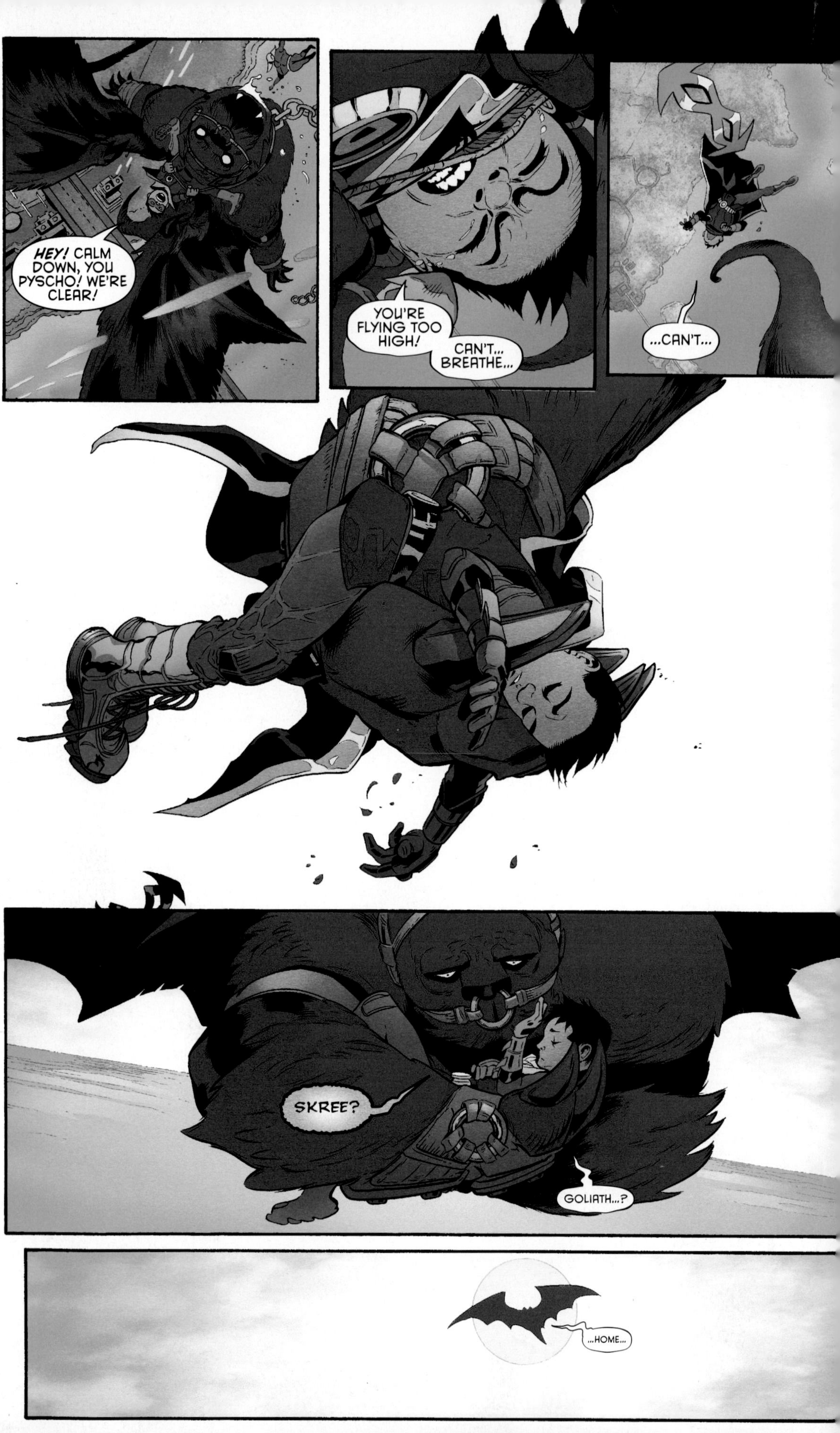
HEY! CALM DOWN, YOU PYSCHO! WE'RE CLEAR!
YOU'RE FLYING TOO HIGH!
CAN'T... BREATHE...
...CAN'T...
SKREE?
GOLIATH...?
...HOME...

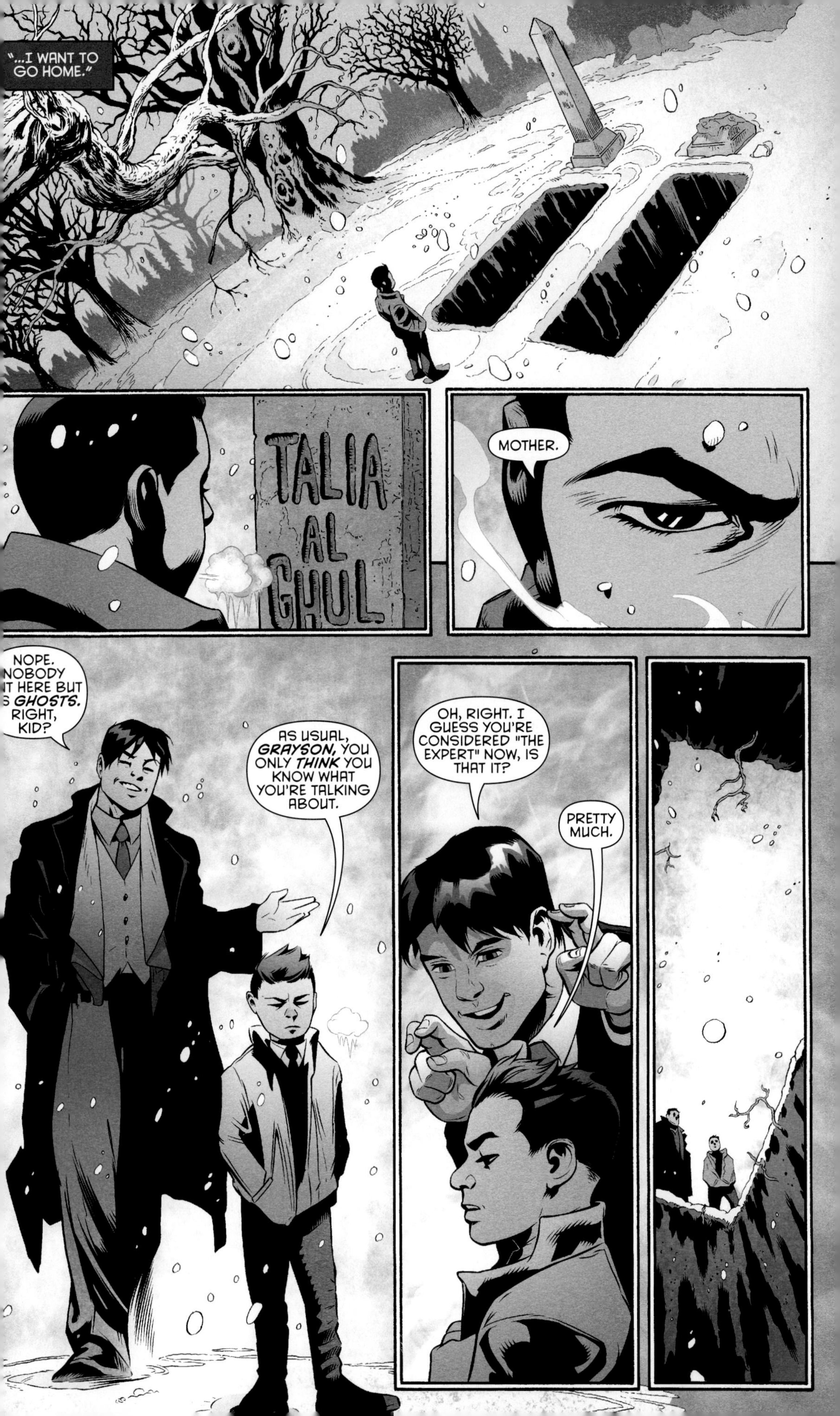
"...I WANT TO GO HOME."
TALIA AL GHUL
MOTHER.
NOPE. NOBODY ...T HERE BUT ...S GHOSTS. RIGHT, KID?
AS USUAL, GRAYSON, YOU ONLY THINK YOU KNOW WHAT YOU'RE TALKING ABOUT.
OH, RIGHT. I GUESS YOU'RE CONSIDERED "THE EXPERT" NOW, IS THAT IT?
PRETTY MUCH.

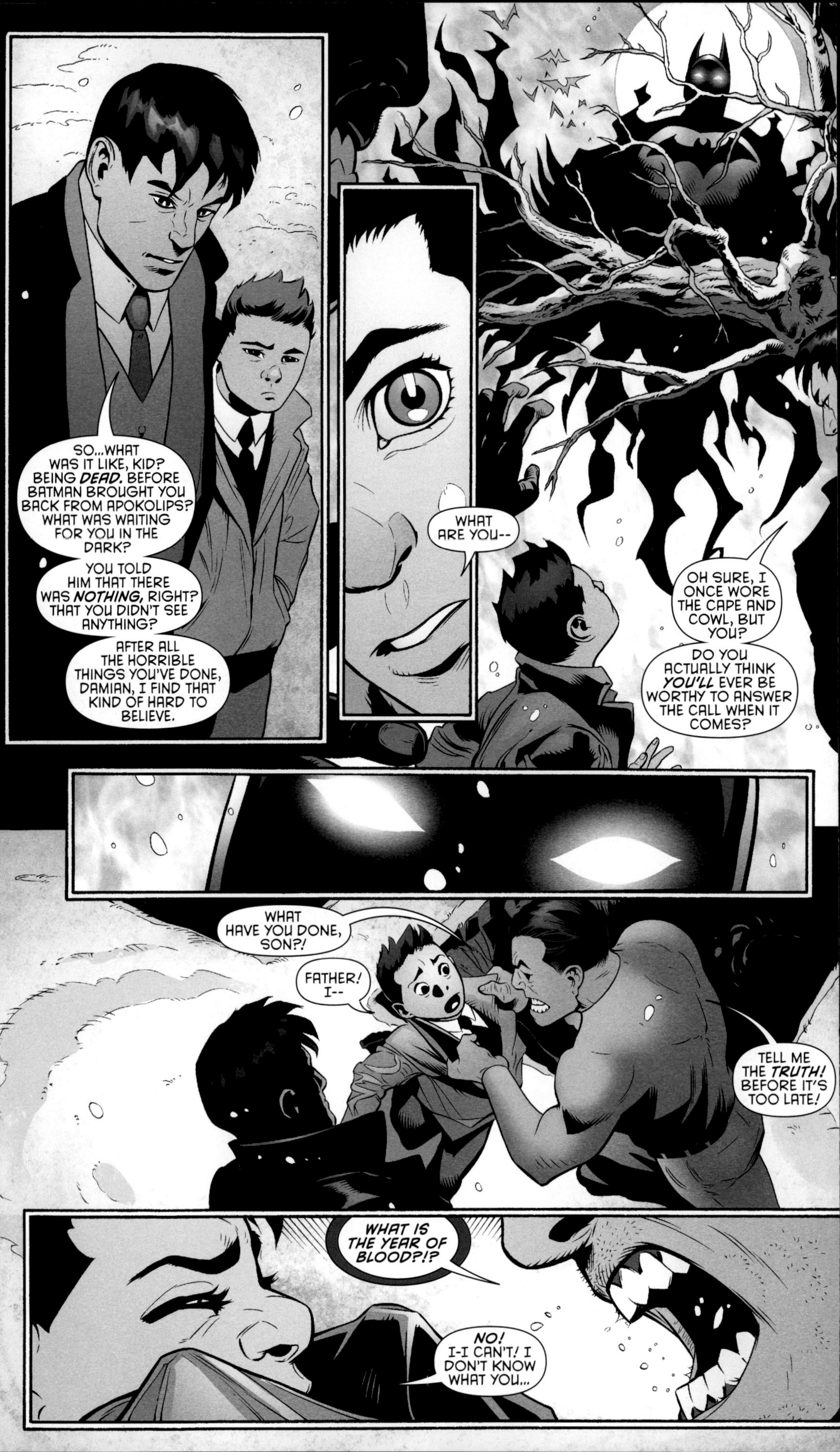
SO...WHAT WAS IT LIKE, KID? BEING DEAD. BEFORE BATMAN BROUGHT YOU BACK FROM APOKOLIPS? WHAT WAS WAITING FOR YOU IN THE DARK?
YOU TOLD HIM THAT THERE WAS NOTHING, RIGHT? THAT YOU DIDN'T SEE ANYTHING?
AFTER ALL THE HORRIBLE THINGS YOU'VE DONE, DAMIAN, I FIND THAT KIND OF HARD TO BELIEVE.
WHAT ARE YOU--
OH SURE, I ONCE WORE THE CAPE AND COWL, BUT YOU?
DO YOU ACTUALLY THINK YOU'LL EVER BE WORTHY TO ANSWER THE CALL WHEN IT COMES?
WHAT HAVE YOU DONE, SON?!
FATHER! I--
TELL ME THE TRUTH! BEFORE IT'S TOO LATE!
WHAT IS THE YEAR OF BLOOD?!?
NO! I-I CAN'T! I DON'T KNOW WHAT YOU...

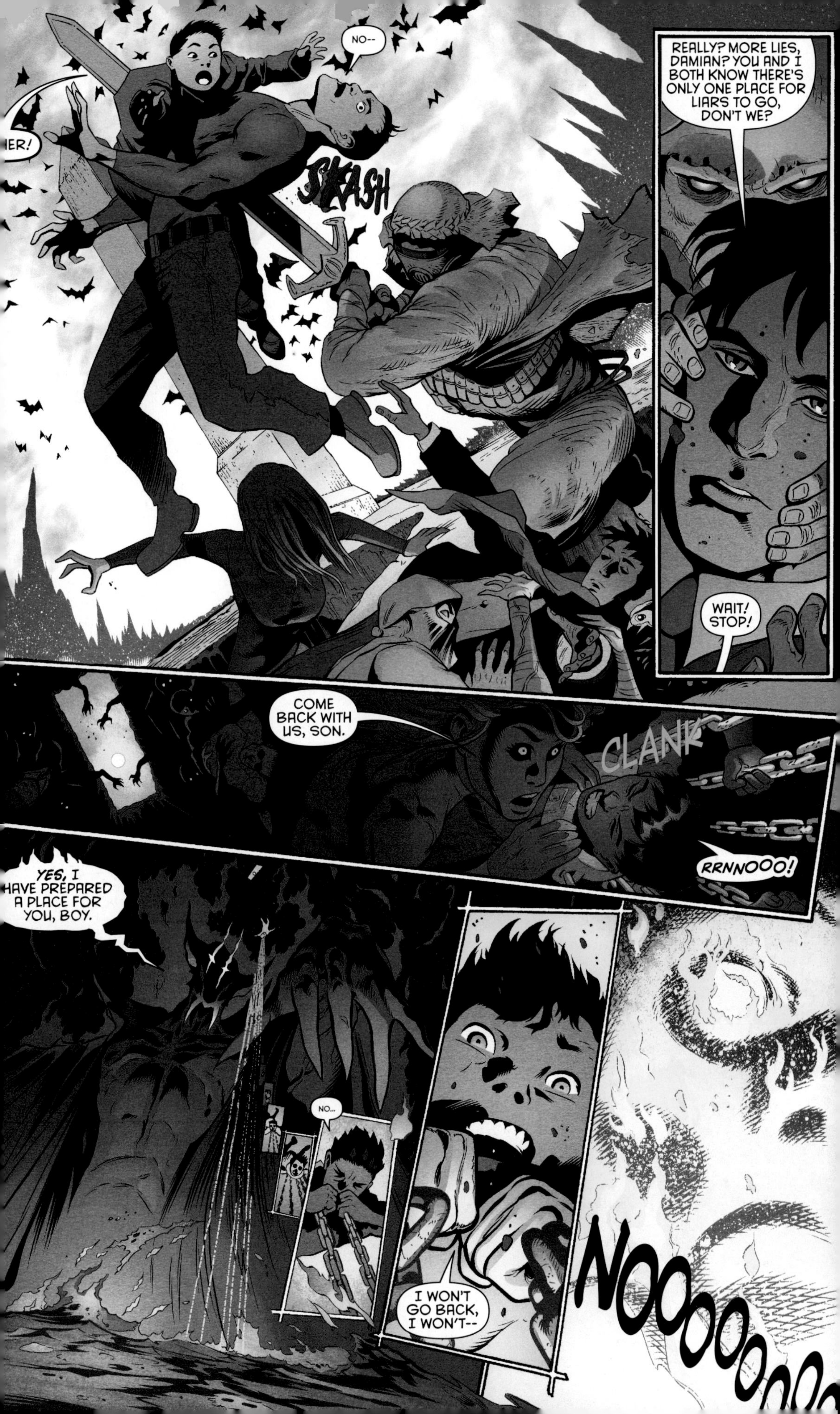

NO--
ER!
SKASH
REALLY? MORE LIES, DAMIAN? YOU AND I BOTH KNOW THERE'S ONLY ONE PLACE FOR LIARS TO GO, DON'T WE?
WAIT! STOP!
COME BACK WITH US, SON.
CLANK
RRNNOOO!
YES, I HAVE PREPARED A PLACE FOR YOU, BOY.
NO...
I WON'T GO BACK, I WON'T--
NOOOOOOOO

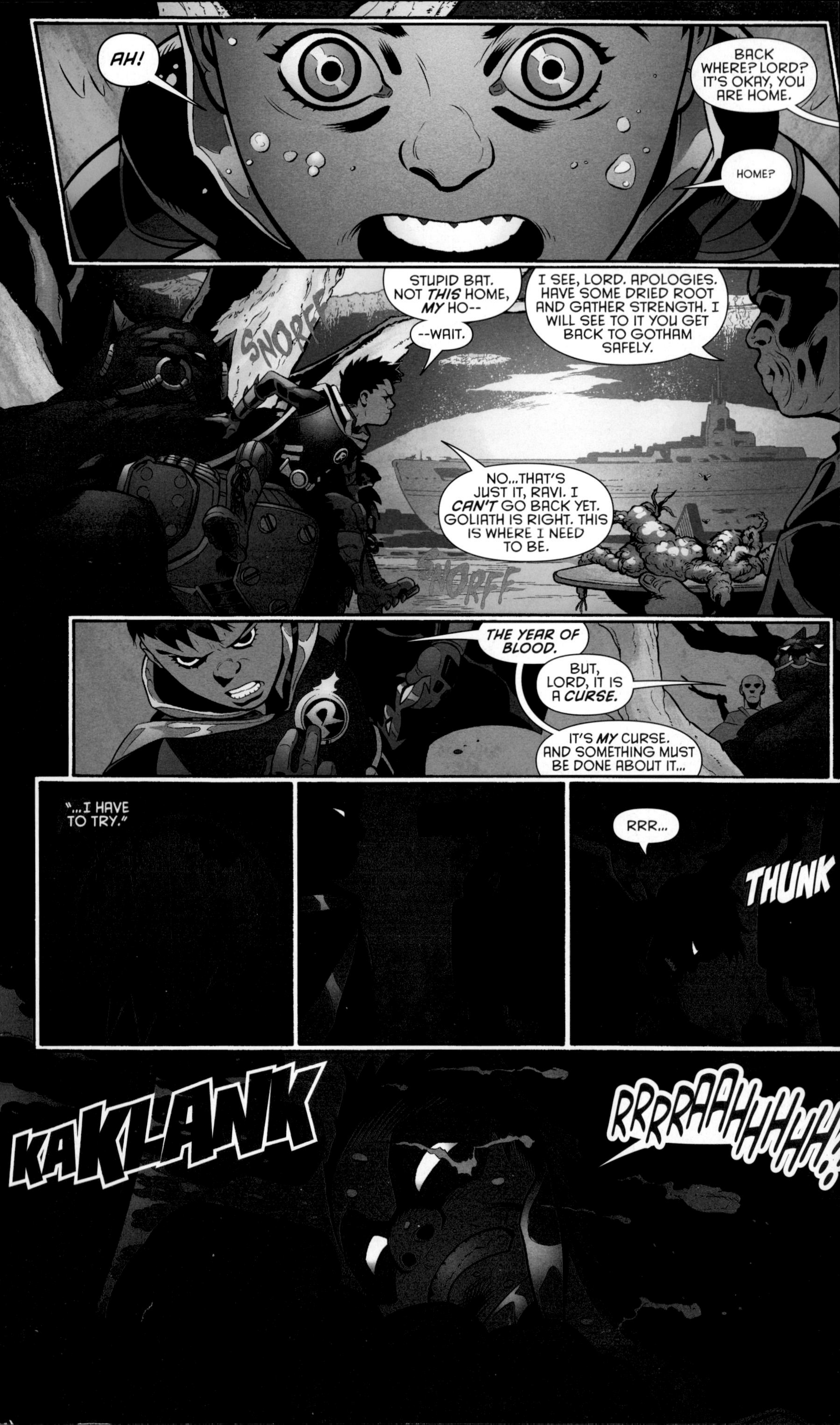
AH!
BACK WHERE? LORD? IT'S OKAY, YOU ARE HOME.
HOME?
STUPID BAT. NOT THIS HOME, MY HO--
--WAIT.
I SEE, LORD. APOLOGIES. HAVE SOME DRIED ROOT AND GATHER STRENGTH. I WILL SEE TO IT YOU GET BACK TO GOTHAM SAFELY.
SNORFF
NO...THAT'S JUST IT, RAVI. I CAN'T GO BACK YET. GOLIATH IS RIGHT. THIS IS WHERE I NEED TO BE.
SNORFF
THE YEAR OF BLOOD.
BUT, LORD, IT IS A CURSE.
IT'S MY CURSE. AND SOMETHING MUST BE DONE ABOUT IT...
"...I HAVE TO TRY."
RRR...
THUNK
KAKLANK
RRRRAAHHHHH!

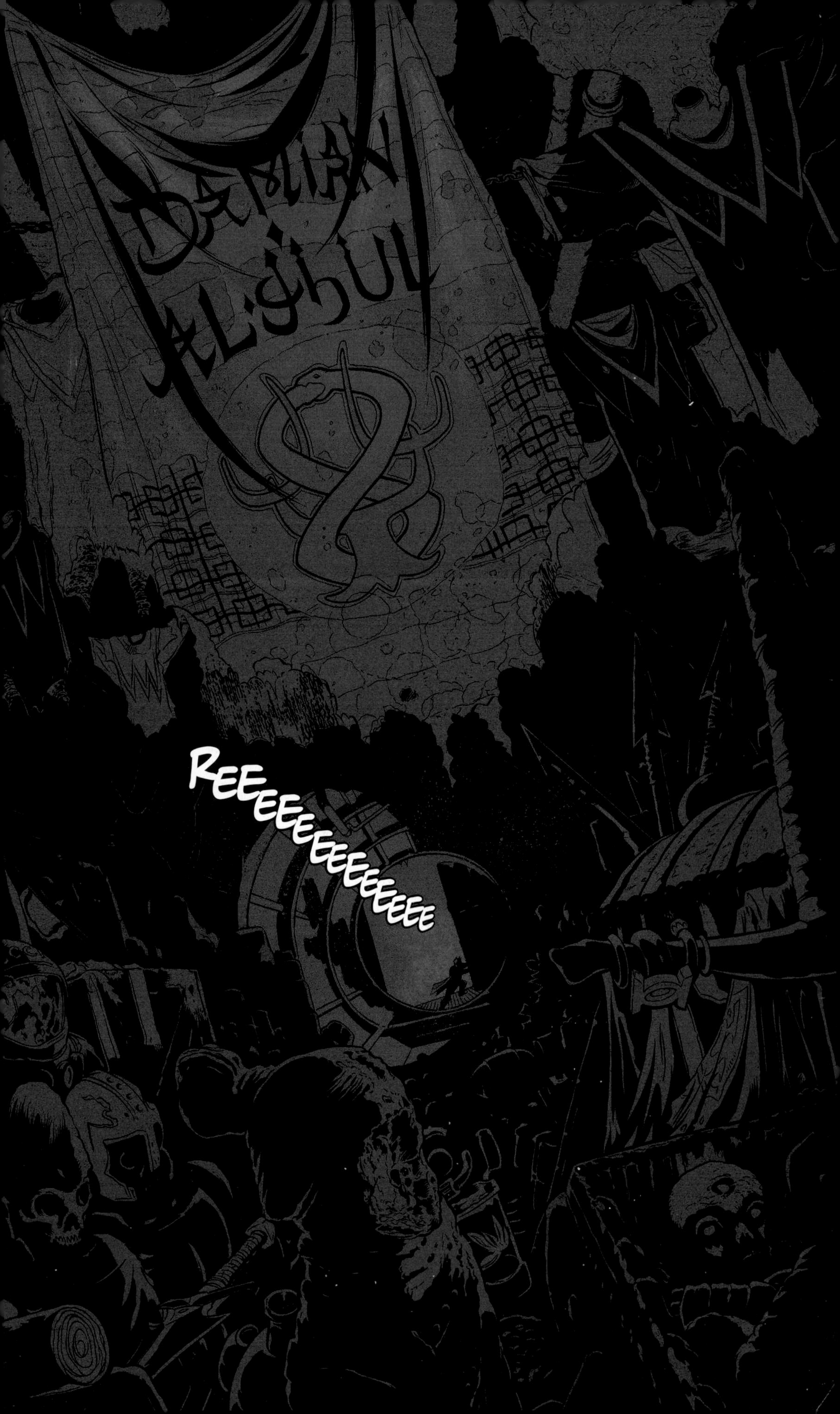
DAMIAN AL GHUL
REEEEEEEEEEEEEEE

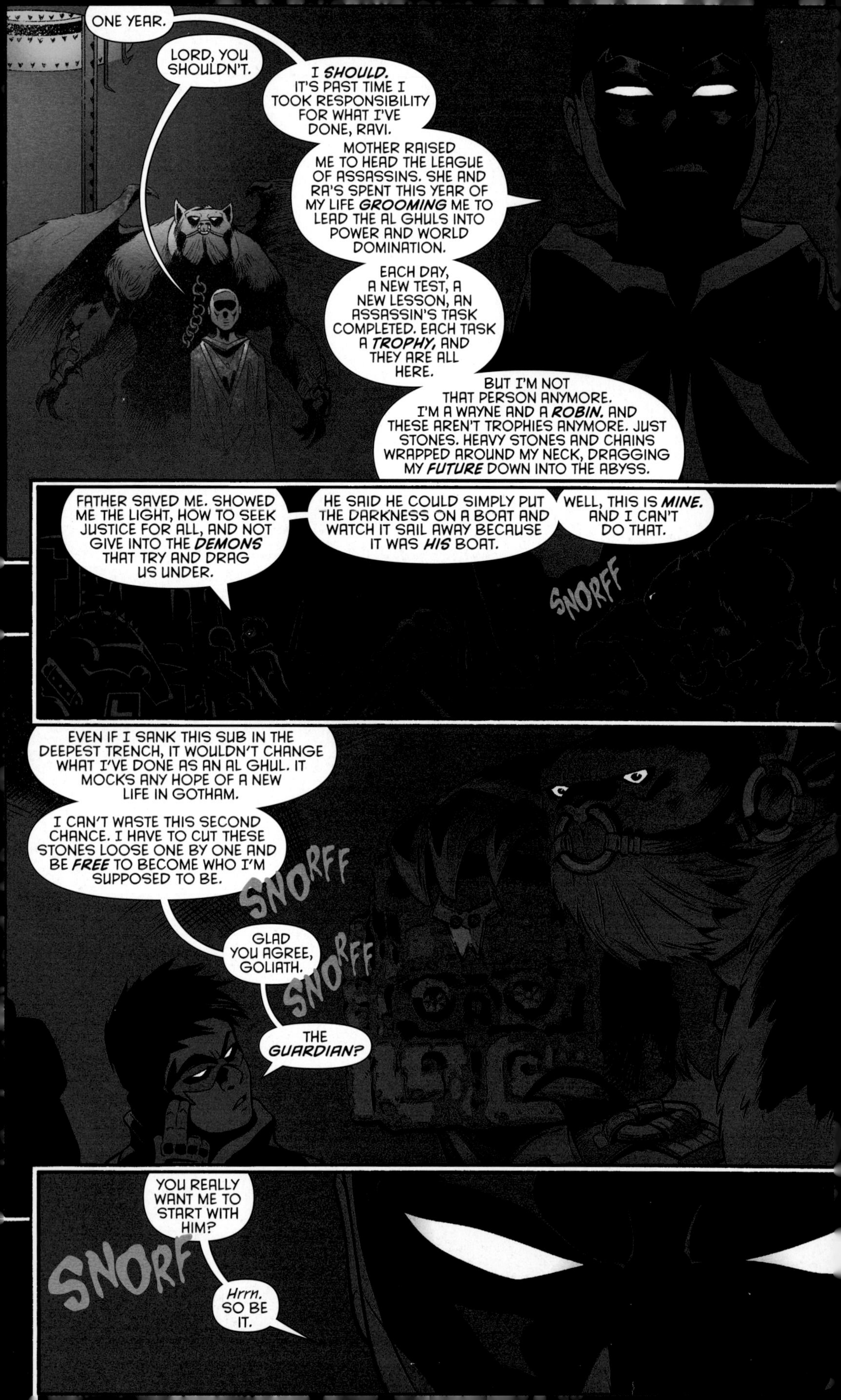
ONE YEAR.
LORD, YOU SHOULDN'T.
I *SHOULD.* IT'S PAST TIME I TOOK RESPONSIBILITY FOR WHAT I'VE DONE, RAVI.
MOTHER RAISED ME TO HEAD THE LEAGUE OF ASSASSINS. SHE AND RA'S SPENT THIS YEAR OF MY LIFE *GROOMING* ME TO LEAD THE AL GHULS INTO POWER AND WORLD DOMINATION.
EACH DAY, A NEW TEST, A NEW LESSON, AN ASSASSIN'S TASK COMPLETED. EACH TASK A *TROPHY,* AND THEY ARE ALL HERE.
BUT I'M NOT THAT PERSON ANYMORE. I'M A WAYNE AND A *ROBIN.* AND THESE AREN'T TROPHIES ANYMORE. JUST STONES. HEAVY STONES AND CHAINS WRAPPED AROUND MY NECK, DRAGGING MY *FUTURE* DOWN INTO THE ABYSS.
FATHER SAVED ME. SHOWED ME THE LIGHT, HOW TO SEEK JUSTICE FOR ALL, AND NOT GIVE INTO THE *DEMONS* THAT TRY AND DRAG US UNDER.
HE SAID HE COULD SIMPLY PUT THE DARKNESS ON A BOAT AND WATCH IT SAIL AWAY BECAUSE IT WAS *HIS* BOAT.
WELL, THIS IS *MINE.* AND I CAN'T DO THAT.
SNORFF
EVEN IF I SANK THIS SUB IN THE DEEPEST TRENCH, IT WOULDN'T CHANGE WHAT I'VE DONE AS AN AL GHUL. IT MOCKS ANY HOPE OF A NEW LIFE IN GOTHAM.
I CAN'T WASTE THIS SECOND CHANCE. I HAVE TO CUT THESE STONES LOOSE ONE BY ONE AND BE *FREE* TO BECOME WHO I'M SUPPOSED TO BE.
SNORFF
GLAD YOU AGREE, GOLIATH.
SNORFF
THE *GUARDIAN?*
YOU REALLY WANT ME TO START WITH HIM?
SNORF
Hrrn. SO BE IT.

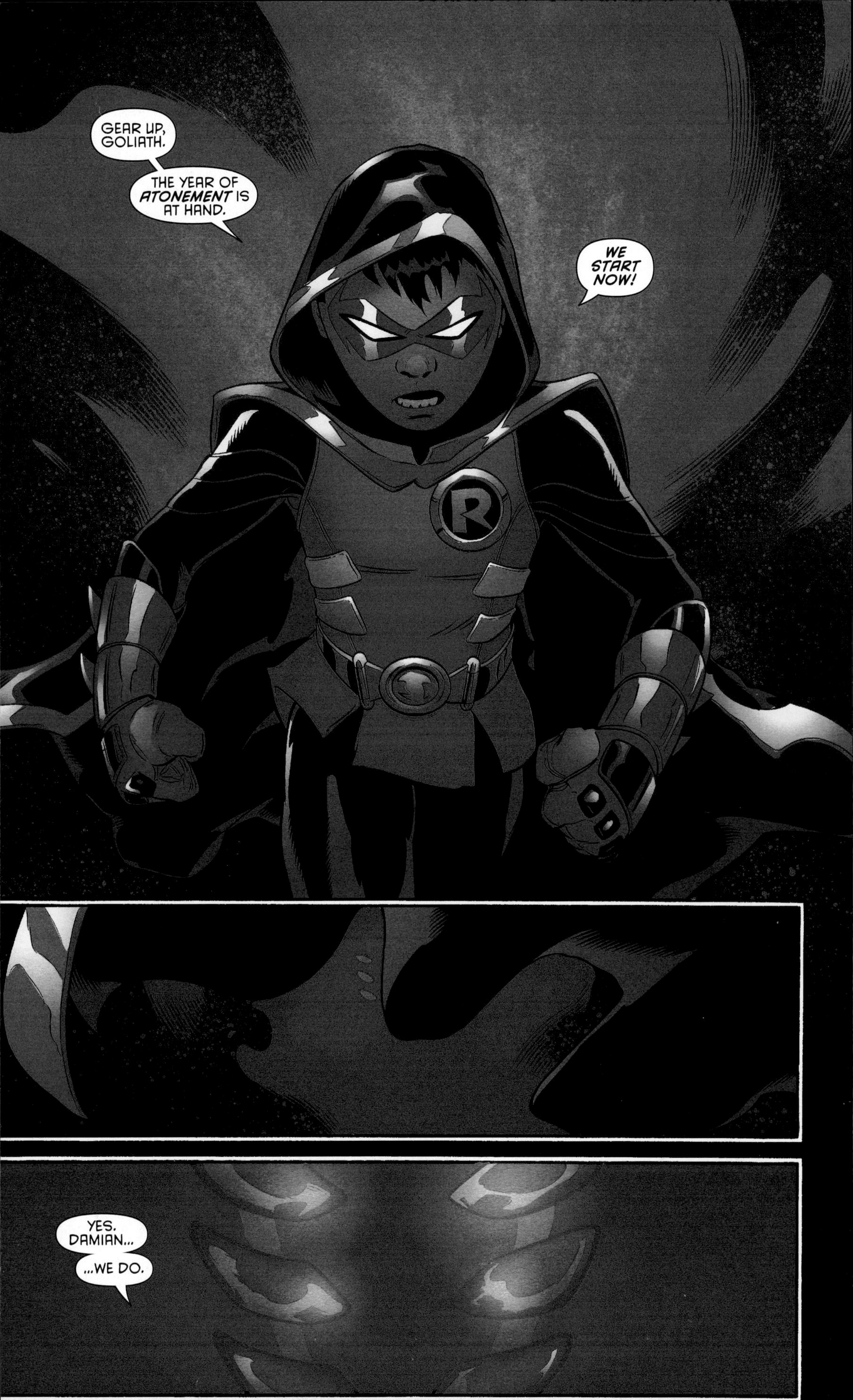
GEAR UP, GOLIATH.
THE YEAR OF *ATONEMENT* IS AT HAND.
WE START NOW!
YES. DAMIAN...
...WE DO.

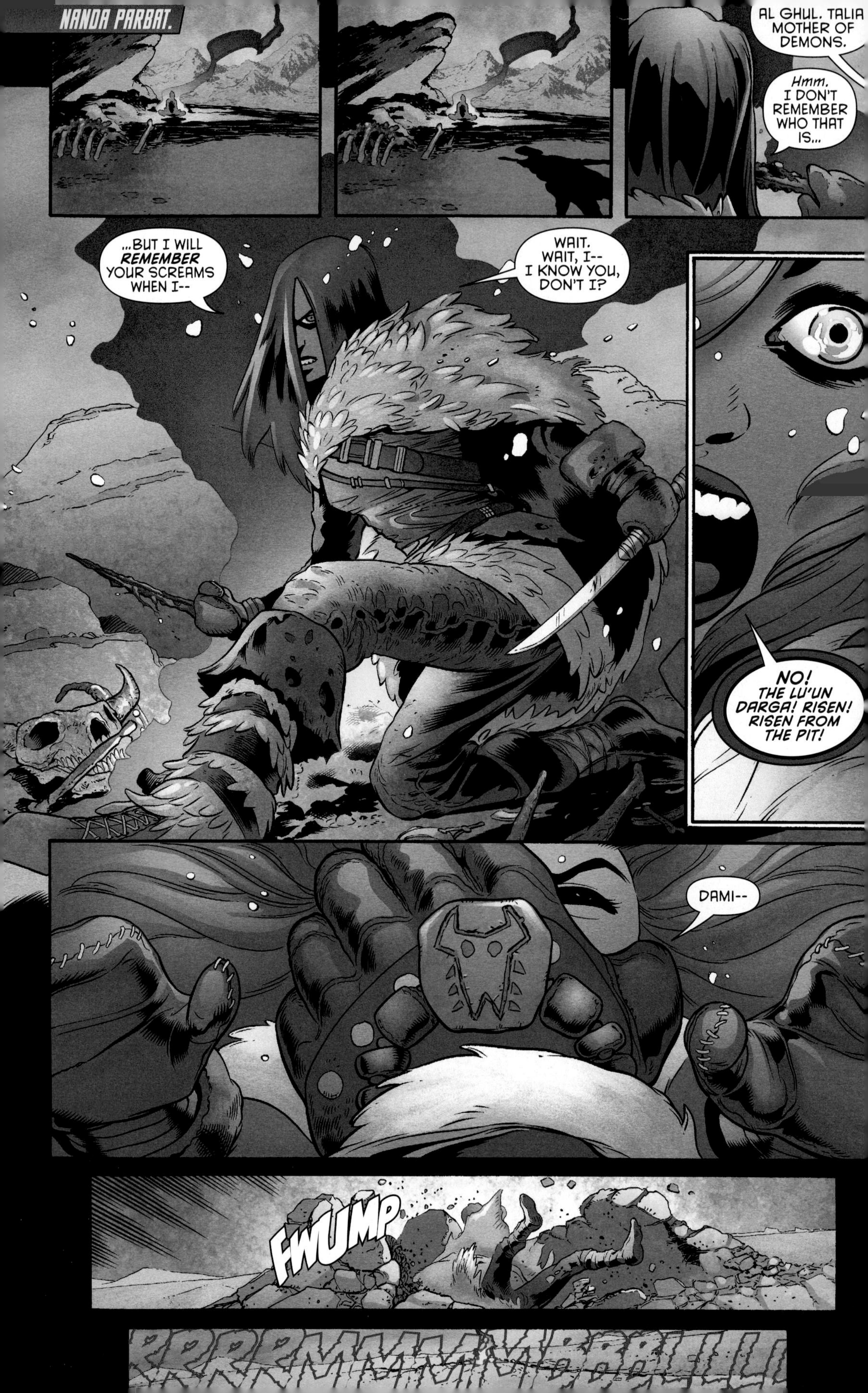
NANDA PARBAT.
AL GHUL. TALIA MOTHER OF DEMONS.
Hmm. I DON'T REMEMBER WHO THAT IS...
...BUT I WILL REMEMBER YOUR SCREAMS WHEN I--
WAIT. WAIT, I-- I KNOW YOU, DON'T I?
NO! THE LU'UN DARGA! RISEN! RISEN FROM THE PIT!
DAMI--
FWUMP

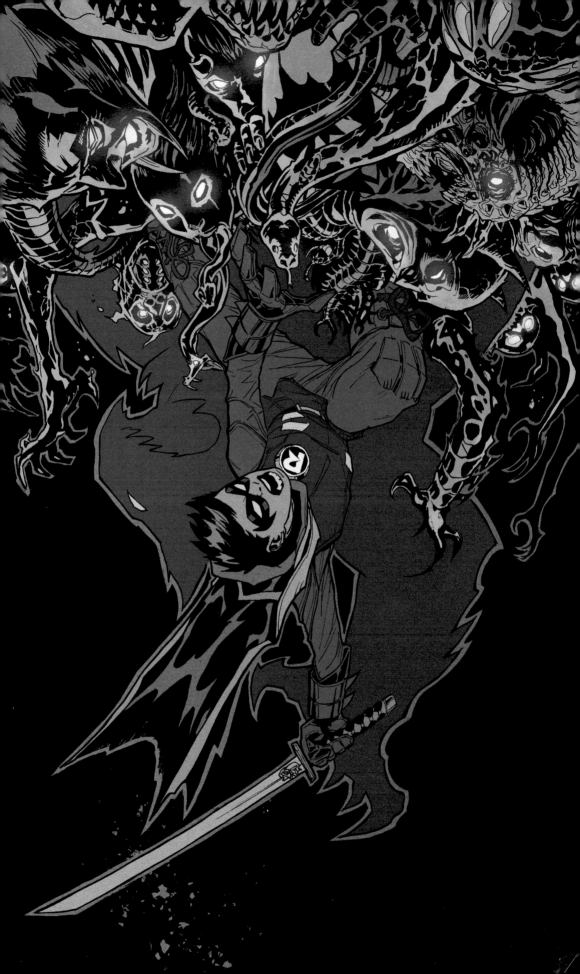

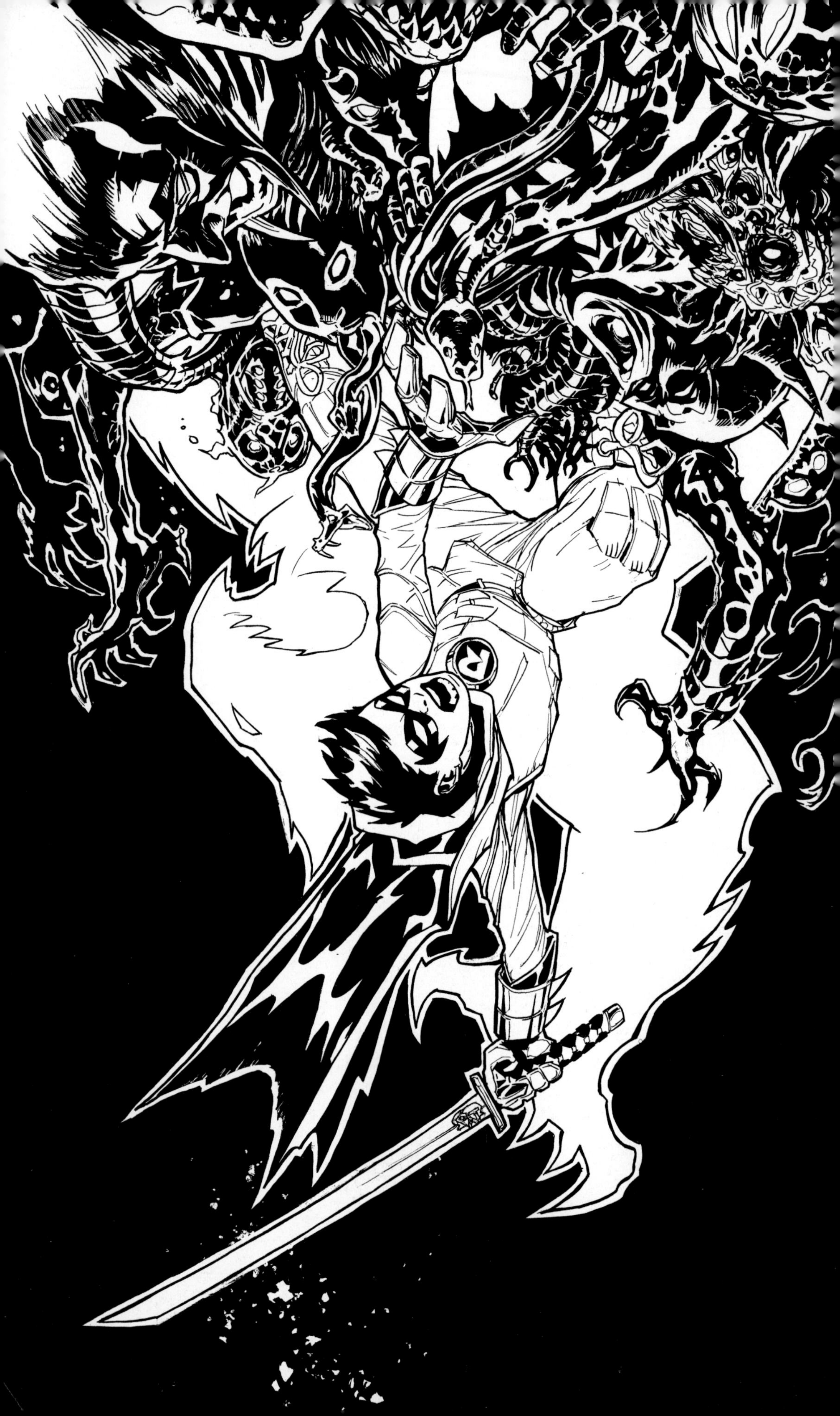

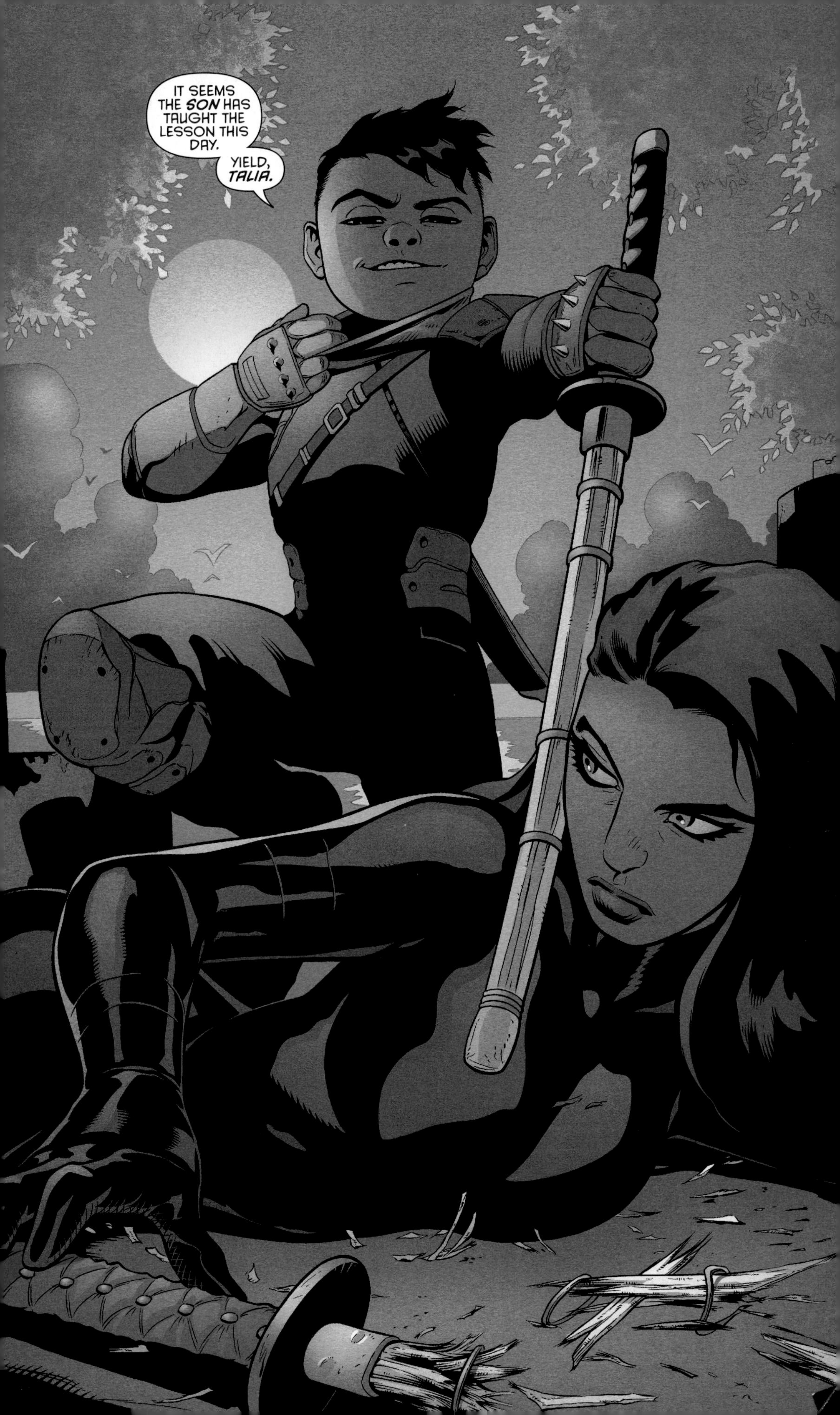
IT SEEMS THE SON HAS TAUGHT THE LESSON THIS DAY.
YIELD, TALIA.

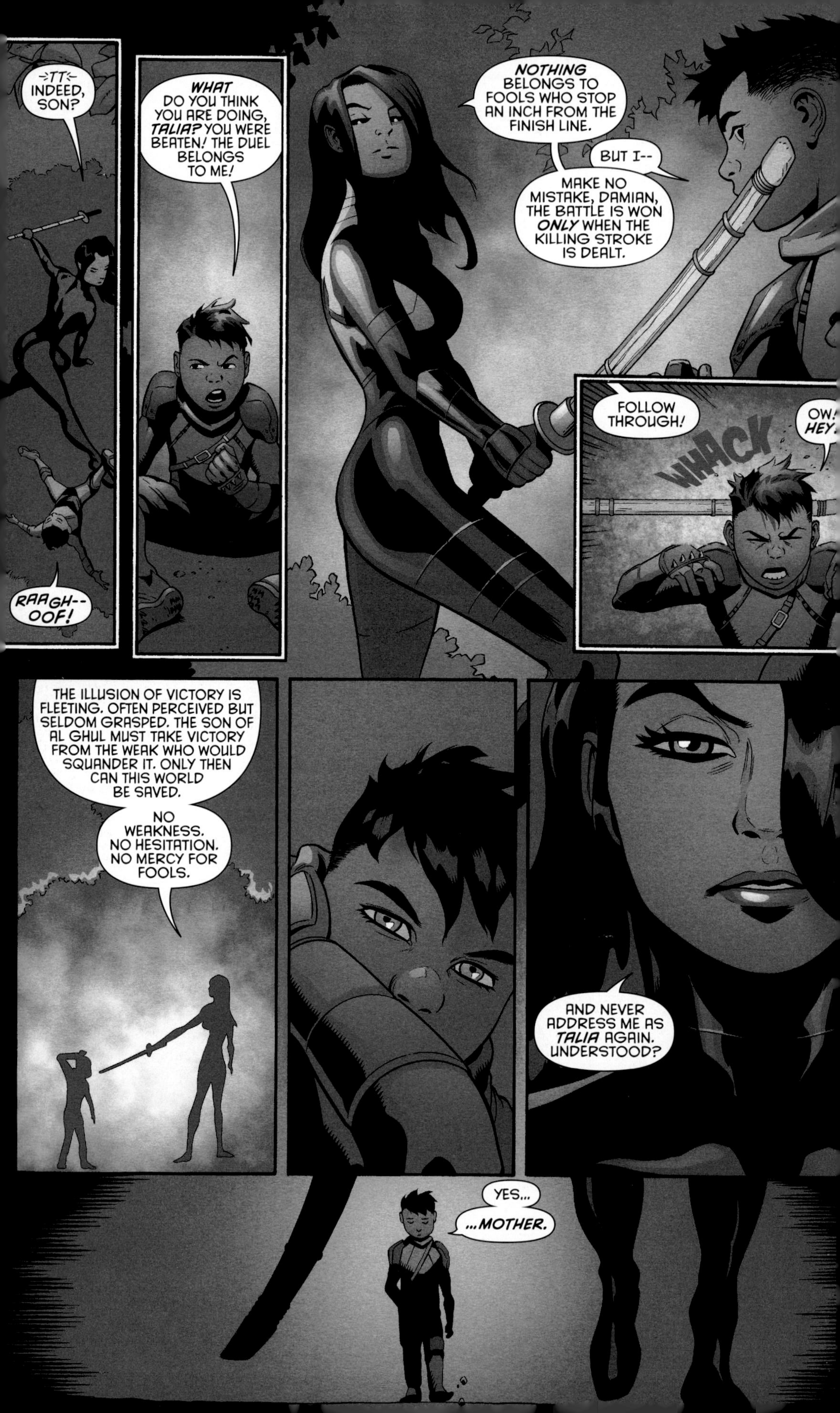

-TT- INDEED, SON?
RAAGH-- OOF!
WHAT DO YOU THINK YOU ARE DOING, TALIA? YOU WERE BEATEN! THE DUEL BELONGS TO ME!
NOTHING BELONGS TO FOOLS WHO STOP AN INCH FROM THE FINISH LINE.
BUT I--
MAKE NO MISTAKE, DAMIAN, THE BATTLE IS WON ONLY WHEN THE KILLING STROKE IS DEALT.
FOLLOW THROUGH!
WHACK
OW! HEY!
THE ILLUSION OF VICTORY IS FLEETING. OFTEN PERCEIVED BUT SELDOM GRASPED. THE SON OF AL GHUL MUST TAKE VICTORY FROM THE WEAK WHO WOULD SQUANDER IT. ONLY THEN CAN THIS WORLD BE SAVED.
NO WEAKNESS. NO HESITATION. NO MERCY FOR FOOLS.
AND NEVER ADDRESS ME AS TALIA AGAIN. UNDERSTOOD?
YES...
...MOTHER.

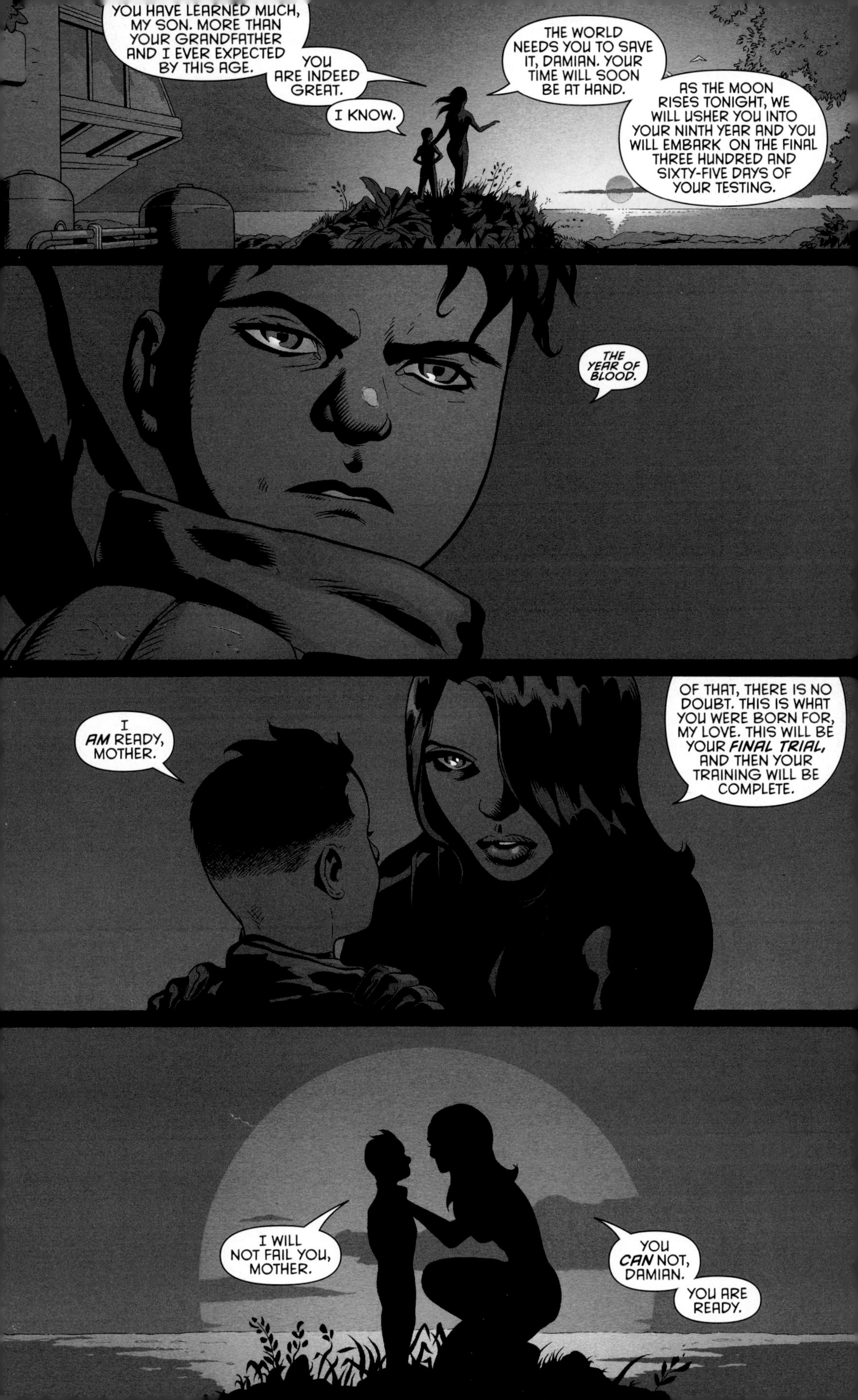
YOU HAVE LEARNED MUCH, MY SON. MORE THAN YOUR GRANDFATHER AND I EVER EXPECTED BY THIS AGE.
YOU ARE INDEED GREAT.
I KNOW.
THE WORLD NEEDS YOU TO SAVE IT, DAMIAN. YOUR TIME WILL SOON BE AT HAND.
AS THE MOON RISES TONIGHT, WE WILL USHER YOU INTO YOUR NINTH YEAR AND YOU WILL EMBARK ON THE FINAL THREE HUNDRED AND SIXTY-FIVE DAYS OF YOUR TESTING.
THE YEAR OF BLOOD.
I AM READY, MOTHER.
OF THAT, THERE IS NO DOUBT. THIS IS WHAT YOU WERE BORN FOR, MY LOVE. THIS WILL BE YOUR FINAL TRIAL, AND THEN YOUR TRAINING WILL BE COMPLETE.
I WILL NOT FAIL YOU, MOTHER.
YOU CAN NOT, DAMIAN.
YOU ARE READY.

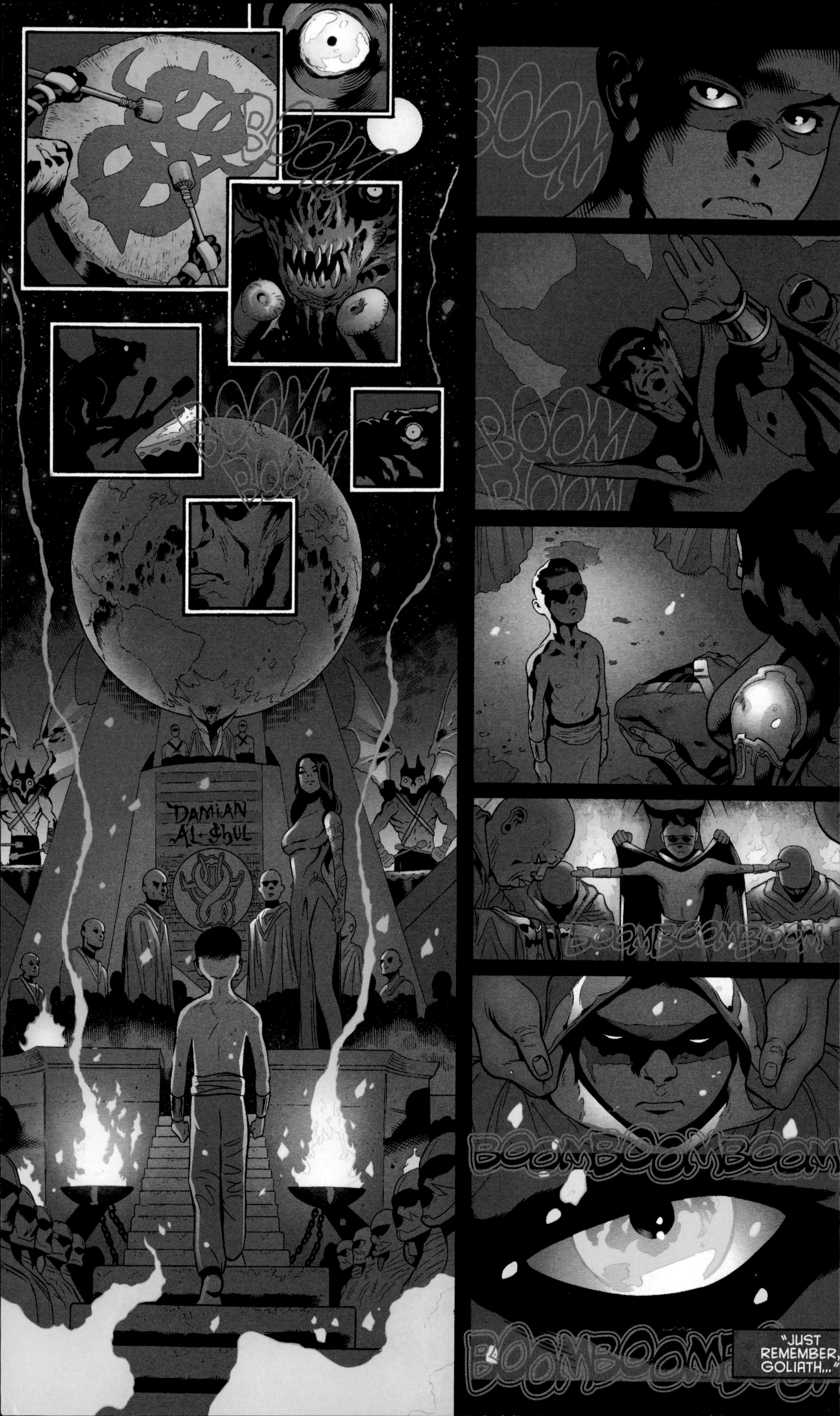
BOOM
BOOM
BOOM
BOOM
DAMIAN AL-GHUL
BOOM
BOOM
BOOM
BOOM
BOOMBOOMBOOM
BOOMBOOMBOOM
BOOMBOOMBOOM
"JUST REMEMBER, GOLIATH..."

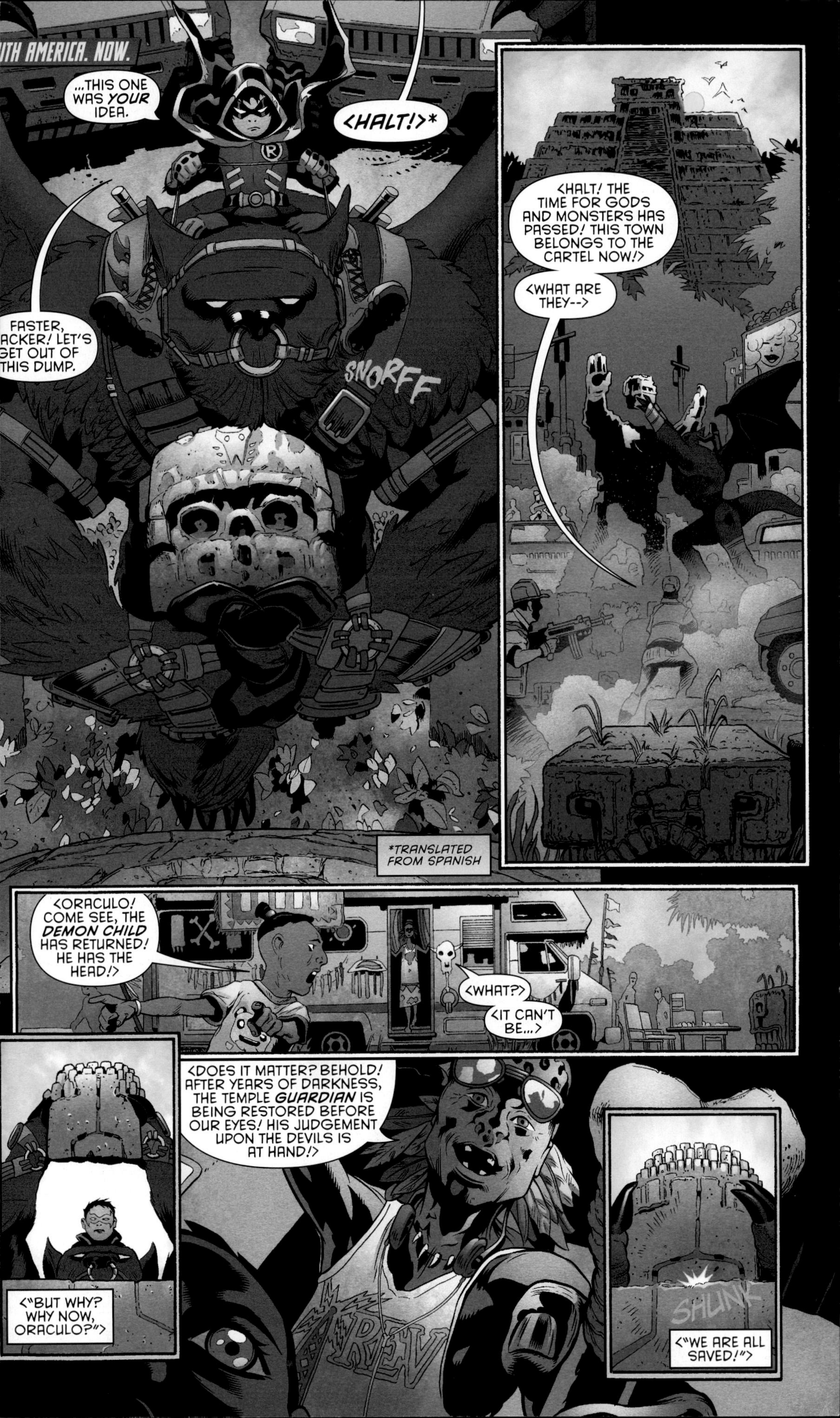

...TH AMERICA. NOW.
...THIS ONE WAS *YOUR* IDEA.
<HALT!>*
FASTER, ...ACKER! LET'S GET OUT OF THIS DUMP.
SNORFF
<HALT! THE TIME FOR GODS AND MONSTERS HAS PASSED! THIS TOWN BELONGS TO THE CARTEL NOW!>
<WHAT ARE THEY-->
*TRANSLATED FROM SPANISH
<ORACULO! COME SEE, THE *DEMON CHILD* HAS RETURNED! HE HAS THE HEAD!>
<WHAT?>
<IT CAN'T BE...>
<DOES IT MATTER? BEHOLD! AFTER YEARS OF DARKNESS, THE TEMPLE *GUARDIAN* IS BEING RESTORED BEFORE OUR EYES! HIS JUDGEMENT UPON THE DEVILS IS AT HAND!>
<"BUT WHY? WHY NOW, ORACULO?">
SHUNK
<"WE ARE ALL SAVED!">

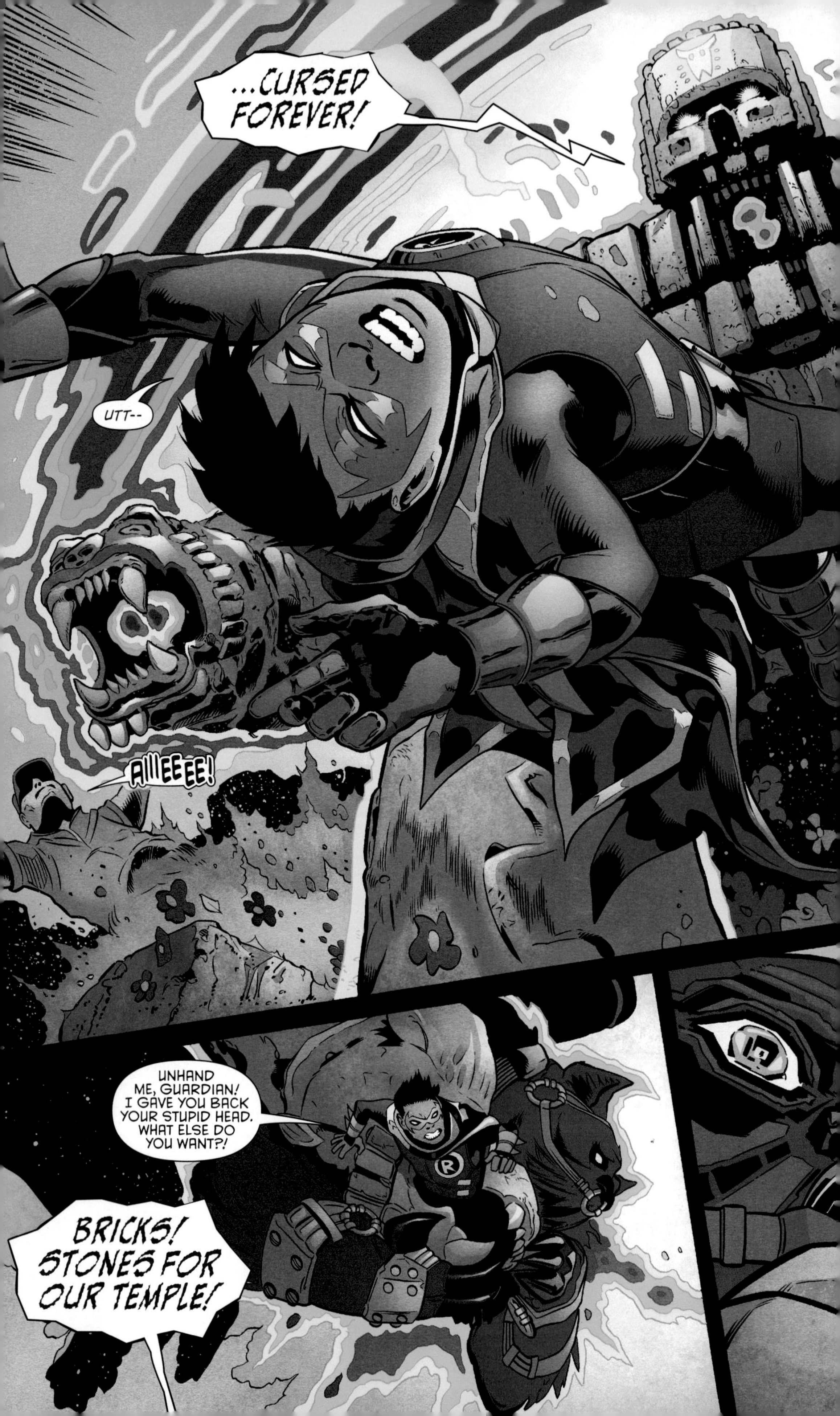
...CURSED FOREVER!
UTT--
AIIIEEEEE!
UNHAND ME, GUARDIAN! I GAVE YOU BACK YOUR STUPID HEAD. WHAT ELSE DO YOU WANT?!
BRICKS! STONES FOR OUR TEMPLE!

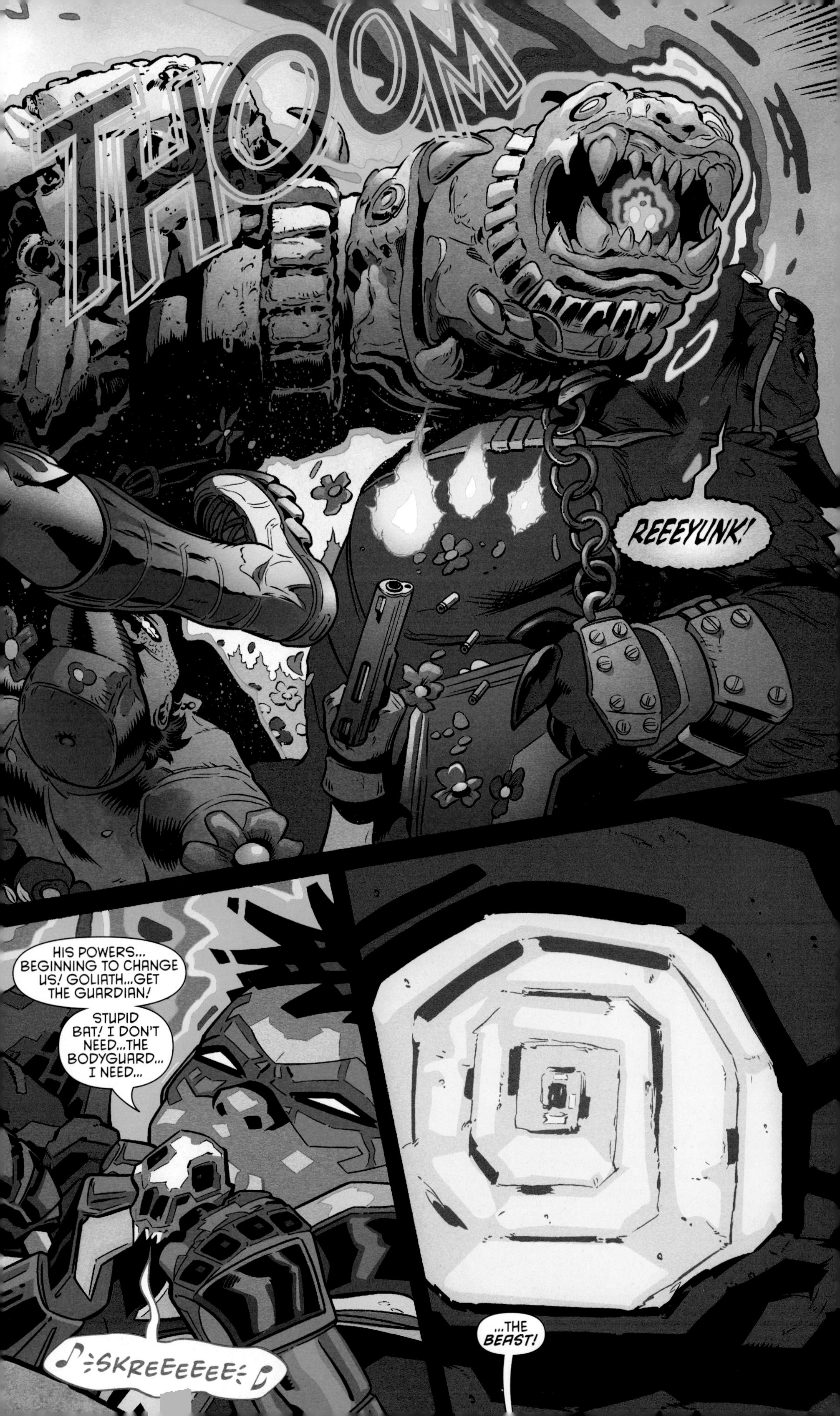
THOOM
REEEYUNK!
HIS POWERS... BEGINNING TO CHANGE US! GOLIATH...GET THE GUARDIAN!
STUPID BAT! I DON'T NEED...THE BODYGUARD... I NEED...
...THE BEAST!
SKREEEEEEE

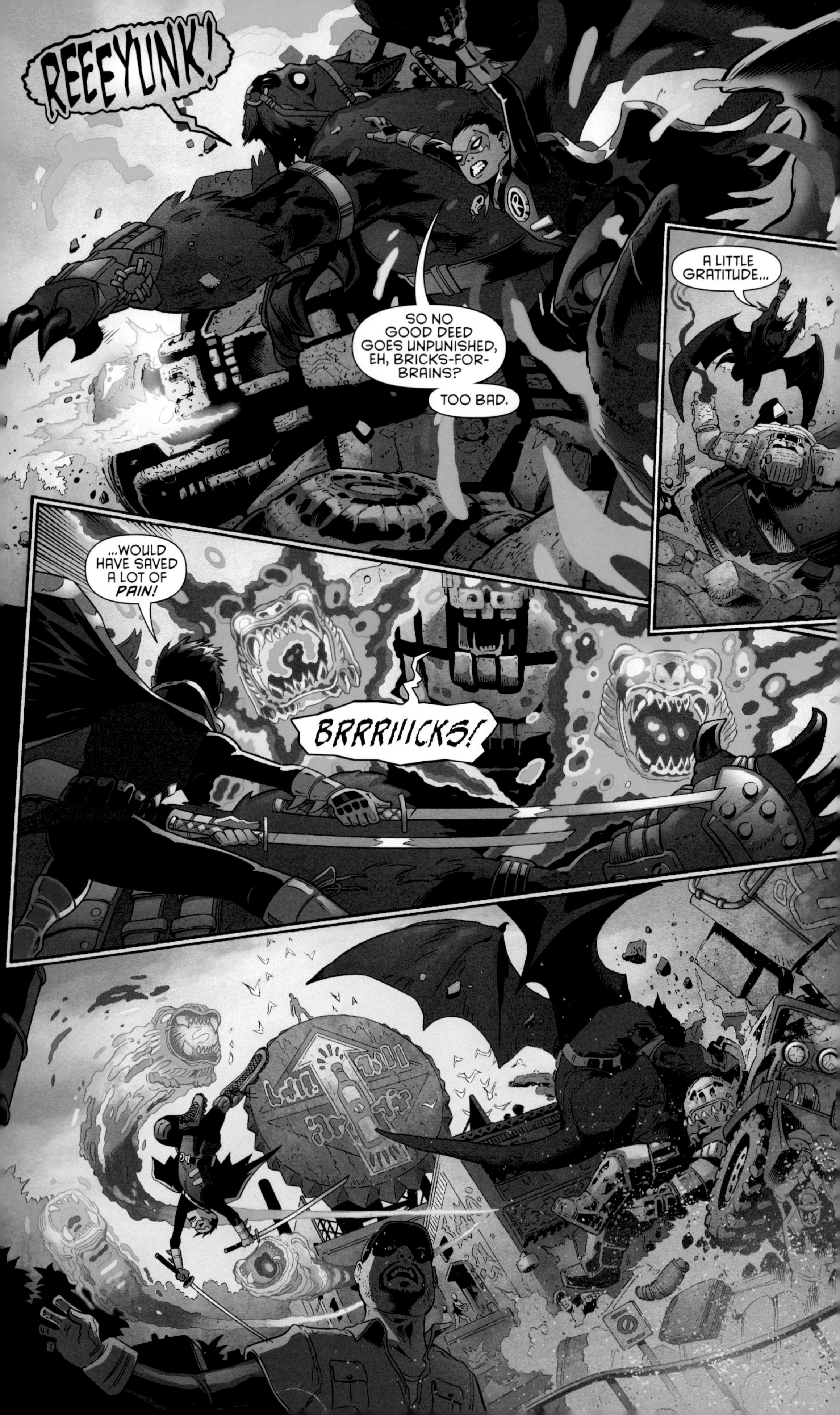
REEEYUNK!
SO NO GOOD DEED GOES UNPUNISHED, EH, BRICKS-FOR-BRAINS?
TOO BAD.
A LITTLE GRATITUDE...
...WOULD HAVE SAVED A LOT OF *PAIN!*
BRRRIIICKS!

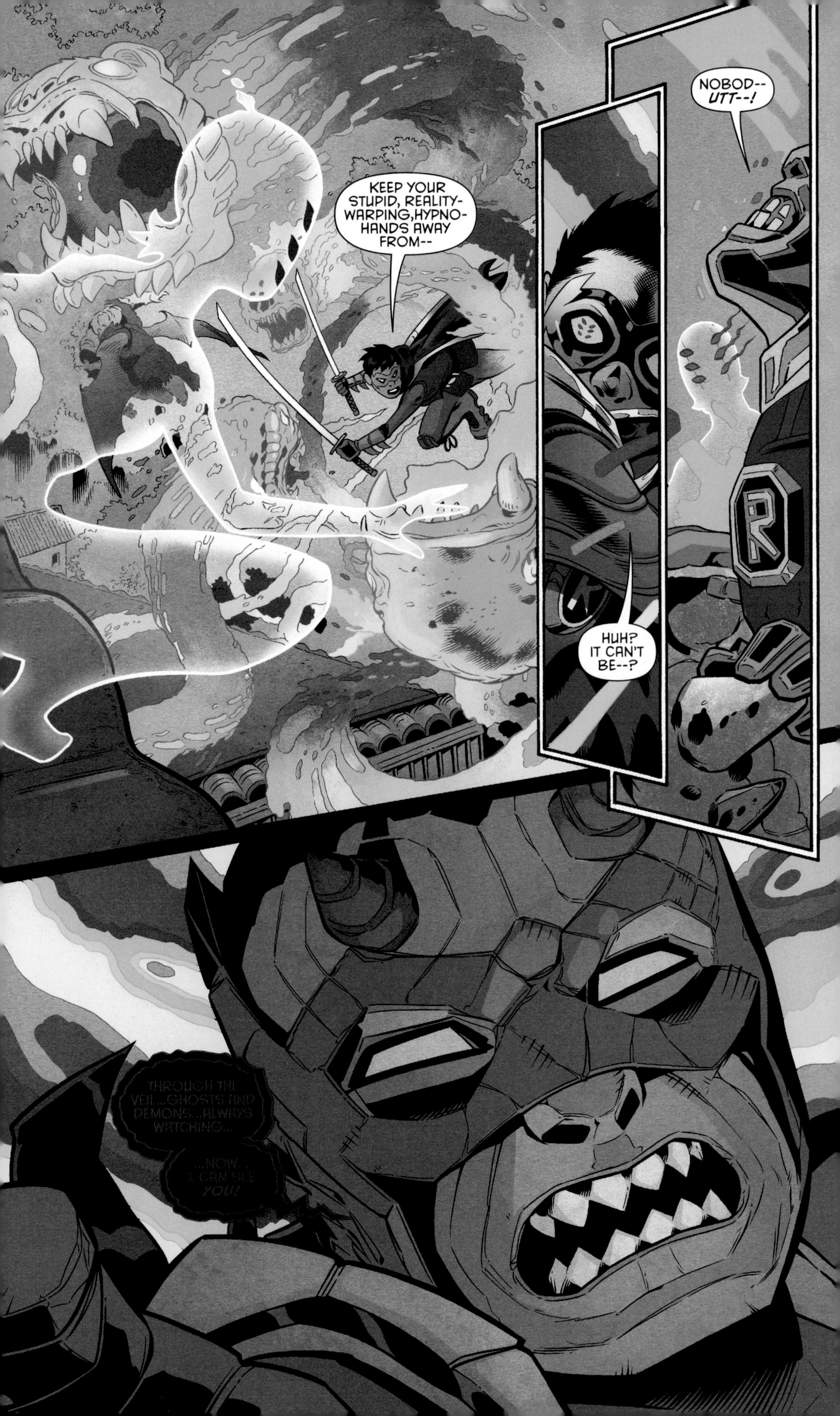
KEEP YOUR STUPID, REALITY-WARPING, HYPNO-HANDS AWAY FROM--
NOBOD--
UTT--!
HUH? IT CAN'T BE--?
THROUGH THE VEIL...GHOSTS AND DEMONS...ALWAYS WATCHING...
...NOW... I CAN SEE YOU!

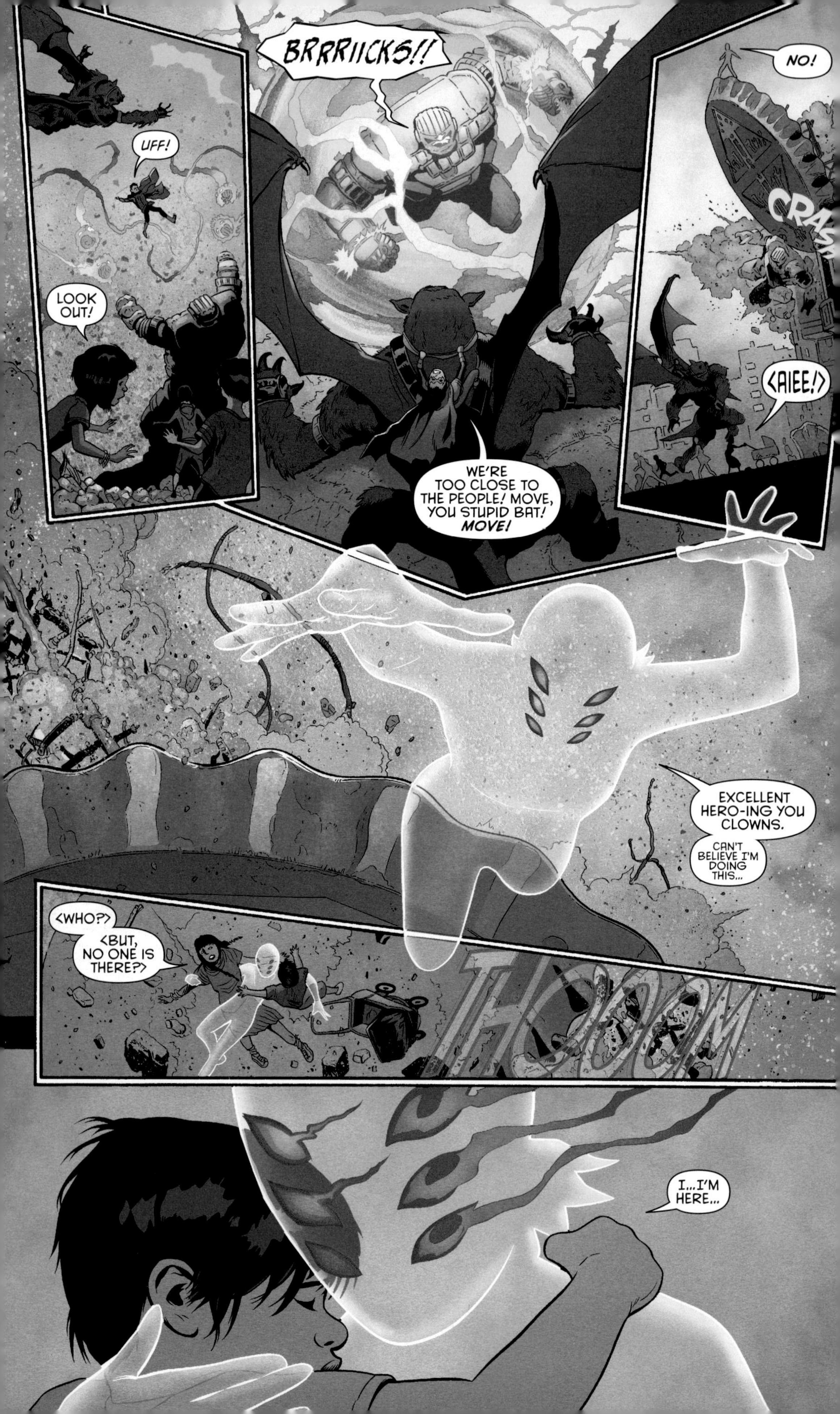
UFF!
LOOK OUT!
BRRRIICKS!!
WE'RE TOO CLOSE TO THE PEOPLE! MOVE, YOU STUPID BAT! *MOVE!*
NO!
CRASH
<AIEE!>
EXCELLENT HERO-ING YOU CLOWNS.
CAN'T BELIEVE I'M DOING THIS...
<WHO?>
<BUT, NO ONE IS THERE?>
THOOOM
I...I'M HERE...

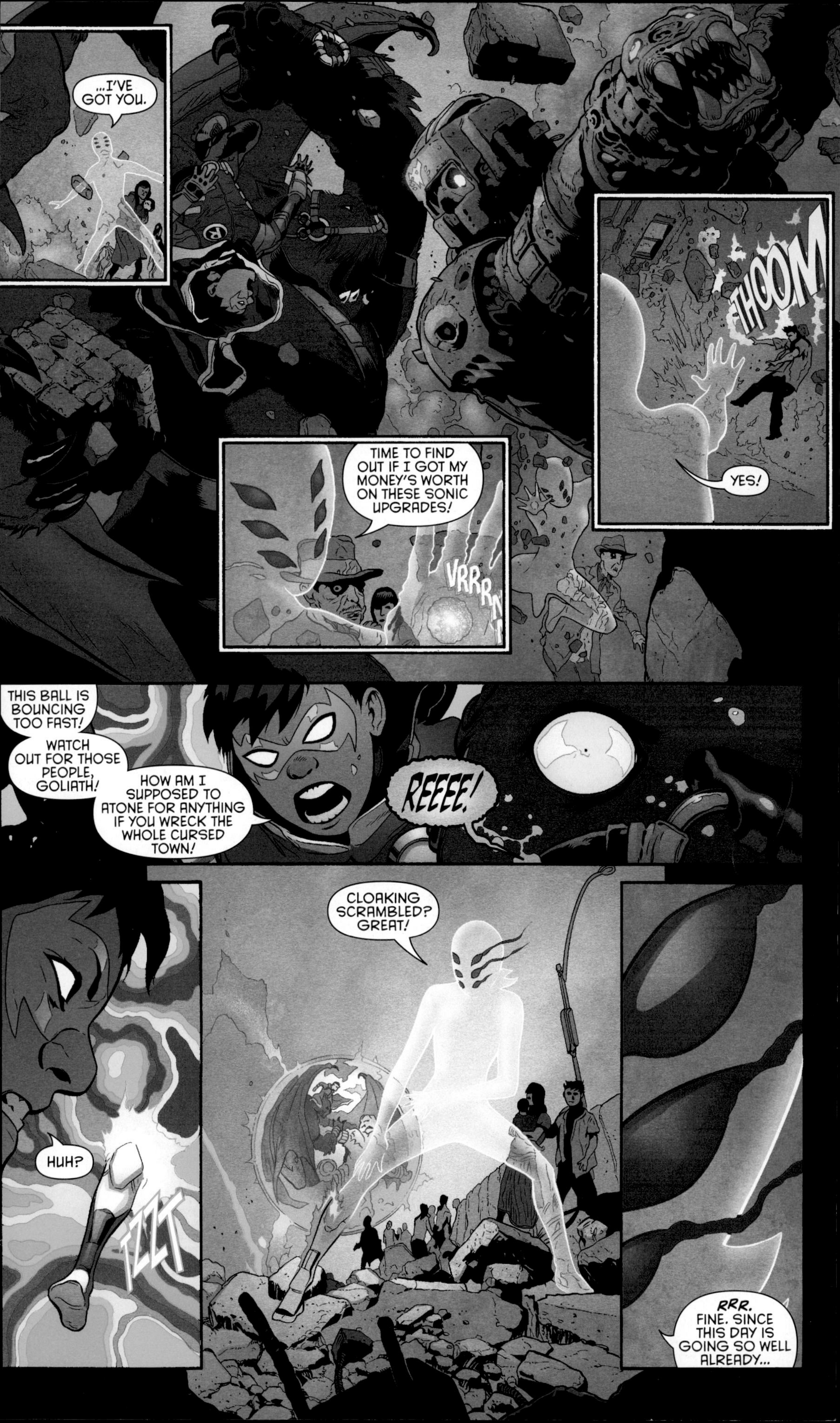
...I'VE GOT YOU.
THOOM
YES!
TIME TO FIND OUT IF I GOT MY MONEY'S WORTH ON THESE SONIC UPGRADES!
VRRRN
THIS BALL IS BOUNCING TOO FAST!
WATCH OUT FOR THOSE PEOPLE, GOLIATH!
HOW AM I SUPPOSED TO ATONE FOR ANYTHING IF YOU WRECK THE WHOLE CURSED TOWN!
REEEE!
HUH?
FZZT
CLOAKING SCRAMBLED? GREAT!
RRR. FINE. SINCE THIS DAY IS GOING SO WELL ALREADY...

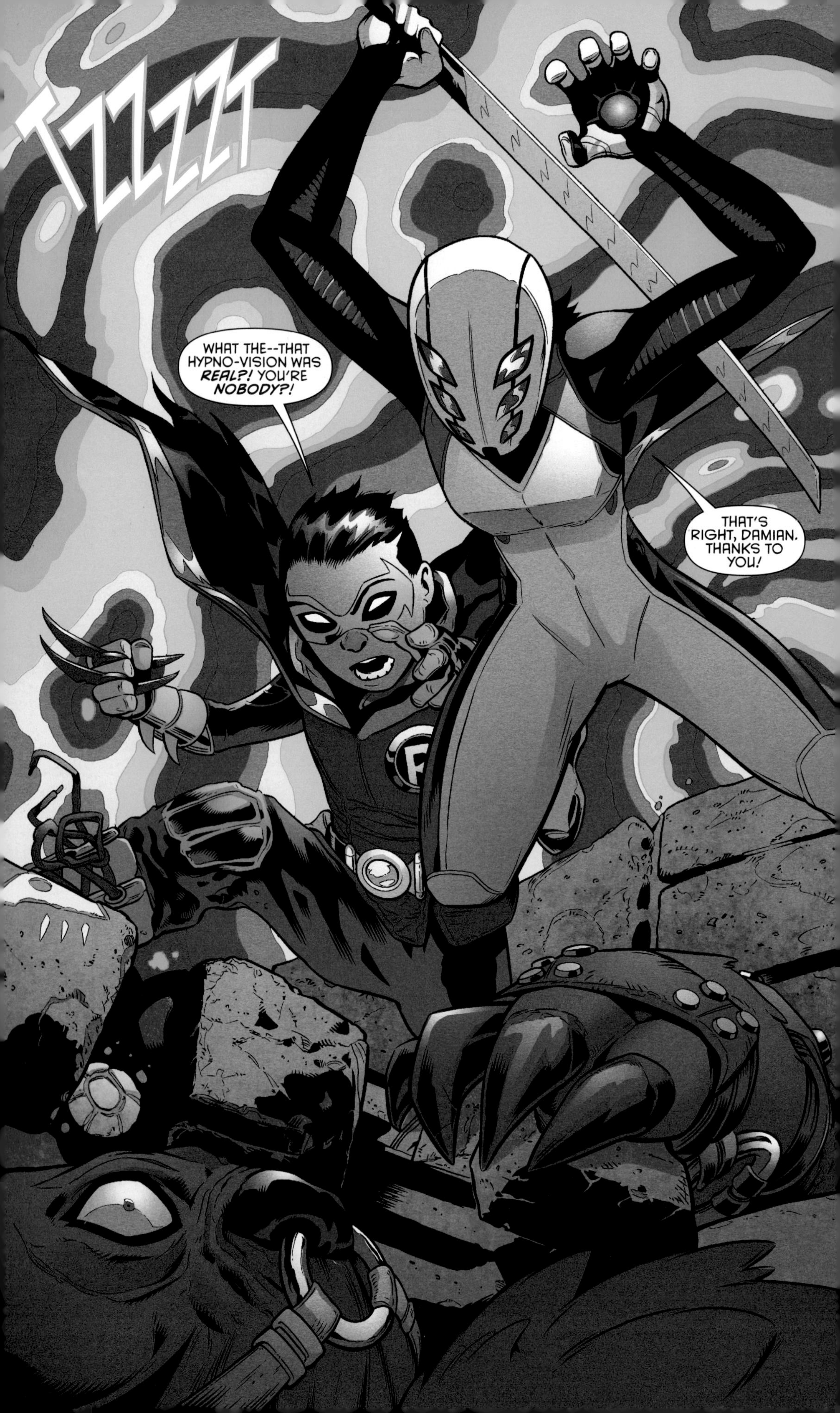
TZZZZZT
WHAT THE--THAT HYPNO-VISION WAS REAL?! YOU'RE NOBODY?!
THAT'S RIGHT, DAMIAN. THANKS TO YOU!

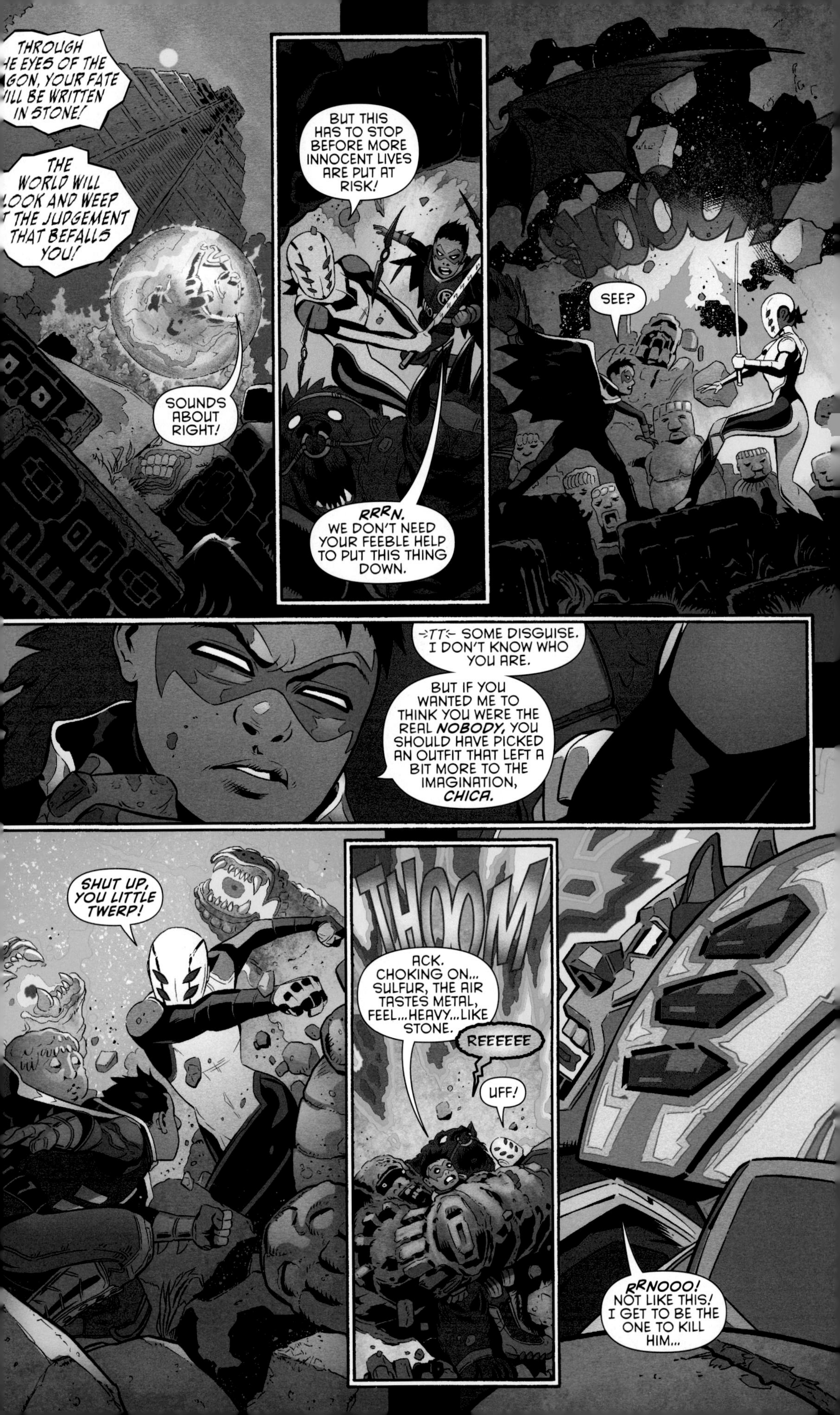
THROUGH HE EYES OF THE AGON, YOUR FATE ILL BE WRITTEN IN STONE!
THE WORLD WILL OOK AND WEEP T THE JUDGEMENT THAT BEFALLS YOU!
SOUNDS ABOUT RIGHT!
BUT THIS HAS TO STOP BEFORE MORE INNOCENT LIVES ARE PUT AT RISK!
RRRN. WE DON'T NEED YOUR FEEBLE HELP TO PUT THIS THING DOWN.
SEE?
-TT- SOME DISGUISE. I DON'T KNOW WHO YOU ARE.
BUT IF YOU WANTED ME TO THINK YOU WERE THE REAL NOBODY, YOU SHOULD HAVE PICKED AN OUTFIT THAT LEFT A BIT MORE TO THE IMAGINATION, CHICA.
SHUT UP, YOU LITTLE TWERP!
THOOM
ACK. CHOKING ON... SULFUR, THE AIR TASTES METAL, FEEL...HEAVY...LIKE STONE.
REEEEEE
UFF!
RRNOOO! NOT LIKE THIS! I GET TO BE THE ONE TO KILL HIM...

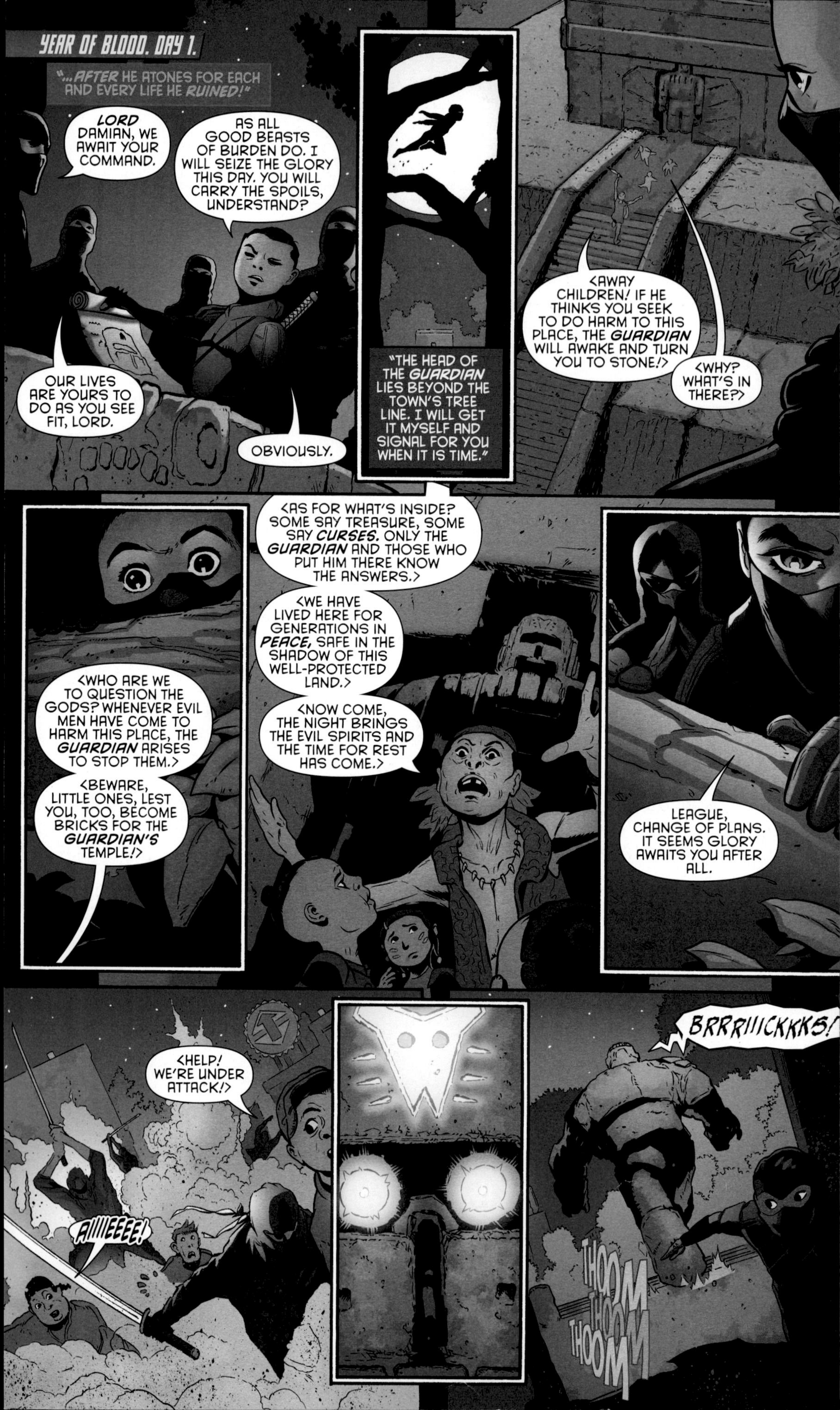
YEAR OF BLOOD. DAY 1.
"...AFTER HE ATONES FOR EACH AND EVERY LIFE HE RUINED!"
LORD DAMIAN, WE AWAIT YOUR COMMAND.
AS ALL GOOD BEASTS OF BURDEN DO. I WILL SEIZE THE GLORY THIS DAY. YOU WILL CARRY THE SPOILS, UNDERSTAND?
OUR LIVES ARE YOURS TO DO AS YOU SEE FIT, LORD.
OBVIOUSLY.
"THE HEAD OF THE GUARDIAN LIES BEYOND THE TOWN'S TREE LINE. I WILL GET IT MYSELF AND SIGNAL FOR YOU WHEN IT IS TIME."
<AWAY CHILDREN! IF HE THINKS YOU SEEK TO DO HARM TO THIS PLACE, THE GUARDIAN WILL AWAKE AND TURN YOU TO STONE!>
<WHY? WHAT'S IN THERE?>
<AS FOR WHAT'S INSIDE? SOME SAY TREASURE, SOME SAY CURSES. ONLY THE GUARDIAN AND THOSE WHO PUT HIM THERE KNOW THE ANSWERS.>
<WE HAVE LIVED HERE FOR GENERATIONS IN PEACE, SAFE IN THE SHADOW OF THIS WELL-PROTECTED LAND.>
<WHO ARE WE TO QUESTION THE GODS? WHENEVER EVIL MEN HAVE COME TO HARM THIS PLACE, THE GUARDIAN ARISES TO STOP THEM.>
<BEWARE, LITTLE ONES, LEST YOU, TOO, BECOME BRICKS FOR THE GUARDIAN'S TEMPLE!>
<NOW COME, THE NIGHT BRINGS THE EVIL SPIRITS AND THE TIME FOR REST HAS COME.>
LEAGUE, CHANGE OF PLANS. IT SEEMS GLORY AWAITS YOU AFTER ALL.
<HELP! WE'RE UNDER ATTACK!>
AIIIEEEE!
BRRRIIICKKKS!
THOOM THOOM THOOM

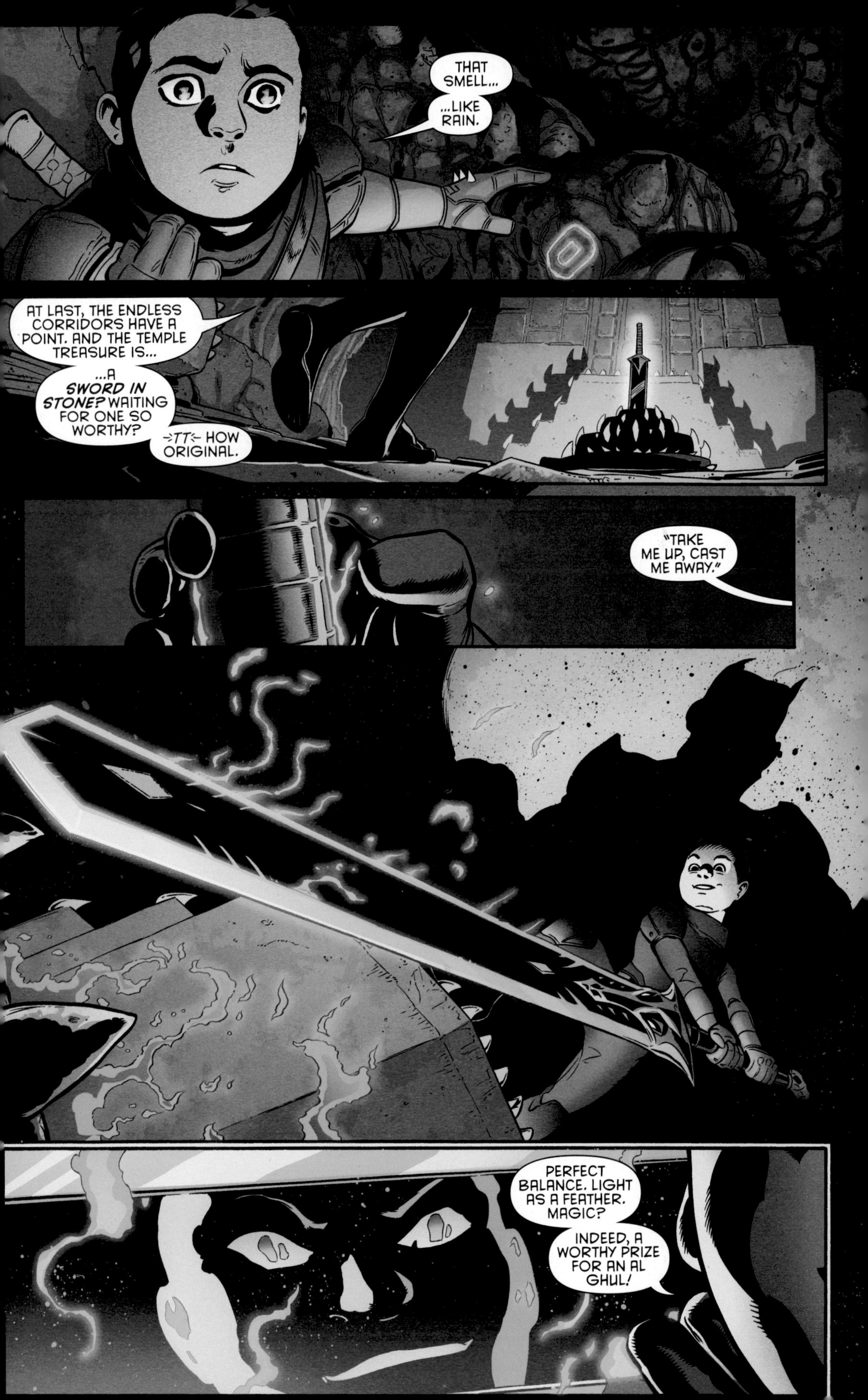
THAT SMELL...
...LIKE RAIN.
AT LAST, THE ENDLESS CORRIDORS HAVE A POINT. AND THE TEMPLE TREASURE IS...
...A SWORD IN STONE? WAITING FOR ONE SO WORTHY?
-TT- HOW ORIGINAL.
"TAKE ME UP, CAST ME AWAY."
PERFECT BALANCE. LIGHT AS A FEATHER. MAGIC?
INDEED, A WORTHY PRIZE FOR AN AL GHUL!

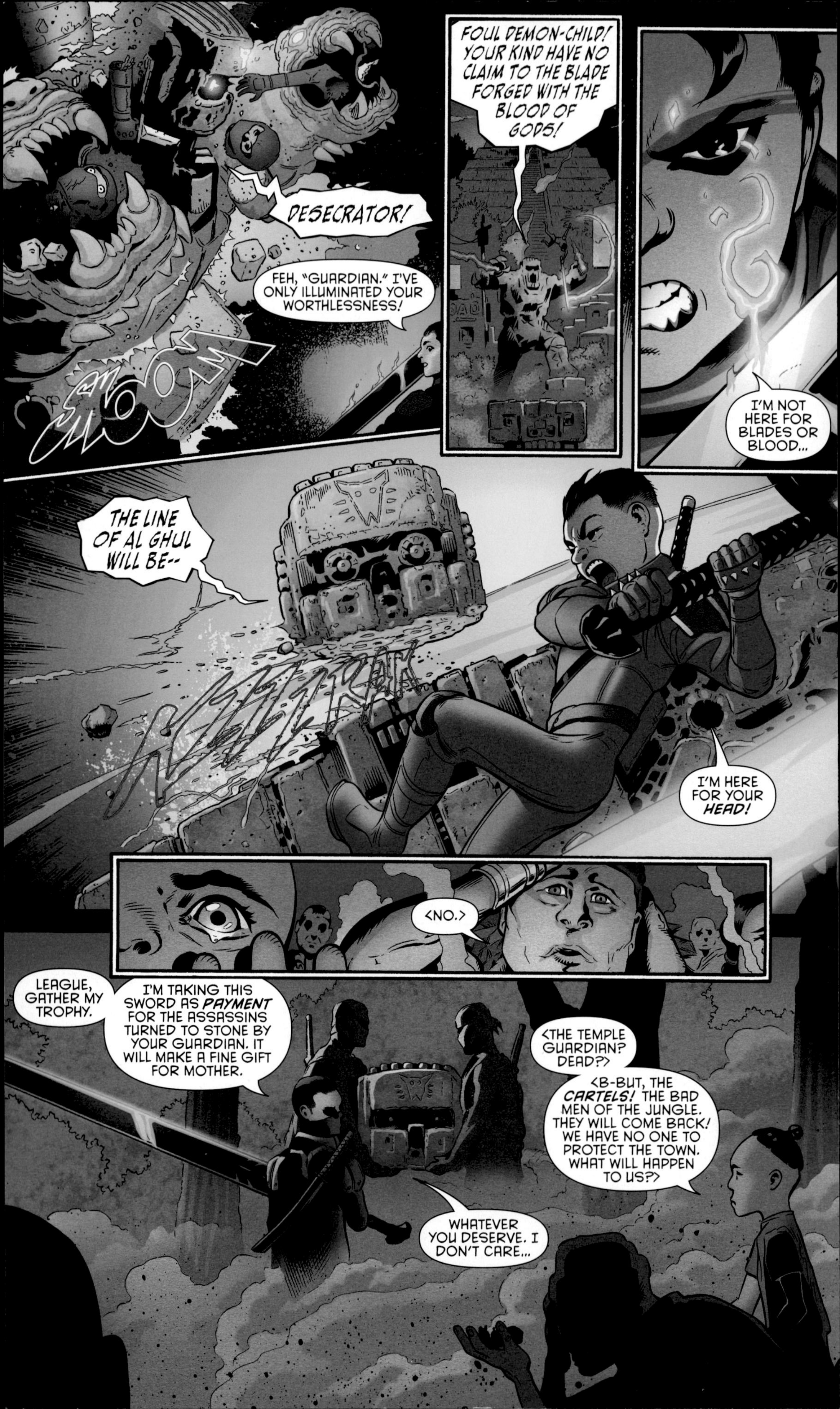
DESECRATOR!
FEH, "GUARDIAN." I'VE ONLY ILLUMINATED YOUR WORTHLESSNESS!
FOUL DEMON-CHILD! YOUR KIND HAVE NO CLAIM TO THE BLADE FORGED WITH THE BLOOD OF GODS!
I'M NOT HERE FOR BLADES OR BLOOD...
THE LINE OF AL GHUL WILL BE--
I'M HERE FOR YOUR HEAD!
<NO.>
LEAGUE, GATHER MY TROPHY.
I'M TAKING THIS SWORD AS PAYMENT FOR THE ASSASSINS TURNED TO STONE BY YOUR GUARDIAN. IT WILL MAKE A FINE GIFT FOR MOTHER.
<THE TEMPLE GUARDIAN? DEAD?>
<B-BUT, THE CARTELS! THE BAD MEN OF THE JUNGLE. THEY WILL COME BACK! WE HAVE NO ONE TO PROTECT THE TOWN. WHAT WILL HAPPEN TO US?>
WHATEVER YOU DESERVE. I DON'T CARE...

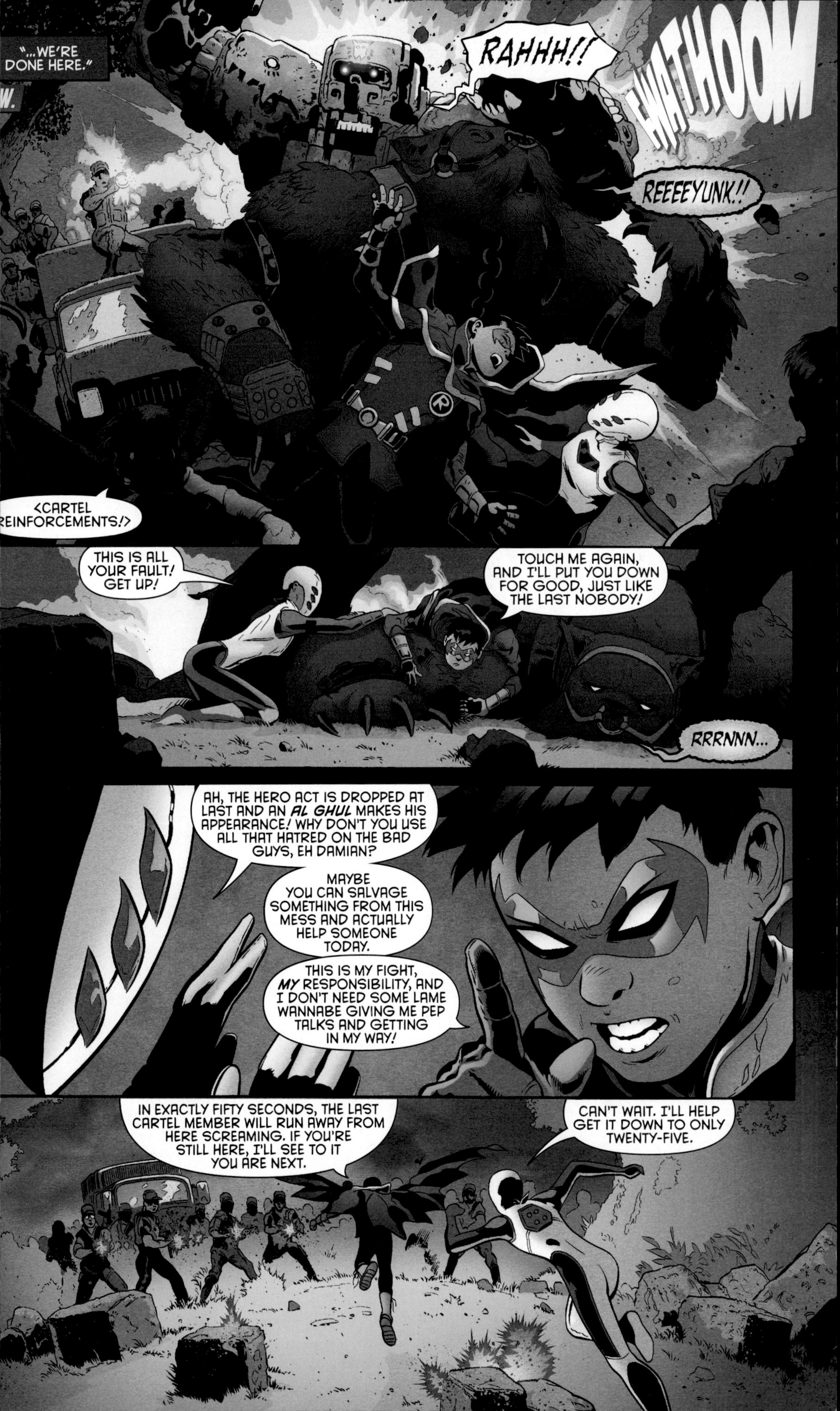

"...WE'RE DONE HERE."
RAHHH!!
FWATHOOM
REEEEYUNK!!
<CARTEL REINFORCEMENTS!>
THIS IS ALL YOUR FAULT! GET UP!
TOUCH ME AGAIN, AND I'LL PUT YOU DOWN FOR GOOD, JUST LIKE THE LAST NOBODY!
RRRNNN...
AH, THE HERO ACT IS DROPPED AT LAST AND AN *AL GHUL* MAKES HIS APPEARANCE! WHY DON'T YOU USE ALL THAT HATRED ON THE BAD GUYS, EH DAMIAN?
MAYBE YOU CAN SALVAGE SOMETHING FROM THIS MESS AND ACTUALLY HELP SOMEONE TODAY.
THIS IS MY FIGHT, *MY* RESPONSIBILITY, AND I DON'T NEED SOME LAME WANNABE GIVING ME PEP TALKS AND GETTING IN MY WAY!
IN EXACTLY FIFTY SECONDS, THE LAST CARTEL MEMBER WILL RUN AWAY FROM HERE SCREAMING. IF YOU'RE STILL HERE, I'LL SEE TO IT YOU ARE NEXT.
CAN'T WAIT. I'LL HELP GET IT DOWN TO ONLY TWENTY-FIVE.

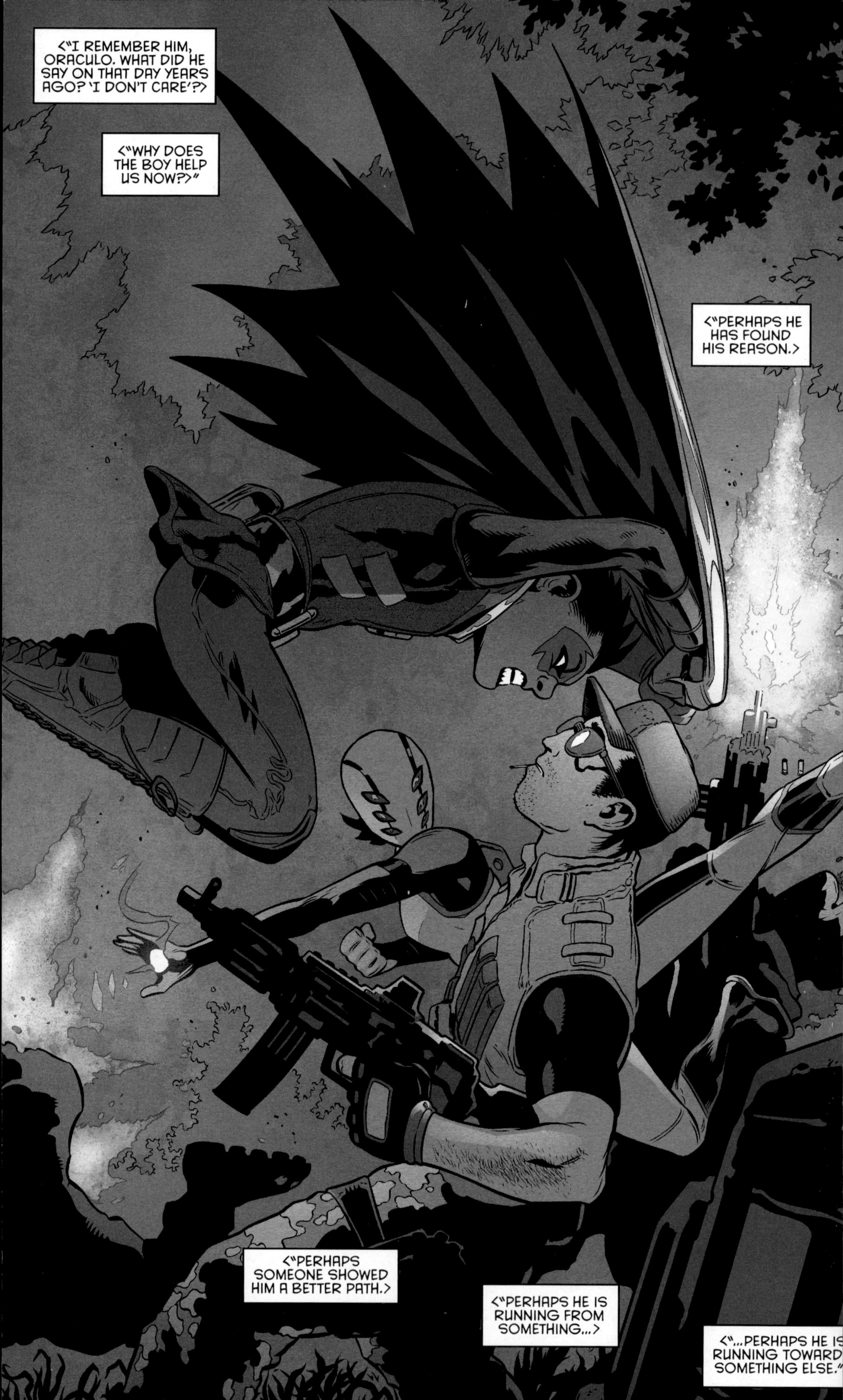

<"I REMEMBER HIM, ORACULO. WHAT DID HE SAY ON THAT DAY YEARS AGO? 'I DON'T CARE'?>
<"WHY DOES THE BOY HELP US NOW?>"
<"PERHAPS HE HAS FOUND HIS REASON.>
<"PERHAPS SOMEONE SHOWED HIM A BETTER PATH.>
<"PERHAPS HE IS RUNNING FROM SOMETHING...>
<"...PERHAPS HE IS RUNNING TOWARD SOMETHING ELSE."

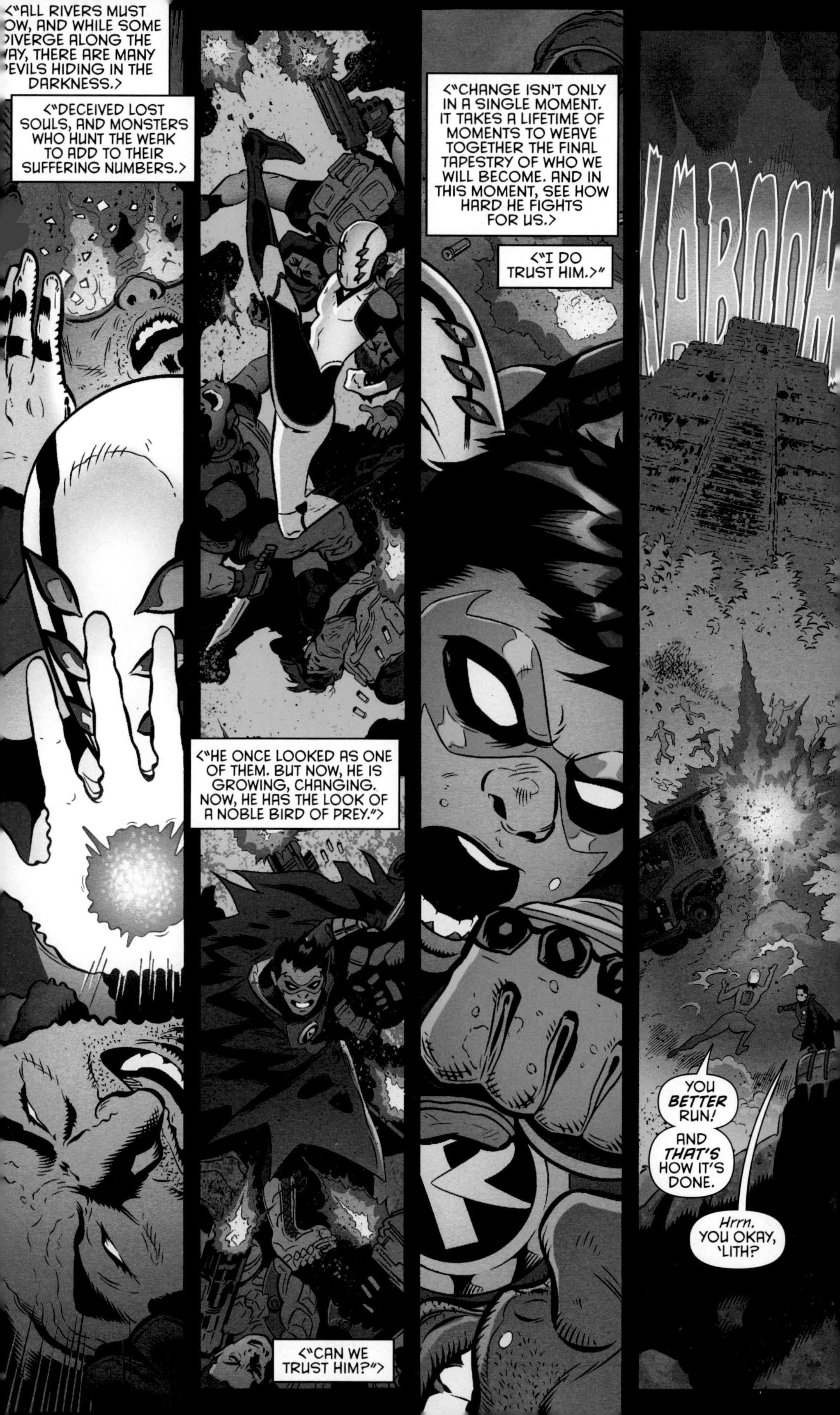

<"ALL RIVERS MUST
OW, AND WHILE SOME
IVERGE ALONG THE
AY, THERE ARE MANY
EVILS HIDING IN THE
DARKNESS.>
<"DECEIVED LOST SOULS, AND MONSTERS WHO HUNT THE WEAK TO ADD TO THEIR SUFFERING NUMBERS.>
<"HE ONCE LOOKED AS ONE OF THEM. BUT NOW, HE IS GROWING, CHANGING. NOW, HE HAS THE LOOK OF A NOBLE BIRD OF PREY.">
<"CAN WE TRUST HIM?">
<"CHANGE ISN'T ONLY IN A SINGLE MOMENT. IT TAKES A LIFETIME OF MOMENTS TO WEAVE TOGETHER THE FINAL TAPESTRY OF WHO WE WILL BECOME. AND IN THIS MOMENT, SEE HOW HARD HE FIGHTS FOR US.>
<"I DO TRUST HIM.>"
KABOOM
YOU *BETTER* RUN!
AND *THAT'S* HOW IT'S DONE.
Hrrn. YOU OKAY, 'LITH?

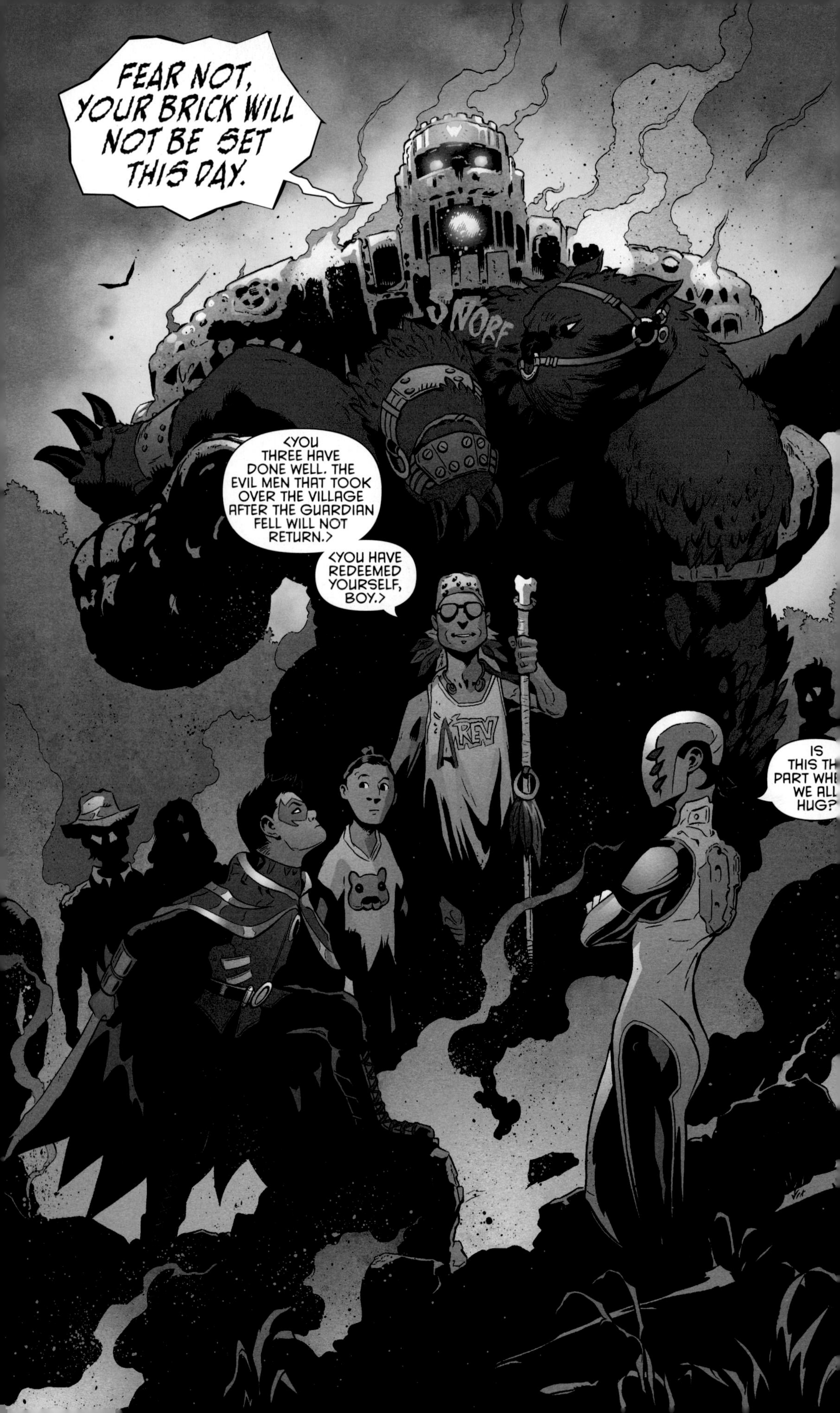
FEAR NOT, YOUR BRICK WILL NOT BE SET THIS DAY.
SNORF
<YOU THREE HAVE DONE WELL. THE EVIL MEN THAT TOOK OVER THE VILLAGE AFTER THE GUARDIAN FELL WILL NOT RETURN.>
<YOU HAVE REDEEMED YOURSELF, BOY.>
IS THIS TH PART WHE WE ALL HUG?

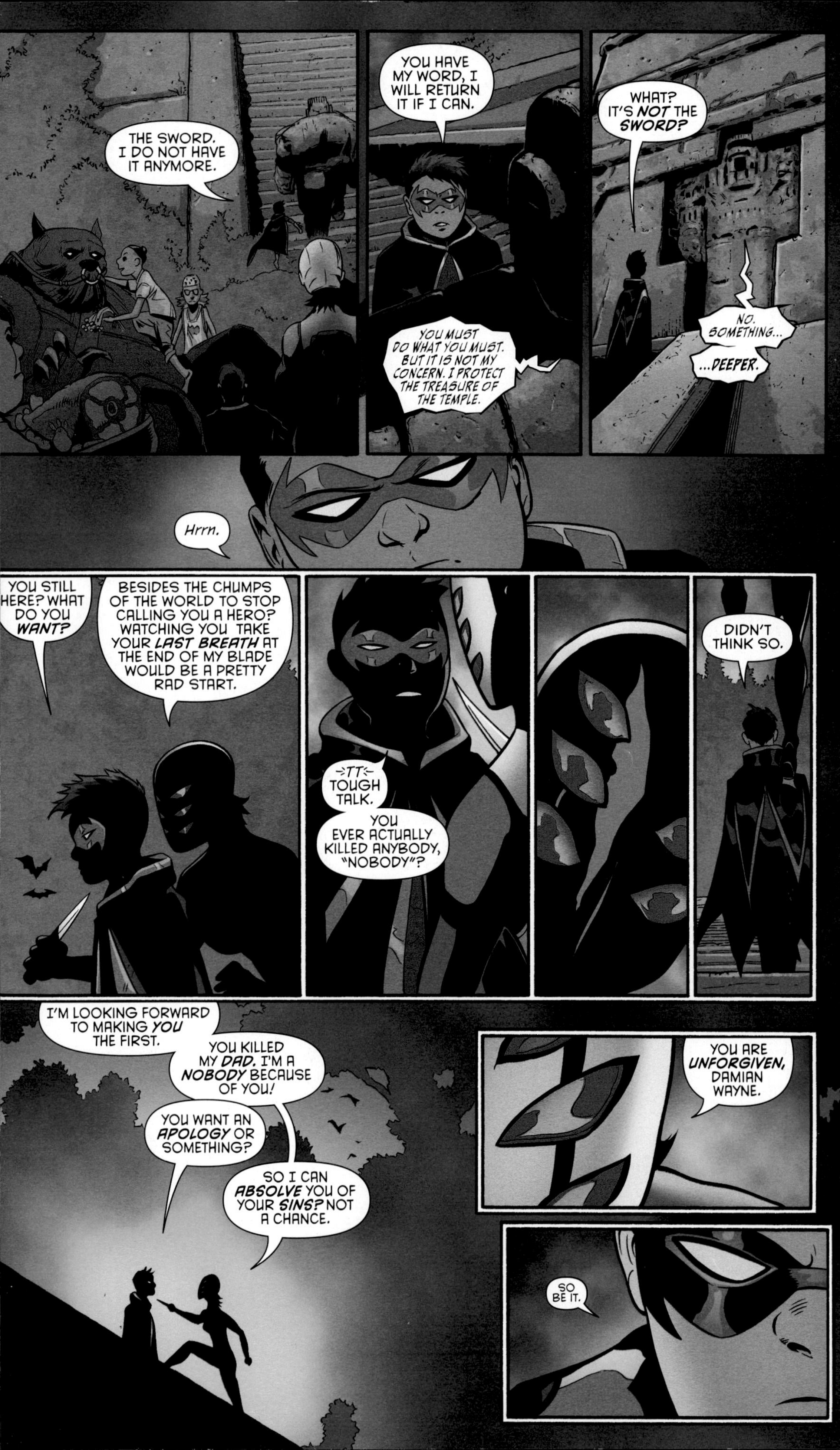
THE SWORD. I DO NOT HAVE IT ANYMORE.
YOU HAVE MY WORD, I WILL RETURN IT IF I CAN.
YOU MUST DO WHAT YOU MUST. BUT IT IS NOT MY CONCERN. I PROTECT THE TREASURE OF THE TEMPLE.
WHAT? IT'S NOT THE SWORD?
NO. SOMETHING...
...DEEPER.
Hrrn.
YOU STILL HERE? WHAT DO YOU WANT?
BESIDES THE CHUMPS OF THE WORLD TO STOP CALLING YOU A HERO? WATCHING YOU TAKE YOUR LAST BREATH AT THE END OF MY BLADE WOULD BE A PRETTY RAD START.
-TT- TOUGH TALK.
YOU EVER ACTUALLY KILLED ANYBODY, "NOBODY"?
DIDN'T THINK SO.
I'M LOOKING FORWARD TO MAKING YOU THE FIRST.
YOU KILLED MY DAD. I'M A NOBODY BECAUSE OF YOU!
YOU WANT AN APOLOGY OR SOMETHING?
SO I CAN ABSOLVE YOU OF YOUR SINS? NOT A CHANCE.
YOU ARE UNFORGIVEN, DAMIAN WAYNE.
SO BE IT.

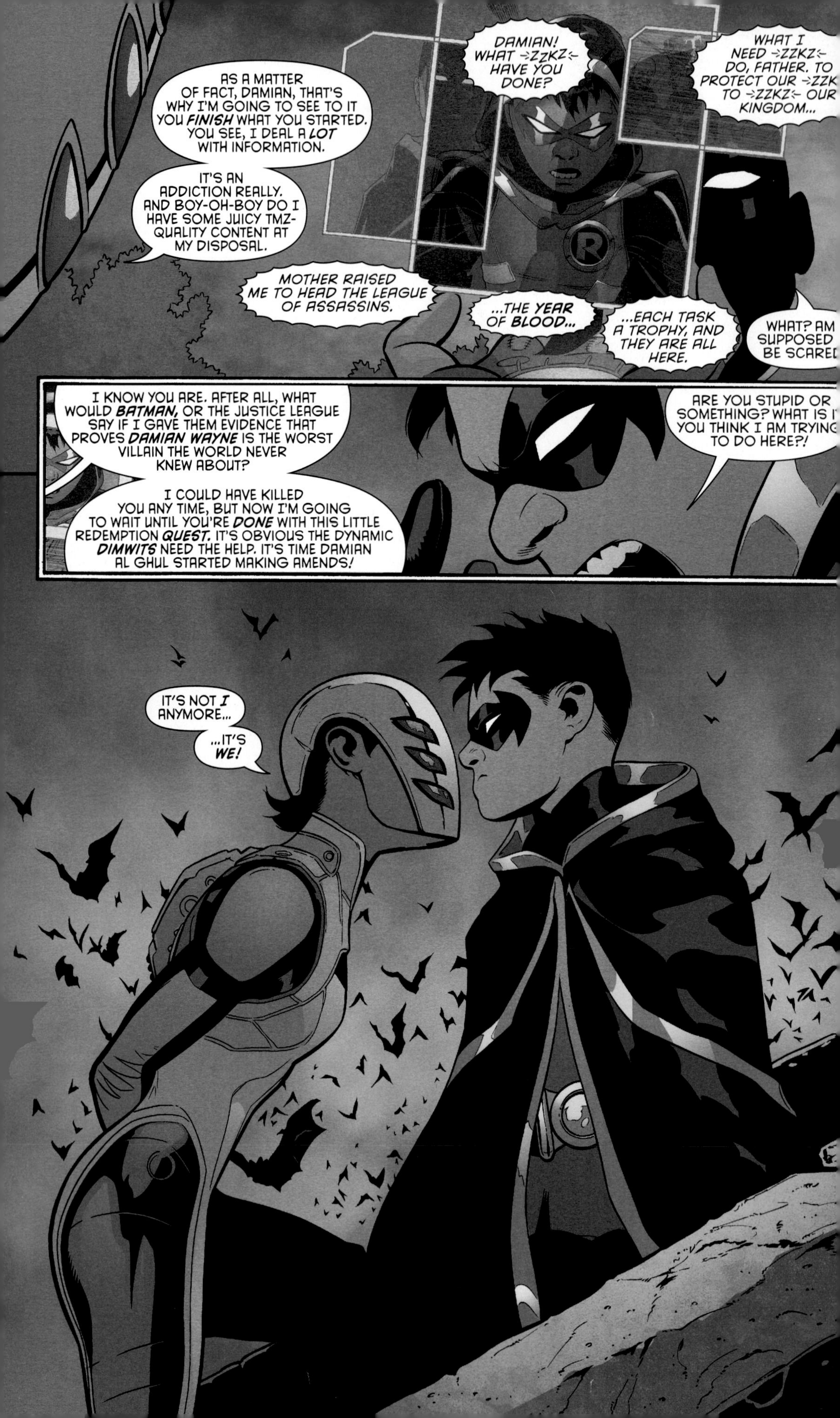
AS A MATTER OF FACT, DAMIAN, THAT'S WHY I'M GOING TO SEE TO IT YOU FINISH WHAT YOU STARTED. YOU SEE, I DEAL A LOT WITH INFORMATION.
IT'S AN ADDICTION REALLY. AND BOY-OH-BOY DO I HAVE SOME JUICY TMZ-QUALITY CONTENT AT MY DISPOSAL.
DAMIAN! WHAT ZZKZ HAVE YOU DONE?
WHAT I NEED ZZKZ DO, FATHER. TO PROTECT OUR ZZK TO ZZKZ OUR KINGDOM...
MOTHER RAISED ME TO HEAD THE LEAGUE OF ASSASSINS.
...THE YEAR OF BLOOD...
...EACH TASK A TROPHY, AND THEY ARE ALL HERE.
WHAT? AM SUPPOSED BE SCARED
I KNOW YOU ARE. AFTER ALL, WHAT WOULD BATMAN, OR THE JUSTICE LEAGUE SAY IF I GAVE THEM EVIDENCE THAT PROVES DAMIAN WAYNE IS THE WORST VILLAIN THE WORLD NEVER KNEW ABOUT?
I COULD HAVE KILLED YOU ANY TIME, BUT NOW I'M GOING TO WAIT UNTIL YOU'RE DONE WITH THIS LITTLE REDEMPTION QUEST. IT'S OBVIOUS THE DYNAMIC DIMWITS NEED THE HELP. IT'S TIME DAMIAN AL GHUL STARTED MAKING AMENDS!
ARE YOU STUPID OR SOMETHING? WHAT IS I YOU THINK I AM TRYING TO DO HERE?!
IT'S NOT I ANYMORE...
...IT'S WE!

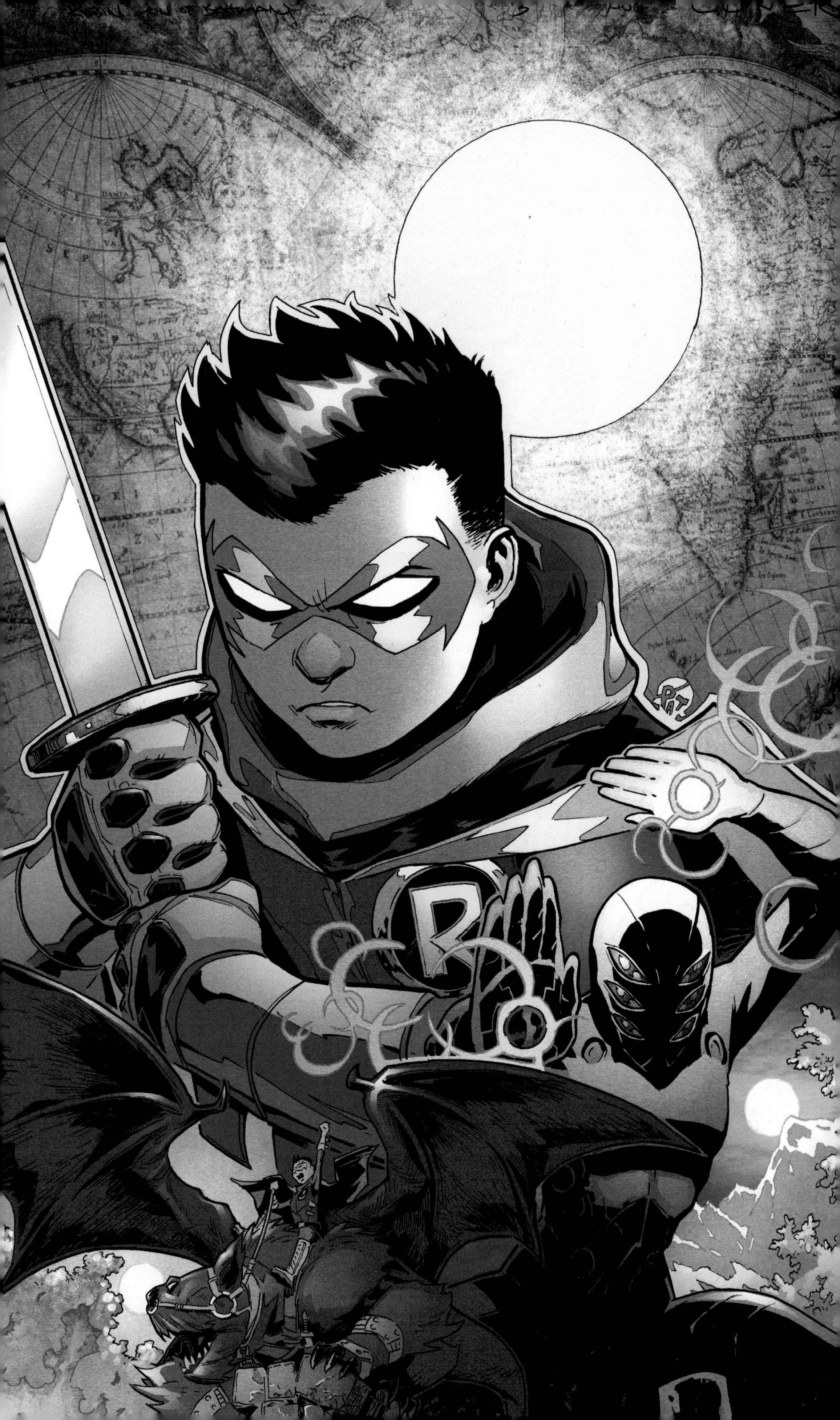

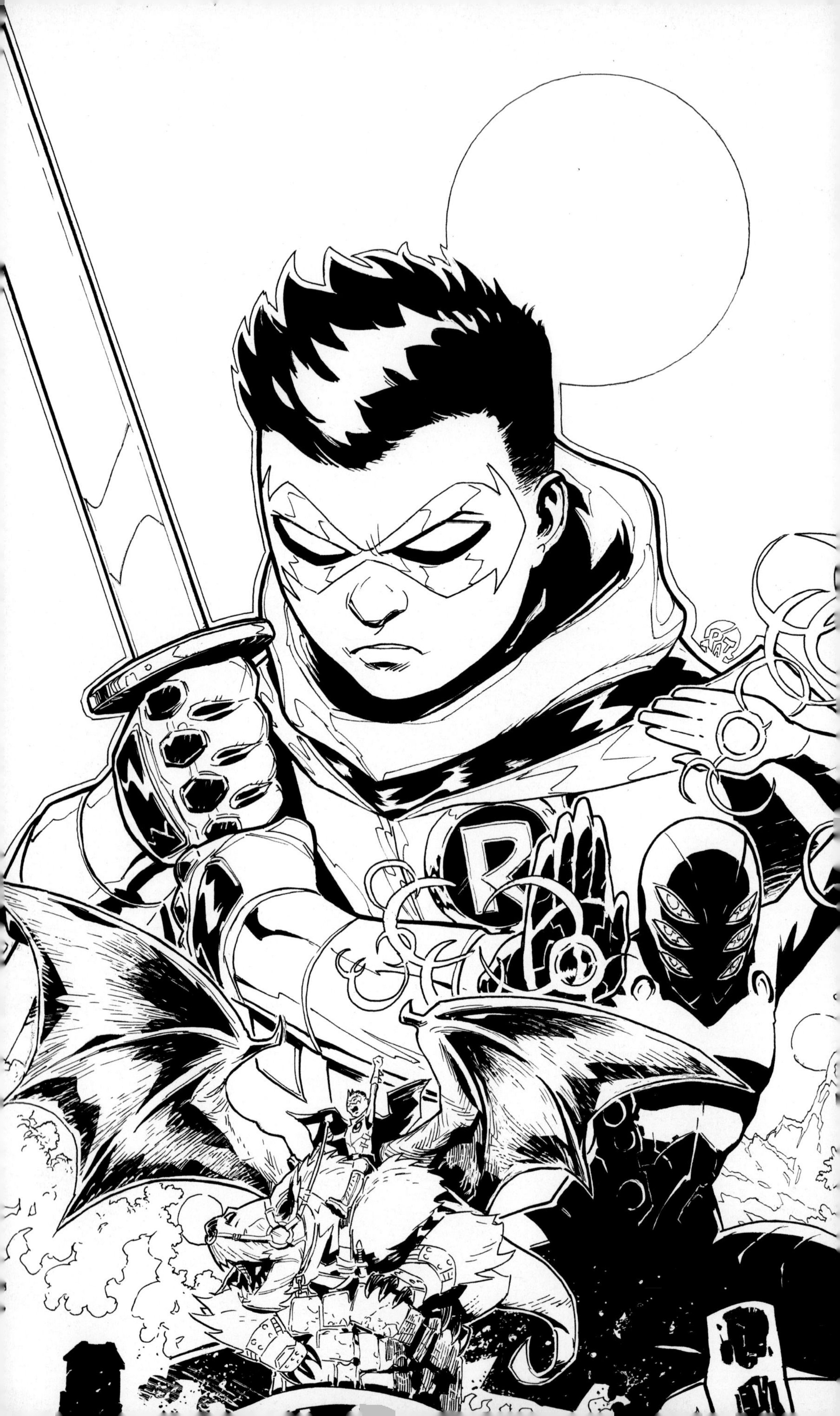

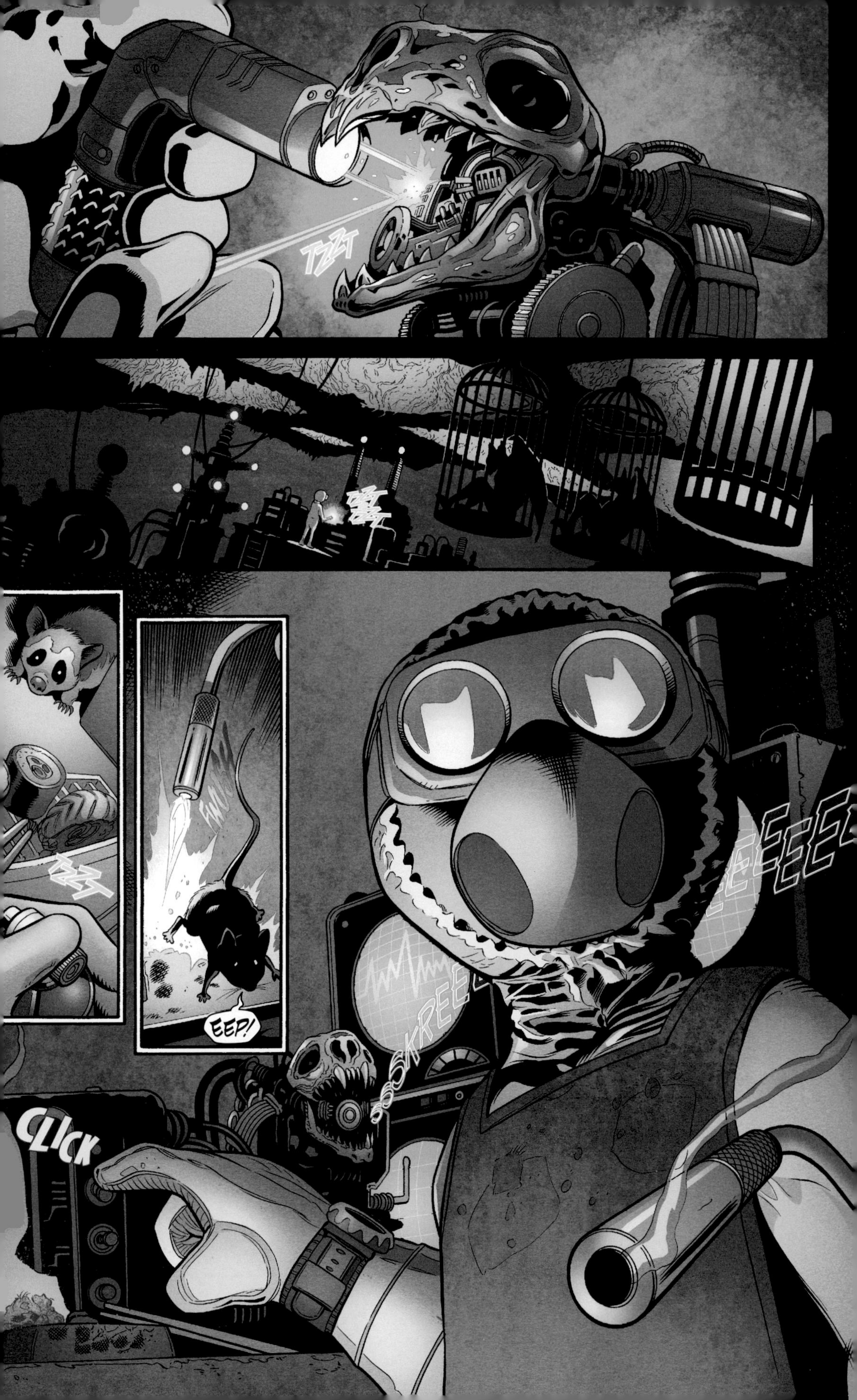
TZZT
TZZT TZZT
TZZT
EEP!
SSSKREEE
EEEEEE
CLICK

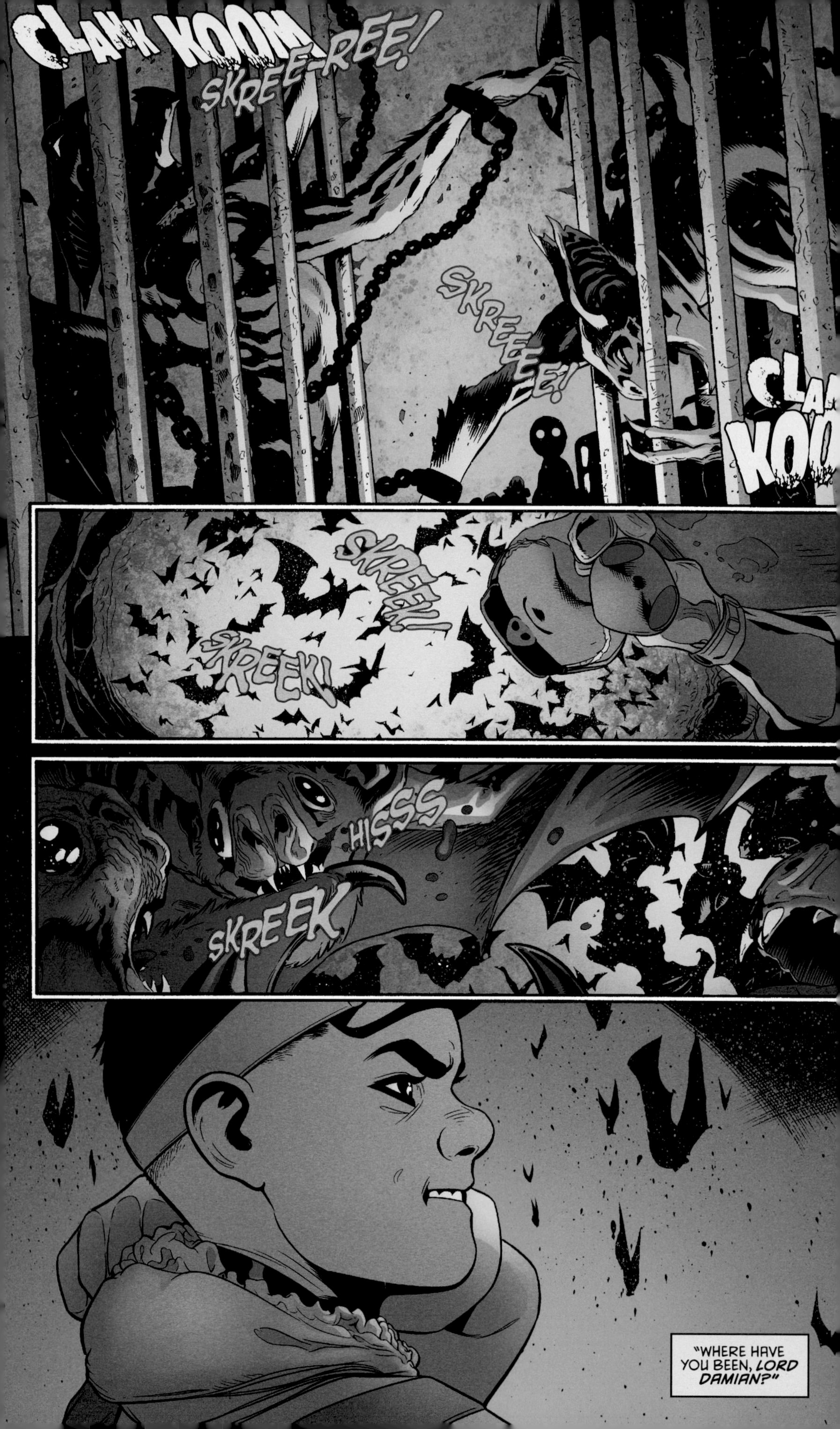
CLANK KOOM
SKREE-REE!
SKREEEEEE!
CLA
KOO
SKREEK!
SKREEK!
HISSS
SKREEK
"WHERE HAVE YOU BEEN, *LORD DAMIAN?*"

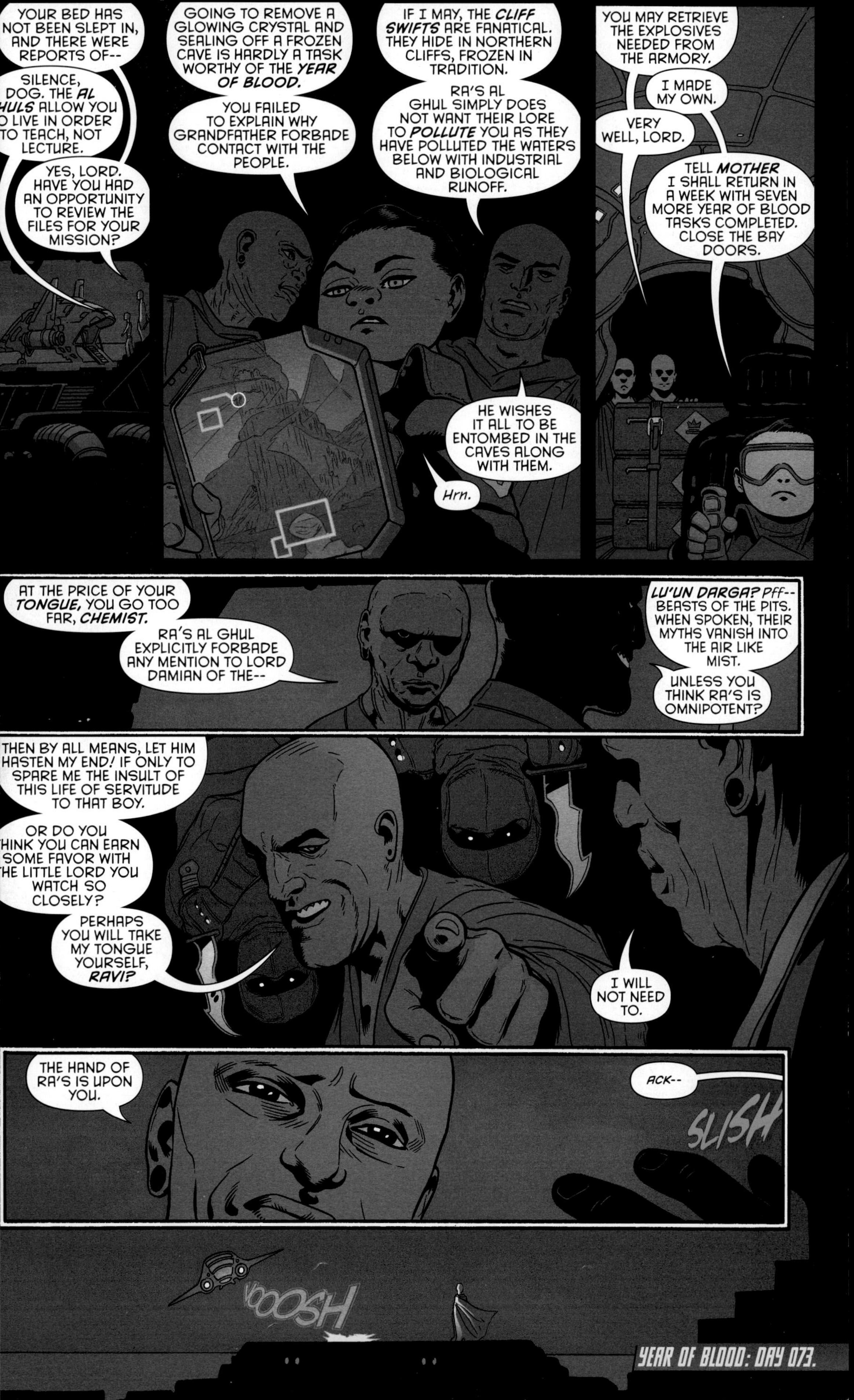
YOUR BED HAS NOT BEEN SLEPT IN, AND THERE WERE REPORTS OF--
SILENCE, DOG. THE AL GHULS ALLOW YOU TO LIVE IN ORDER TO TEACH, NOT LECTURE.
YES, LORD. HAVE YOU HAD AN OPPORTUNITY TO REVIEW THE FILES FOR YOUR MISSION?
GOING TO REMOVE A GLOWING CRYSTAL AND SEALING OFF A FROZEN CAVE IS HARDLY A TASK WORTHY OF THE YEAR OF BLOOD.
YOU FAILED TO EXPLAIN WHY GRANDFATHER FORBADE CONTACT WITH THE PEOPLE.
IF I MAY, THE CLIFF SWIFTS ARE FANATICAL. THEY HIDE IN NORTHERN CLIFFS, FROZEN IN TRADITION.
RA'S AL GHUL SIMPLY DOES NOT WANT THEIR LORE TO POLLUTE YOU AS THEY HAVE POLLUTED THE WATERS BELOW WITH INDUSTRIAL AND BIOLOGICAL RUNOFF.
HE WISHES IT ALL TO BE ENTOMBED IN THE CAVES ALONG WITH THEM.
Hrn.
YOU MAY RETRIEVE THE EXPLOSIVES NEEDED FROM THE ARMORY.
I MADE MY OWN.
VERY WELL, LORD.
TELL MOTHER I SHALL RETURN IN A WEEK WITH SEVEN MORE YEAR OF BLOOD TASKS COMPLETED. CLOSE THE BAY DOORS.
AT THE PRICE OF YOUR TONGUE, YOU GO TOO FAR, CHEMIST.
RA'S AL GHUL EXPLICITLY FORBADE ANY MENTION TO LORD DAMIAN OF THE--
LU'UN DARGA? Pff-- BEASTS OF THE PITS. WHEN SPOKEN, THEIR MYTHS VANISH INTO THE AIR LIKE MIST.
UNLESS YOU THINK RA'S IS OMNIPOTENT?
THEN BY ALL MEANS, LET HIM HASTEN MY END! IF ONLY TO SPARE ME THE INSULT OF THIS LIFE OF SERVITUDE TO THAT BOY.
OR DO YOU THINK YOU CAN EARN SOME FAVOR WITH THE LITTLE LORD YOU WATCH SO CLOSELY?
PERHAPS YOU WILL TAKE MY TONGUE YOURSELF, RAVI?
I WILL NOT NEED TO.
THE HAND OF RA'S IS UPON YOU.
ACK--
SLISH
VOOOSH
YEAR OF BLOOD: DAY 073.

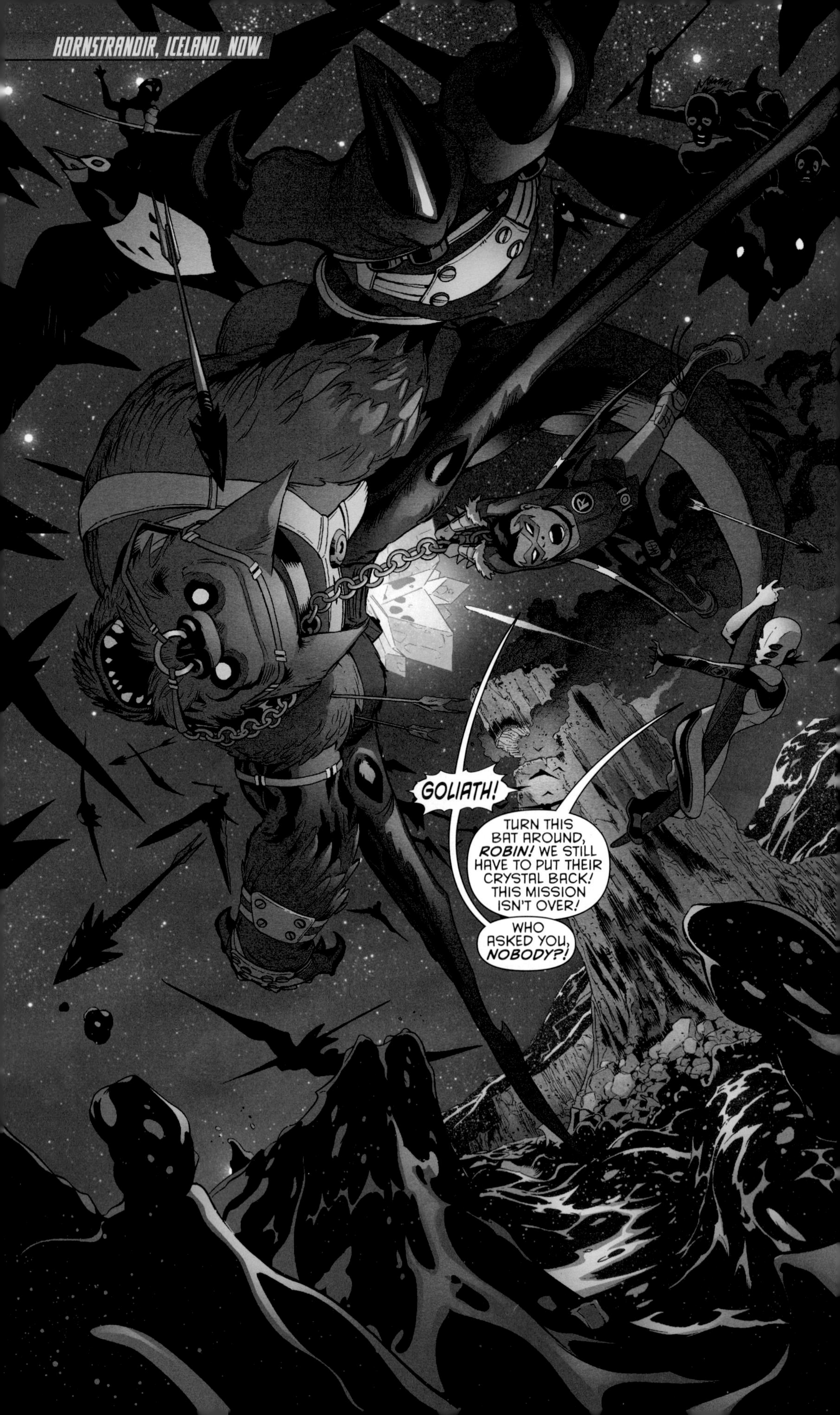
HORNSTRANDIR, ICELAND. NOW.
GOLIATH!
TURN THIS BAT AROUND, ROBIN! WE STILL HAVE TO PUT THEIR CRYSTAL BACK! THIS MISSION ISN'T OVER!
WHO ASKED YOU, NOBODY?!

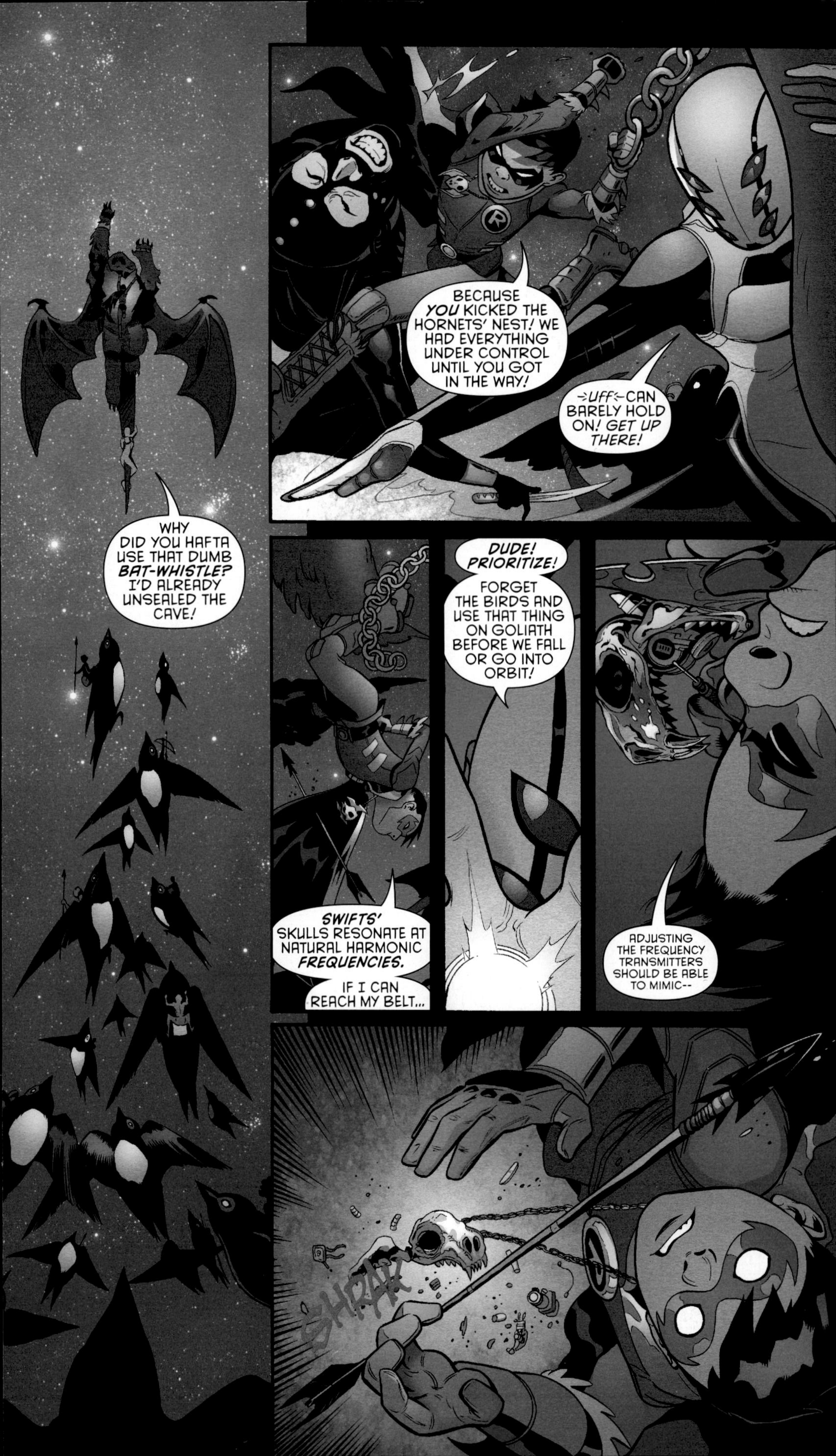
WHY DID YOU HAFTA USE THAT DUMB BAT-WHISTLE? I'D ALREADY UNSEALED THE CAVE!
BECAUSE YOU KICKED THE HORNETS' NEST! WE HAD EVERYTHING UNDER CONTROL UNTIL YOU GOT IN THE WAY!
UFF--CAN BARELY HOLD ON! GET UP THERE!
SWIFTS' SKULLS RESONATE AT NATURAL HARMONIC FREQUENCIES.
IF I CAN REACH MY BELT...
DUDE! PRIORITIZE!
FORGET THE BIRDS AND USE THAT THING ON GOLIATH BEFORE WE FALL OR GO INTO ORBIT!
ADJUSTING THE FREQUENCY TRANSMITTERS SHOULD BE ABLE TO MIMIC--
SHRAK

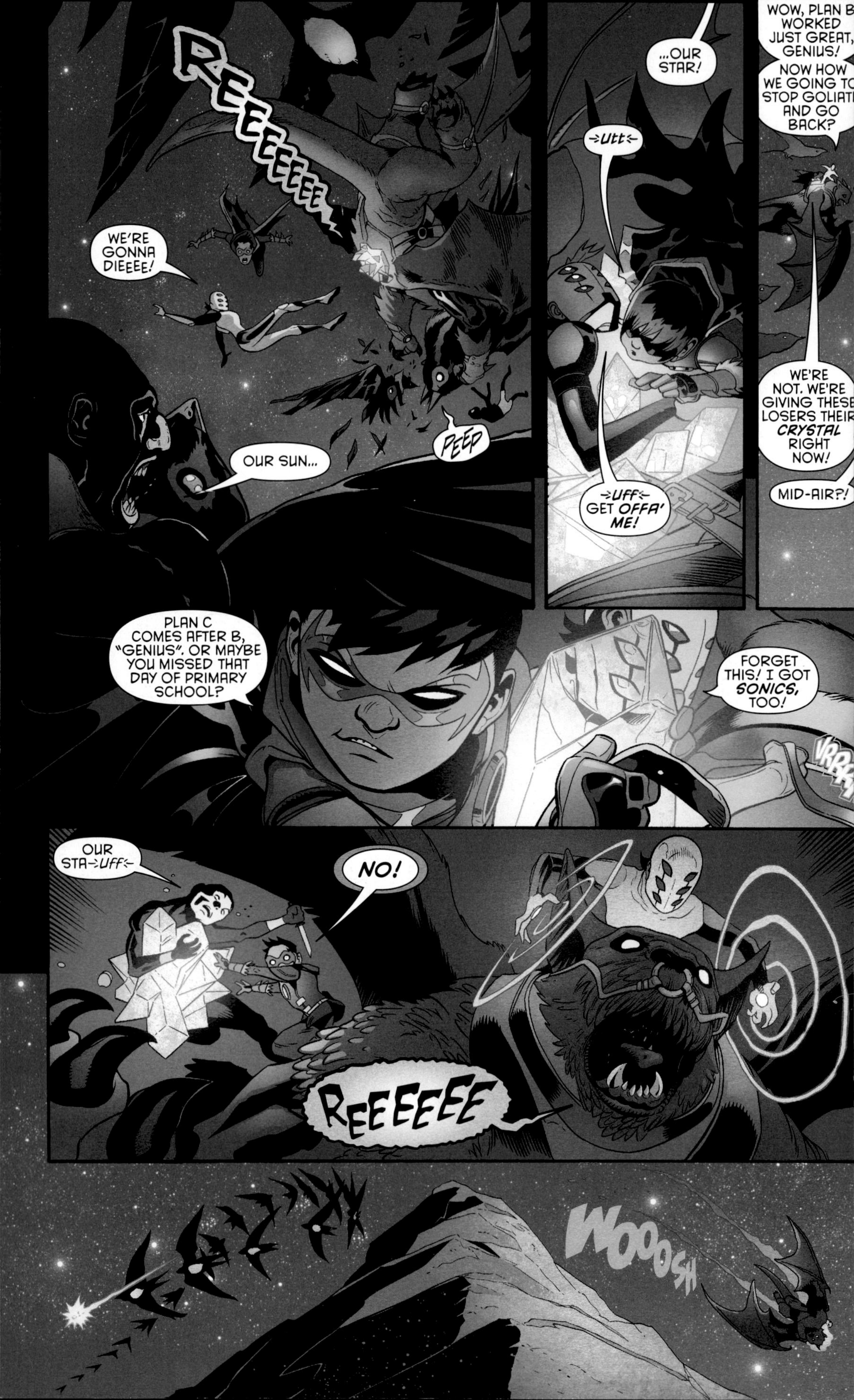
REEEEEEEE
WE'RE GONNA DIEEEE!
OUR SUN...
PEEP
...OUR STAR!
UTT
UFF GET OFFA' ME!
WOW, PLAN B WORKED JUST GREAT, GENIUS!
NOW HOW WE GOING TO STOP GOLIATH AND GO BACK?
WE'RE NOT. WE'RE GIVING THESE LOSERS THEIR CRYSTAL RIGHT NOW!
MID-AIR?!
PLAN C COMES AFTER B, "GENIUS". OR MAYBE YOU MISSED THAT DAY OF PRIMARY SCHOOL?
FORGET THIS! I GOT SONICS, TOO!
OUR STA-UFF
NO!
REEEEEE
WOOOSH

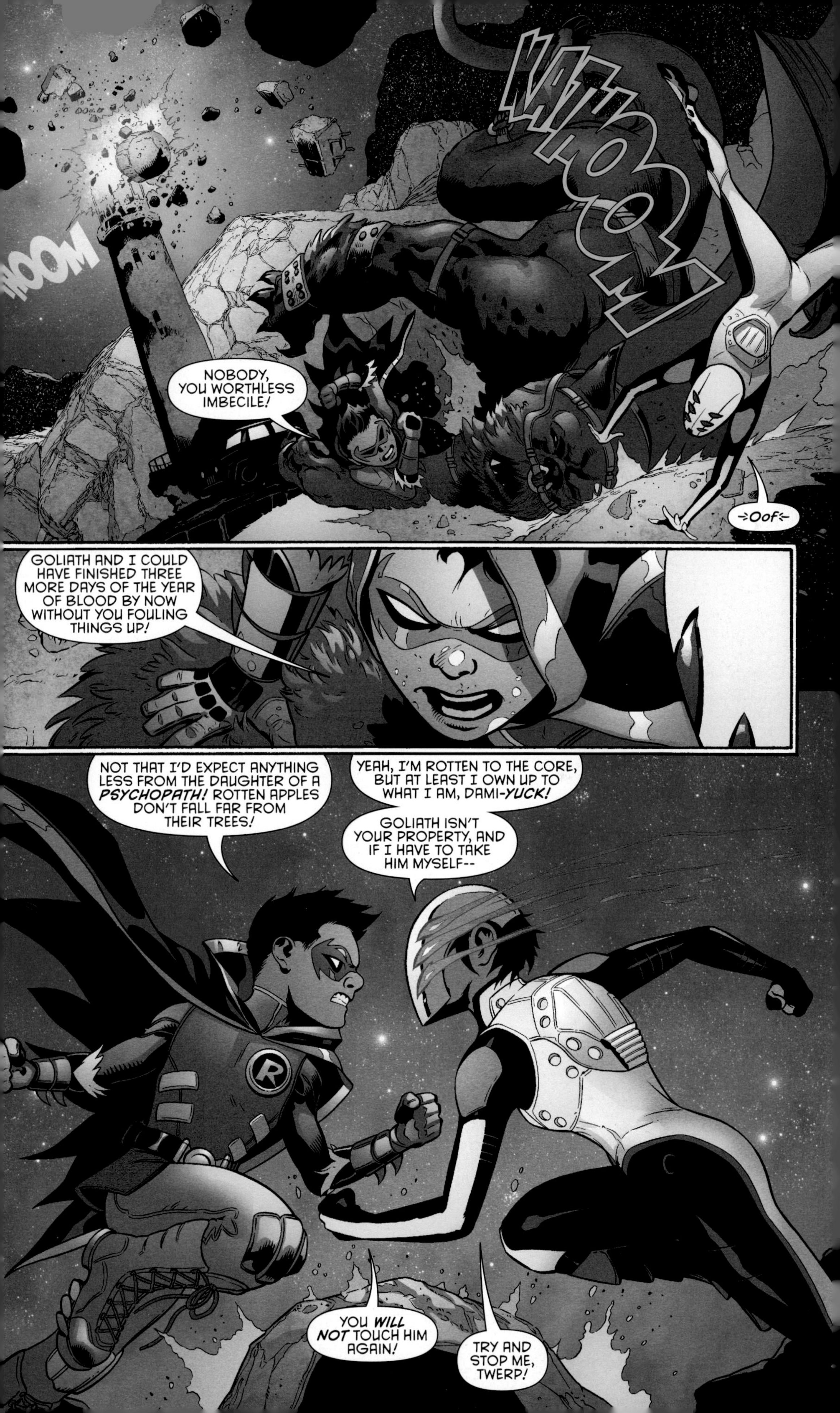
NOBODY, YOU WORTHLESS IMBECILE!
Oof
GOLIATH AND I COULD HAVE FINISHED THREE MORE DAYS OF THE YEAR OF BLOOD BY NOW WITHOUT YOU FOULING THINGS UP!
NOT THAT I'D EXPECT ANYTHING LESS FROM THE DAUGHTER OF A *PSYCHOPATH!* ROTTEN APPLES DON'T FALL FAR FROM THEIR TREES!
YEAH, I'M ROTTEN TO THE CORE, BUT AT LEAST I OWN UP TO WHAT I AM, DAMI-*YUCK!*
GOLIATH ISN'T YOUR PROPERTY, AND IF I HAVE TO TAKE HIM MYSELF--
YOU ***WILL NOT*** TOUCH HIM AGAIN!
TRY AND STOP ME, TWERP!

VRBN

HAI!

CLOAKING? DID YOU LEARN ANYTHING BESIDES YOUR FATHER'S TRICKS? IT DIDN'T SAVE HIM! IT WON'T SAVE YOU!

RAAH!

KRACK

PREDICTABLE.

THUMPTA THUMPTA THUMPTA

PEDESTRIAN AT BEST. TRY GIVING ME A REASON TO BREAK A SWEAT.

FHUMP

POPS NEVER TAUGHT ME HIS MOVES. LEARNED WATCHING HIM FROM THE SHADOWS.

RECENTLY, I'VE LEARNED A VERY SPECIAL TWO-FINGERED ATTACK. THE ONE HE TAUGHT YOU...AND YOU USED ON HIM!

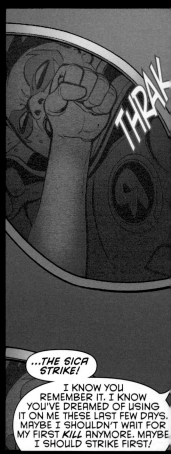

THRAK

...THE SICA STRIKE!

I KNOW YOU REMEMBER IT. I KNOW YOU'VE DREAMED OF USING IT ON ME THESE LAST FEW DAYS. MAYBE I SHOULDN'T WAIT FOR MY FIRST KILL ANYMORE. MAYBE I SHOULD STRIKE FIRST!

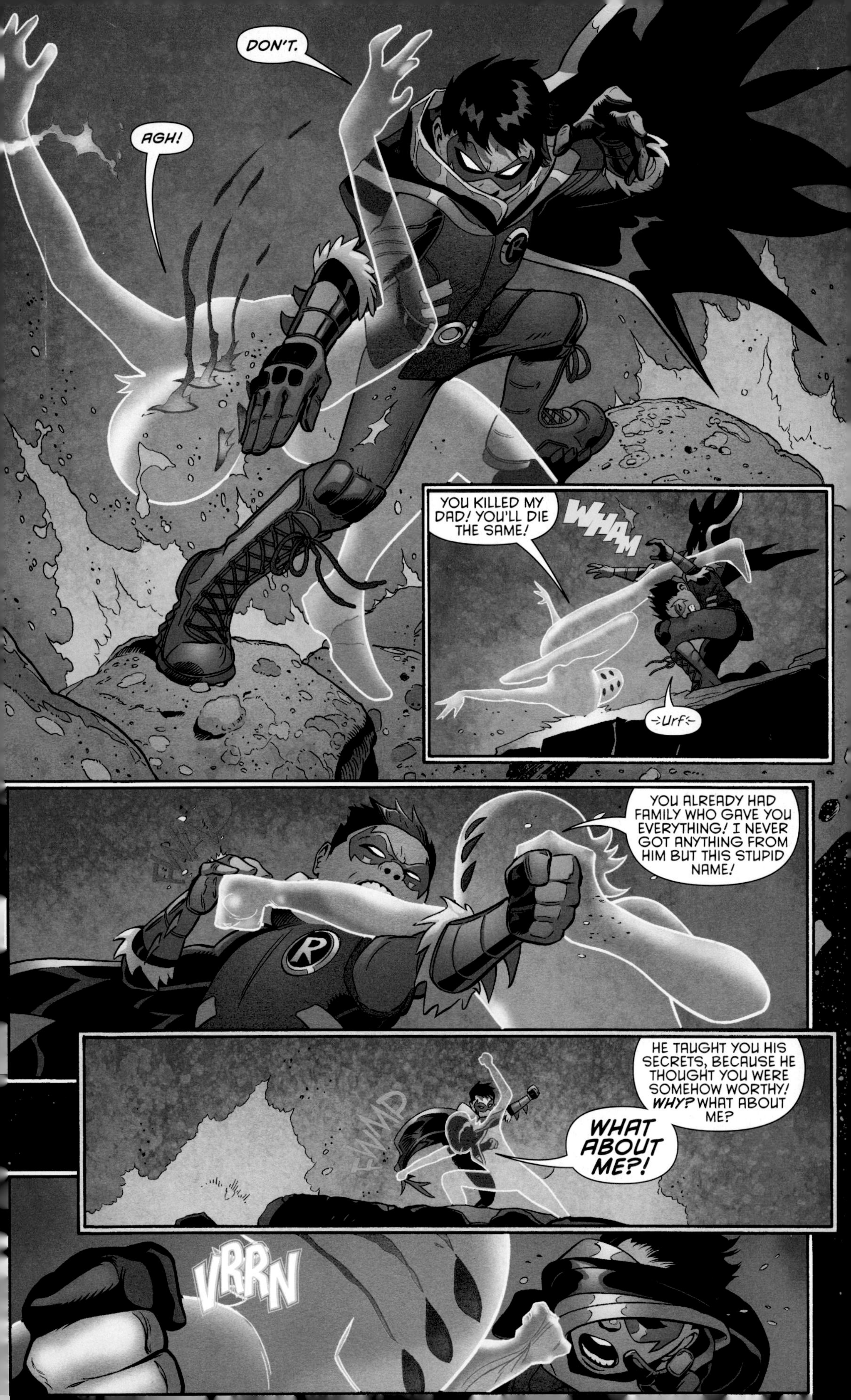

DON'T.
AGH!
YOU KILLED MY DAD! YOU'LL DIE THE SAME!
WHAM
Urf
YOU ALREADY HAD FAMILY WHO GAVE YOU EVERYTHING! I NEVER GOT ANYTHING FROM HIM BUT THIS STUPID NAME!
HE TAUGHT YOU HIS SECRETS, BECAUSE HE THOUGHT YOU WERE SOMEHOW WORTHY! WHY? WHAT ABOUT ME?
WHAT ABOUT ME?!
FWMP
VRRN

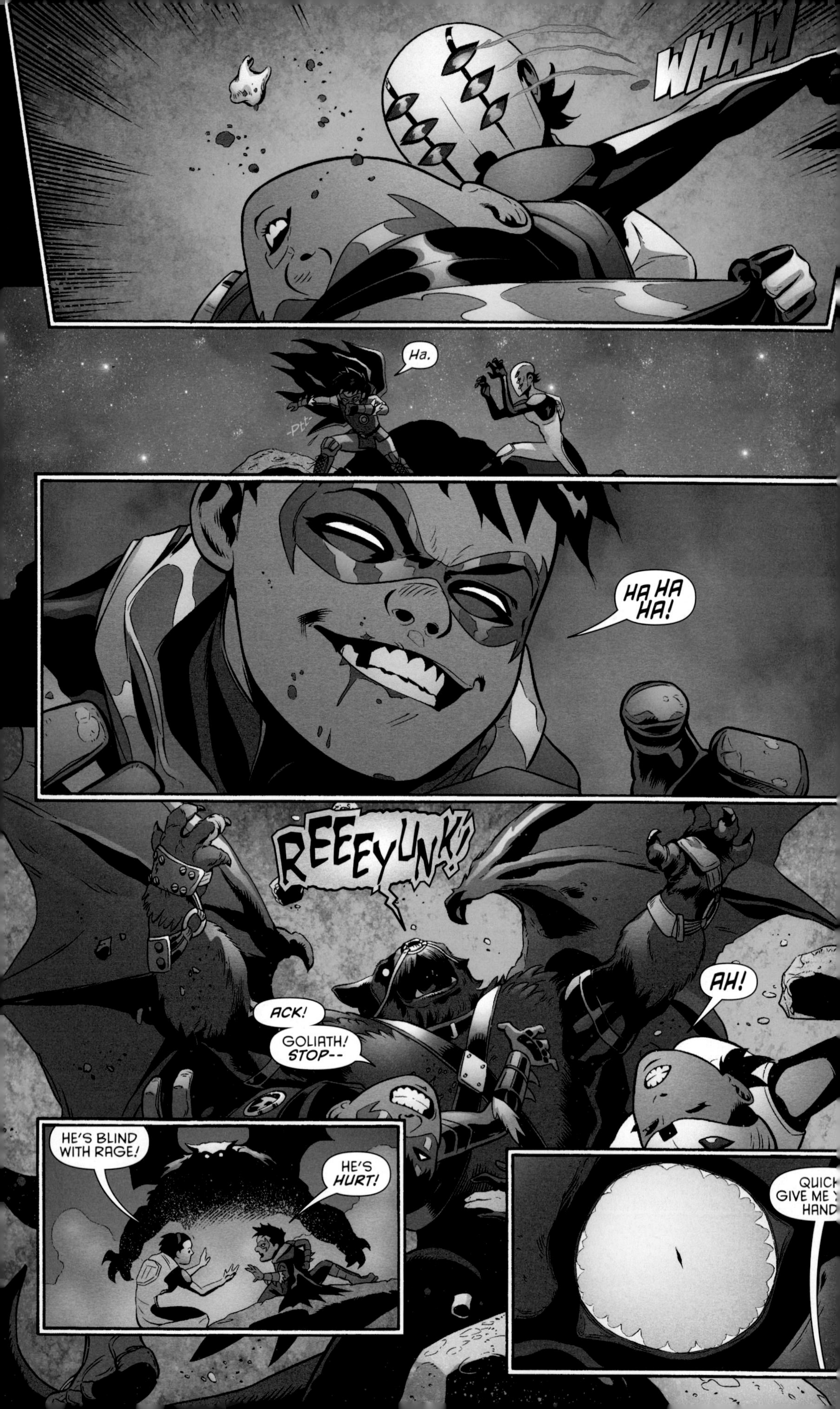

WHAM
Ha.
-Ptt-
HA HA HA!
REEEYUNK!
ACK!
GOLIATH! STOP--
AH!
HE'S BLIND WITH RAGE!
HE'S HURT!
QUICK GIVE ME Y HAND

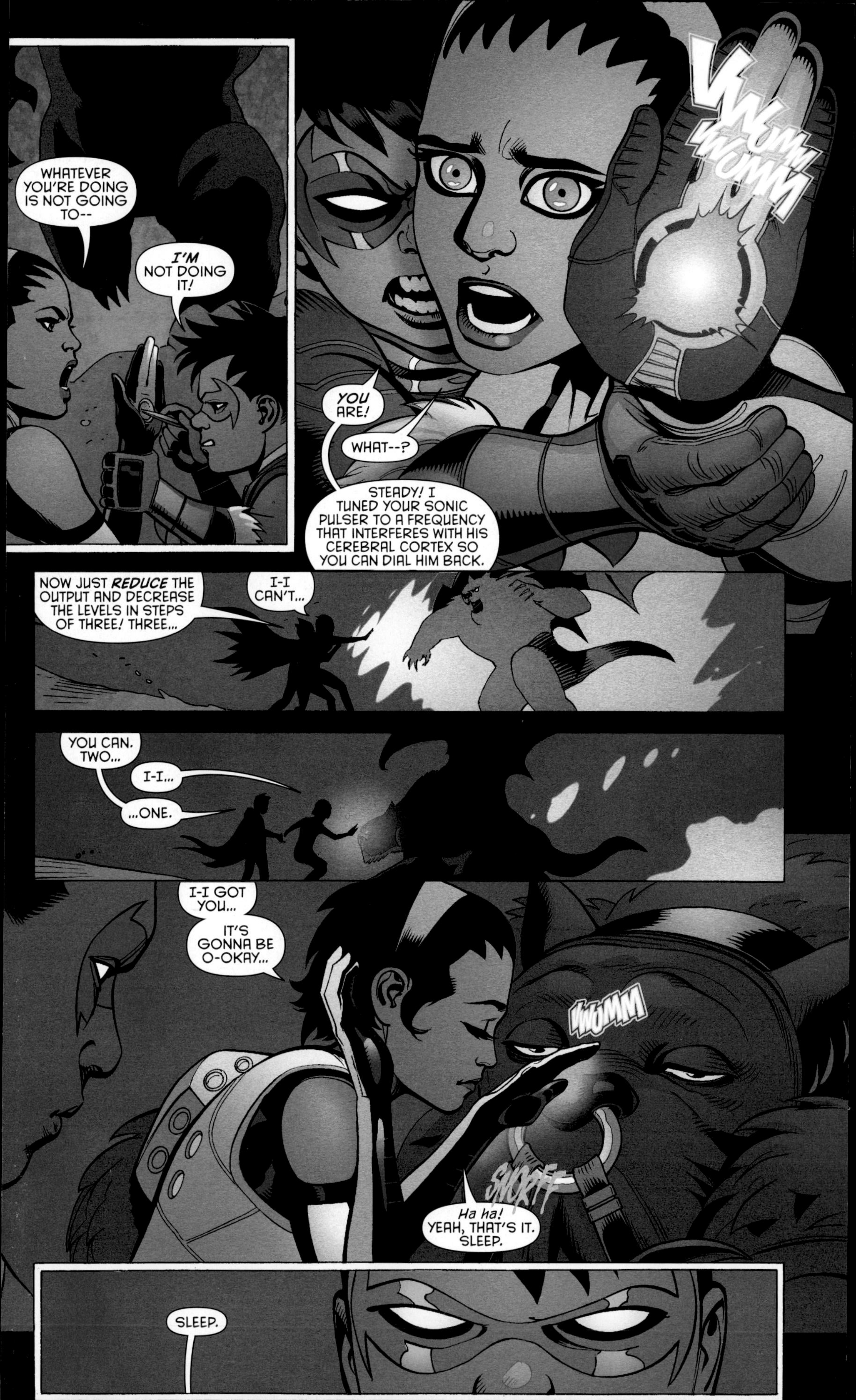
WHATEVER YOU'RE DOING IS NOT GOING TO--
I'M NOT DOING IT!
VWUMM WUMM
YOU ARE!
WHAT--?
STEADY! I TUNED YOUR SONIC PULSER TO A FREQUENCY THAT INTERFERES WITH HIS CEREBRAL CORTEX SO YOU CAN DIAL HIM BACK.
NOW JUST REDUCE THE OUTPUT AND DECREASE THE LEVELS IN STEPS OF THREE! THREE...
I-I CAN'T...
YOU CAN. TWO...
I-I...
...ONE.
I-I GOT YOU...
IT'S GONNA BE O-OKAY...
VWOMM
SNORFF
Ha ha! YEAH, THAT'S IT. SLEEP.
SLEEP.

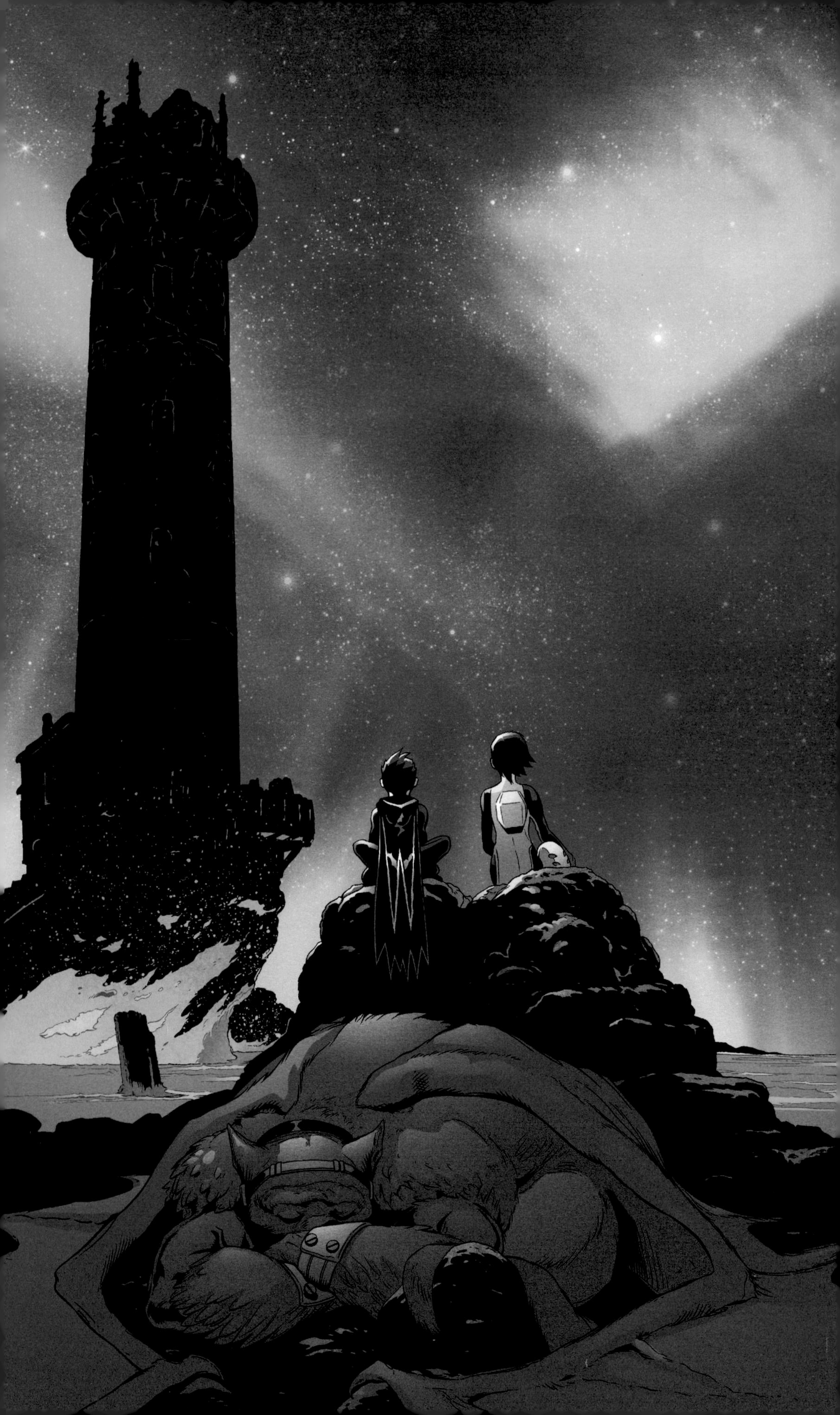

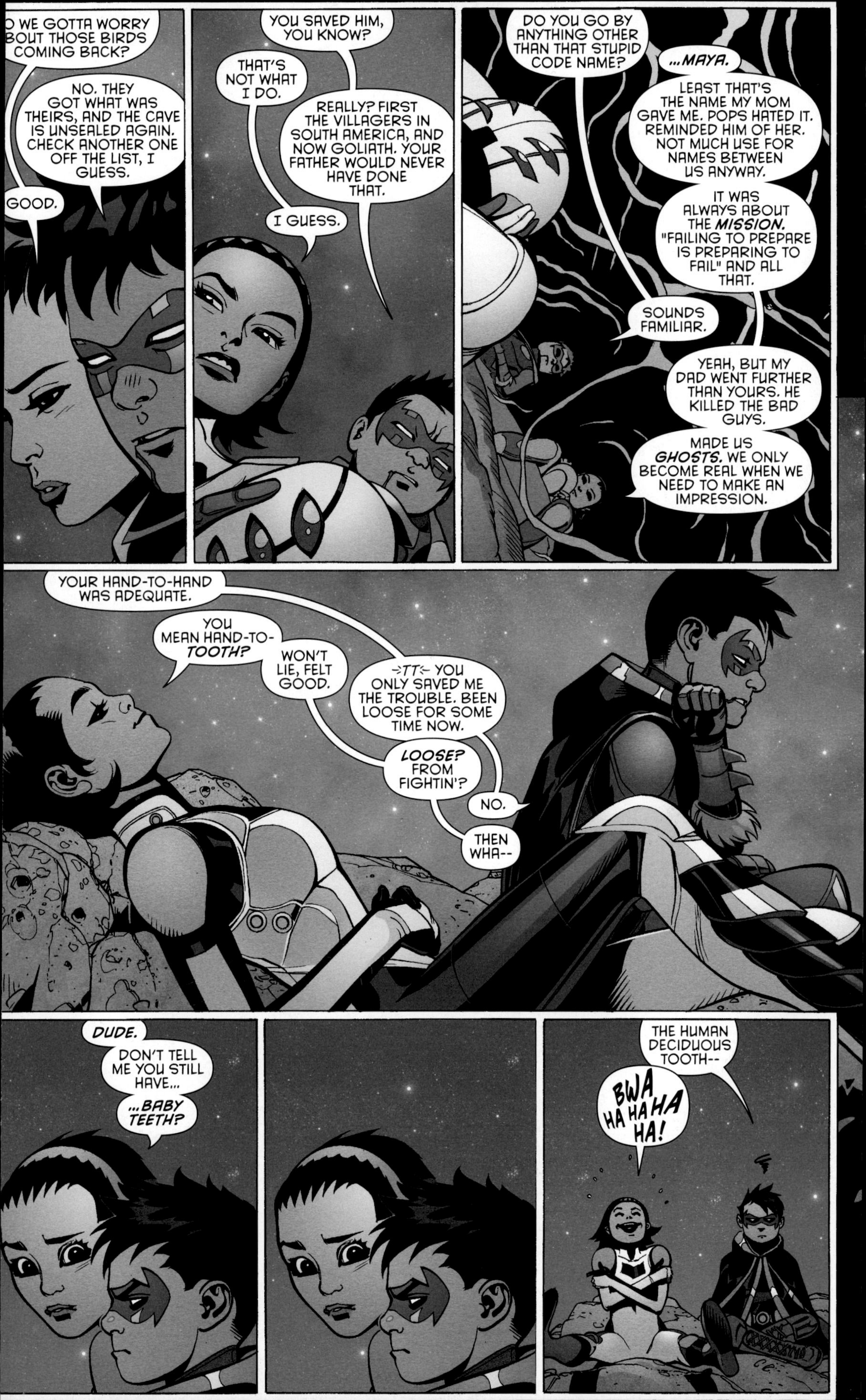
O WE GOTTA WORRY BOUT THOSE BIRDS COMING BACK?
NO. THEY GOT WHAT WAS THEIRS, AND THE CAVE IS UNSEALED AGAIN. CHECK ANOTHER ONE OFF THE LIST, I GUESS.
GOOD.
YOU SAVED HIM, YOU KNOW?
THAT'S NOT WHAT I DO.
REALLY? FIRST THE VILLAGERS IN SOUTH AMERICA, AND NOW GOLIATH. YOUR FATHER WOULD NEVER HAVE DONE THAT.
I GUESS.
DO YOU GO BY ANYTHING OTHER THAN THAT STUPID CODE NAME?
...MAYA.
LEAST THAT'S THE NAME MY MOM GAVE ME. POPS HATED IT. REMINDED HIM OF HER. NOT MUCH USE FOR NAMES BETWEEN US ANYWAY.
IT WAS ALWAYS ABOUT THE MISSION. "FAILING TO PREPARE IS PREPARING TO FAIL" AND ALL THAT.
SOUNDS FAMILIAR.
YEAH, BUT MY DAD WENT FURTHER THAN YOURS. HE KILLED THE BAD GUYS.
MADE US GHOSTS. WE ONLY BECOME REAL WHEN WE NEED TO MAKE AN IMPRESSION.
YOUR HAND-TO-HAND WAS ADEQUATE.
YOU MEAN HAND-TO-TOOTH?
WON'T LIE, FELT GOOD.
-TT- YOU ONLY SAVED ME THE TROUBLE. BEEN LOOSE FOR SOME TIME NOW.
LOOSE? FROM FIGHTIN'?
NO.
THEN WHA--
DUDE.
DON'T TELL ME YOU STILL HAVE...
...BABY TEETH?
THE HUMAN DECIDUOUS TOOTH--
BWA HA HA HA HA HA!

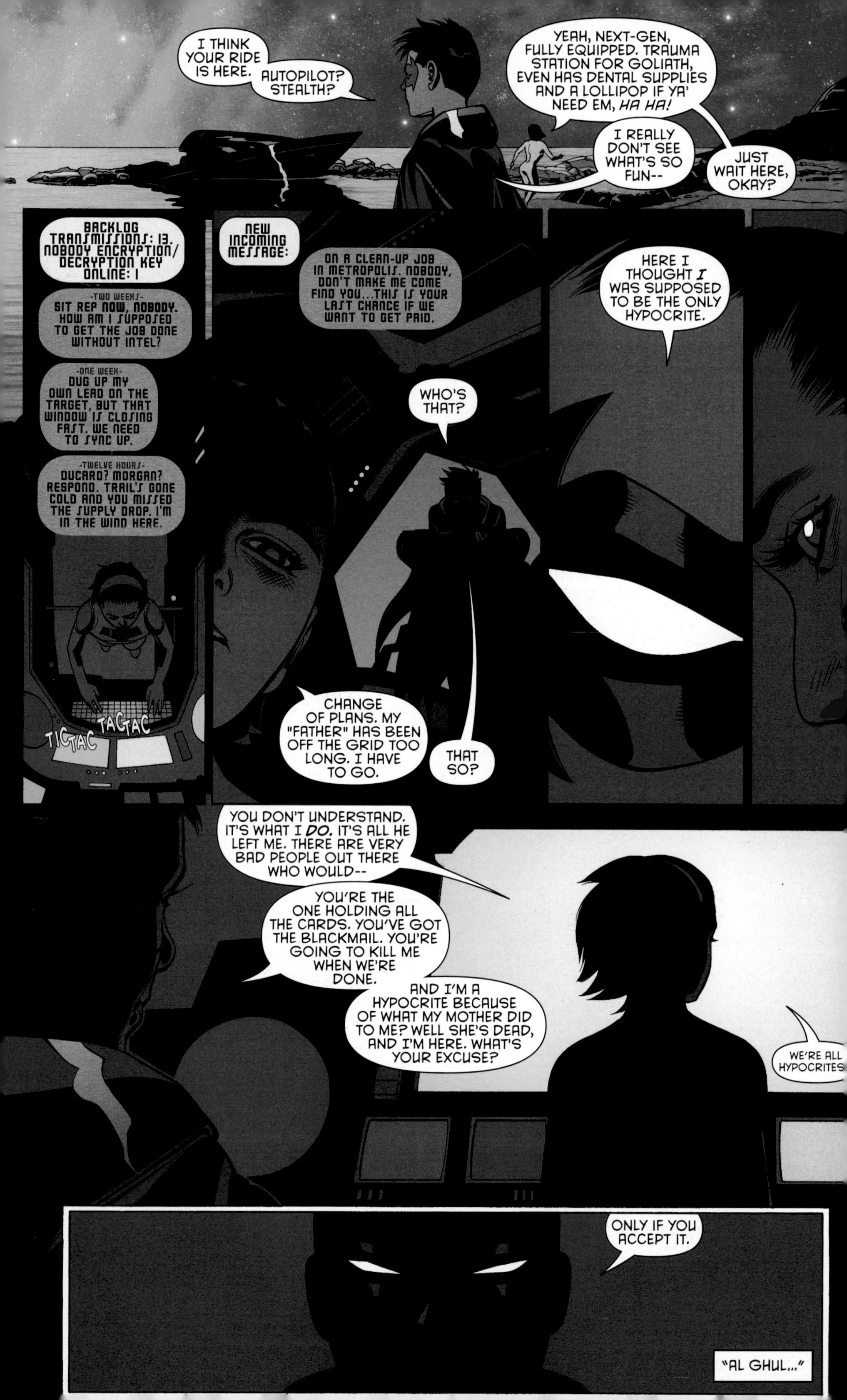
I THINK YOUR RIDE IS HERE.
AUTOPILOT? STEALTH?
YEAH, NEXT-GEN, FULLY EQUIPPED. TRAUMA STATION FOR GOLIATH, EVEN HAS DENTAL SUPPLIES AND A LOLLIPOP IF YA' NEED EM, HA HA!
I REALLY DON'T SEE WHAT'S SO FUN--
JUST WAIT HERE, OKAY?
BACKLOG TRANSMISSIONS: 13. NOBODY ENCRYPTION/ DECRYPTION KEY ONLINE: 1
-TWO WEEKS-
SIT REP NOW, NOBODY. HOW AM I SUPPOSED TO GET THE JOB DONE WITHOUT INTEL?
-ONE WEEK-
DUG UP MY OWN LEAD ON THE TARGET, BUT THAT WINDOW IS CLOSING FAST. WE NEED TO SYNC UP.
-TWELVE HOURS-
DUCARD? MORGAN? RESPOND. TRAIL'S GONE COLD AND YOU MISSED THE SUPPLY DROP. I'M IN THE WIND HERE.
TIC TAC TAC TAC
NEW INCOMING MESSAGE:
ON A CLEAN-UP JOB IN METROPOLIS. NOBODY, DON'T MAKE ME COME FIND YOU...THIS IS YOUR LAST CHANCE IF WE WANT TO GET PAID.
WHO'S THAT?
CHANGE OF PLANS. MY "FATHER" HAS BEEN OFF THE GRID TOO LONG. I HAVE TO GO.
THAT SO?
HERE I THOUGHT I WAS SUPPOSED TO BE THE ONLY HYPOCRITE.
YOU DON'T UNDERSTAND. IT'S WHAT I DO. IT'S ALL HE LEFT ME. THERE ARE VERY BAD PEOPLE OUT THERE WHO WOULD--
YOU'RE THE ONE HOLDING ALL THE CARDS. YOU'VE GOT THE BLACKMAIL. YOU'RE GOING TO KILL ME WHEN WE'RE DONE.
AND I'M A HYPOCRITE BECAUSE OF WHAT MY MOTHER DID TO ME? WELL SHE'S DEAD, AND I'M HERE. WHAT'S YOUR EXCUSE?
WE'RE ALL HYPOCRITES
ONLY IF YOU ACCEPT IT.
"AL GHUL..."

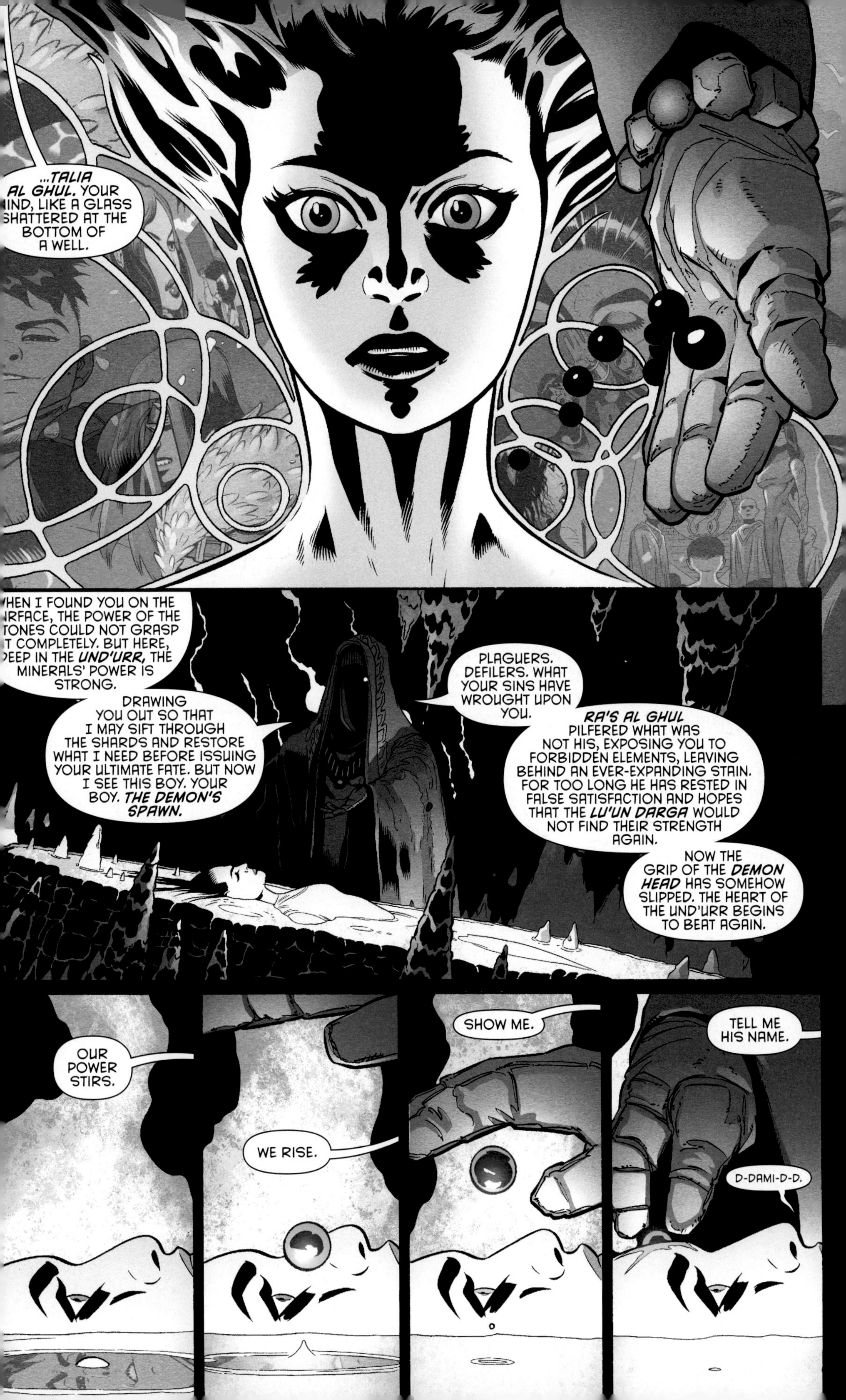

...TALIA AL GHUL. YOUR MIND, LIKE A GLASS SHATTERED AT THE BOTTOM OF A WELL.
WHEN I FOUND YOU ON THE SURFACE, THE POWER OF THE STONES COULD NOT GRASP IT COMPLETELY. BUT HERE, DEEP IN THE UND'URR, THE MINERALS' POWER IS STRONG.
DRAWING YOU OUT SO THAT I MAY SIFT THROUGH THE SHARDS AND RESTORE WHAT I NEED BEFORE ISSUING YOUR ULTIMATE FATE. BUT NOW I SEE THIS BOY. YOUR BOY. THE DEMON'S SPAWN.
PLAGUERS. DEFILERS. WHAT YOUR SINS HAVE WROUGHT UPON YOU.
RA'S AL GHUL PILFERED WHAT WAS NOT HIS, EXPOSING YOU TO FORBIDDEN ELEMENTS, LEAVING BEHIND AN EVER-EXPANDING STAIN. FOR TOO LONG HE HAS RESTED IN FALSE SATISFACTION AND HOPES THAT THE LU'UN DARGA WOULD NOT FIND THEIR STRENGTH AGAIN.
NOW THE GRIP OF THE DEMON HEAD HAS SOMEHOW SLIPPED. THE HEART OF THE UND'URR BEGINS TO BEAT AGAIN.
OUR POWER STIRS.
WE RISE.
SHOW ME.
TELL ME HIS NAME.
D-DAMI-D-D.

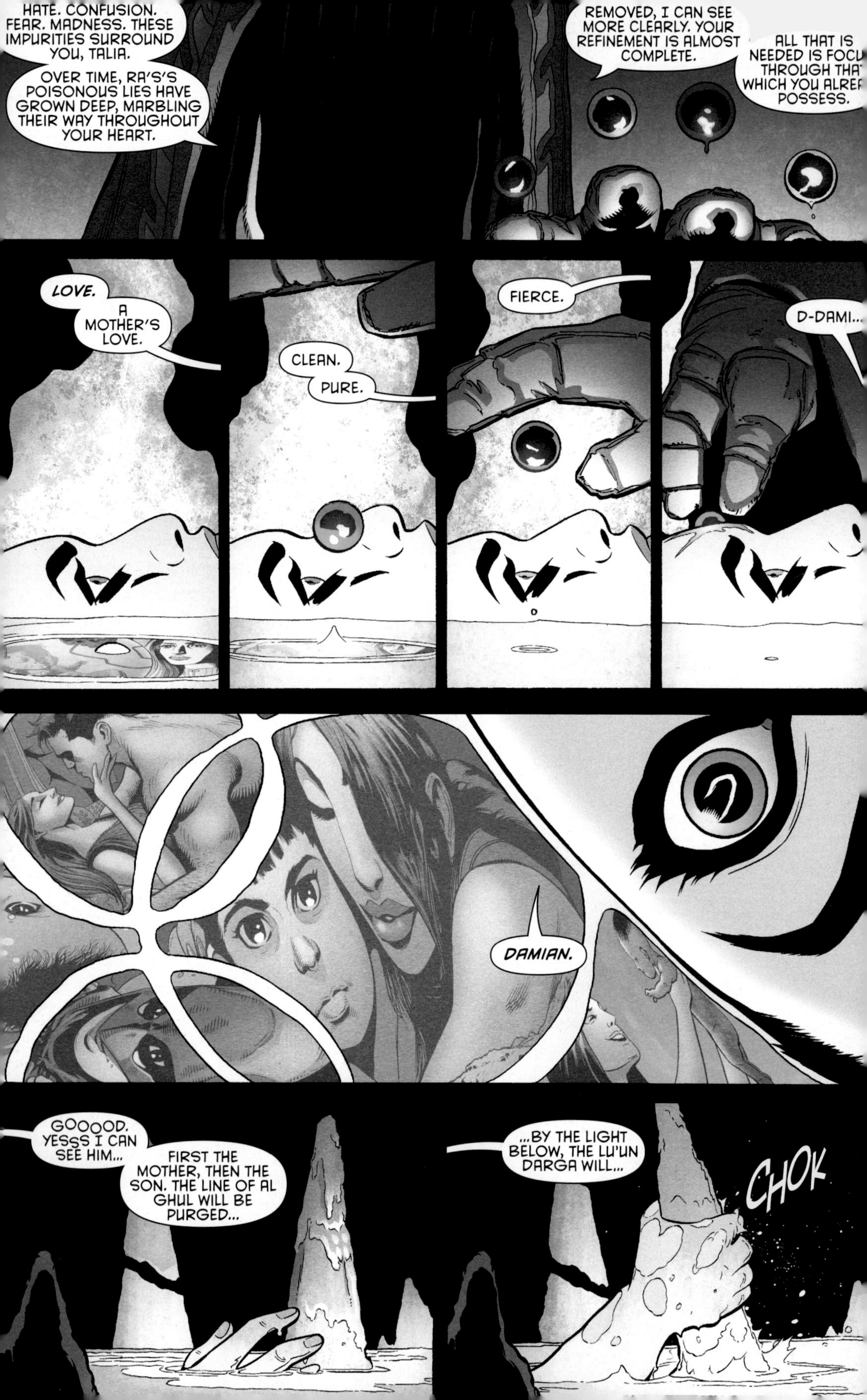
HATE. CONFUSION. FEAR. MADNESS. THESE IMPURITIES SURROUND YOU, TALIA.
OVER TIME, RA'S'S POISONOUS LIES HAVE GROWN DEEP, MARBLING THEIR WAY THROUGHOUT YOUR HEART.
REMOVED, I CAN SEE MORE CLEARLY. YOUR REFINEMENT IS ALMOST COMPLETE.
LOVE.
A MOTHER'S LOVE.
CLEAN.
PURE.
FIERCE.
D-DAMI...
DAMIAN.
GOOOOOD. YESSS I CAN SEE HIM...
FIRST THE MOTHER, THEN THE SON. THE LINE OF AL GHUL WILL BE PURGED...
...BY THE LIGHT BELOW, THE LU'UN DARGA WILL...
CHOK

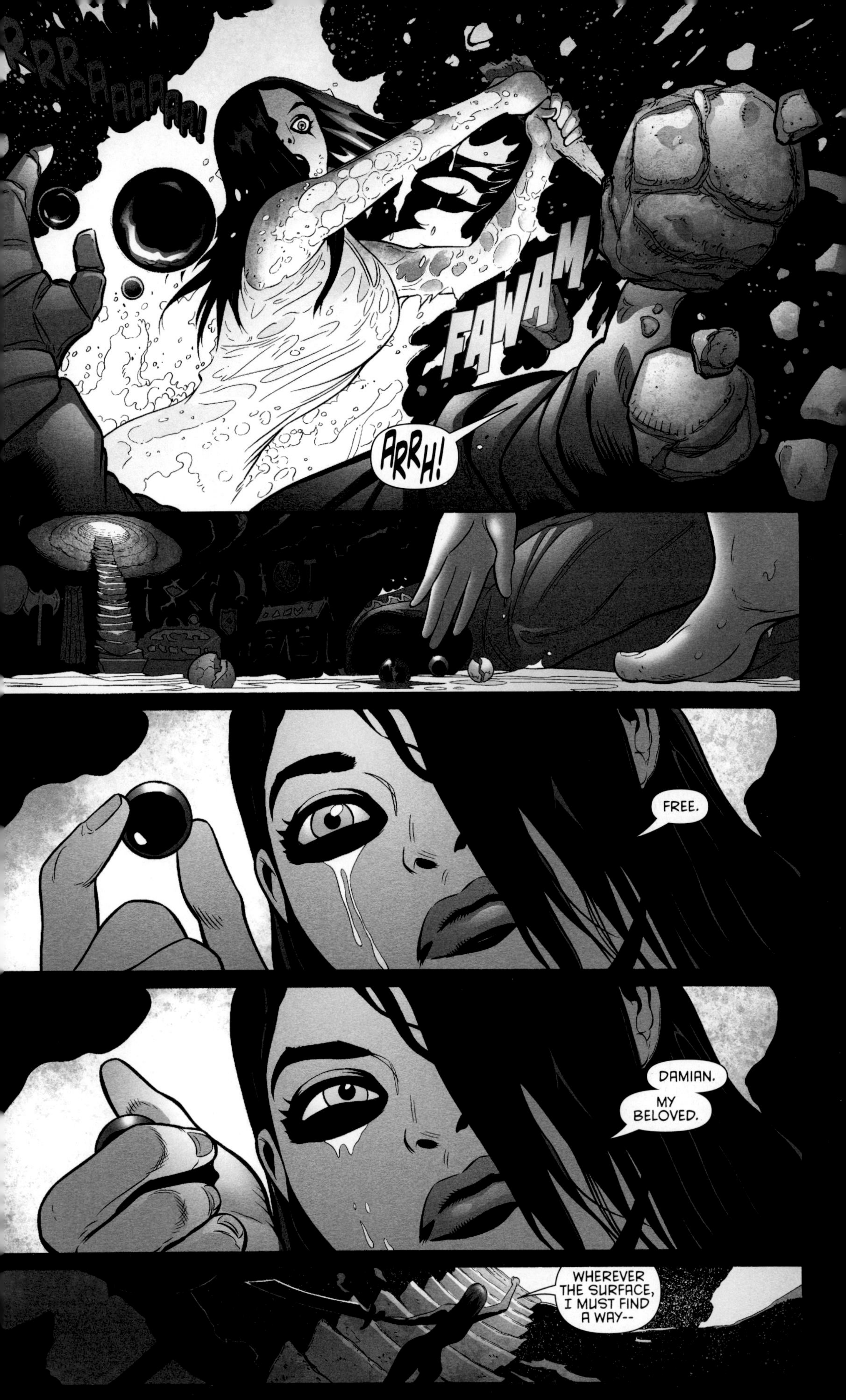
RRRAAAAAAH!
FAWAM
ARRH!
FREE.
DAMIAN.
MY BELOVED.
WHEREVER THE SURFACE, I MUST FIND A WAY--

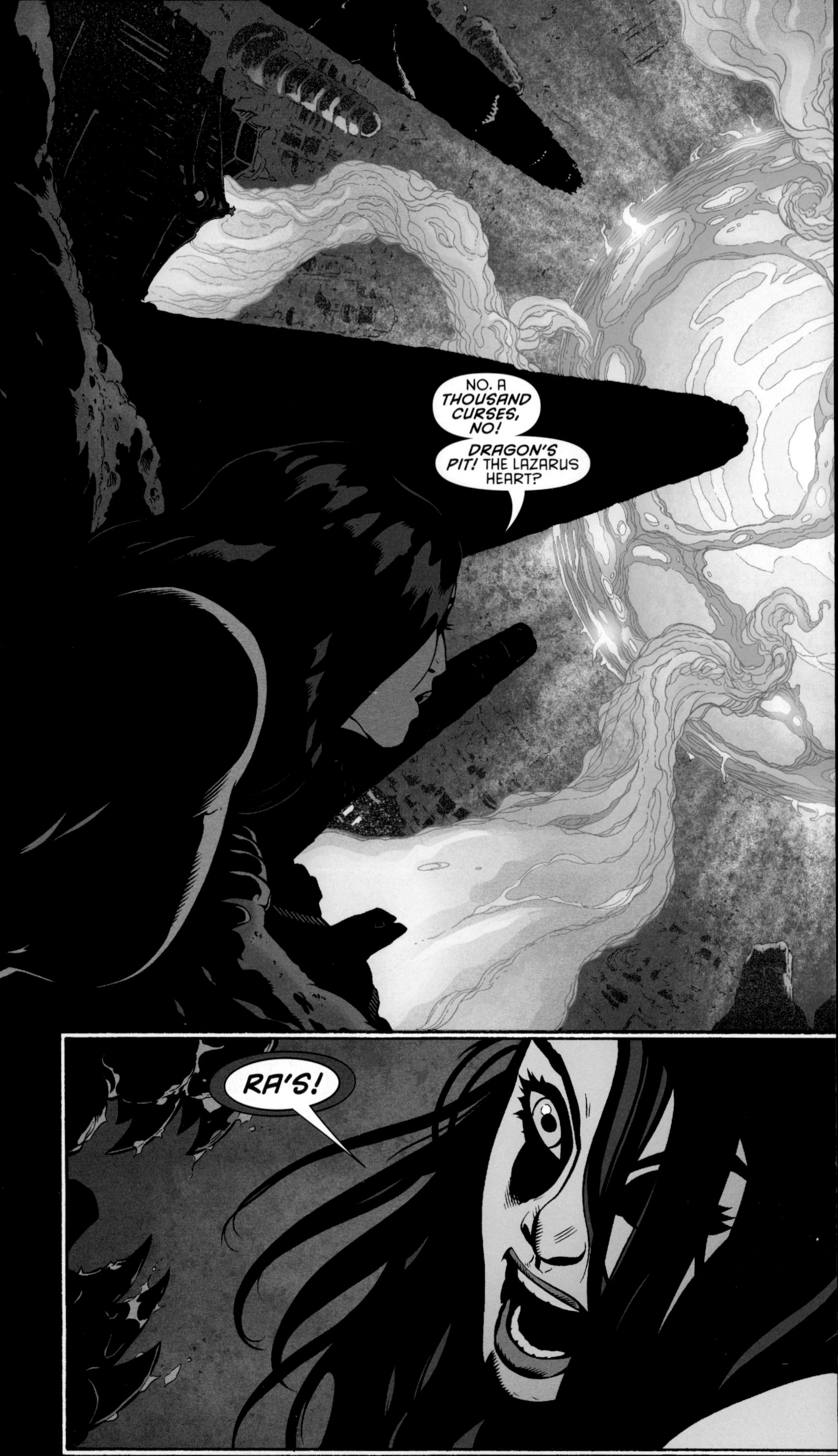
NO. A *THOUSAND CURSES*, NO!
DRAGON'S PIT! THE LAZARUS HEART?
RA'S!

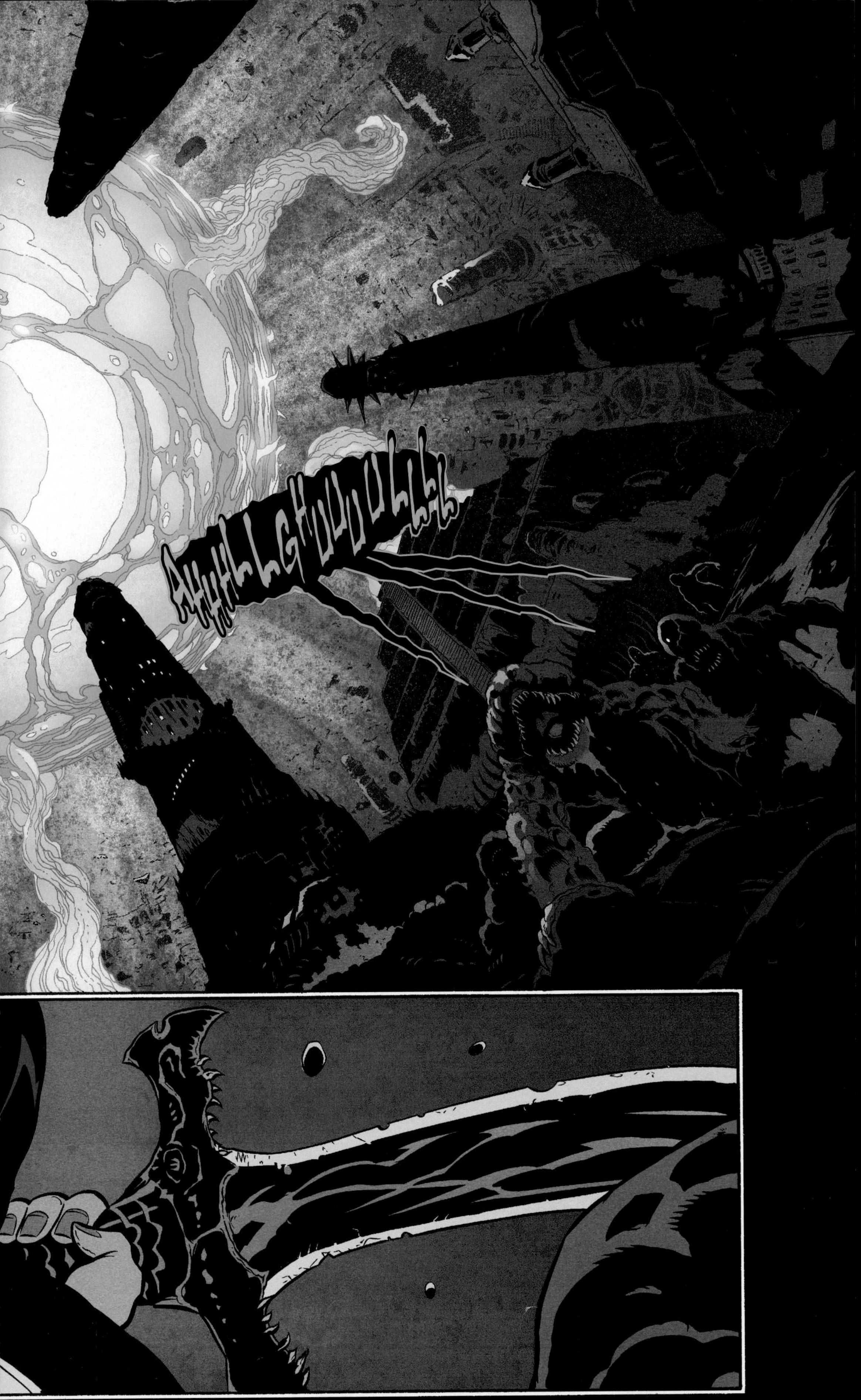
AHHLLGHUUUULLL

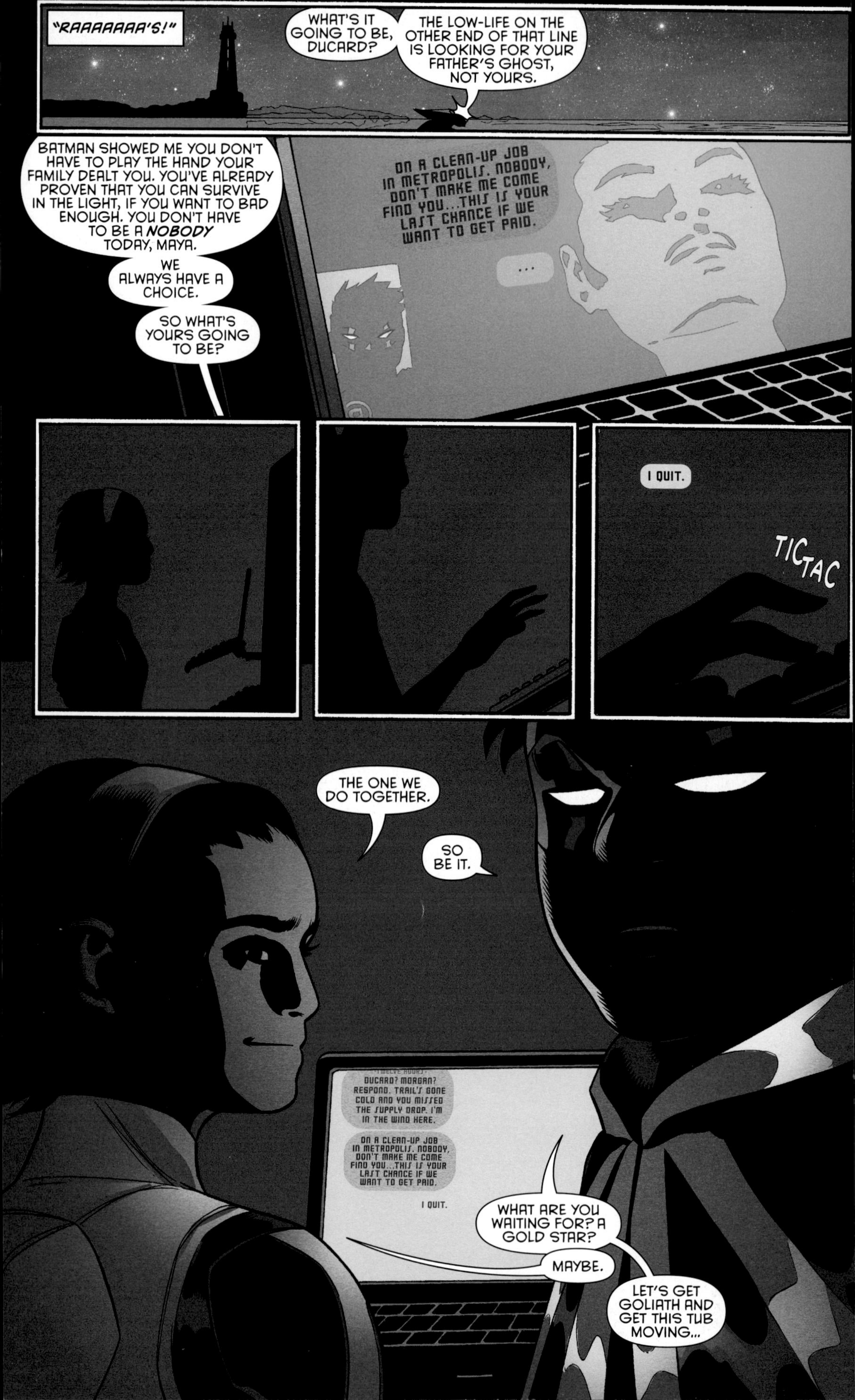
"RAAAAAAA'S!"
WHAT'S IT GOING TO BE, DUCARD?
THE LOW-LIFE ON THE OTHER END OF THAT LINE IS LOOKING FOR YOUR FATHER'S GHOST, NOT YOURS.
BATMAN SHOWED ME YOU DON'T HAVE TO PLAY THE HAND YOUR FAMILY DEALT YOU. YOU'VE ALREADY PROVEN THAT YOU CAN SURVIVE IN THE LIGHT, IF YOU WANT TO BAD ENOUGH. YOU DON'T HAVE TO BE A *NOBODY* TODAY, MAYA.
ON A CLEAN-UP JOB IN METROPOLIS. NOBODY, DON'T MAKE ME COME FIND YOU...THIS IS YOUR LAST CHANCE IF WE WANT TO GET PAID.
...
WE ALWAYS HAVE A CHOICE.
SO WHAT'S YOURS GOING TO BE?
I QUIT.
TIC TAC
DUCARD? MORGAN? RESPOND. TRAIL'S GONE COLD AND YOU MISSED THE SUPPLY DROP. I'M IN THE WIND HERE.
ON A CLEAN-UP JOB IN METROPOLIS. NOBODY, DON'T MAKE ME COME FIND YOU...THIS IS YOUR LAST CHANCE IF WE WANT TO GET PAID.
I QUIT.
THE ONE WE DO TOGETHER.
SO BE IT.
WHAT ARE YOU WAITING FOR? A GOLD STAR?
MAYBE.
LET'S GET GOLIATH AND GET THIS TUB MOVING...

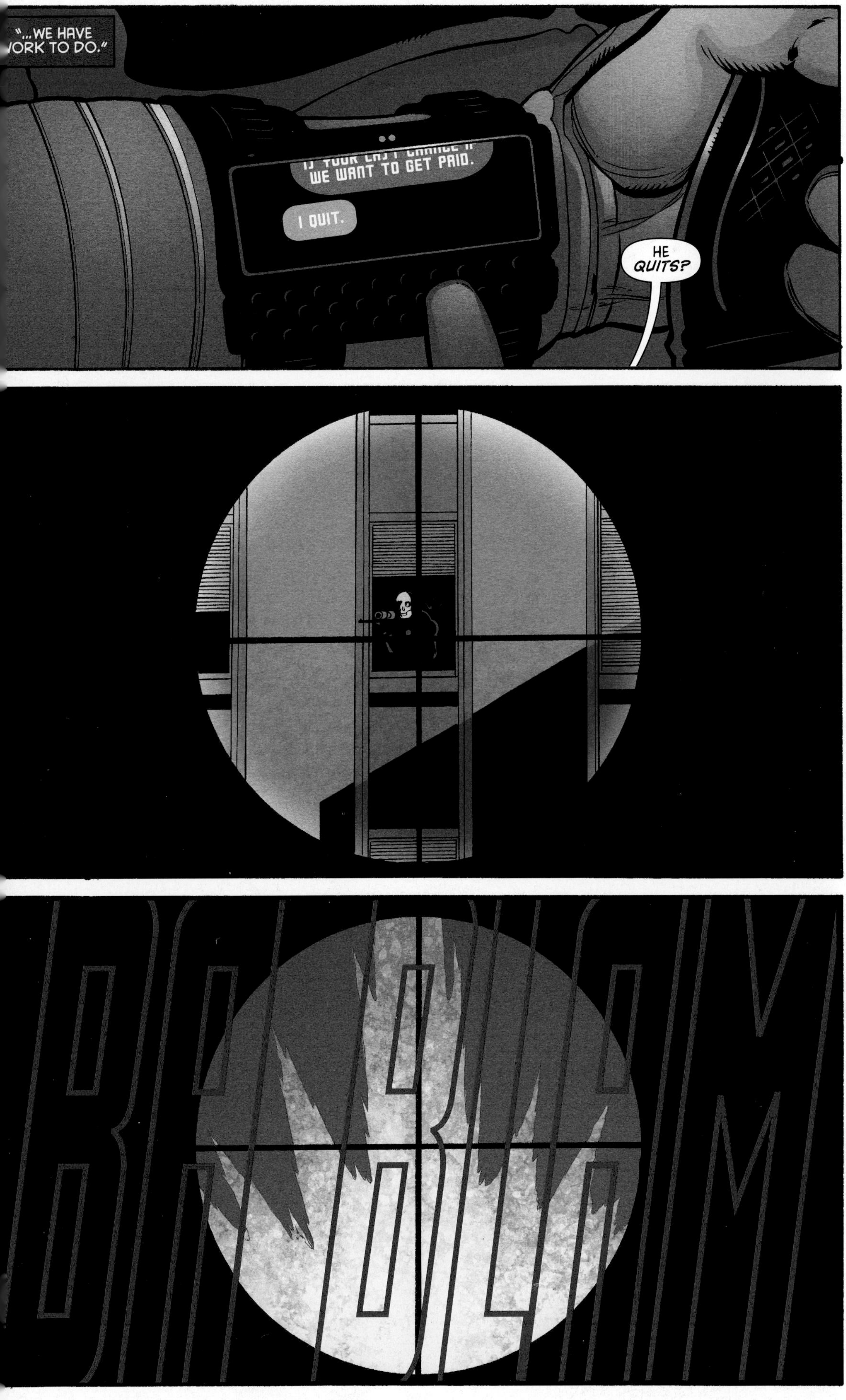
"...WE HAVE WORK TO DO."
WE WANT TO GET PAID.
I QUIT.
HE QUITS?

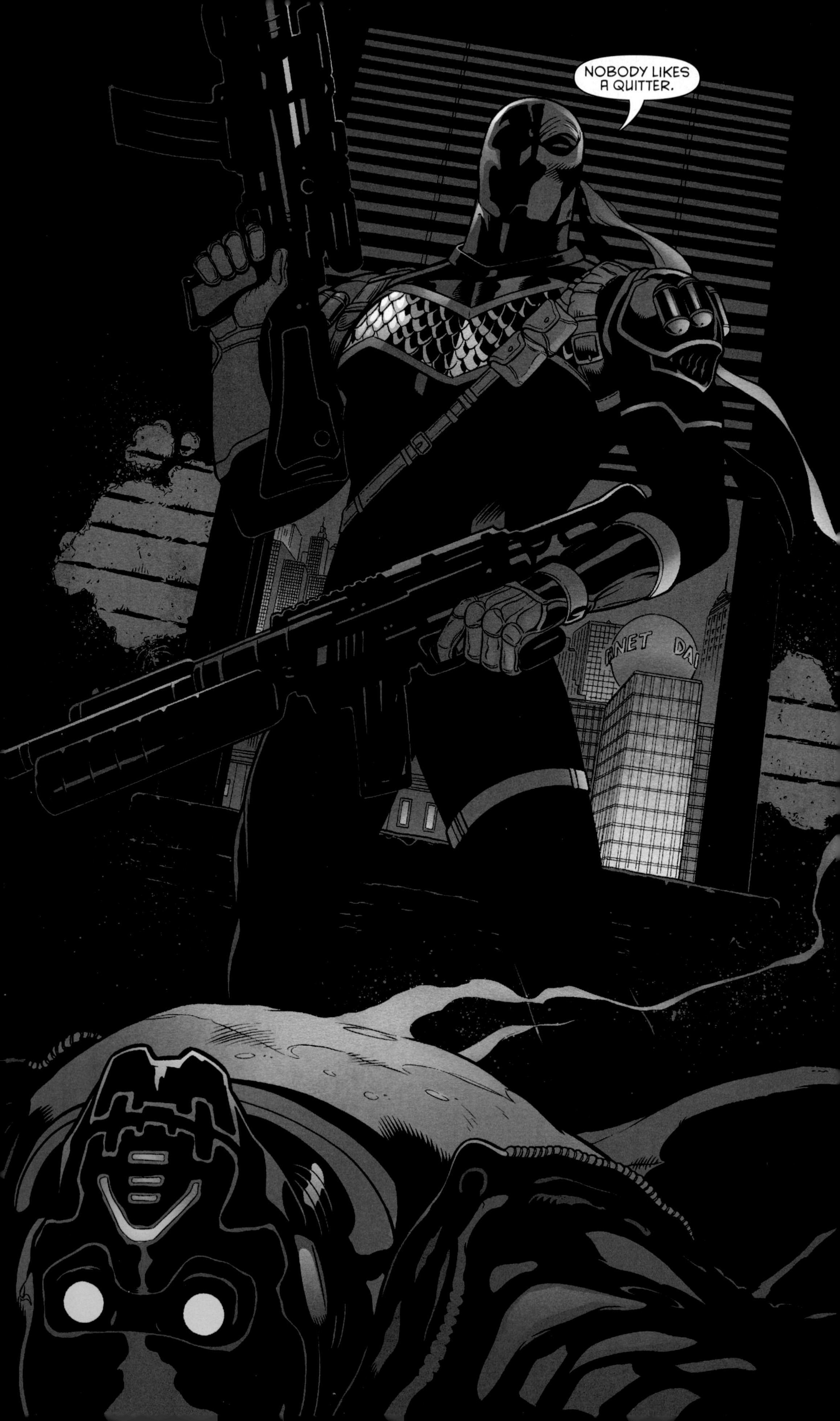
NOBODY LIKES A QUITTER.

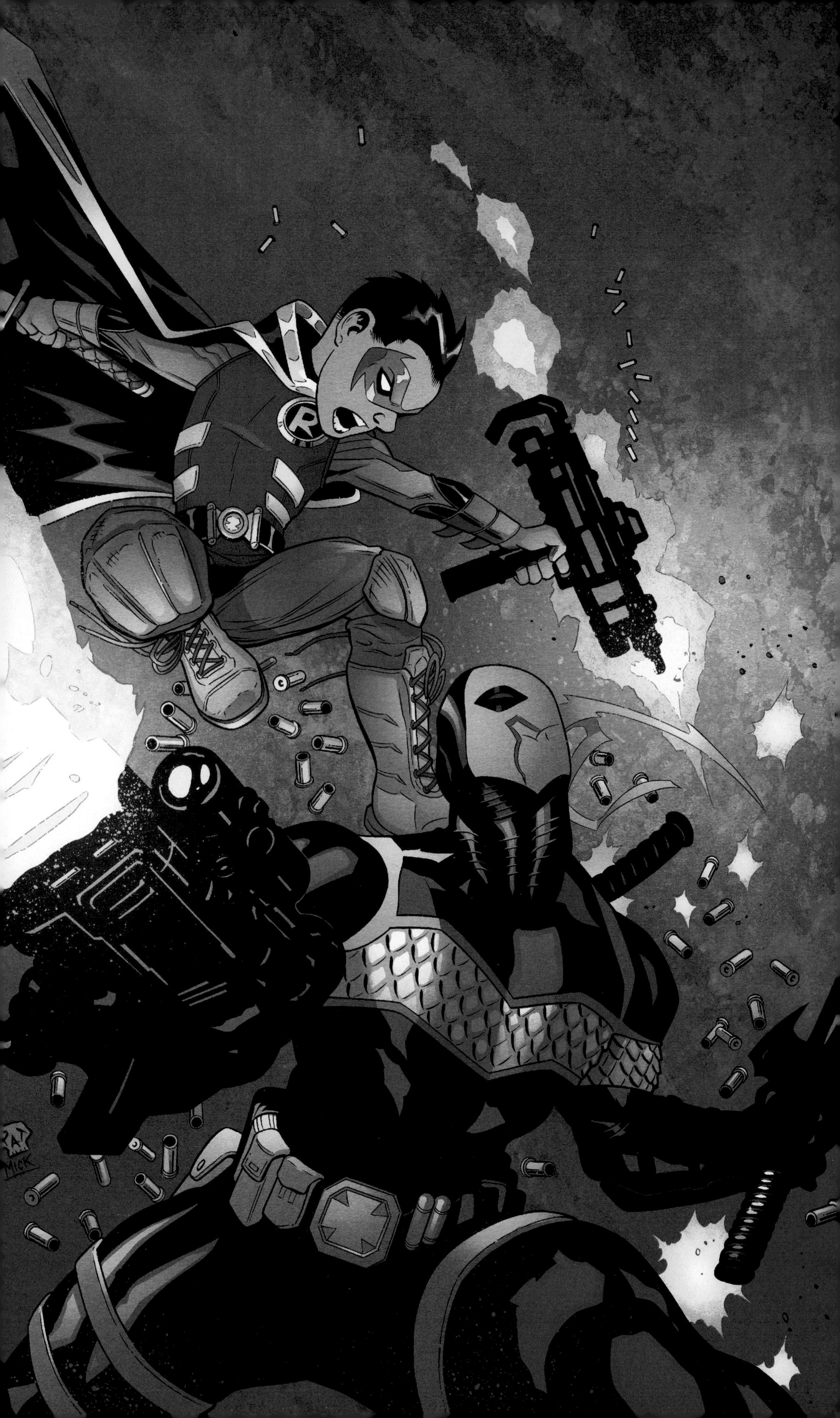

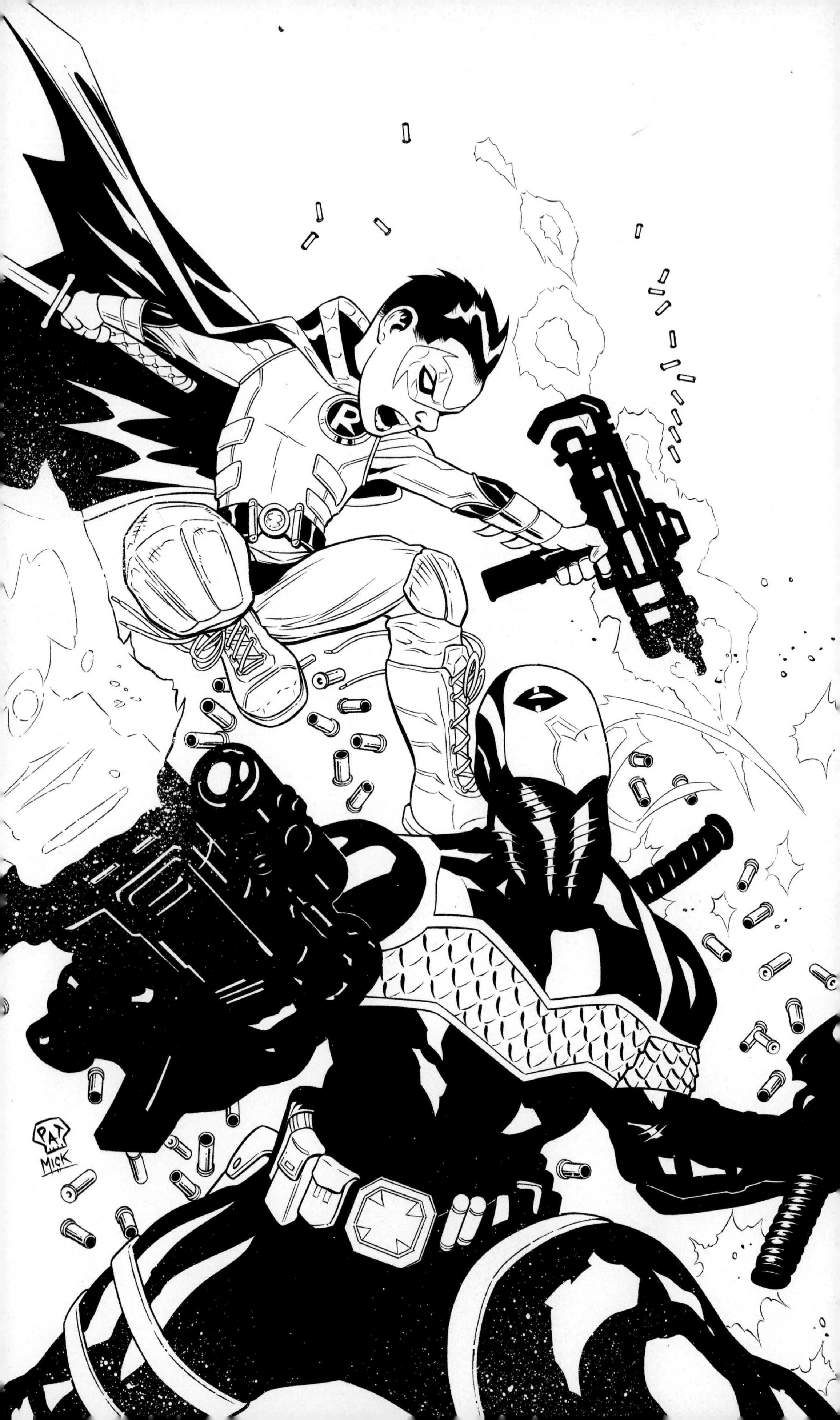
PAT
MICK

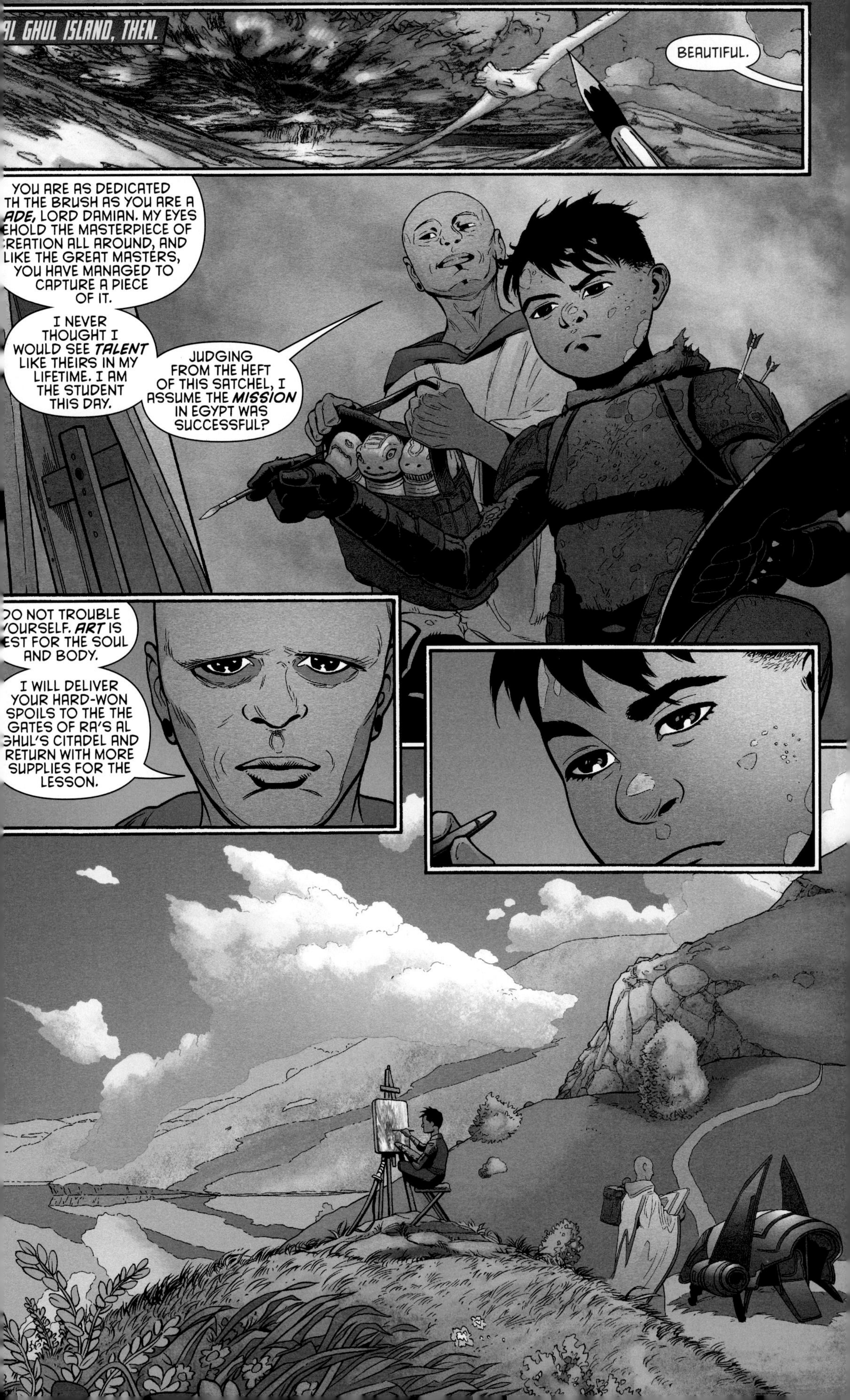

AL GHUL ISLAND, THEN.
BEAUTIFUL.
YOU ARE AS DEDICATED TH THE BRUSH AS YOU ARE A ADE, LORD DAMIAN. MY EYES EHOLD THE MASTERPIECE OF CREATION ALL AROUND, AND LIKE THE GREAT MASTERS, YOU HAVE MANAGED TO CAPTURE A PIECE OF IT.
I NEVER THOUGHT I WOULD SEE TALENT LIKE THEIRS IN MY LIFETIME. I AM THE STUDENT THIS DAY.
JUDGING FROM THE HEFT OF THIS SATCHEL, I ASSUME THE MISSION IN EGYPT WAS SUCCESSFUL?
DO NOT TROUBLE YOURSELF. ART IS EST FOR THE SOUL AND BODY.
I WILL DELIVER YOUR HARD-WON SPOILS TO THE THE GATES OF RA'S AL GHUL'S CITADEL AND RETURN WITH MORE SUPPLIES FOR THE LESSON.

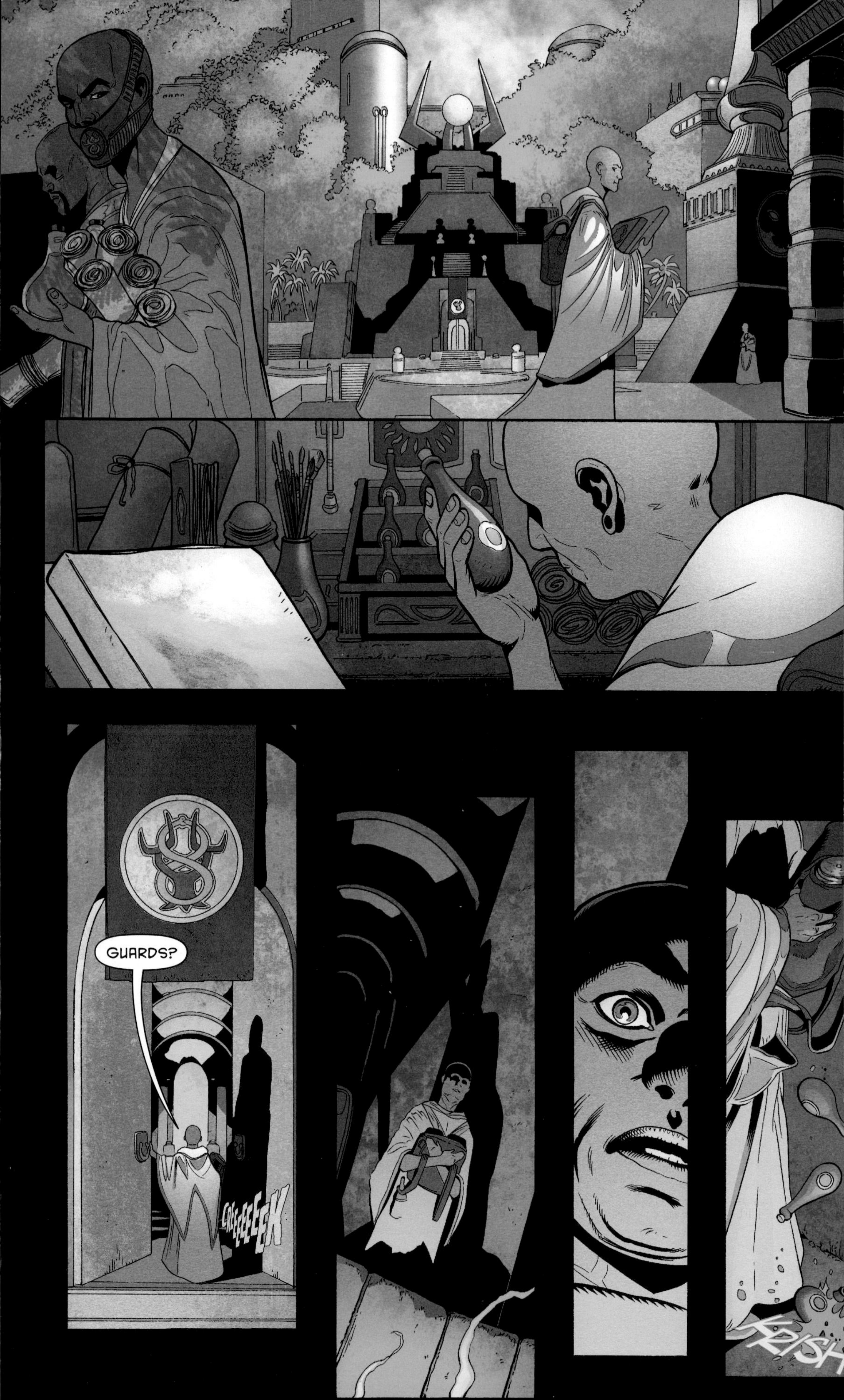
GUARDS?
CREEEEEEEK
KRISH

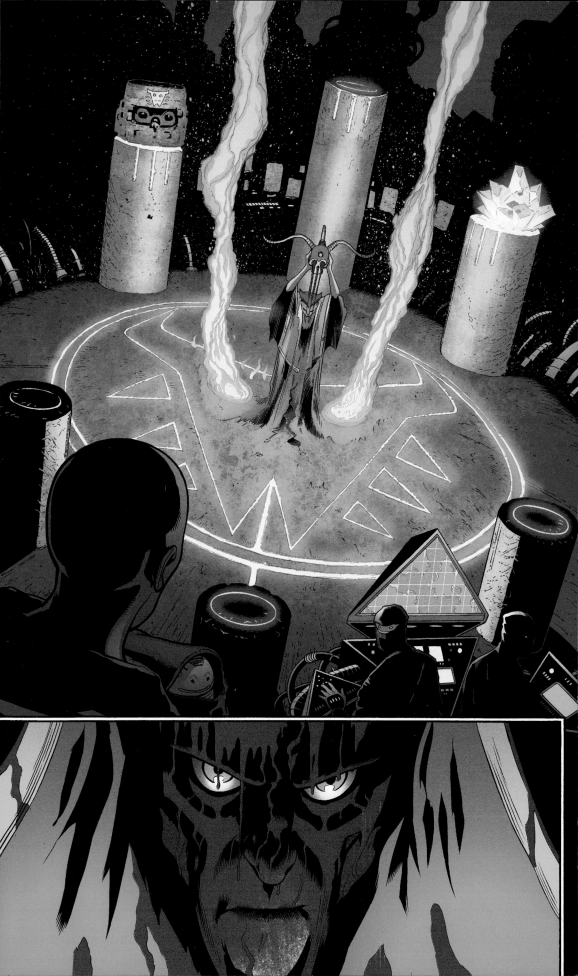

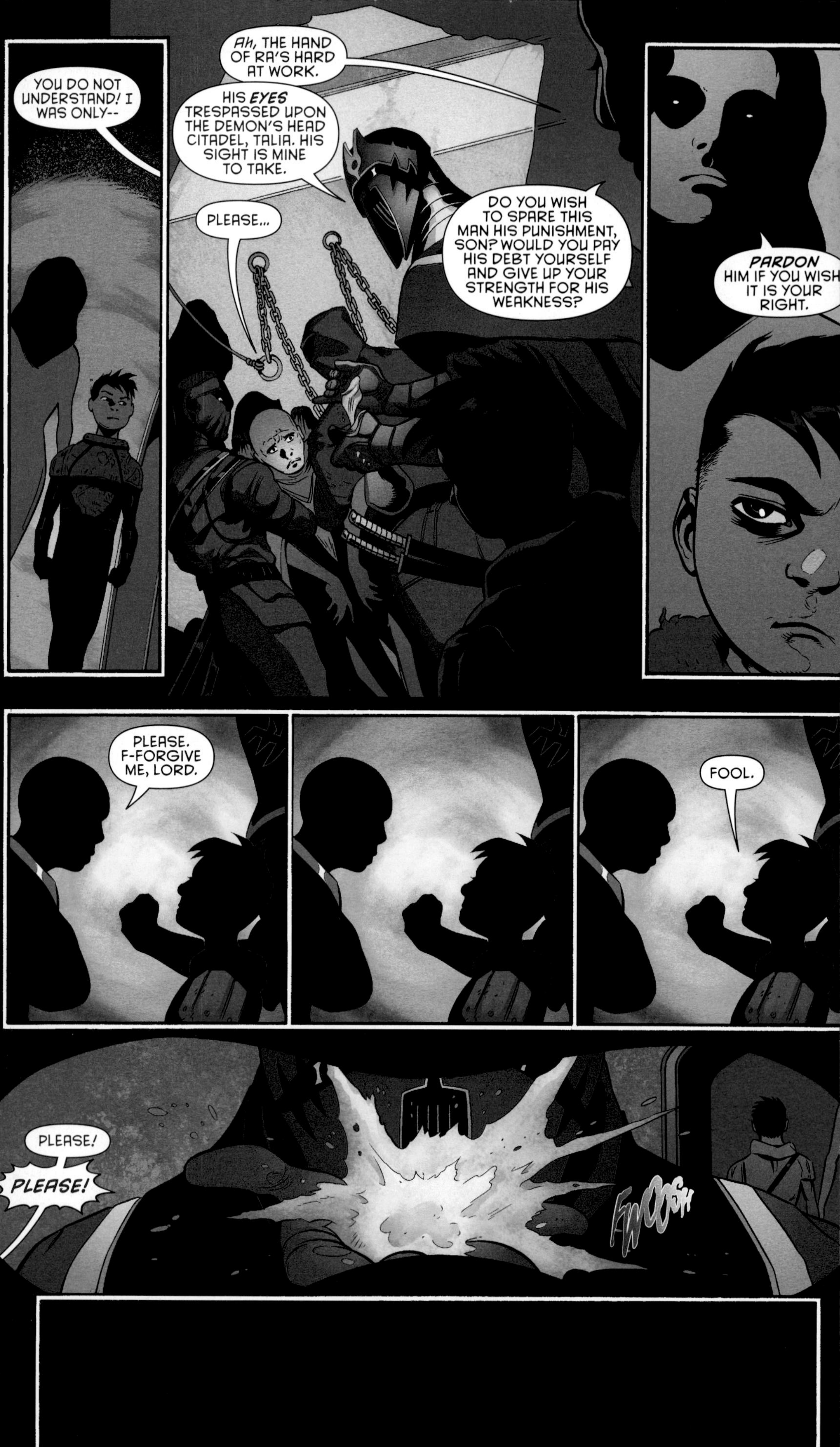
YOU DO NOT UNDERSTAND! I WAS ONLY--
Ah, THE HAND OF RA'S HARD AT WORK.
HIS EYES TRESPASSED UPON THE DEMON'S HEAD CITADEL, TALIA. HIS SIGHT IS MINE TO TAKE.
PLEASE...
DO YOU WISH TO SPARE THIS MAN HIS PUNISHMENT, SON? WOULD YOU PAY HIS DEBT YOURSELF AND GIVE UP YOUR STRENGTH FOR HIS WEAKNESS?
PARDON HIM IF YOU WISH IT IS YOUR RIGHT.
PLEASE. F-FORGIVE ME, LORD.
FOOL.
PLEASE!
PLEASE!
FWOOSH

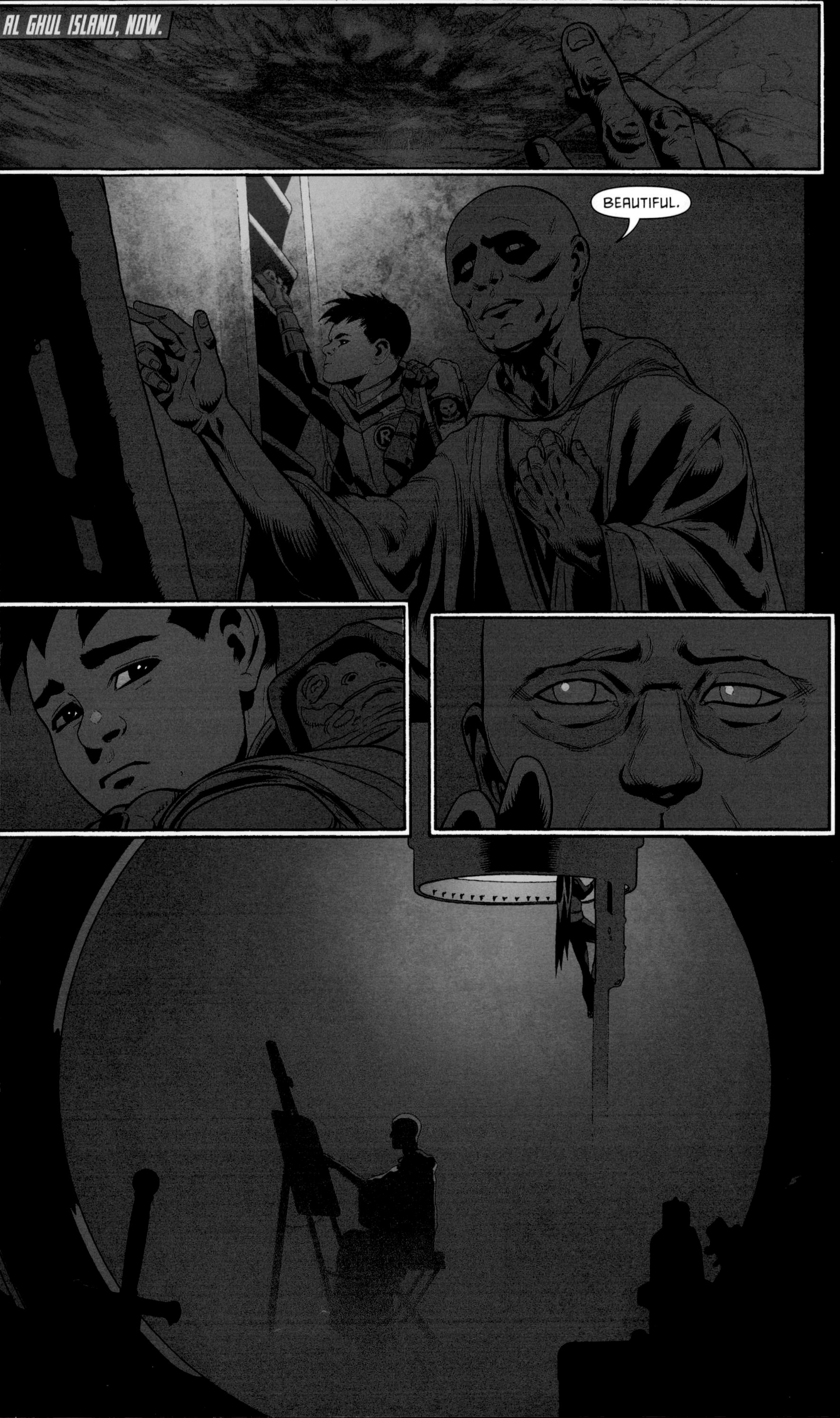
AL GHUL ISLAND, NOW.
BEAUTIFUL.

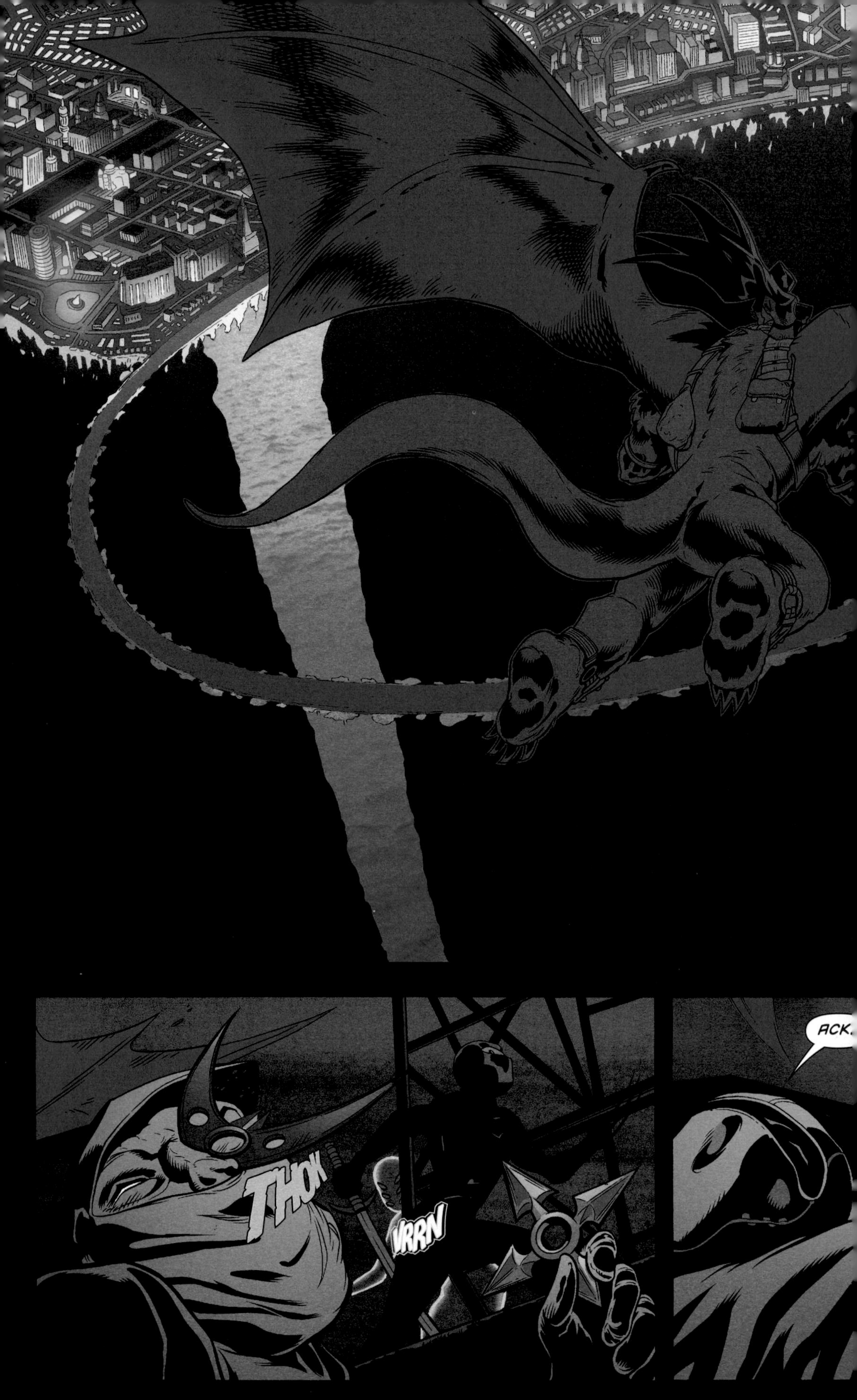
THOK
VRRN
ACK.

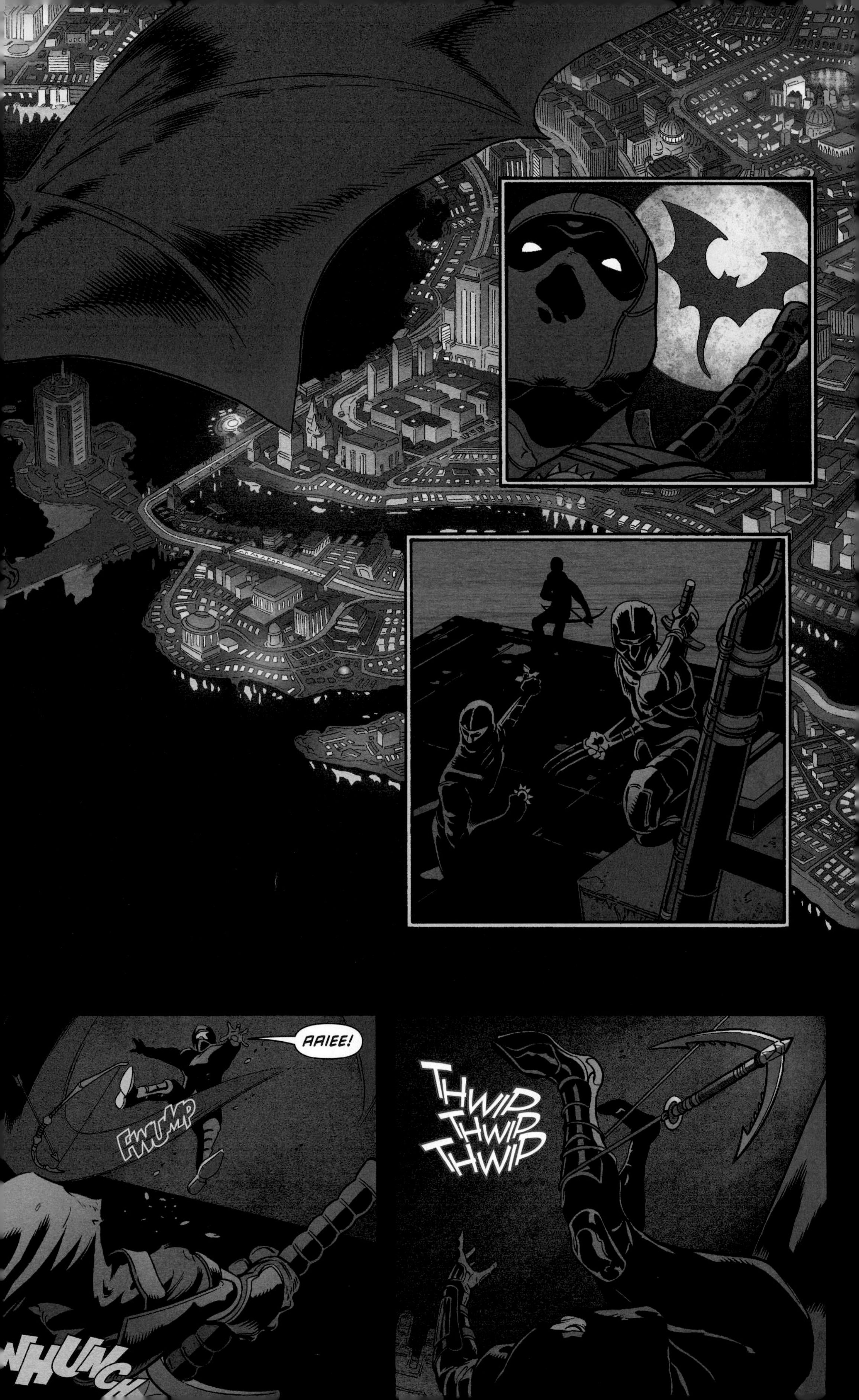
AAIEE!
FWUMP
THWIP THWIP THWIP
NHUNCH

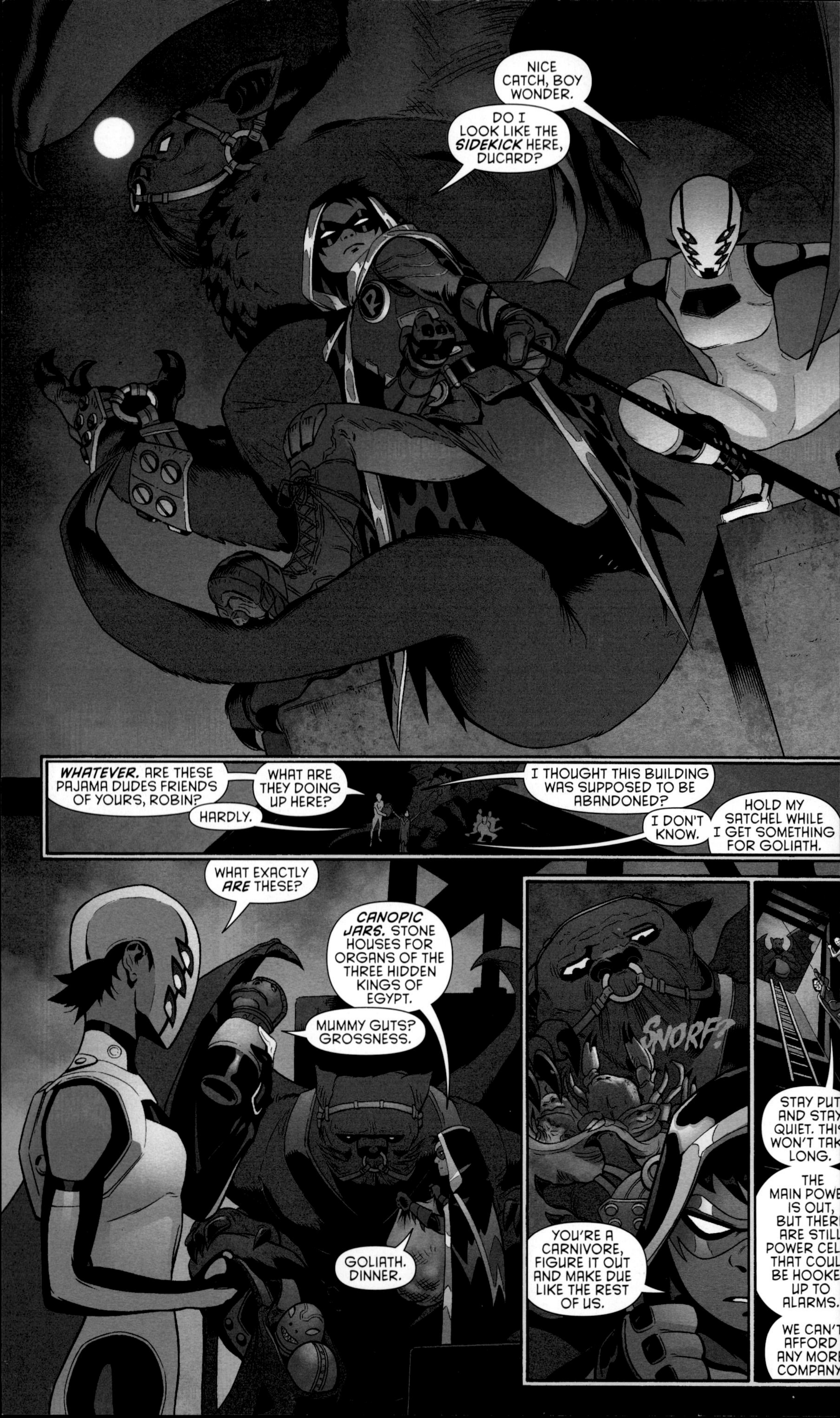
NICE CATCH, BOY WONDER.
DO I LOOK LIKE THE *SIDEKICK* HERE, DUCARD?
WHATEVER. ARE THESE PAJAMA DUDES FRIENDS OF YOURS, ROBIN?
HARDLY.
WHAT ARE THEY DOING UP HERE?
I THOUGHT THIS BUILDING WAS SUPPOSED TO BE ABANDONED?
I DON'T KNOW.
HOLD MY SATCHEL WHILE I GET SOMETHING FOR GOLIATH.
WHAT EXACTLY *ARE* THESE?
CANOPIC JARS. STONE HOUSES FOR ORGANS OF THE THREE HIDDEN KINGS OF EGYPT.
MUMMY GUTS? GROSSNESS.
GOLIATH. DINNER.
SNORF?
YOU'RE A CARNIVORE, FIGURE IT OUT AND MAKE DUE LIKE THE REST OF US.

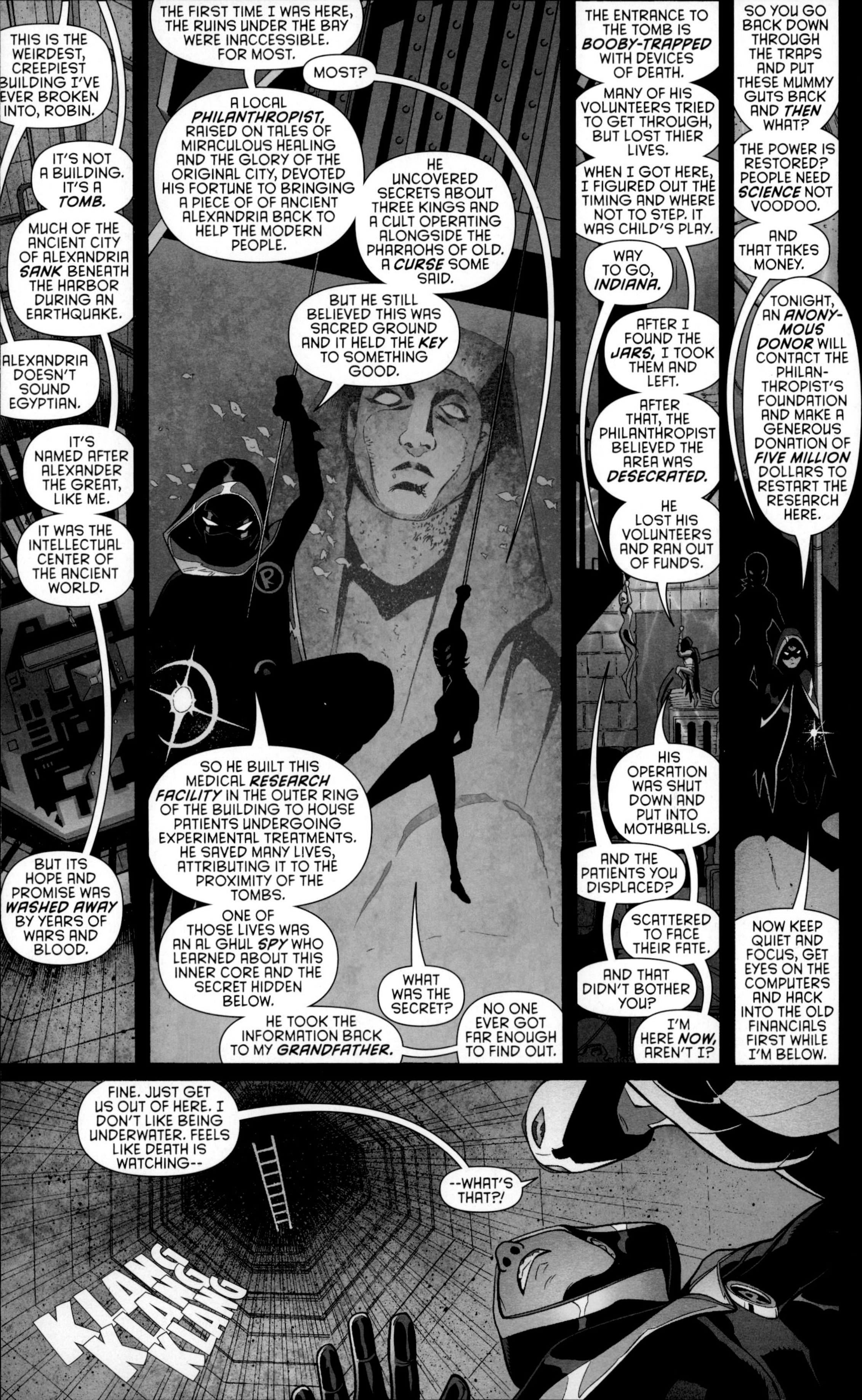
THIS IS THE WEIRDEST, CREEPIEST BUILDING I'VE EVER BROKEN INTO, ROBIN.
IT'S NOT A BUILDING. IT'S A TOMB.
MUCH OF THE ANCIENT CITY OF ALEXANDRIA SANK BENEATH THE HARBOR DURING AN EARTHQUAKE.
ALEXANDRIA DOESN'T SOUND EGYPTIAN.
IT'S NAMED AFTER ALEXANDER THE GREAT, LIKE ME.
IT WAS THE INTELLECTUAL CENTER OF THE ANCIENT WORLD.
BUT ITS HOPE AND PROMISE WAS WASHED AWAY BY YEARS OF WARS AND BLOOD.
THE FIRST TIME I WAS HERE, THE RUINS UNDER THE BAY WERE INACCESSIBLE. FOR MOST.
MOST?
A LOCAL PHILANTHROPIST, RAISED ON TALES OF MIRACULOUS HEALING AND THE GLORY OF THE ORIGINAL CITY, DEVOTED HIS FORTUNE TO BRINGING A PIECE OF OF ANCIENT ALEXANDRIA BACK TO HELP THE MODERN PEOPLE.
HE UNCOVERED SECRETS ABOUT THREE KINGS AND A CULT OPERATING ALONGSIDE THE PHARAOHS OF OLD. A CURSE SOME SAID.
BUT HE STILL BELIEVED THIS WAS SACRED GROUND AND IT HELD THE KEY TO SOMETHING GOOD.
SO HE BUILT THIS MEDICAL RESEARCH FACILITY IN THE OUTER RING OF THE BUILDING TO HOUSE PATIENTS UNDERGOING EXPERIMENTAL TREATMENTS. HE SAVED MANY LIVES, ATTRIBUTING IT TO THE PROXIMITY OF THE TOMBS.
ONE OF THOSE LIVES WAS AN AL GHUL SPY WHO LEARNED ABOUT THIS INNER CORE AND THE SECRET HIDDEN BELOW.
WHAT WAS THE SECRET?
HE TOOK THE INFORMATION BACK TO MY GRANDFATHER.
NO ONE EVER GOT FAR ENOUGH TO FIND OUT.
THE ENTRANCE TO THE TOMB IS BOOBY-TRAPPED WITH DEVICES OF DEATH.
MANY OF HIS VOLUNTEERS TRIED TO GET THROUGH, BUT LOST THIER LIVES.
WHEN I GOT HERE, I FIGURED OUT THE TIMING AND WHERE NOT TO STEP. IT WAS CHILD'S PLAY.
WAY TO GO, INDIANA.
AFTER I FOUND THE JARS, I TOOK THEM AND LEFT.
AFTER THAT, THE PHILANTHROPIST BELIEVED THE AREA WAS DESECRATED.
HE LOST HIS VOLUNTEERS AND RAN OUT OF FUNDS.
HIS OPERATION WAS SHUT DOWN AND PUT INTO MOTHBALLS.
AND THE PATIENTS YOU DISPLACED?
SCATTERED TO FACE THEIR FATE.
AND THAT DIDN'T BOTHER YOU?
I'M HERE NOW, AREN'T I?
SO YOU GO BACK DOWN THROUGH THE TRAPS AND PUT THESE MUMMY GUTS BACK AND THEN WHAT?
THE POWER IS RESTORED? PEOPLE NEED SCIENCE NOT VOODOO.
AND THAT TAKES MONEY.
TONIGHT, AN ANONYMOUS DONOR WILL CONTACT THE PHILANTHROPIST'S FOUNDATION AND MAKE A GENEROUS DONATION OF FIVE MILLION DOLLARS TO RESTART THE RESEARCH HERE.
NOW KEEP QUIET AND FOCUS, GET EYES ON THE COMPUTERS AND HACK INTO THE OLD FINANCIALS FIRST WHILE I'M BELOW.
FINE. JUST GET US OUT OF HERE. I DON'T LIKE BEING UNDERWATER. FEELS LIKE DEATH IS WATCHING--
--WHAT'S THAT?!
KLANG KLANG KLANG

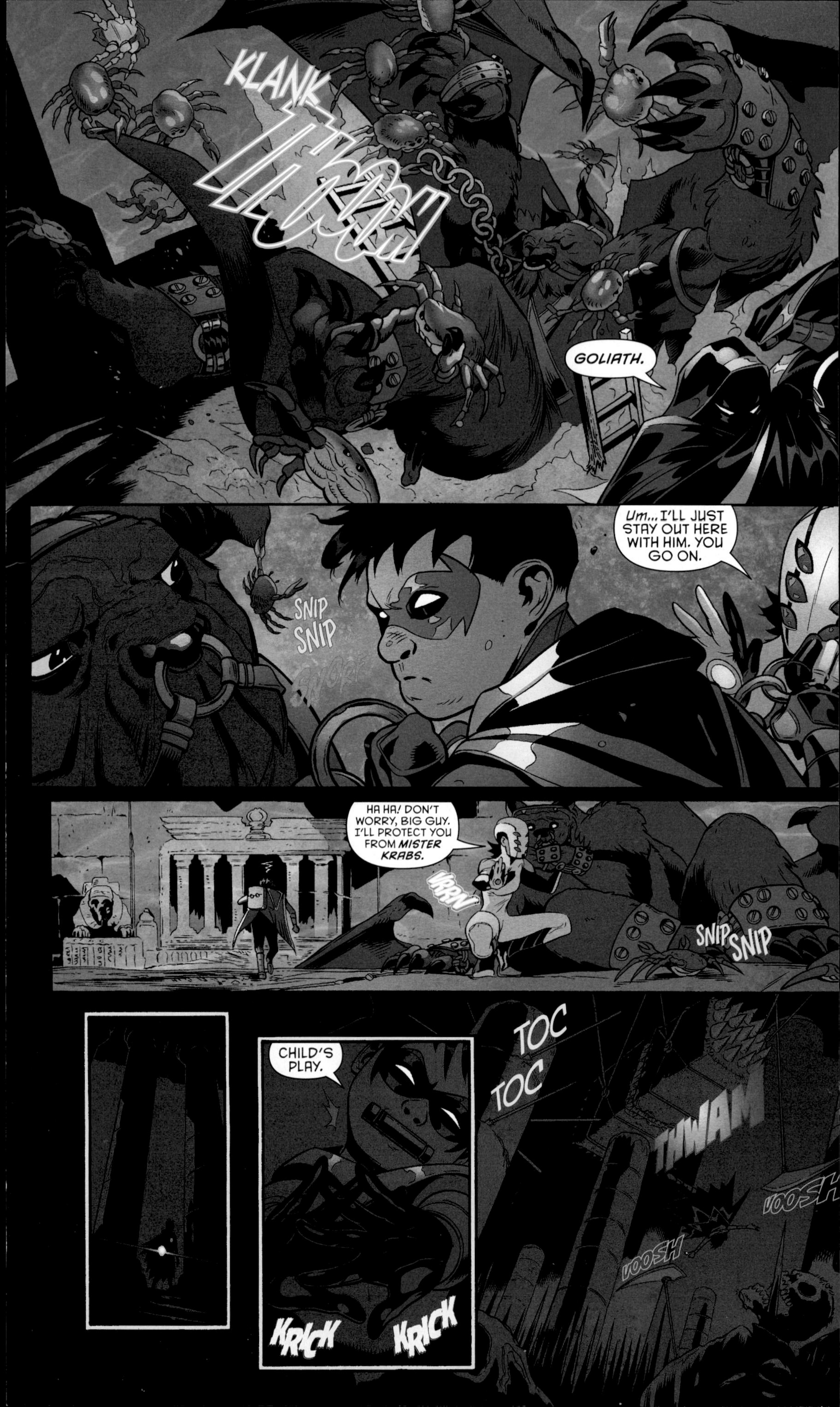
KLANK
THOOM
GOLIATH.
Um... I'LL JUST STAY OUT HERE WITH HIM. YOU GO ON.
SNIP SNIP
SNORF
HA HA! DON'T WORRY, BIG GUY. I'LL PROTECT YOU FROM MISTER KRABS.
VRRN
SNIP SNIP
CHILD'S PLAY.
KRICK KRICK
TOC TOC
THWAM
VOOSH
VOOSH

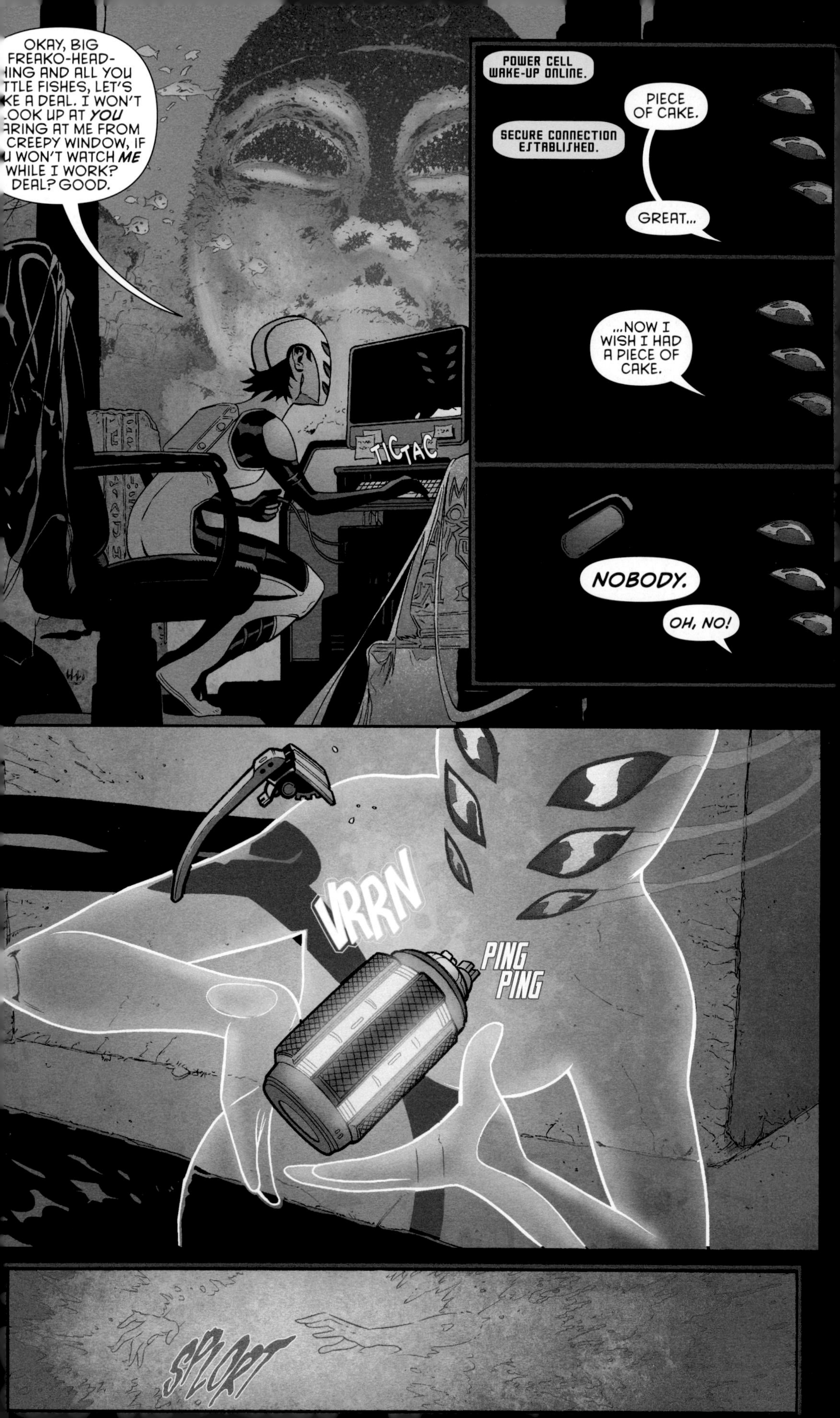
OKAY, BIG FREAKO-HEAD-HING AND ALL YOU TTLE FISHES, LET'S KE A DEAL. I WON'T OOK UP AT *YOU* ARING AT ME FROM CREEPY WINDOW, IF U WON'T WATCH *ME* WHILE I WORK? DEAL? GOOD.
TIC TAC
POWER CELL WAKE-UP ONLINE.
PIECE OF CAKE.
SECURE CONNECTION ESTABLISHED.
GREAT...
...NOW I WISH I HAD A PIECE OF CAKE.
NOBODY.
OH, NO!
VRRN
PING PING
SPLORT

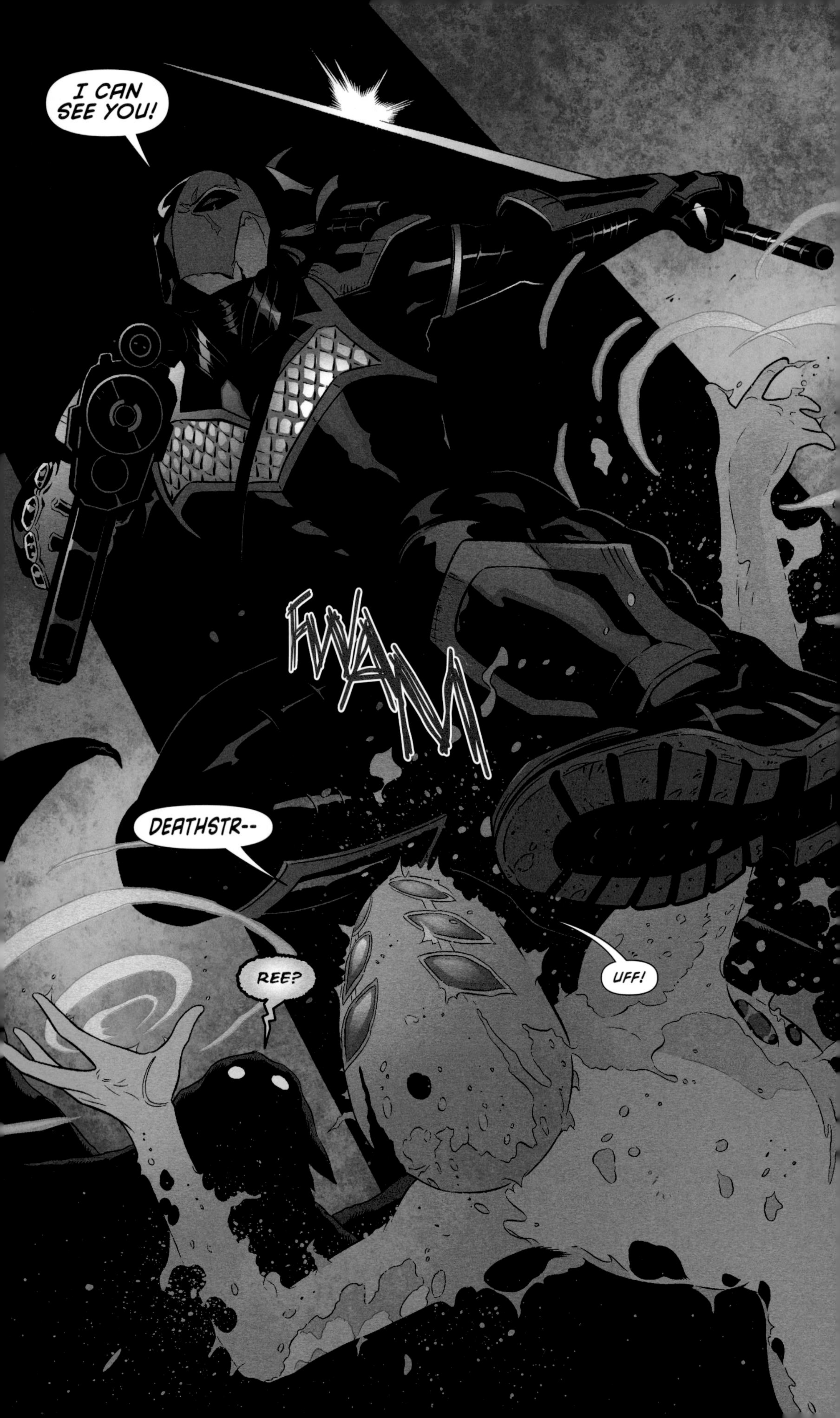
I CAN SEE YOU!
FWAM
DEATHSTR--
REE?
UFF!

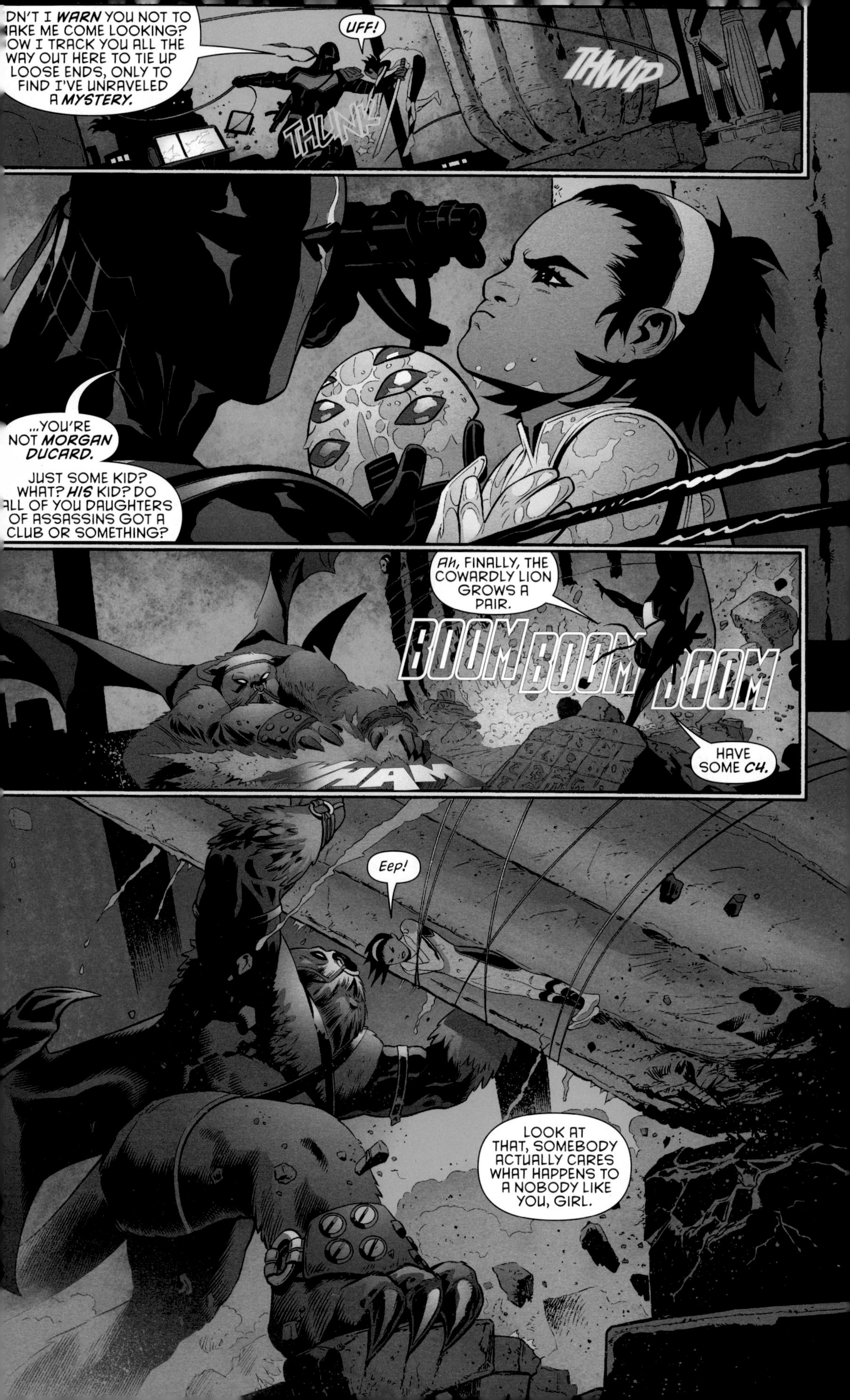
DN'T I WARN YOU NOT TO
AKE ME COME LOOKING?
OW I TRACK YOU ALL THE
WAY OUT HERE TO TIE UP
LOOSE ENDS, ONLY TO
FIND I'VE UNRAVELED
A MYSTERY.
UFF!
THWIP
THUNK
...YOU'RE
NOT MORGAN
DUCARD.
JUST SOME KID?
WHAT? HIS KID? DO
LL OF YOU DAUGHTERS
OF ASSASSINS GOT A
CLUB OR SOMETHING?
Ah, FINALLY, THE
COWARDLY LION
GROWS A
PAIR.
BOOM BOOM DOOM
HAVE
SOME C4.
WHAM
Eep!
LOOK AT
THAT, SOMEBODY
ACTUALLY CARES
WHAT HAPPENS TO
A NOBODY LIKE
YOU, GIRL.

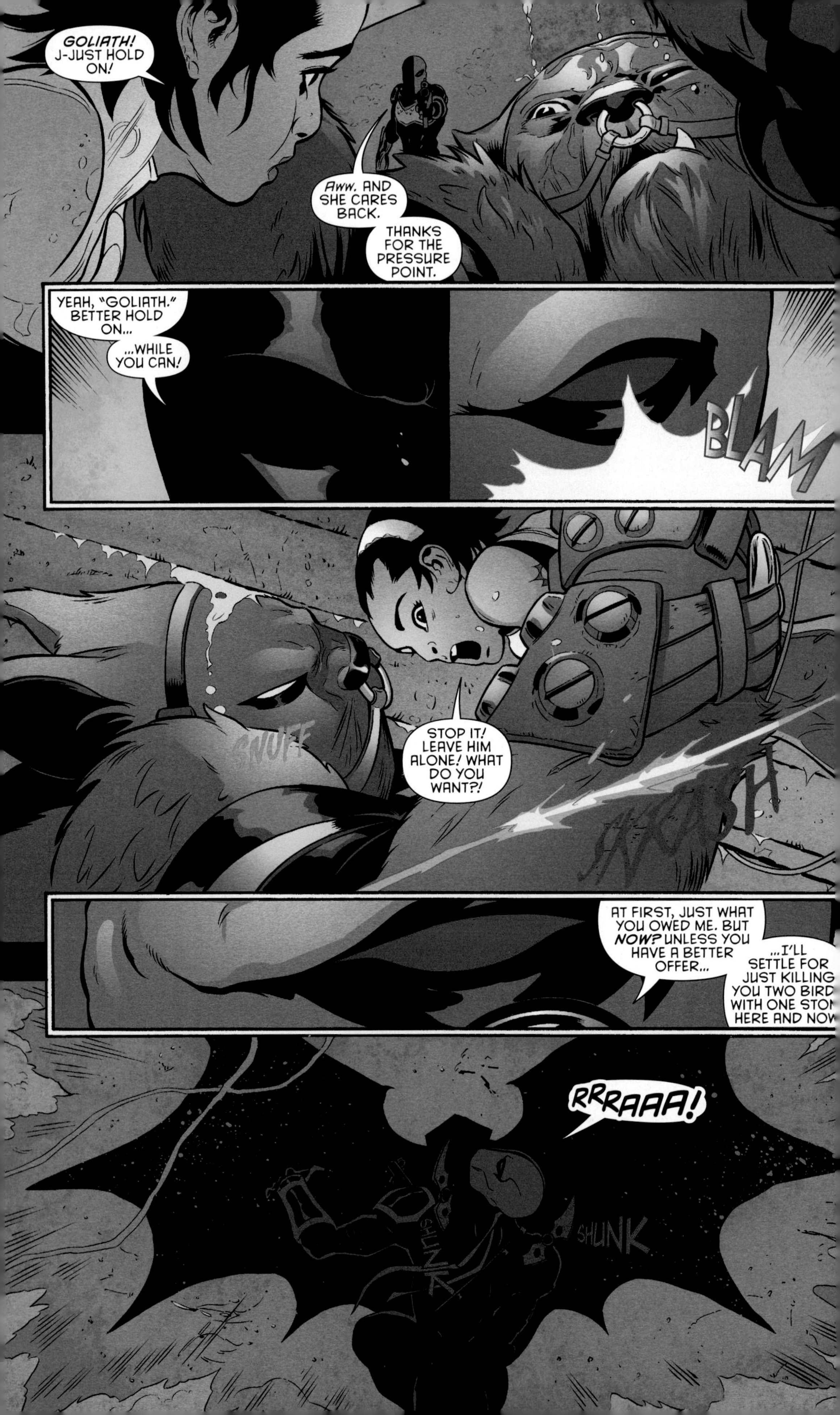
GOLIATH! J-JUST HOLD ON!
AWW. AND SHE CARES BACK.
THANKS FOR THE PRESSURE POINT.
YEAH, "GOLIATH." BETTER HOLD ON...
...WHILE YOU CAN!
BLAM
SNUFF
STOP IT! LEAVE HIM ALONE! WHAT DO YOU WANT?!
AT FIRST, JUST WHAT YOU OWED ME. BUT NOW? UNLESS YOU HAVE A BETTER OFFER...
...I'LL SETTLE FOR JUST KILLING YOU TWO BIRD WITH ONE STON HERE AND NOW
RRRAAA!
SHUNK
SHUNK

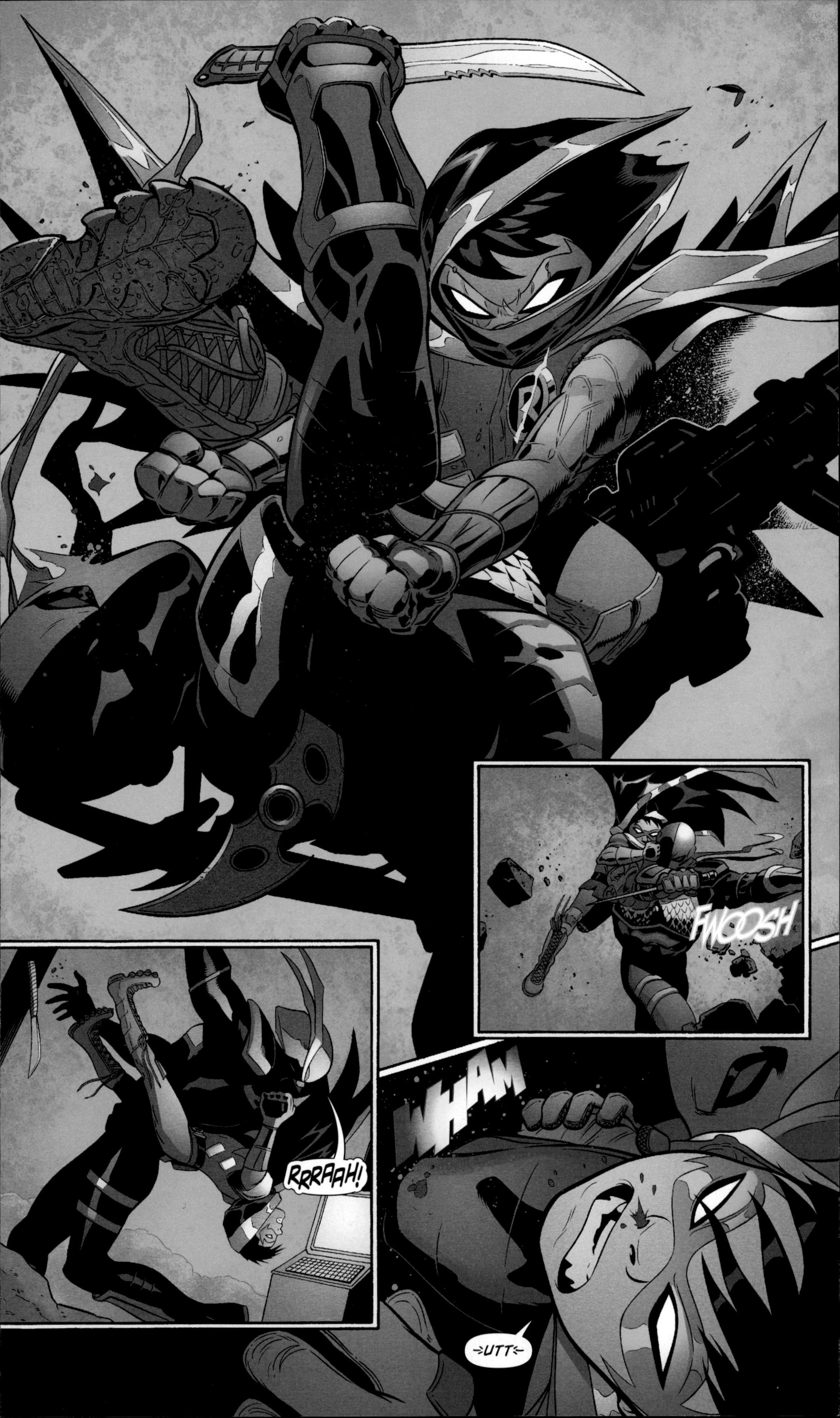
FWOOSH
RRRAAH!
WHAM
UTT

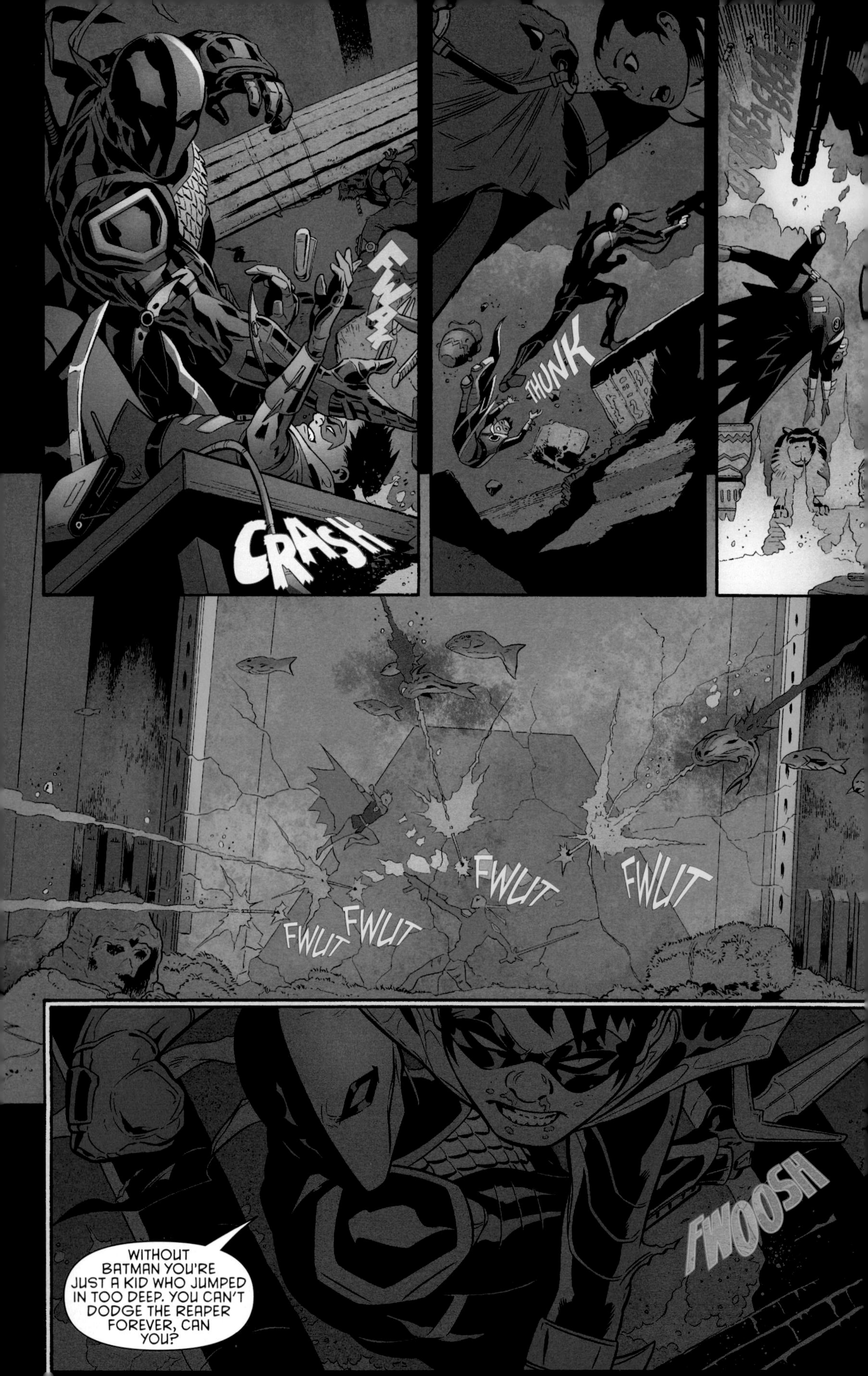
FWAK
CRASH
THUNK
FWUT
FWUT
FWUT
FWUT
WITHOUT BATMAN YOU'RE JUST A KID WHO JUMPED IN TOO DEEP. YOU CAN'T DODGE THE REAPER FOREVER, CAN YOU?
FWOOSH

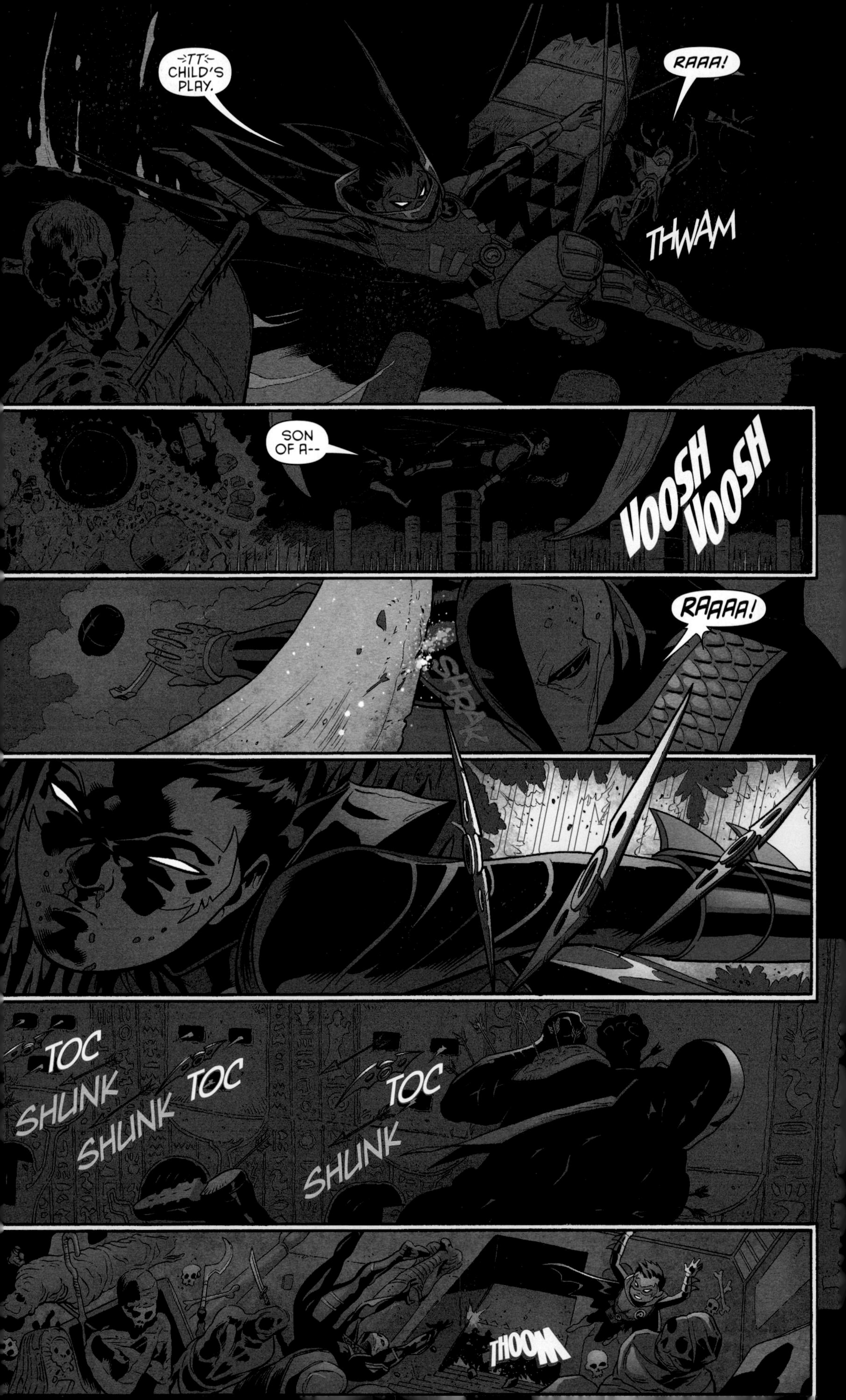
-TT-
CHILD'S PLAY.
RAAA!
THWAM
SON OF A--
VOOSH VOOSH
RAAAA!
TOC
SHUNK
SHUNK TOC
TOC
SHUNK
THOOM

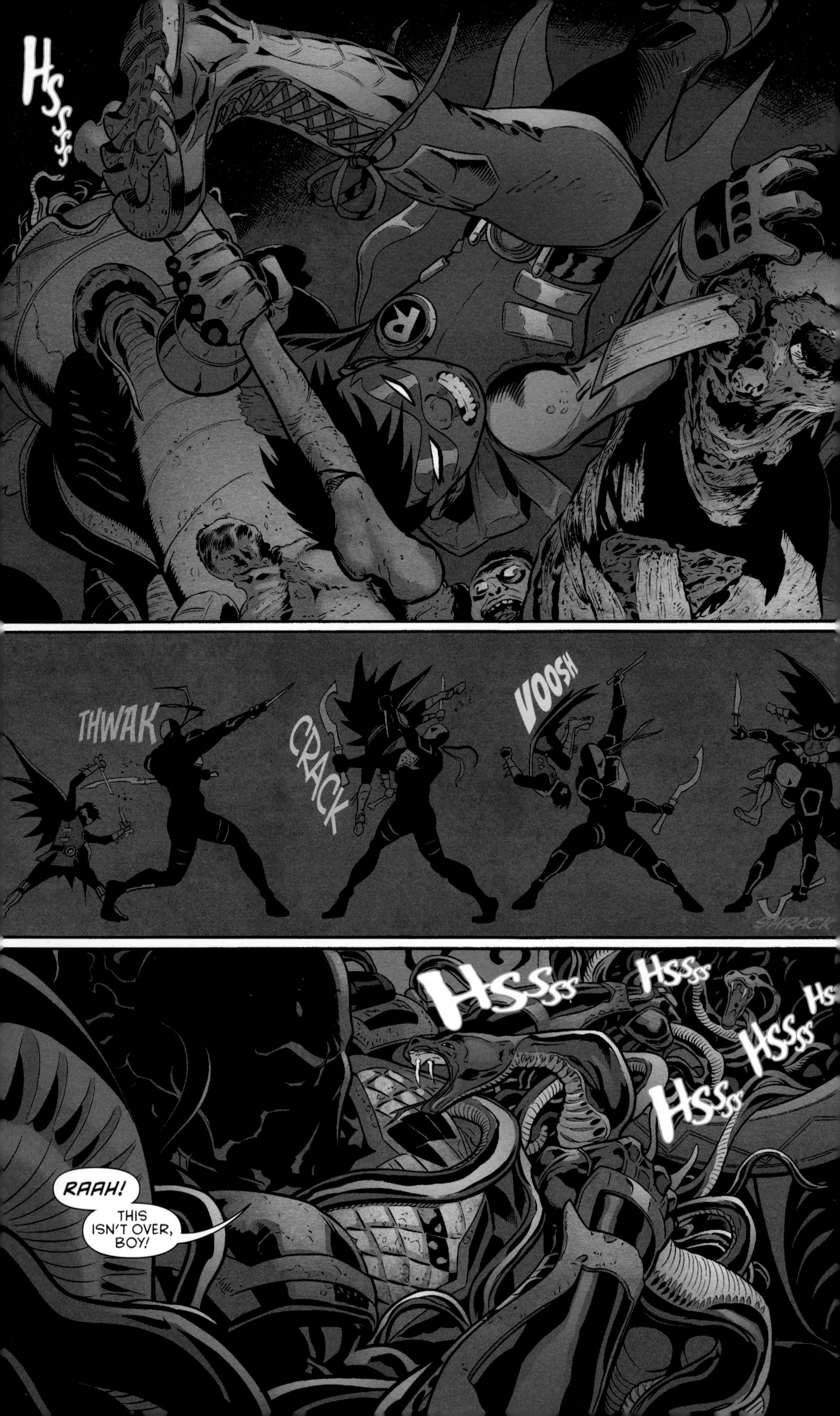
HSSSS
THWAK
CRACK
VOOSH
SHRACK
HSSSSS
HSSSS
HSSSS
HS
HSSSS
RAAH!
THIS ISN'T OVER, BOY!

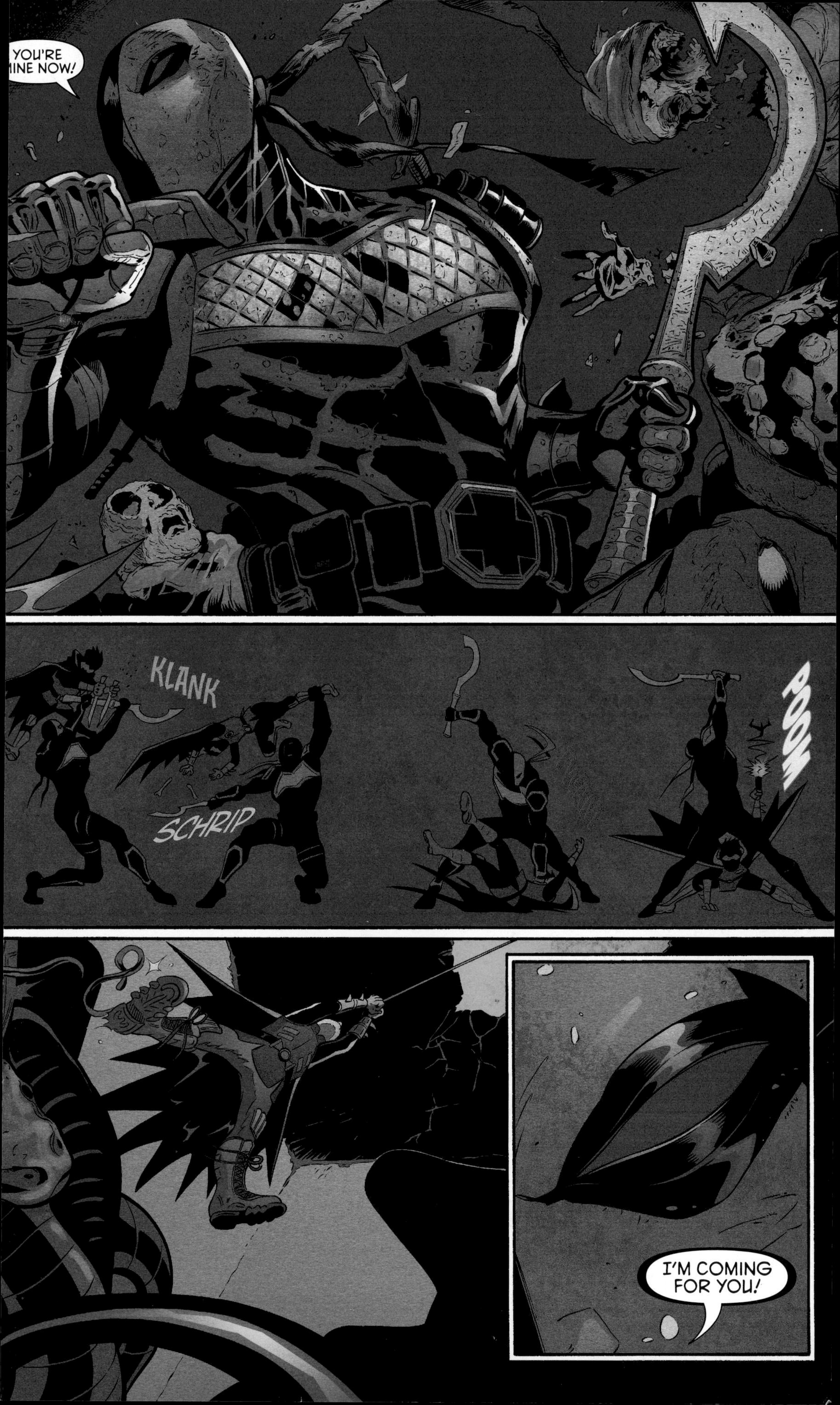
YOU'RE
MINE NOW!
KLANK
SCHRIP
POOM
I'M COMING
FOR YOU!

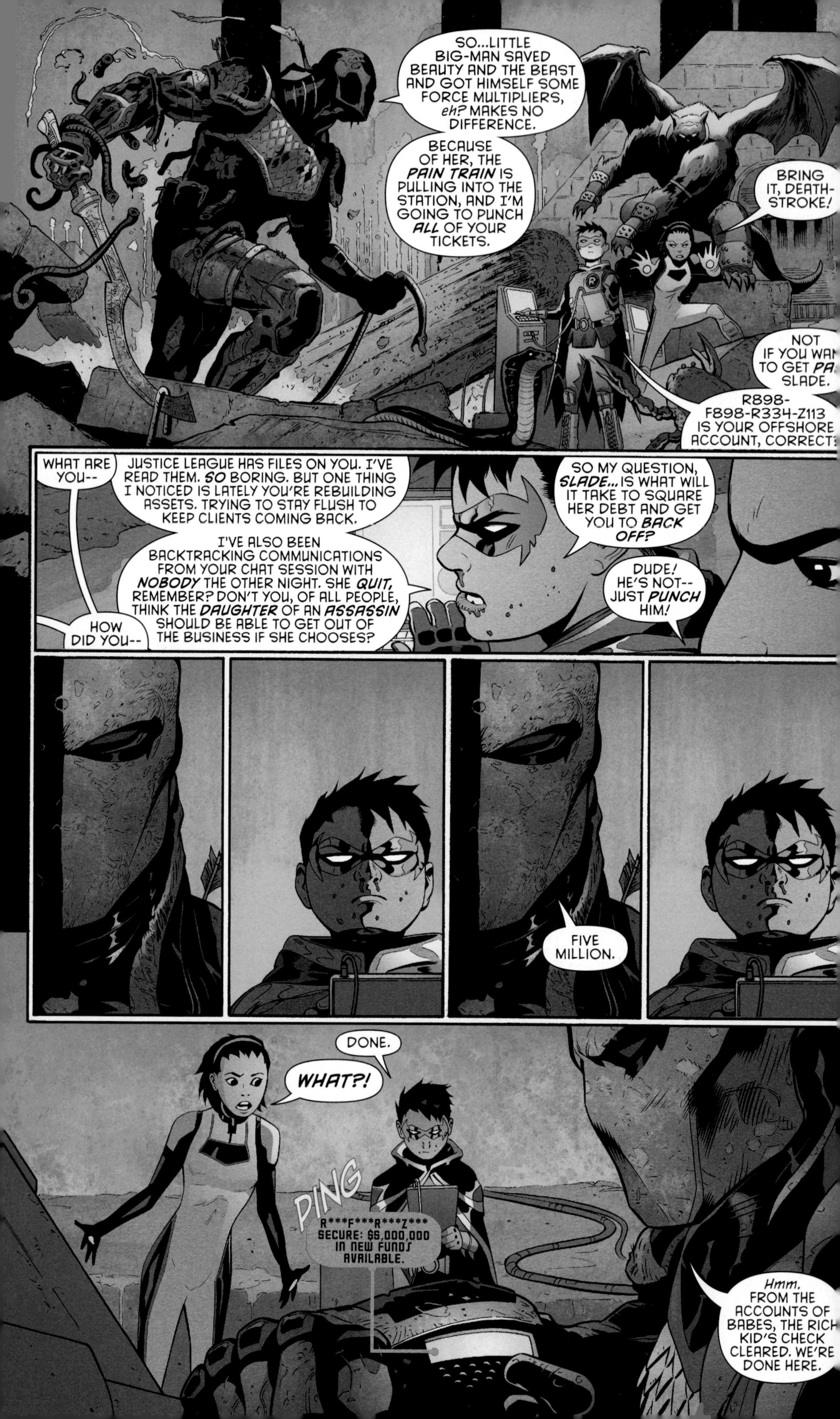

SO...LITTLE BIG-MAN SAVED BEAUTY AND THE BEAST AND GOT HIMSELF SOME FORCE MULTIPLIERS, *eh?* MAKES NO DIFFERENCE.
BECAUSE OF HER, THE *PAIN TRAIN* IS PULLING INTO THE STATION, AND I'M GOING TO PUNCH *ALL* OF YOUR TICKETS.
BRING IT, DEATH-STROKE!
NOT IF YOU WAN TO GET PA SLADE.
R898-F898-R334-Z113 IS YOUR OFFSHORE ACCOUNT, CORRECT?
WHAT ARE YOU--
JUSTICE LEAGUE HAS FILES ON YOU. I'VE READ THEM. *SO* BORING. BUT ONE THING I NOTICED IS LATELY YOU'RE REBUILDING ASSETS. TRYING TO STAY FLUSH TO KEEP CLIENTS COMING BACK.
HOW DID YOU--
I'VE ALSO BEEN BACKTRACKING COMMUNICATIONS FROM YOUR CHAT SESSION WITH *NOBODY* THE OTHER NIGHT. SHE *QUIT,* REMEMBER? DON'T YOU, OF ALL PEOPLE, THINK THE *DAUGHTER* OF AN *ASSASSIN* SHOULD BE ABLE TO GET OUT OF THE BUSINESS IF SHE CHOOSES?
SO MY QUESTION, *SLADE...* IS WHAT WILL IT TAKE TO SQUARE HER DEBT AND GET YOU TO *BACK OFF?*
DUDE! HE'S NOT-- JUST *PUNCH* HIM!
FIVE MILLION.
DONE.
WHAT?!
PING
R***F***R***Z*** SECURE: $5,000,000 IN NEW FUNDS AVAILABLE.
Hmm. FROM THE ACCOUNTS OF BABES, THE RICH KID'S CHECK CLEARED. WE'RE DONE HERE.

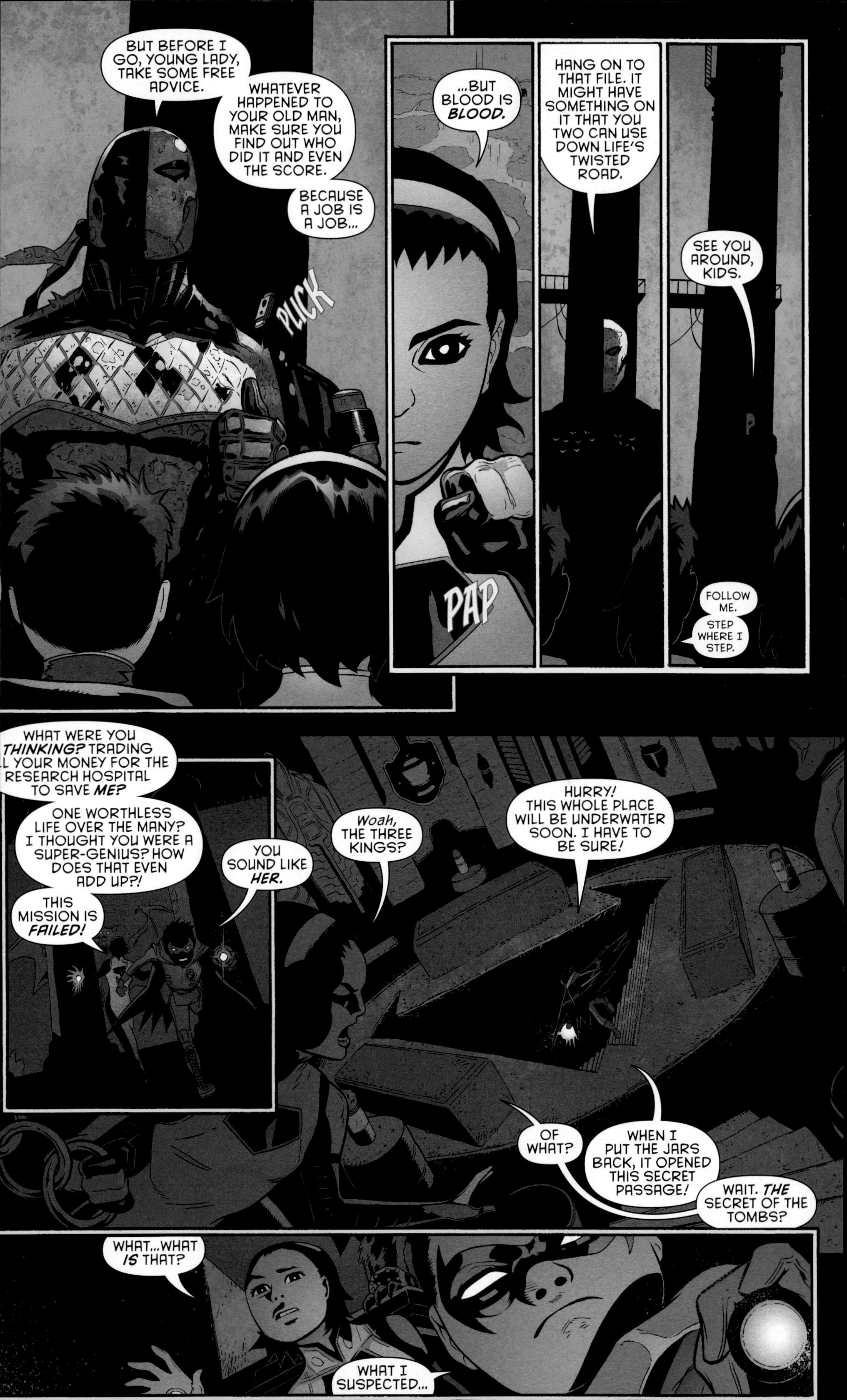
BUT BEFORE I GO, YOUNG LADY, TAKE SOME FREE ADVICE.
WHATEVER HAPPENED TO YOUR OLD MAN, MAKE SURE YOU FIND OUT WHO DID IT AND EVEN THE SCORE.
BECAUSE A JOB IS A JOB...
PLICK
...BUT BLOOD IS BLOOD.
PAP
HANG ON TO THAT FILE. IT MIGHT HAVE SOMETHING ON IT THAT YOU TWO CAN USE DOWN LIFE'S TWISTED ROAD.
SEE YOU AROUND, KIDS.
FOLLOW ME.
STEP WHERE I STEP.
WHAT WERE YOU THINKING? TRADING ALL YOUR MONEY FOR THE RESEARCH HOSPITAL TO SAVE ME?
ONE WORTHLESS LIFE OVER THE MANY? I THOUGHT YOU WERE A SUPER-GENIUS? HOW DOES THAT EVEN ADD UP?!
THIS MISSION IS FAILED!
YOU SOUND LIKE HER.
Woah, THE THREE KINGS?
HURRY! THIS WHOLE PLACE WILL BE UNDERWATER SOON. I HAVE TO BE SURE!
OF WHAT?
WHEN I PUT THE JARS BACK, IT OPENED THIS SECRET PASSAGE!
WAIT. THE SECRET OF THE TOMBS?
WHAT...WHAT IS THAT?
WHAT I SUSPECTED...

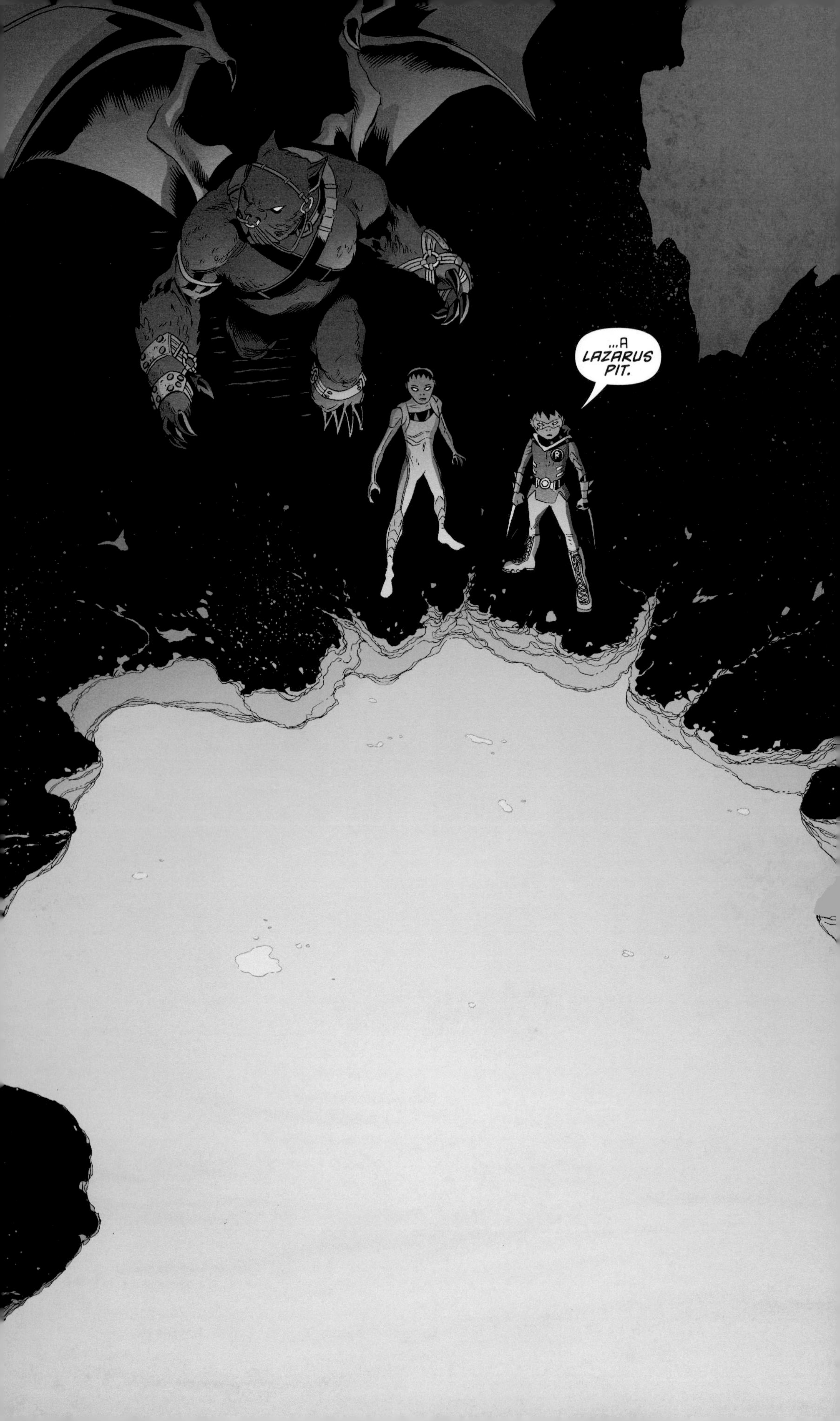
...A LAZARUS PIT.

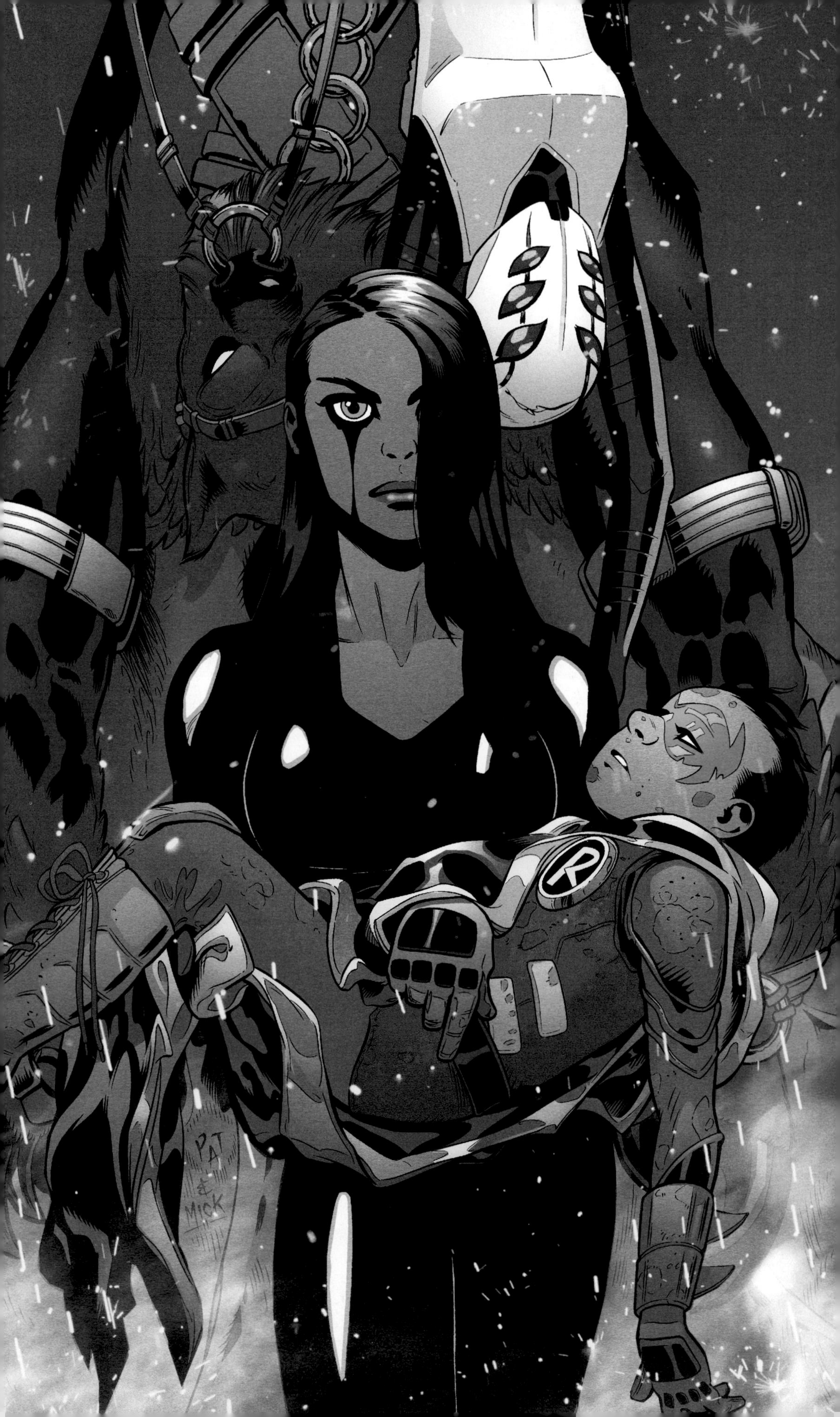
PAT & MICK

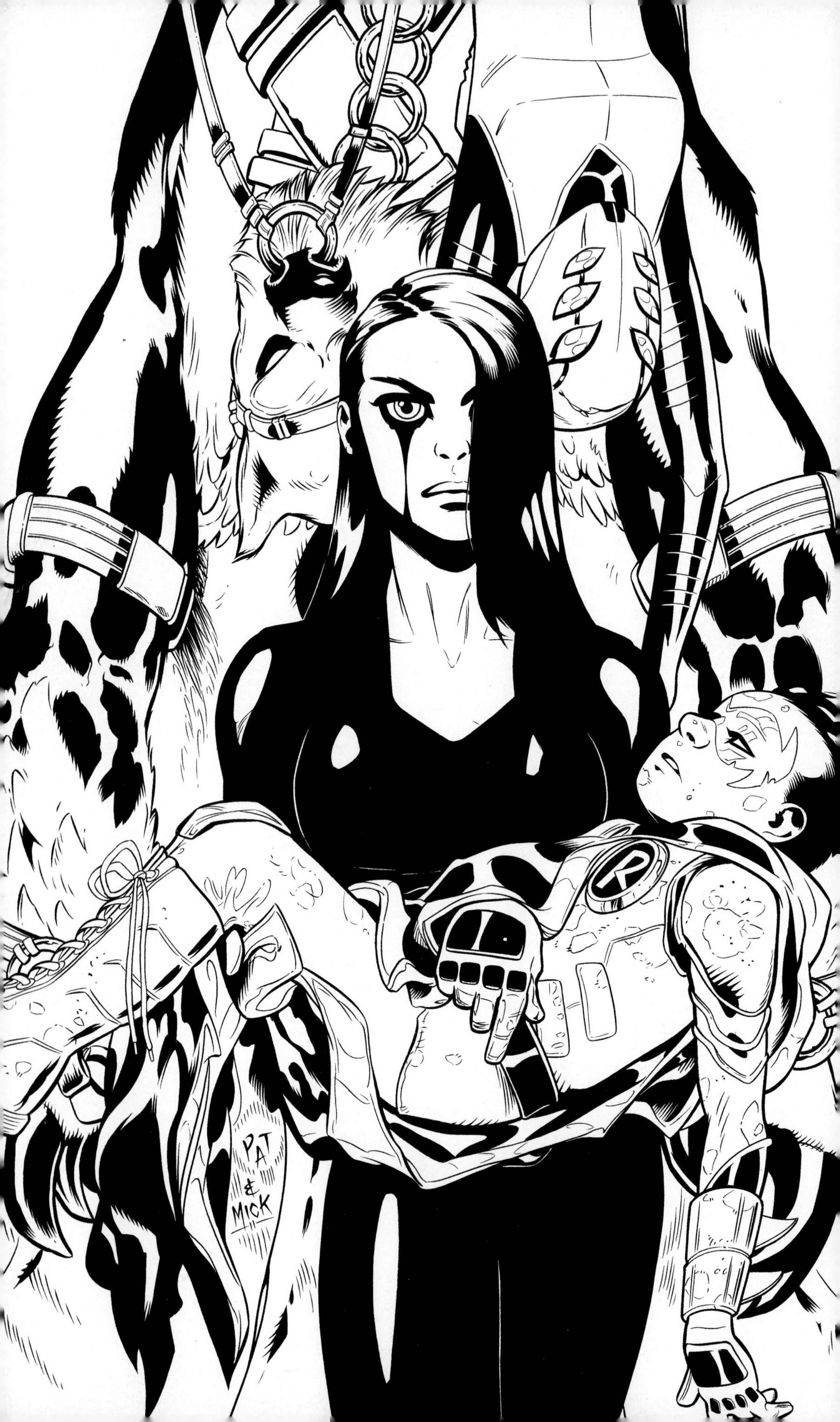
PAT & MICK

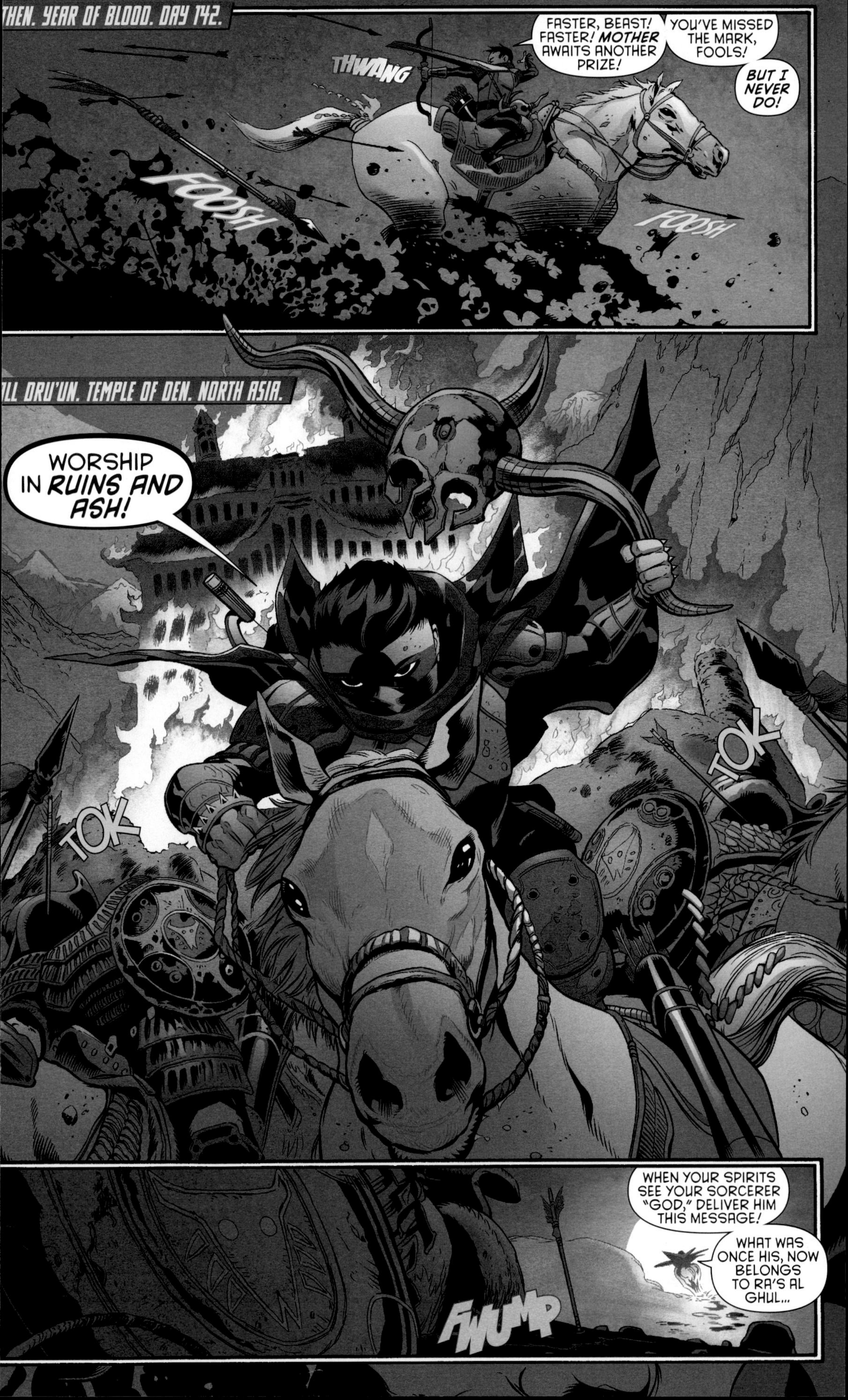
THEN. YEAR OF BLOOD. DAY 142.
FASTER, BEAST! FASTER! MOTHER AWAITS ANOTHER PRIZE!
YOU'VE MISSED THE MARK, FOOLS!
BUT I NEVER DO!
THWANG
FOOSH
FOOSH
LL DRU'UN. TEMPLE OF DEN. NORTH ASIA.
WORSHIP IN RUINS AND ASH!
TOK
TOK
WHEN YOUR SPIRITS SEE YOUR SORCERER "GOD," DELIVER HIM THIS MESSAGE!
WHAT WAS ONCE HIS, NOW BELONGS TO RA'S AL GHUL...
FWUMP

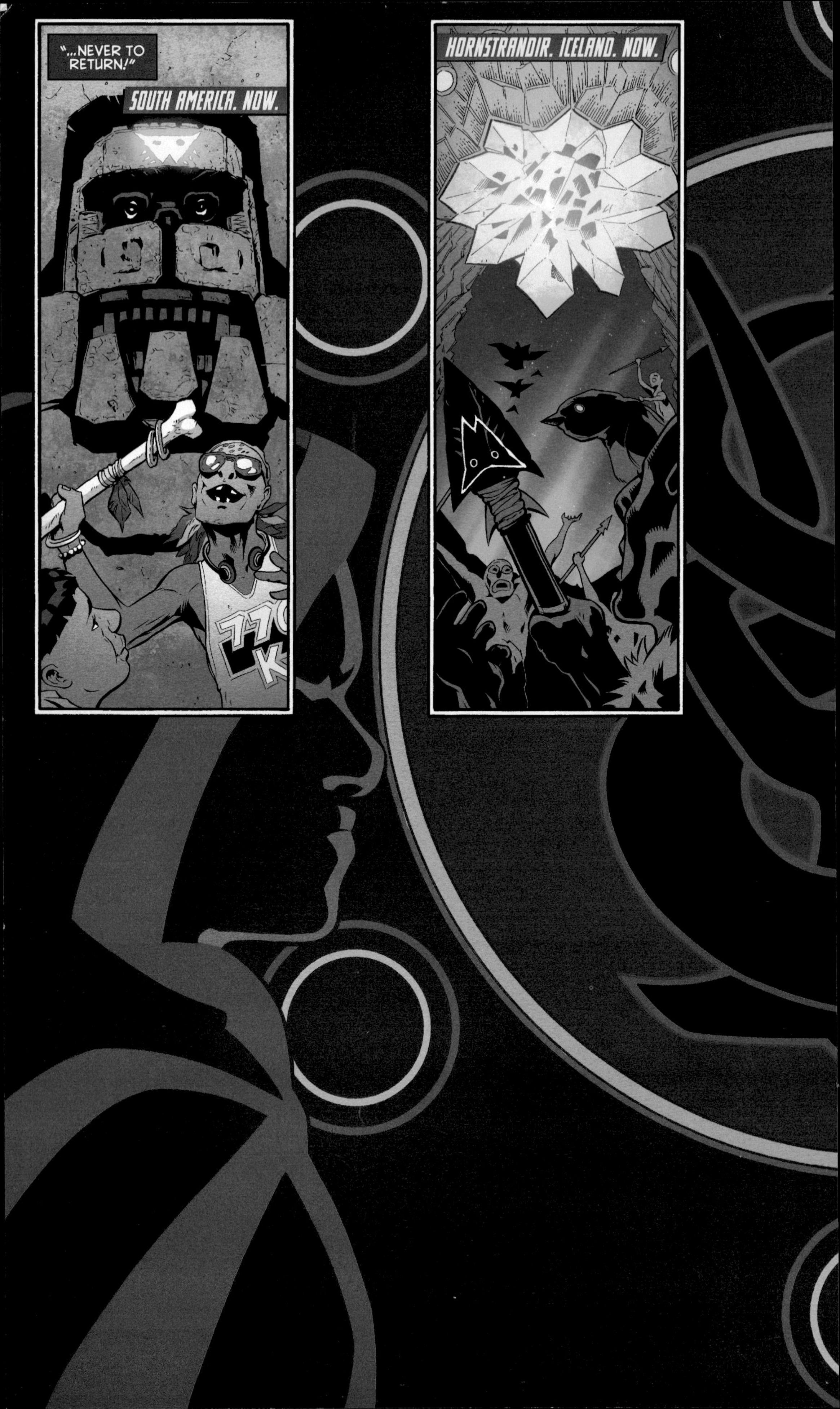

"...NEVER TO RETURN!"
SOUTH AMERICA. NOW.
HORNSTRANDIR. ICELAND. NOW.

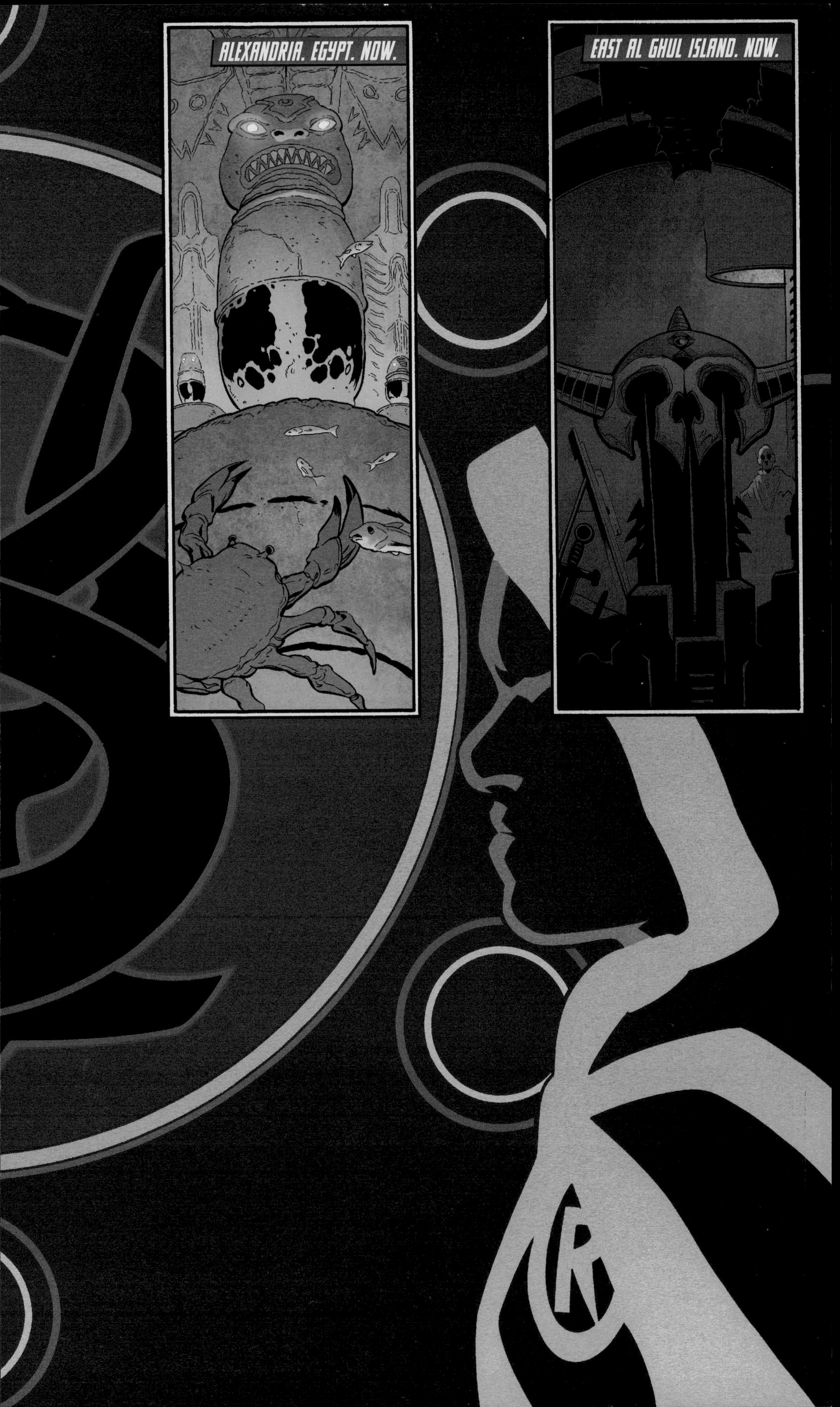
ALEXANDRIA. EGYPT. NOW.
EAST AL GHUL ISLAND. NOW.

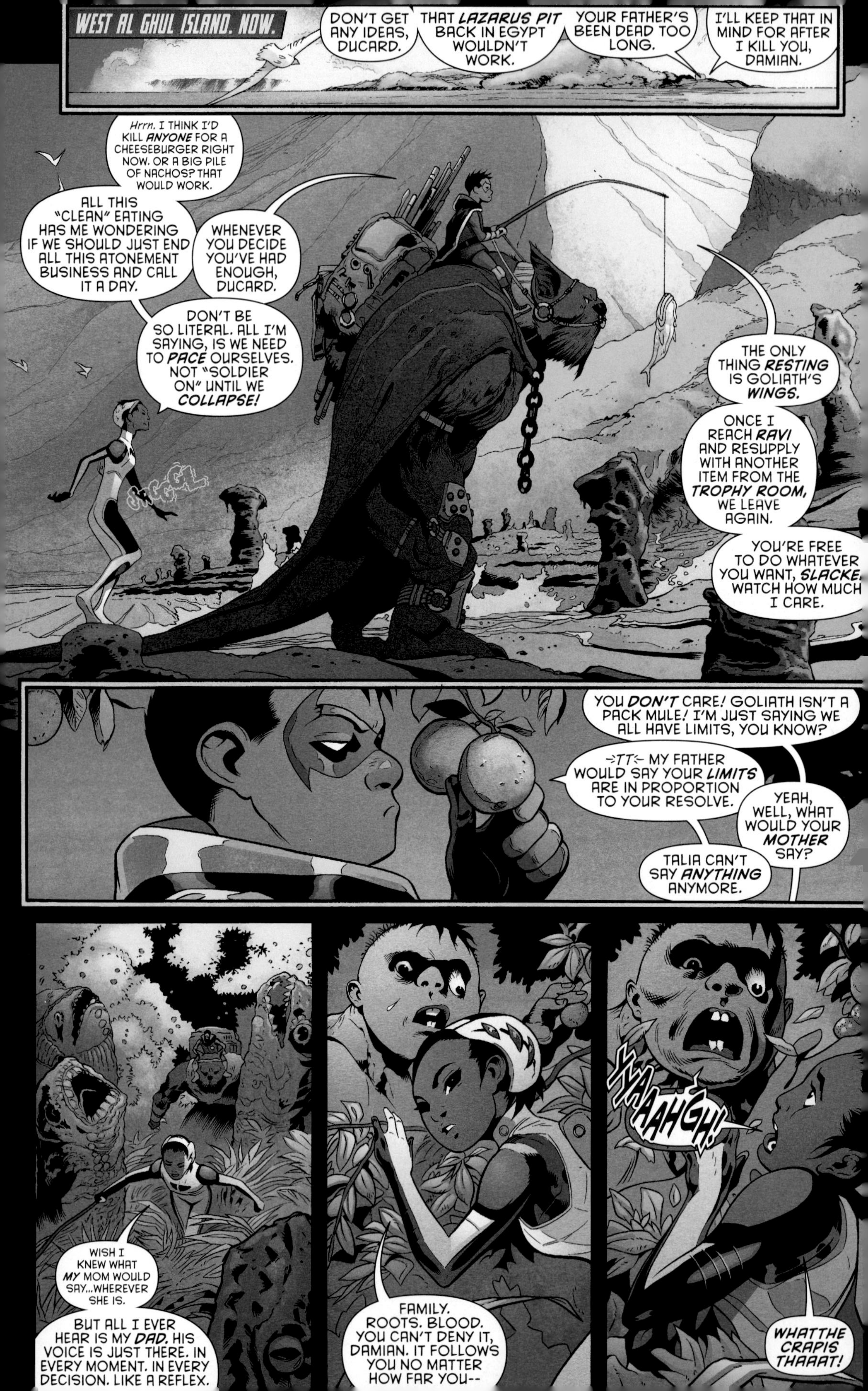
WEST AL GHUL ISLAND. NOW.
DON'T GET ANY IDEAS, DUCARD.
THAT LAZARUS PIT BACK IN EGYPT WOULDN'T WORK.
YOUR FATHER'S BEEN DEAD TOO LONG.
I'LL KEEP THAT IN MIND FOR AFTER I KILL YOU, DAMIAN.
Hrrn. I THINK I'D KILL ANYONE FOR A CHEESEBURGER RIGHT NOW. OR A BIG PILE OF NACHOS? THAT WOULD WORK.
ALL THIS "CLEAN" EATING HAS ME WONDERING IF WE SHOULD JUST END ALL THIS ATONEMENT BUSINESS AND CALL IT A DAY.
WHENEVER YOU DECIDE YOU'VE HAD ENOUGH, DUCARD.
DON'T BE SO LITERAL. ALL I'M SAYING, IS WE NEED TO PACE OURSELVES. NOT "SOLDIER ON" UNTIL WE COLLAPSE!
THE ONLY THING RESTING IS GOLIATH'S WINGS.
ONCE I REACH RAVI AND RESUPPLY WITH ANOTHER ITEM FROM THE TROPHY ROOM, WE LEAVE AGAIN.
YOU'RE FREE TO DO WHATEVER YOU WANT, SLACKE. WATCH HOW MUCH I CARE.
YOU DON'T CARE! GOLIATH ISN'T A PACK MULE! I'M JUST SAYING WE ALL HAVE LIMITS, YOU KNOW?
TT MY FATHER WOULD SAY YOUR LIMITS ARE IN PROPORTION TO YOUR RESOLVE.
YEAH, WELL, WHAT WOULD YOUR MOTHER SAY?
TALIA CAN'T SAY ANYTHING ANYMORE.
WISH I KNEW WHAT MY MOM WOULD SAY...WHEREVER SHE IS.
BUT ALL I EVER HEAR IS MY DAD. HIS VOICE IS JUST THERE. IN EVERY MOMENT. IN EVERY DECISION. LIKE A REFLEX.
FAMILY. ROOTS. BLOOD. YOU CAN'T DENY IT, DAMIAN. IT FOLLOWS YOU NO MATTER HOW FAR YOU--
YYAAAHGH!
WHATTHE CRAPIS THAAAT!

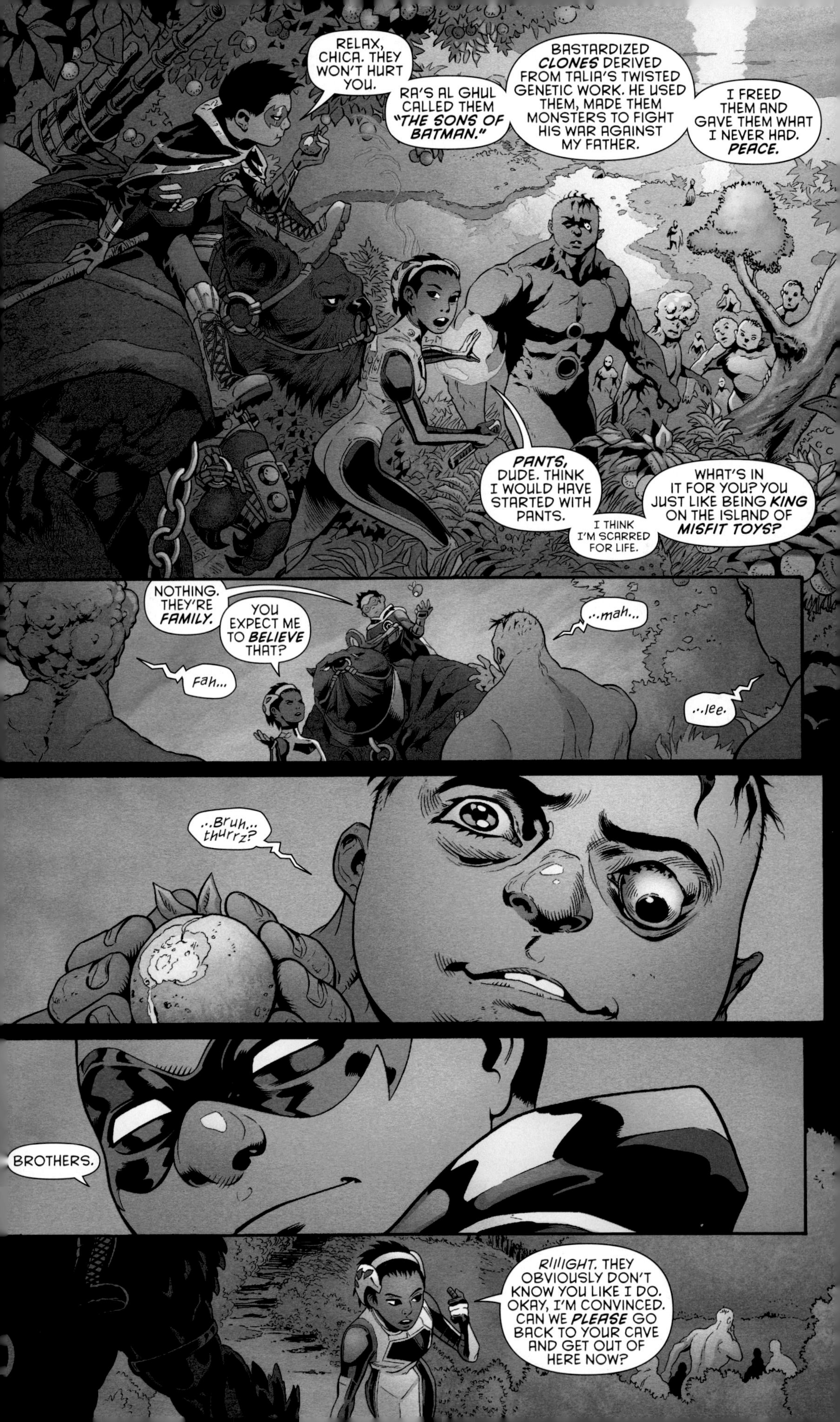

RELAX, CHICA. THEY WON'T HURT YOU.
RA'S AL GHUL CALLED THEM "THE SONS OF BATMAN."
BASTARDIZED CLONES DERIVED FROM TALIA'S TWISTED GENETIC WORK. HE USED THEM, MADE THEM MONSTERS TO FIGHT HIS WAR AGAINST MY FATHER.
I FREED THEM AND GAVE THEM WHAT I NEVER HAD. PEACE.
PANTS, DUDE. THINK I WOULD HAVE STARTED WITH PANTS.
I THINK I'M SCARRED FOR LIFE.
WHAT'S IN IT FOR YOU? YOU JUST LIKE BEING KING ON THE ISLAND OF MISFIT TOYS?
NOTHING. THEY'RE FAMILY.
YOU EXPECT ME TO BELIEVE THAT?
Fah...
...mah...
...lee.
...Bruh... thurrz?
BROTHERS.
RIIIGHT. THEY OBVIOUSLY DON'T KNOW YOU LIKE I DO. OKAY, I'M CONVINCED. CAN WE PLEASE GO BACK TO YOUR CAVE AND GET OUT OF HERE NOW?

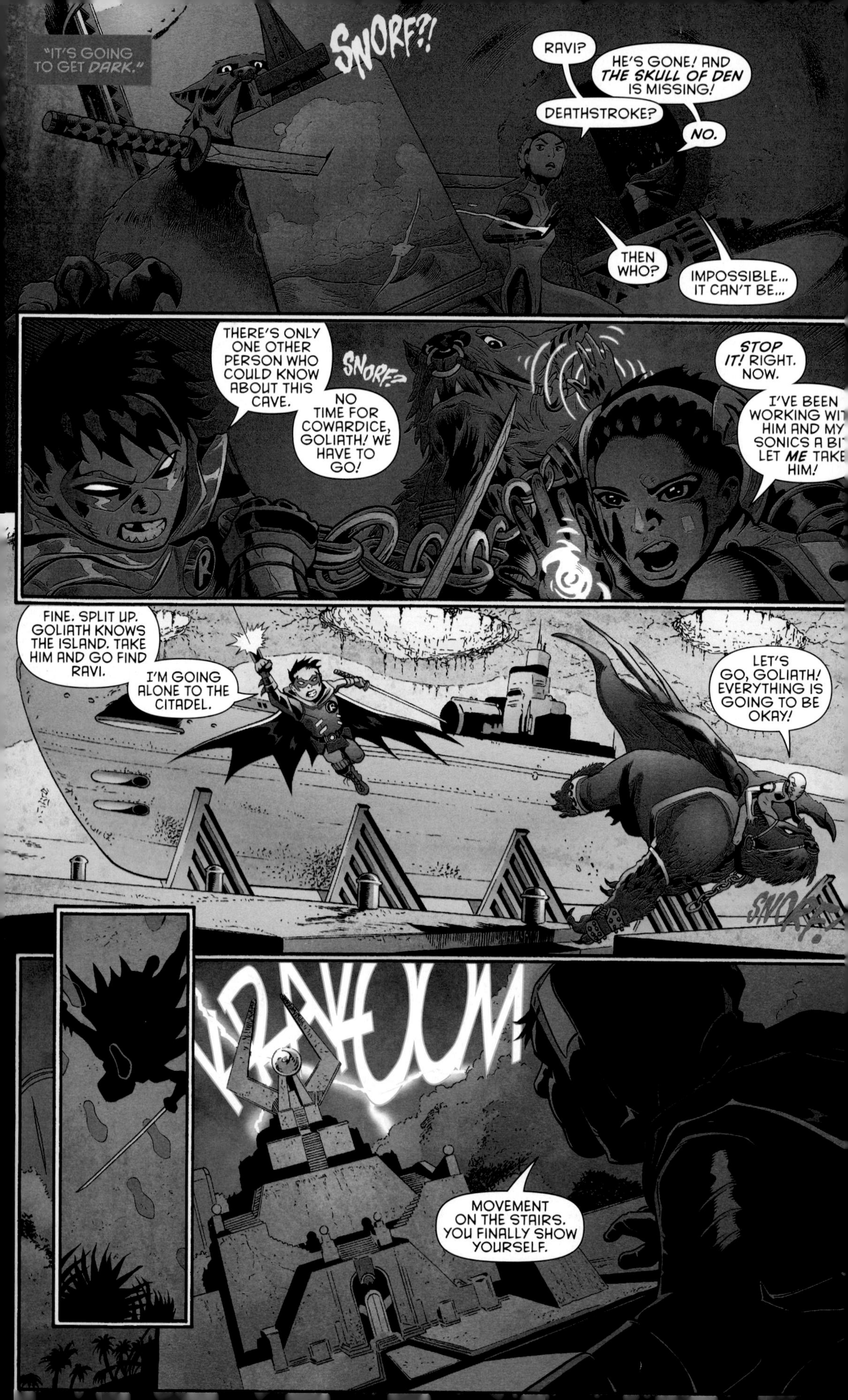
"IT'S GOING TO GET DARK."
SNORF?!
RAVI?
HE'S GONE! AND THE SKULL OF DEN IS MISSING!
DEATHSTROKE?
NO.
THEN WHO?
IMPOSSIBLE... IT CAN'T BE...
THERE'S ONLY ONE OTHER PERSON WHO COULD KNOW ABOUT THIS CAVE.
SNORF?
NO TIME FOR COWARDICE, GOLIATH! WE HAVE TO GO!
STOP IT! RIGHT. NOW.
I'VE BEEN WORKING WITH HIM AND MY SONICS A BIT. LET ME TAKE HIM!
FINE. SPLIT UP. GOLIATH KNOWS THE ISLAND. TAKE HIM AND GO FIND RAVI.
I'M GOING ALONE TO THE CITADEL.
LET'S GO, GOLIATH! EVERYTHING IS GOING TO BE OKAY!
SNORF?!
KRAKOOM
MOVEMENT ON THE STAIRS. YOU FINALLY SHOW YOURSELF.

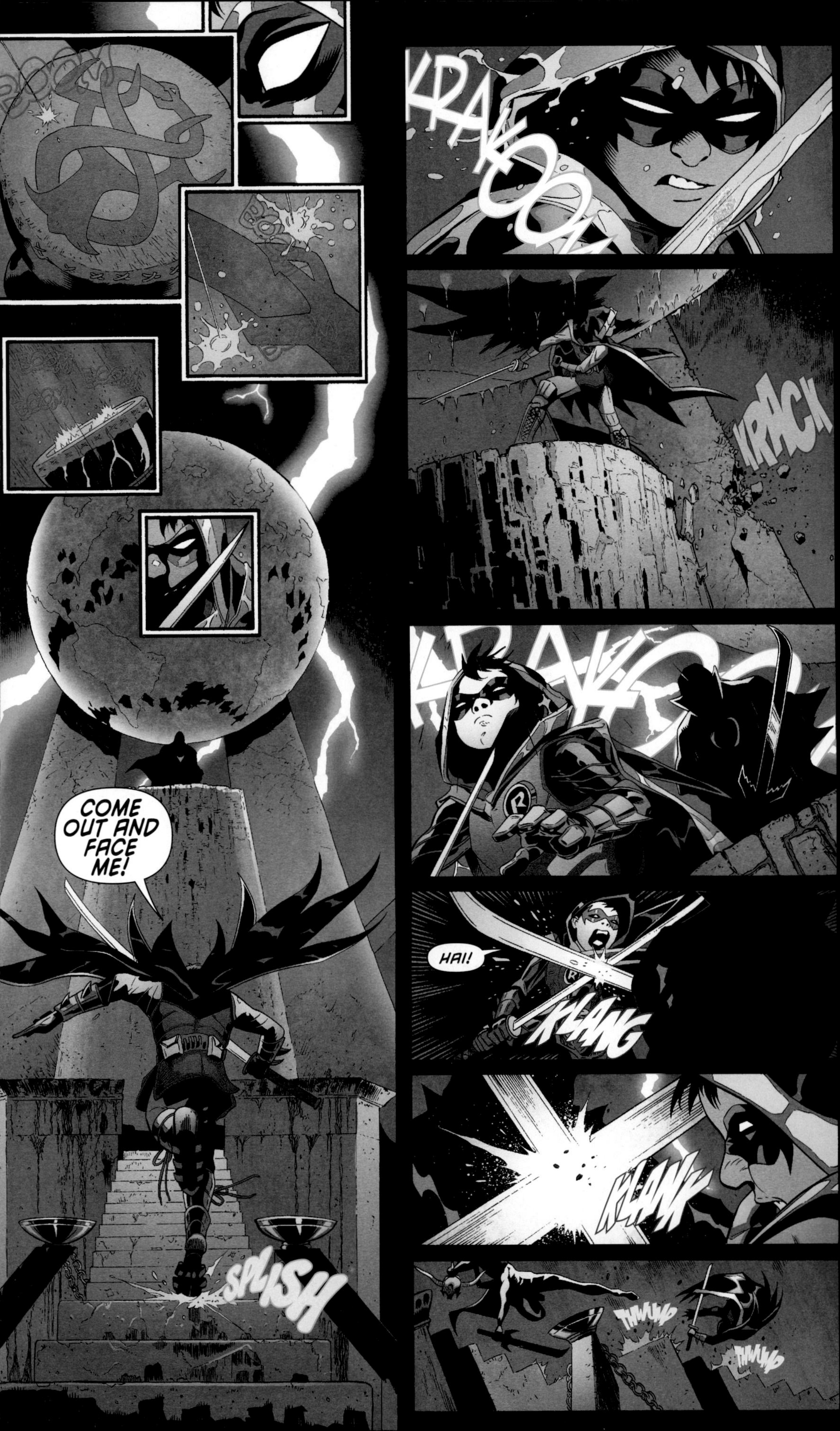
BOOM
BOOM
BOOM
KRAKOOOM
KRACK
KRAKOOOM
COME OUT AND FACE ME!
SPLISH
HAI!
KLANG
KLANK
THWUMP
THWUMP

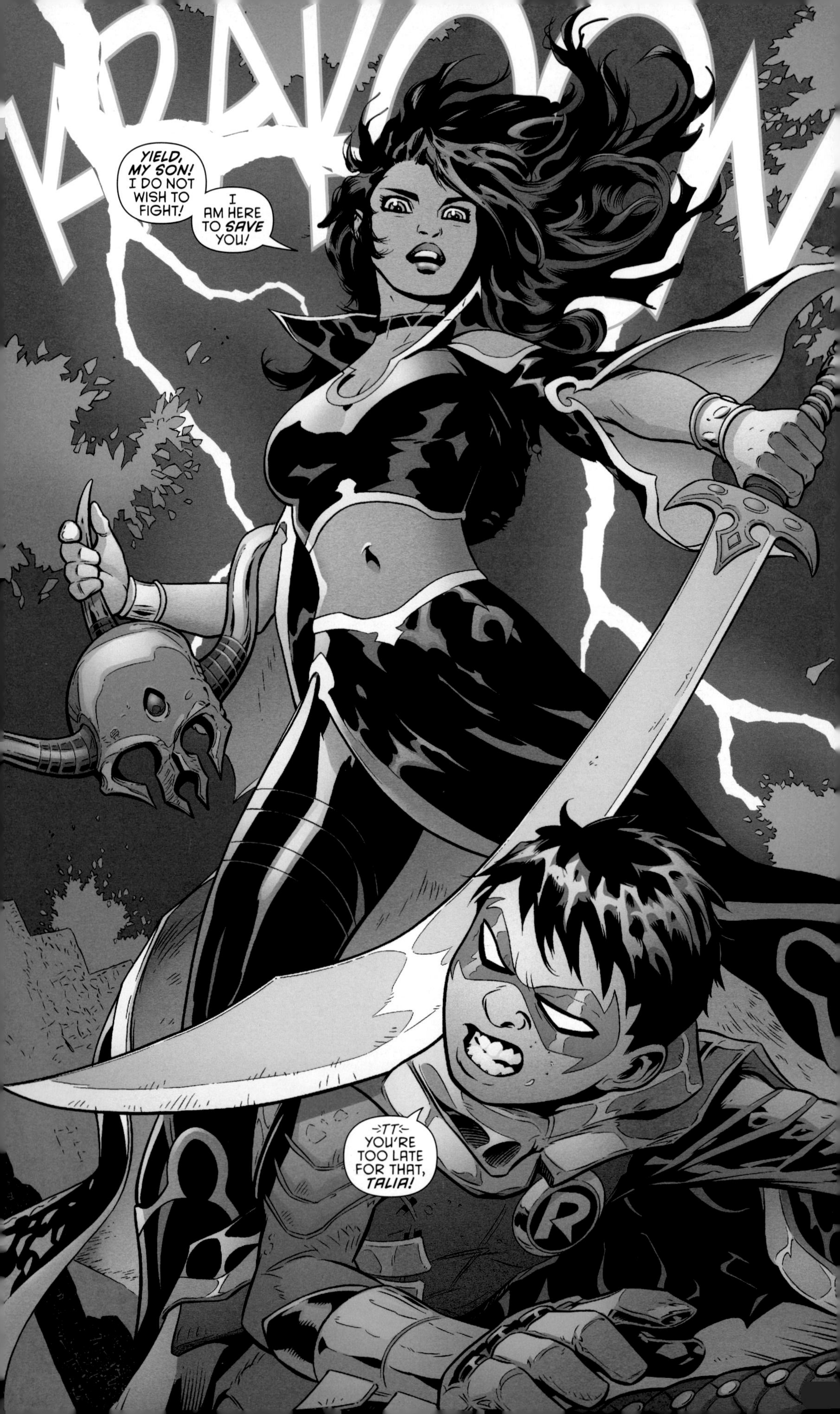

KRAKOOM
YIELD, MY SON! I DO NOT WISH TO FIGHT!
I AM HERE TO SAVE YOU!
-TT- YOU'RE TOO LATE FOR THAT, TALIA!

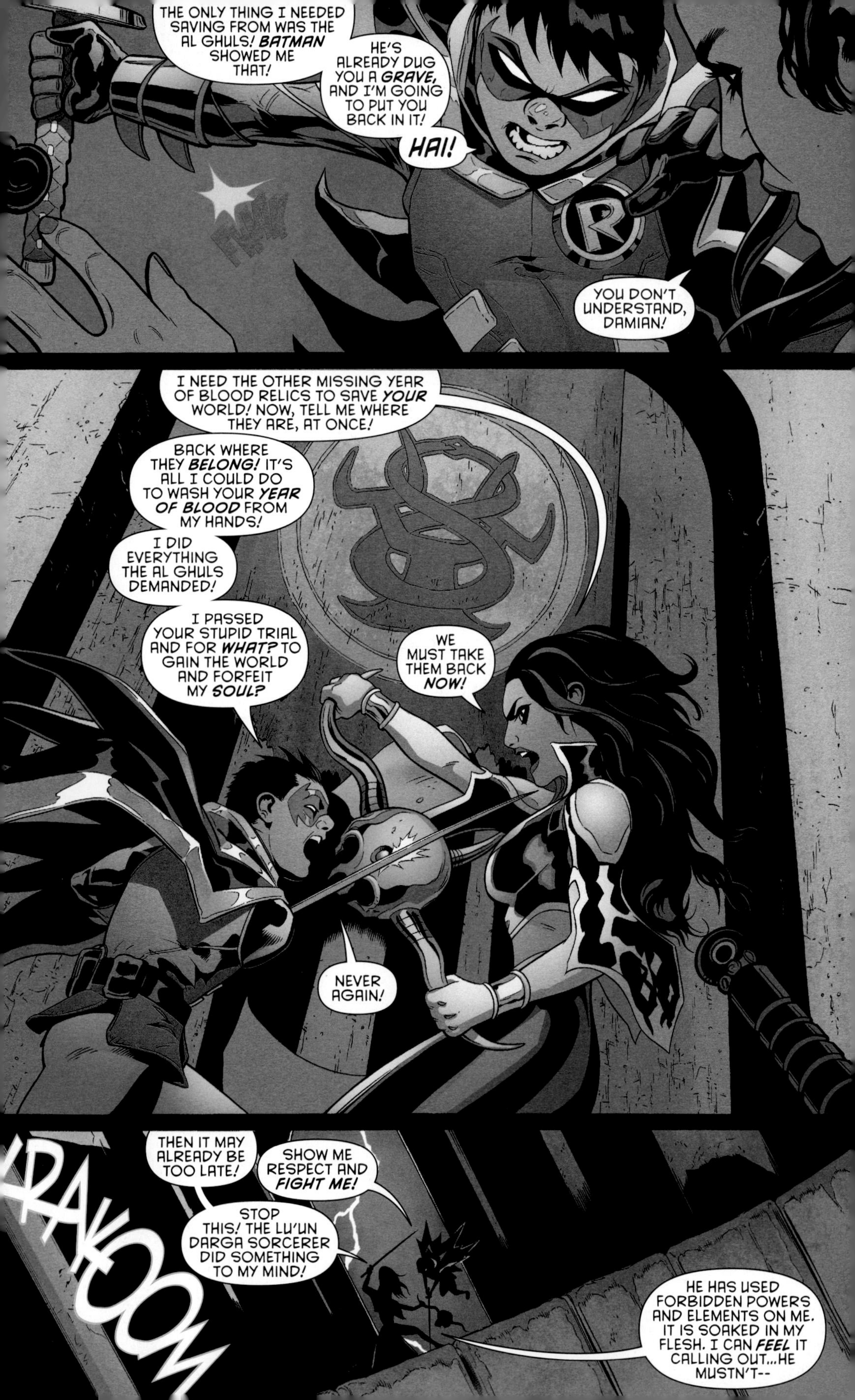
THE ONLY THING I NEEDED SAVING FROM WAS THE AL GHULS! BATMAN SHOWED ME THAT!
HE'S ALREADY DUG YOU A GRAVE, AND I'M GOING TO PUT YOU BACK IN IT!
HAI!
FWAK
YOU DON'T UNDERSTAND, DAMIAN!
I NEED THE OTHER MISSING YEAR OF BLOOD RELICS TO SAVE YOUR WORLD! NOW, TELL ME WHERE THEY ARE, AT ONCE!
BACK WHERE THEY BELONG! IT'S ALL I COULD DO TO WASH YOUR YEAR OF BLOOD FROM MY HANDS!
I DID EVERYTHING THE AL GHULS DEMANDED!
I PASSED YOUR STUPID TRIAL AND FOR WHAT? TO GAIN THE WORLD AND FORFEIT MY SOUL?
WE MUST TAKE THEM BACK NOW!
NEVER AGAIN!
KRAKOOM
THEN IT MAY ALREADY BE TOO LATE!
SHOW ME RESPECT AND FIGHT ME!
STOP THIS! THE LU'UN DARGA SORCERER DID SOMETHING TO MY MIND!
HE HAS USED FORBIDDEN POWERS AND ELEMENTS ON ME. IT IS SOAKED IN MY FLESH. I CAN FEEL IT CALLING OUT...HE MUSTN'T--

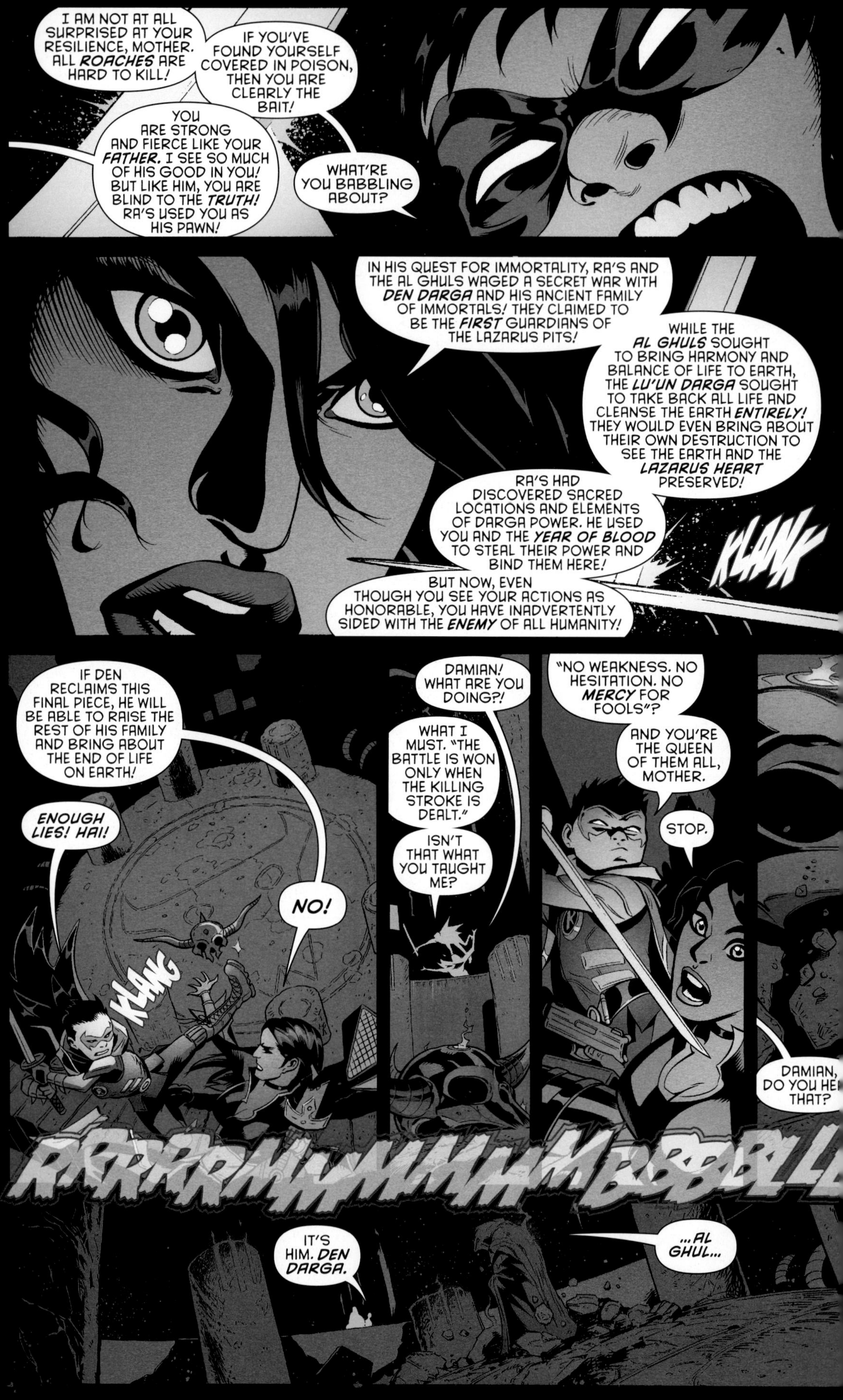
I AM NOT AT ALL SURPRISED AT YOUR RESILIENCE, MOTHER. ALL ROACHES ARE HARD TO KILL!
IF YOU'VE FOUND YOURSELF COVERED IN POISON, THEN YOU ARE CLEARLY THE BAIT!
YOU ARE STRONG AND FIERCE LIKE YOUR FATHER. I SEE SO MUCH OF HIS GOOD IN YOU! BUT LIKE HIM, YOU ARE BLIND TO THE TRUTH! RA'S USED YOU AS HIS PAWN!
WHAT'RE YOU BABBLING ABOUT?
IN HIS QUEST FOR IMMORTALITY, RA'S AND THE AL GHULS WAGED A SECRET WAR WITH DEN DARGA AND HIS ANCIENT FAMILY OF IMMORTALS! THEY CLAIMED TO BE THE FIRST GUARDIANS OF THE LAZARUS PITS!
WHILE THE AL GHULS SOUGHT TO BRING HARMONY AND BALANCE OF LIFE TO EARTH, THE LU'UN DARGA SOUGHT TO TAKE BACK ALL LIFE AND CLEANSE THE EARTH ENTIRELY! THEY WOULD EVEN BRING ABOUT THEIR OWN DESTRUCTION TO SEE THE EARTH AND THE LAZARUS HEART PRESERVED!
RA'S HAD DISCOVERED SACRED LOCATIONS AND ELEMENTS OF DARGA POWER. HE USED YOU AND THE YEAR OF BLOOD TO STEAL THEIR POWER AND BIND THEM HERE!
KLANK
BUT NOW, EVEN THOUGH YOU SEE YOUR ACTIONS AS HONORABLE, YOU HAVE INADVERTENTLY SIDED WITH THE ENEMY OF ALL HUMANITY!
IF DEN RECLAIMS THIS FINAL PIECE, HE WILL BE ABLE TO RAISE THE REST OF HIS FAMILY AND BRING ABOUT THE END OF LIFE ON EARTH!
ENOUGH LIES! HAI!
NO!
KLANG
DAMIAN! WHAT ARE YOU DOING?!
WHAT I MUST. "THE BATTLE IS WON ONLY WHEN THE KILLING STROKE IS DEALT."
ISN'T THAT WHAT YOU TAUGHT ME?
"NO WEAKNESS. NO HESITATION. NO MERCY FOR FOOLS"?
AND YOU'RE THE QUEEN OF THEM ALL, MOTHER.
STOP.
DAMIAN, DO YOU HE THAT?
RRRRRMMMMMMMMMBBBBLL
IT'S HIM. DEN DARGA.
...AL GHUL...

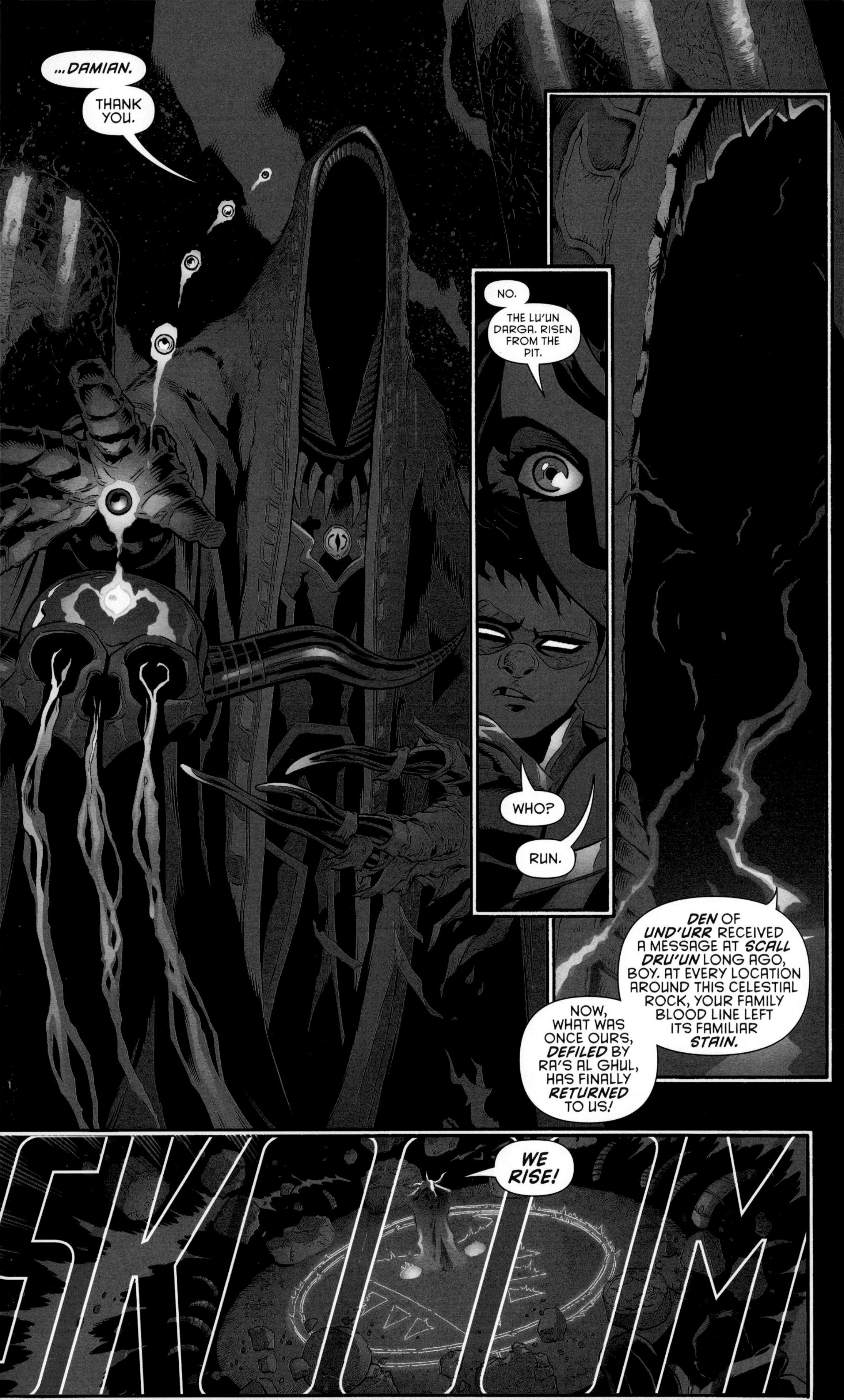

...DAMIAN.
THANK YOU.
NO.
THE LU'UN DARGA. RISEN FROM THE PIT.
WHO?
RUN.
DEN OF UND'URR RECEIVED A MESSAGE AT SCALL DRU'UN LONG AGO, BOY. AT EVERY LOCATION AROUND THIS CELESTIAL ROCK, YOUR FAMILY BLOOD LINE LEFT ITS FAMILIAR STAIN.
NOW, WHAT WAS ONCE OURS, DEFILED BY RA'S AL GHUL, HAS FINALLY RETURNED TO US!
WE RISE!
SKOOOM

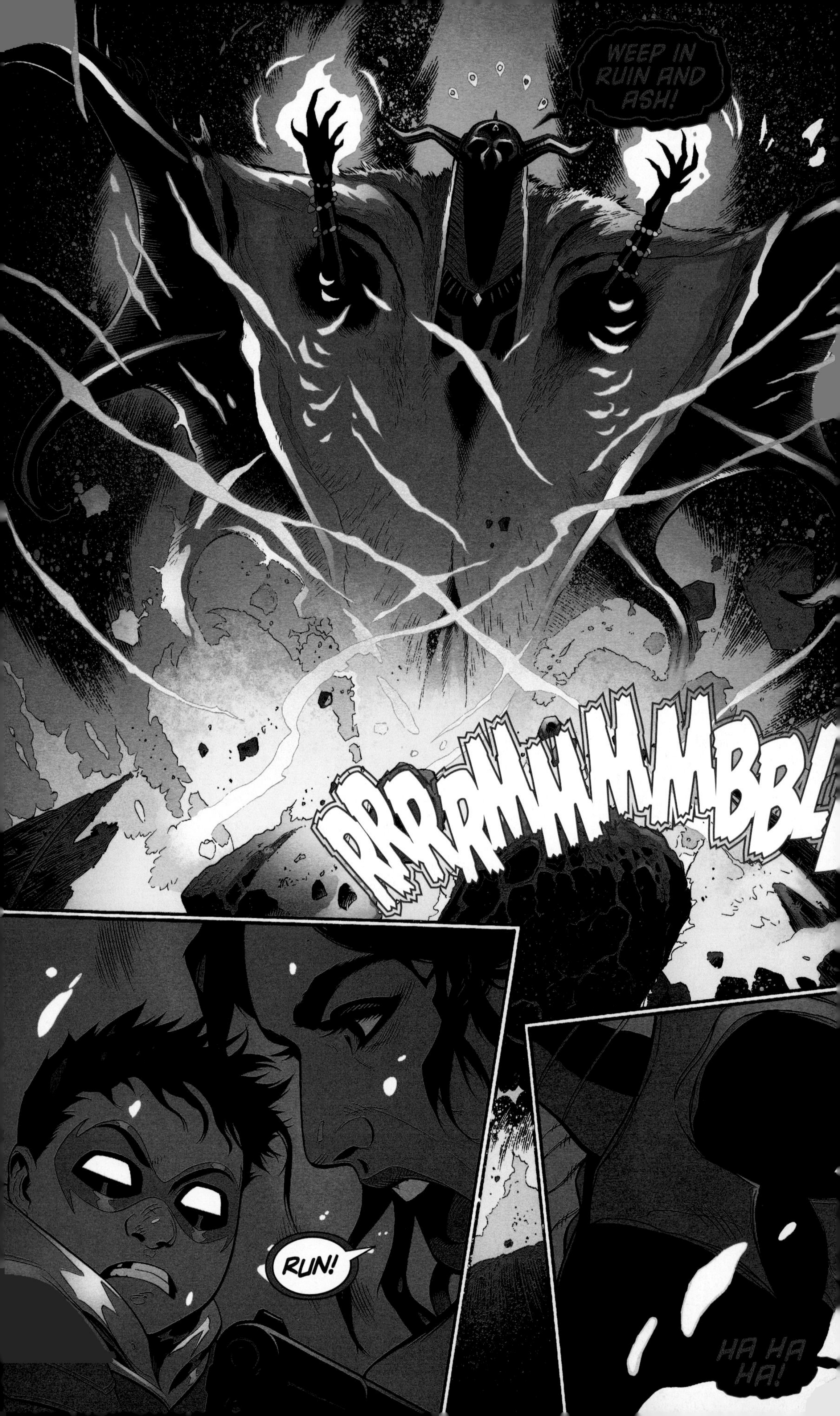
WEEP IN RUIN AND ASH!
RRRHHMMMBBL
RUN!
HA HA HA!

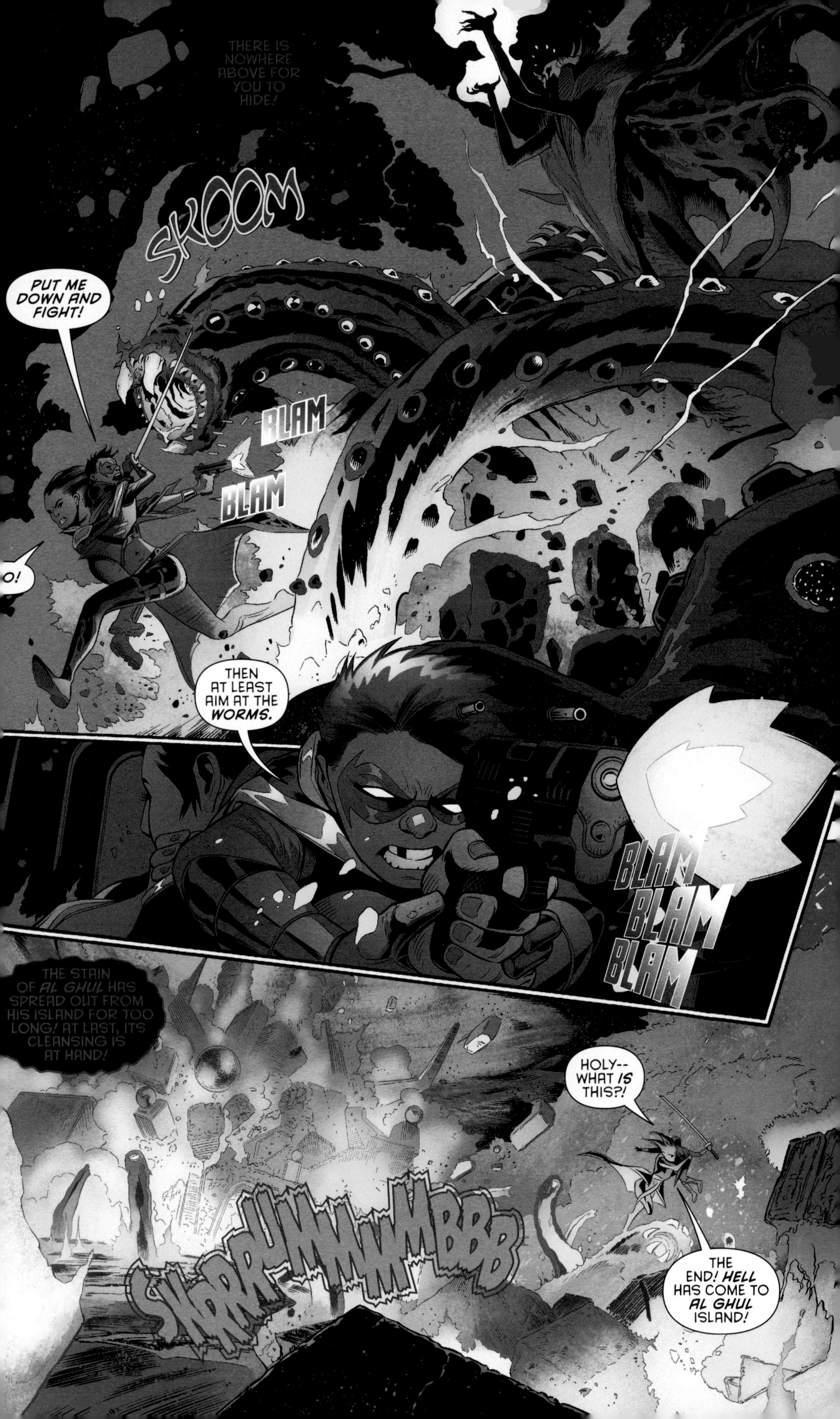
THERE IS NOWHERE ABOVE FOR YOU TO HIDE!
SKOOM
PUT ME DOWN AND FIGHT!
BLAM
BLAM
O!
THEN AT LEAST AIM AT THE *WORMS.*
BLAM
BLAM
BLAM
THE STAIN OF *AL GHUL* HAS SPREAD OUT FROM HIS ISLAND FOR TOO LONG! AT LAST, ITS CLEANSING IS AT HAND!
HOLY-- WHAT *IS* THIS?!
SKRRHMMMMBBB
THE END! *HELL* HAS COME TO *AL GHUL* ISLAND!

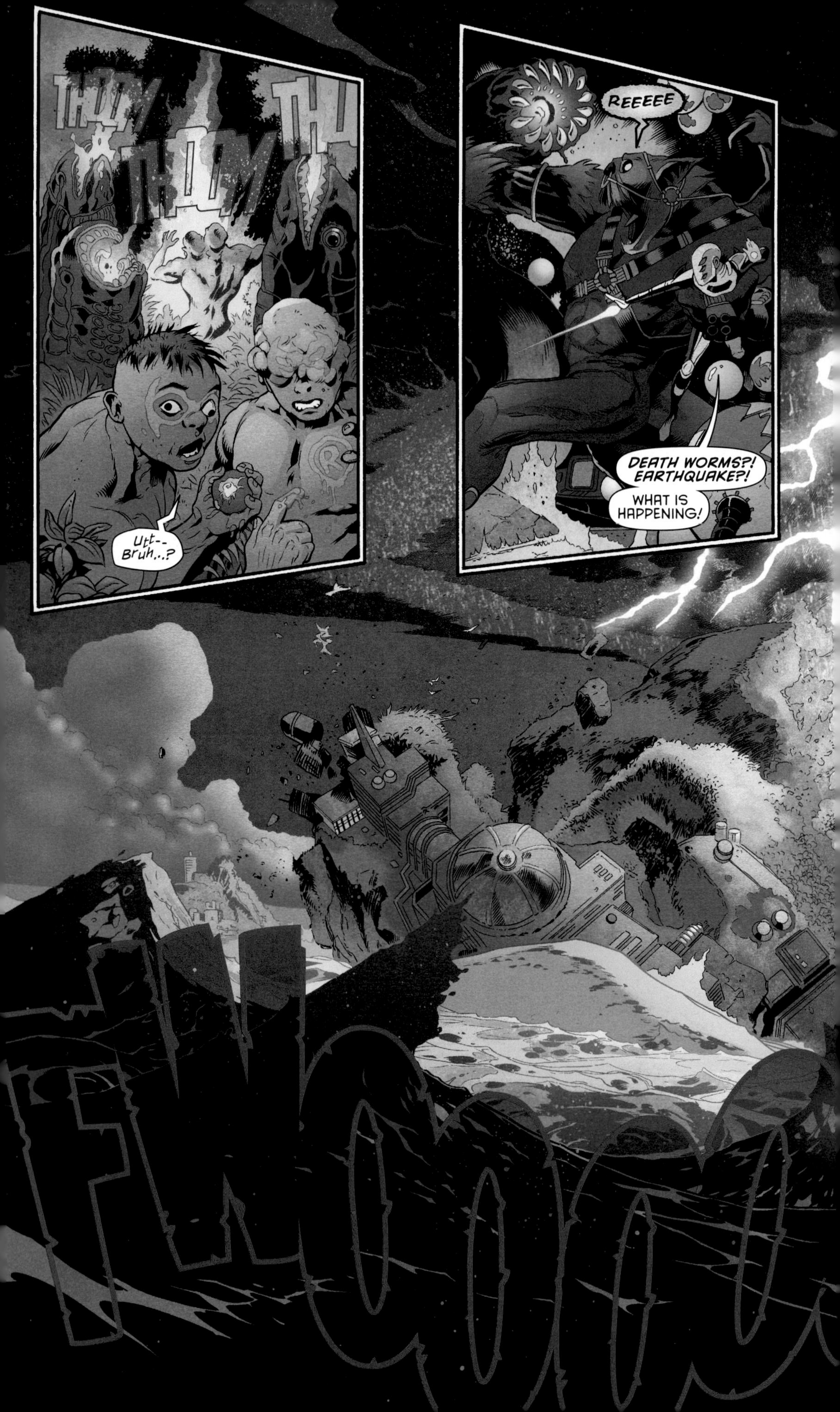

THOM THOM THU
Utt-- Bruh...?
REEEEE
DEATH WORMS?! EARTHQUAKE?!
WHAT IS HAPPENING!
FWOOOO

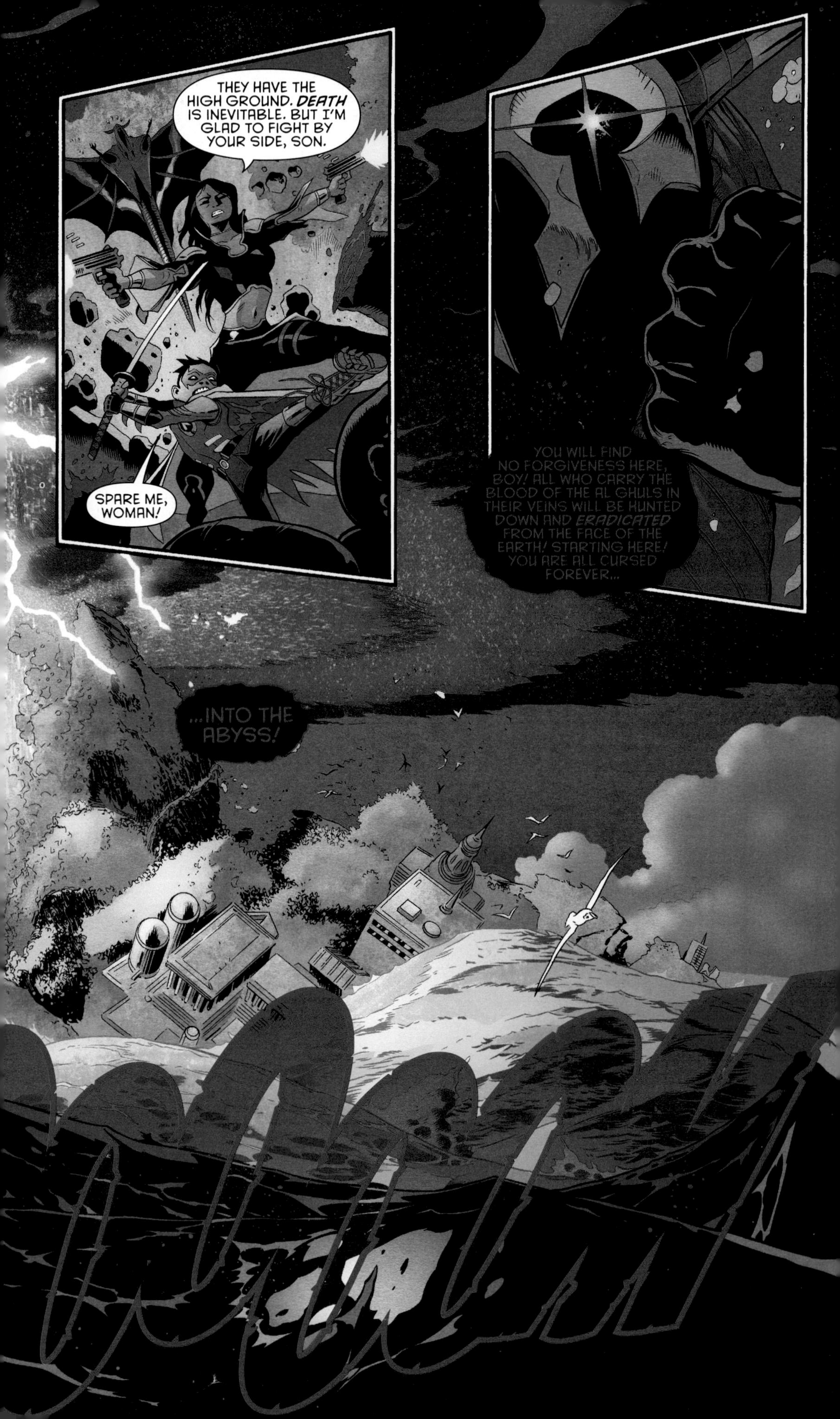
THEY HAVE THE HIGH GROUND. DEATH IS INEVITABLE. BUT I'M GLAD TO FIGHT BY YOUR SIDE, SON.
SPARE ME, WOMAN!
YOU WILL FIND NO FORGIVENESS HERE, BOY! ALL WHO CARRY THE BLOOD OF THE AL GHULS IN THEIR VEINS WILL BE HUNTED DOWN AND ERADICATED FROM THE FACE OF THE EARTH! STARTING HERE! YOU ARE ALL CURSED FOREVER...
...INTO THE ABYSS!

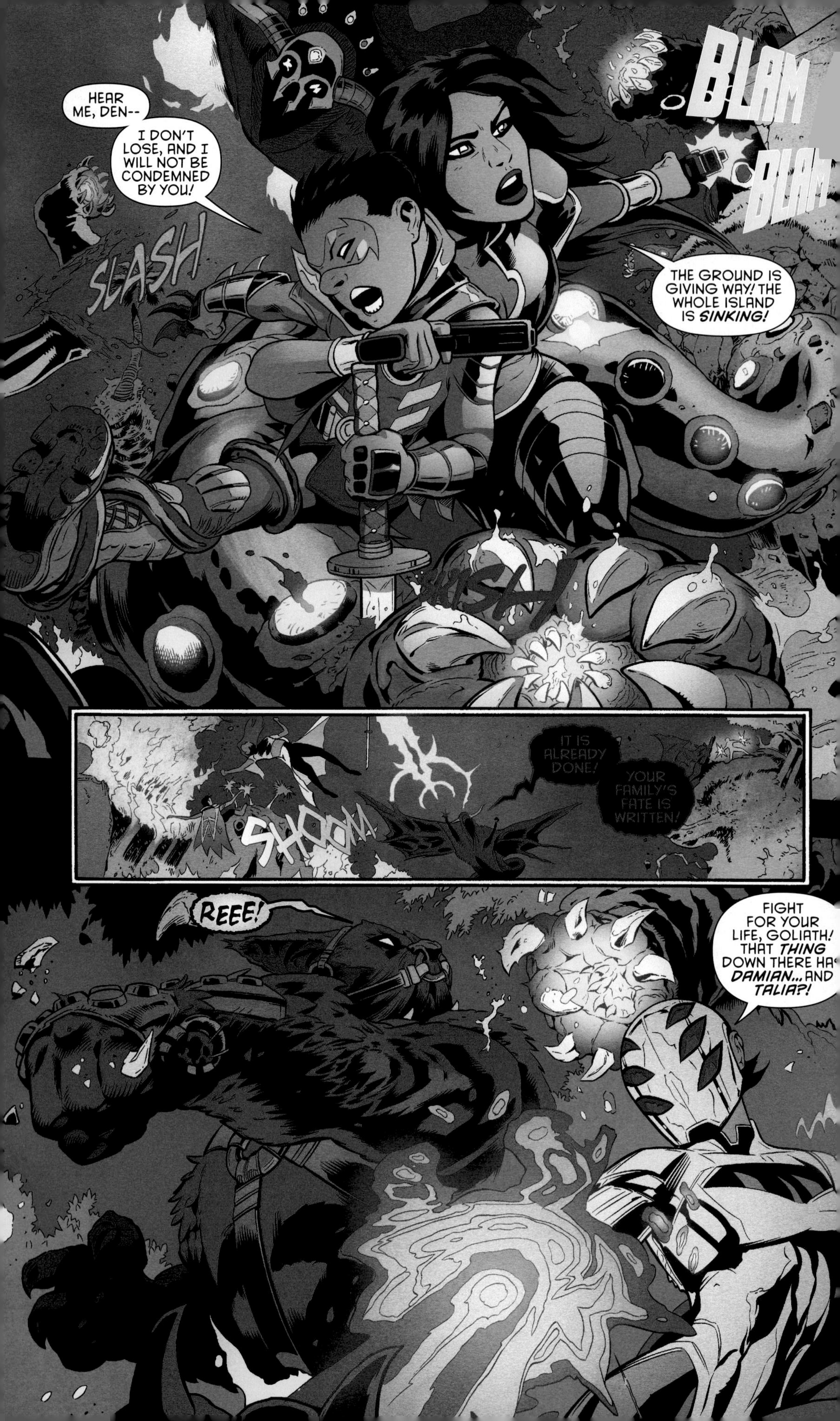
HEAR ME, DEN--
I DON'T LOSE, AND I WILL NOT BE CONDEMNED BY YOU!
BLAM
BLAM
SLASH
THE GROUND IS GIVING WAY! THE WHOLE ISLAND IS SINKING!
SHISH
IT IS ALREADY DONE!
YOUR FAMILY'S FATE IS WRITTEN!
SHOOM
REEE!
FIGHT FOR YOUR LIFE, GOLIATH! THAT THING DOWN THERE HA DAMIAN... AND TALIA?!

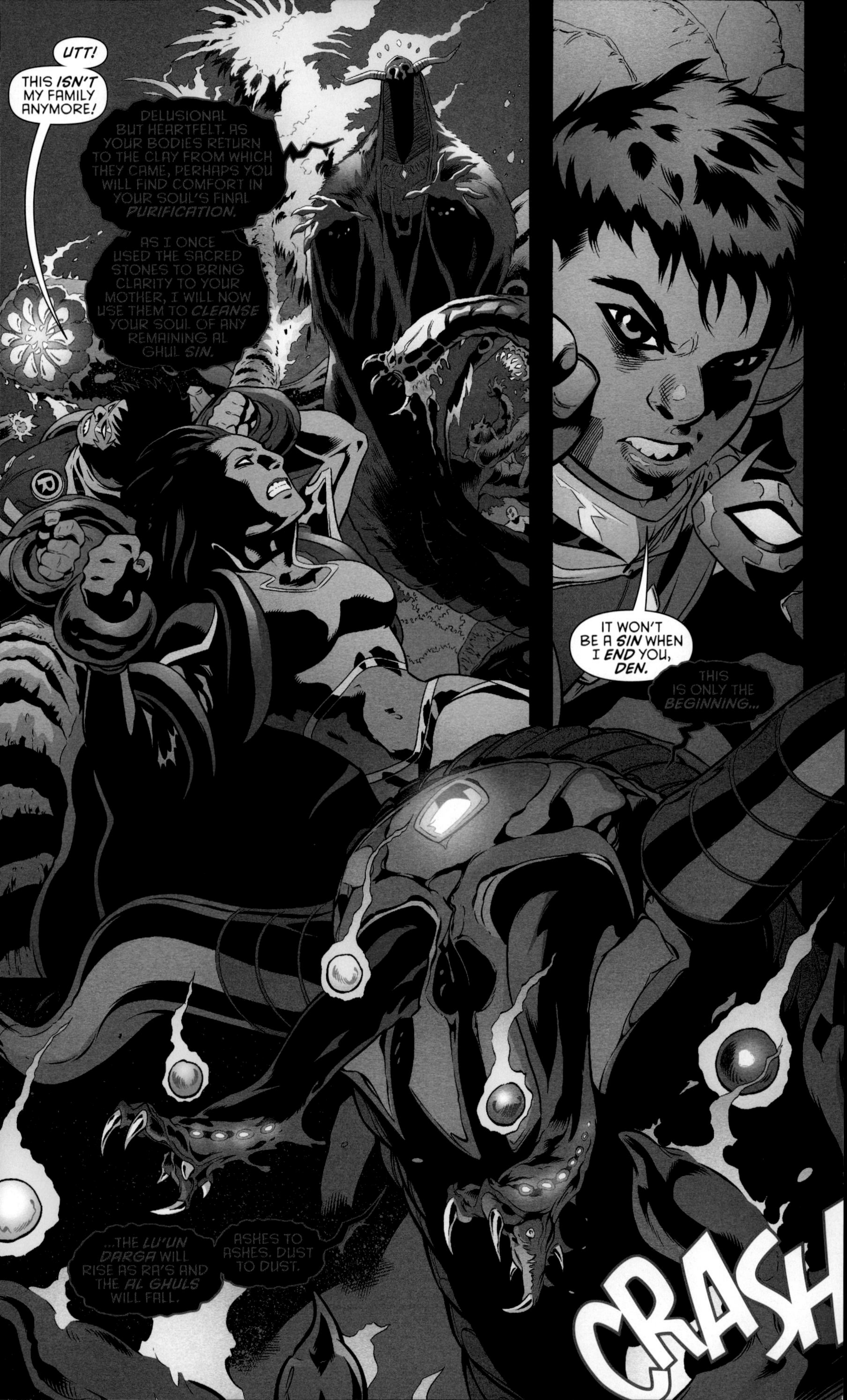
UTT!
THIS ISN'T MY FAMILY ANYMORE!
DELUSIONAL BUT HEARTFELT. AS YOUR BODIES RETURN TO THE CLAY FROM WHICH THEY CAME, PERHAPS YOU WILL FIND COMFORT IN YOUR SOUL'S FINAL PURIFICATION.
AS I ONCE USED THE SACRED STONES TO BRING CLARITY TO YOUR MOTHER, I WILL NOW USE THEM TO CLEANSE YOUR SOUL OF ANY REMAINING AL GHUL SIN.
IT WON'T BE A SIN WHEN I END YOU, DEN.
THIS IS ONLY THE BEGINNING...
...THE LU'UN DARGA WILL RISE AS RA'S AND THE AL GHULS WILL FALL.
ASHES TO ASHES. DUST TO DUST.
CRASH

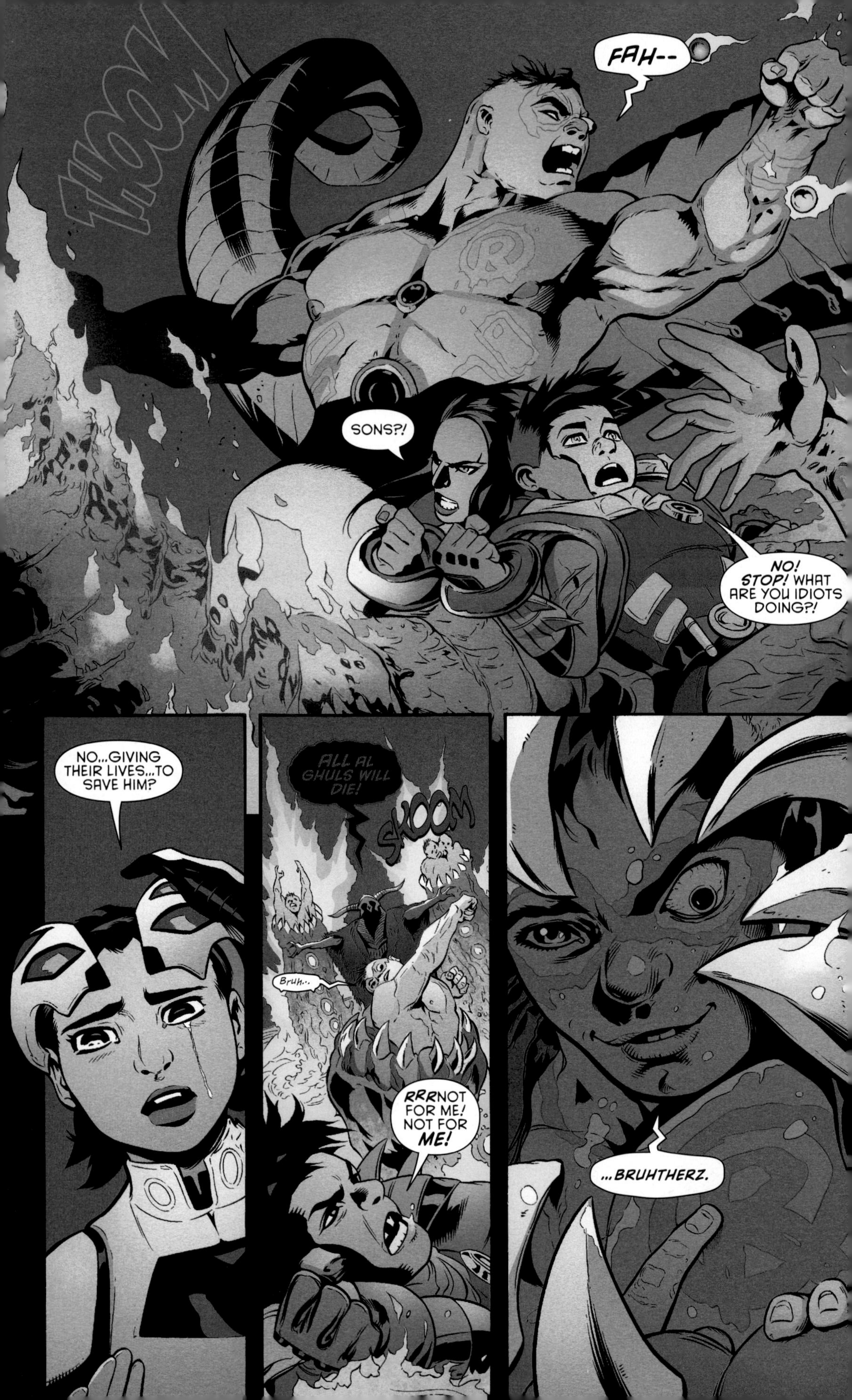
WHOOM!
FAH--
SONS?!
NO! STOP! WHAT ARE YOU IDIOTS DOING?!
NO...GIVING THEIR LIVES...TO SAVE HIM?
ALL AL GHULS WILL DIE!
SKOOM
Bruh..
RRRNOT FOR ME! NOT FOR ME!
...BRUHTHERZ.

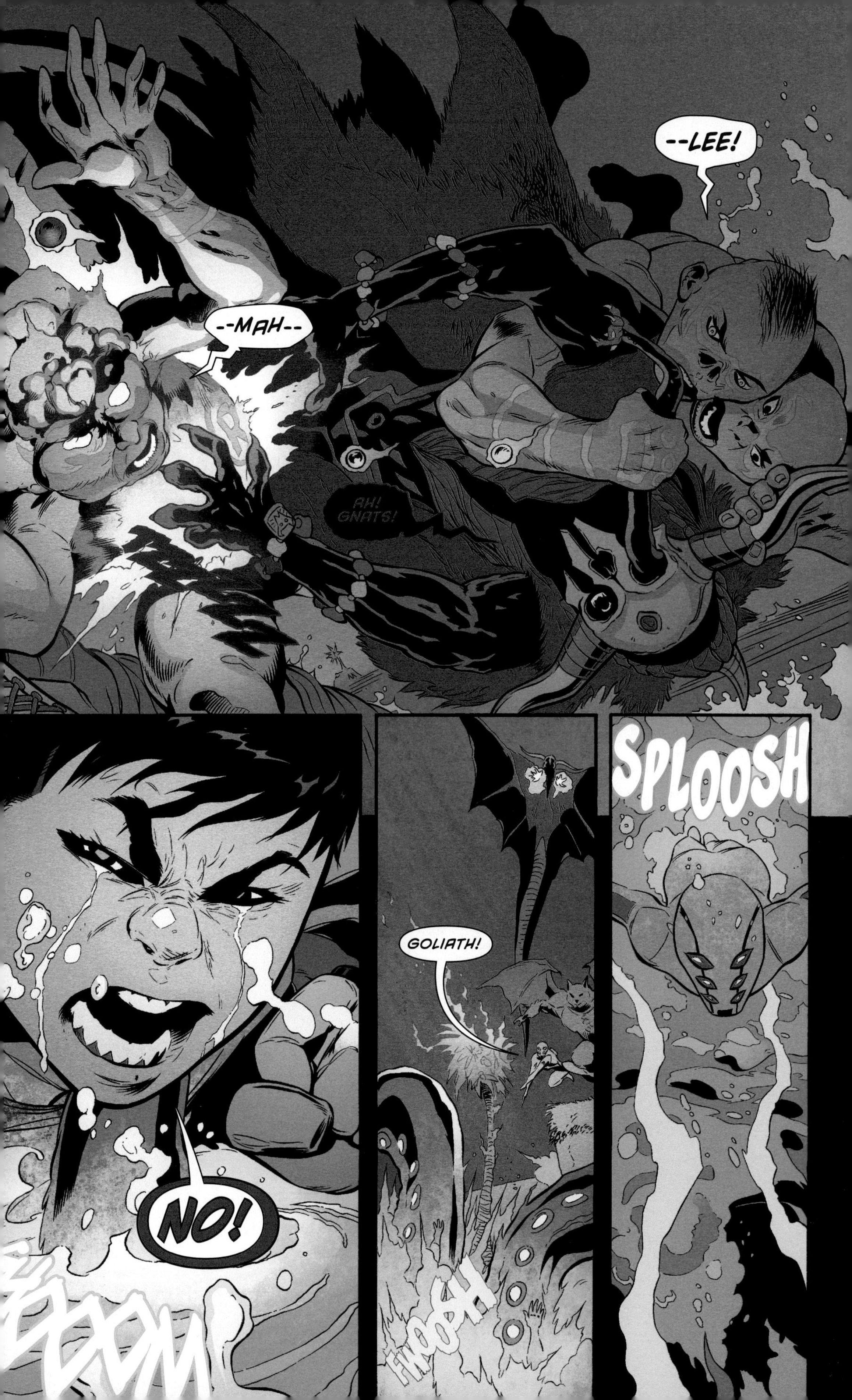
--LEE!
--MAH--
AH! GNATS!
NO!
GOLIATH!
FWOOSH
SPLOOSH

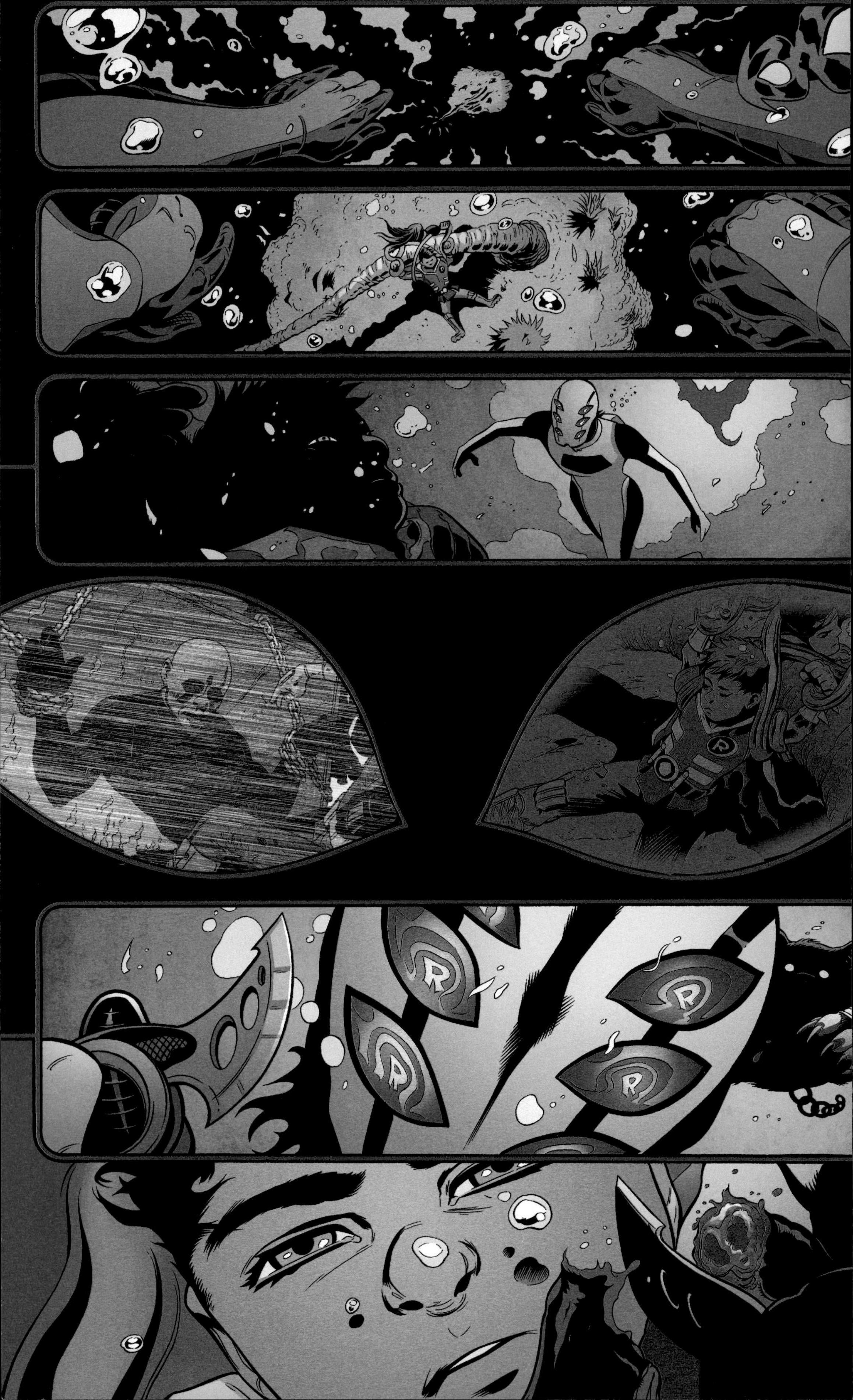

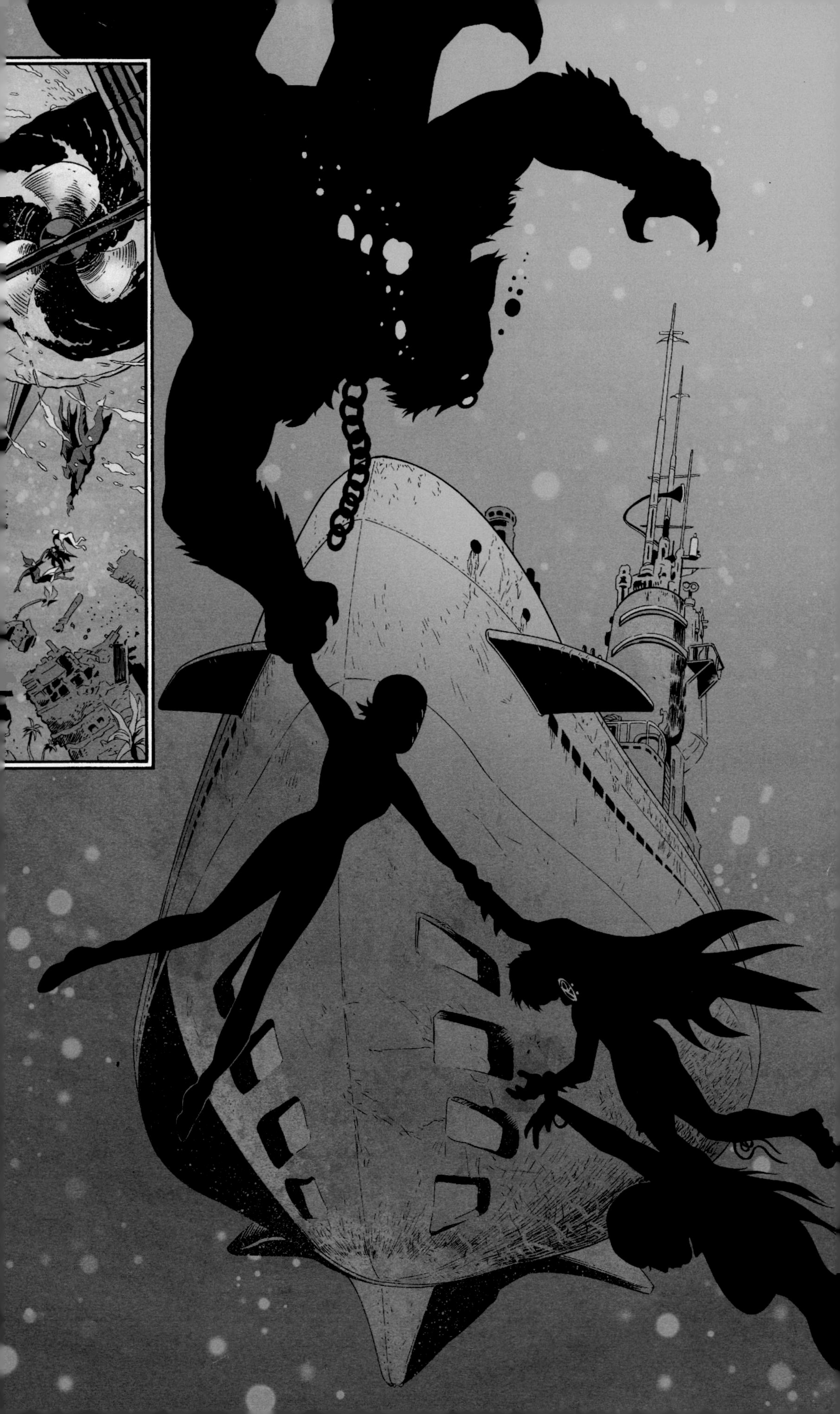

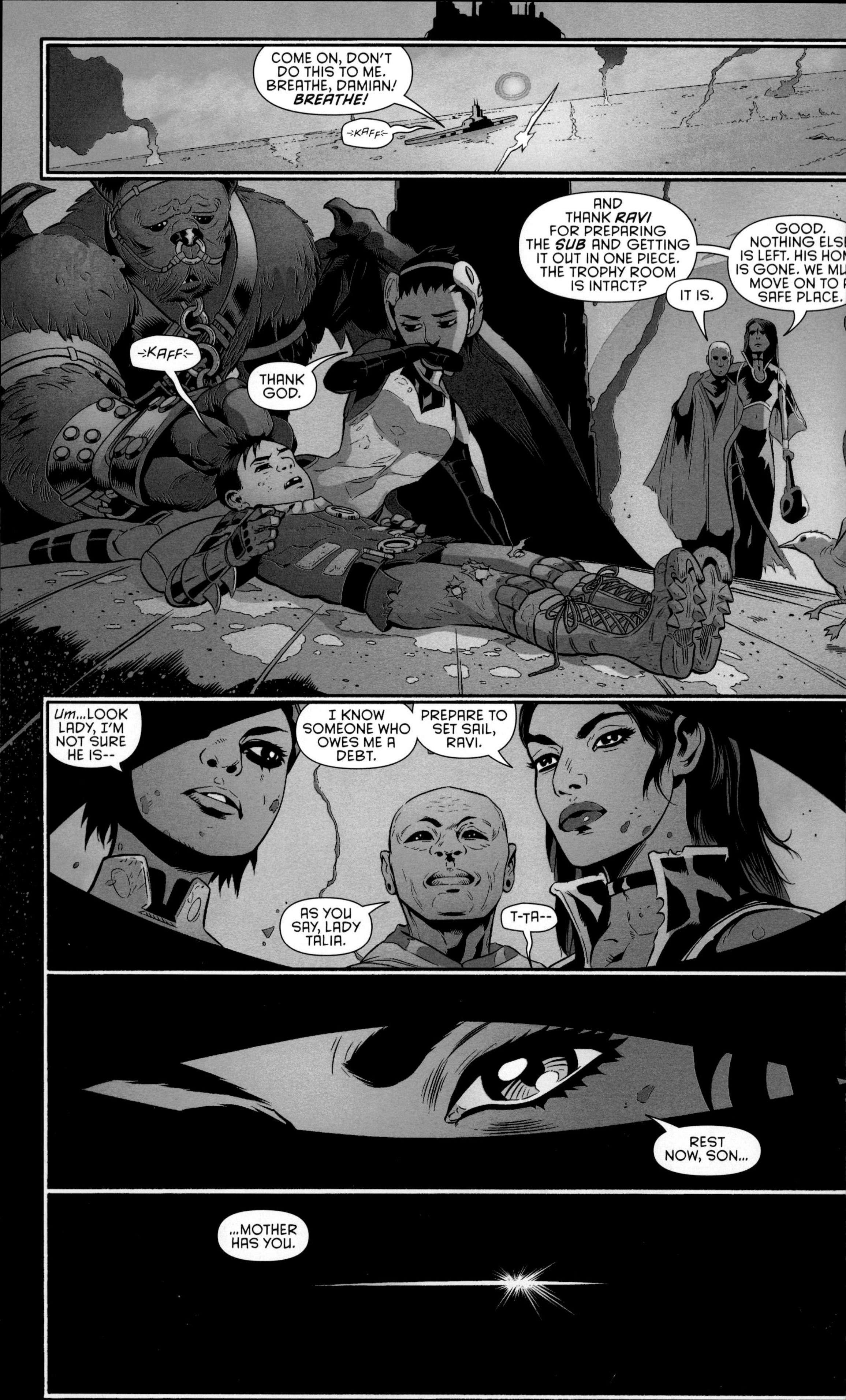
COME ON, DON'T DO THIS TO ME. BREATHE, DAMIAN! BREATHE!
KAFF
KAFF
THANK GOD.
AND THANK RAVI FOR PREPARING THE SUB AND GETTING IT OUT IN ONE PIECE. THE TROPHY ROOM IS INTACT?
IT IS.
GOOD. NOTHING ELSE IS LEFT. HIS HOM IS GONE. WE MU MOVE ON TO A SAFE PLACE.
Um...LOOK LADY, I'M NOT SURE HE IS--
I KNOW SOMEONE WHO OWES ME A DEBT.
PREPARE TO SET SAIL, RAVI.
AS YOU SAY, LADY TALIA.
T-TA--
REST NOW, SON...
...MOTHER HAS YOU.

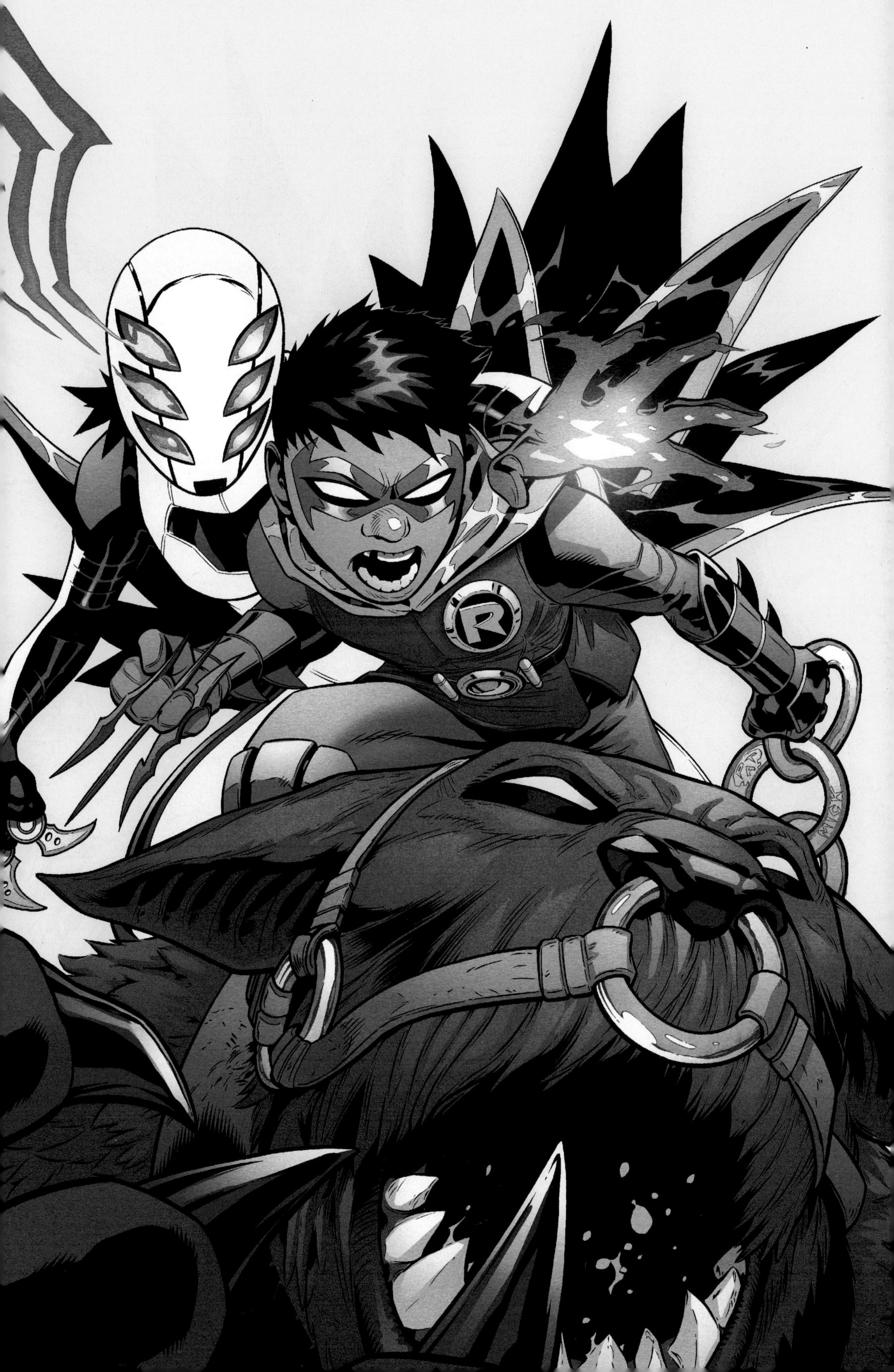

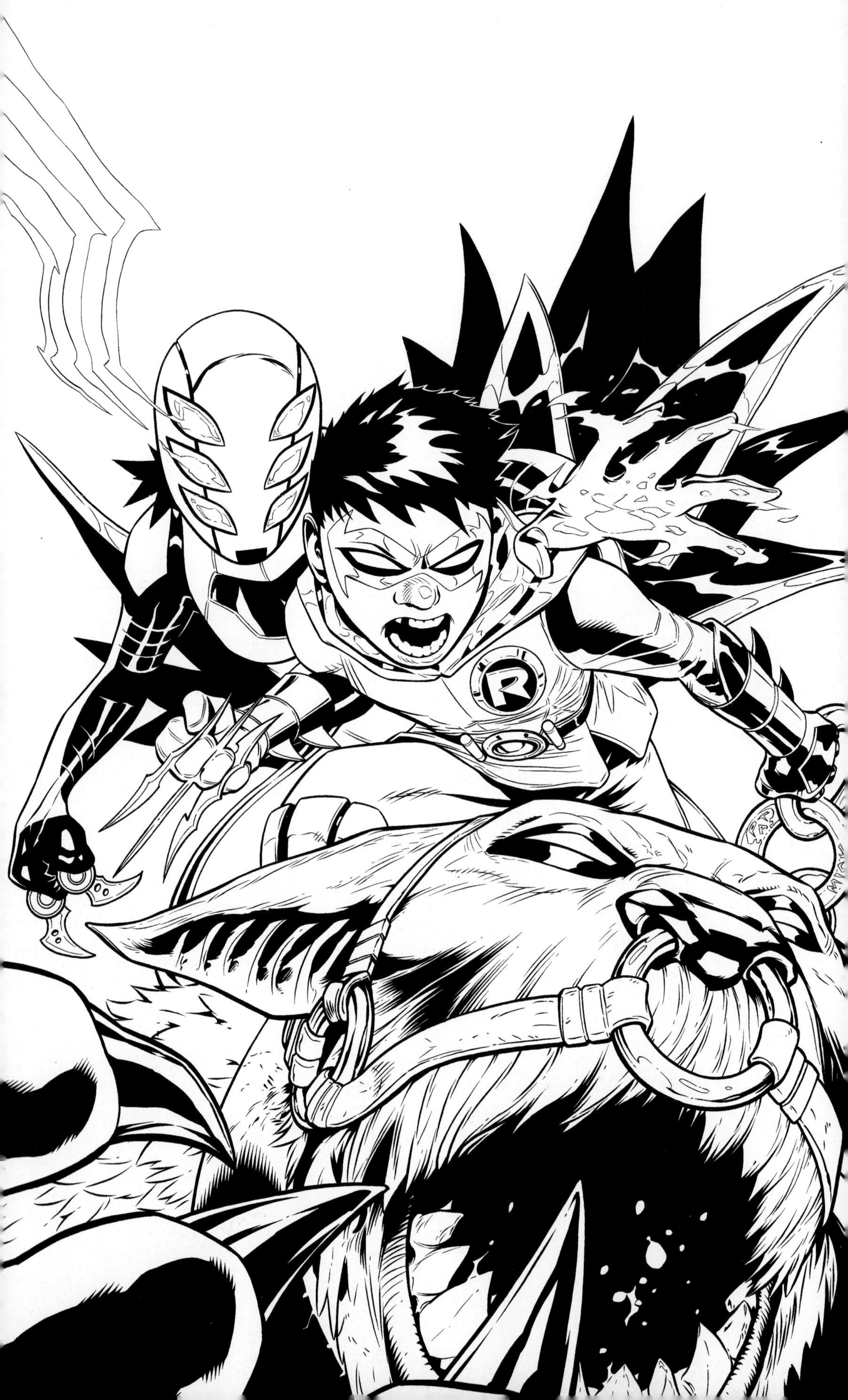

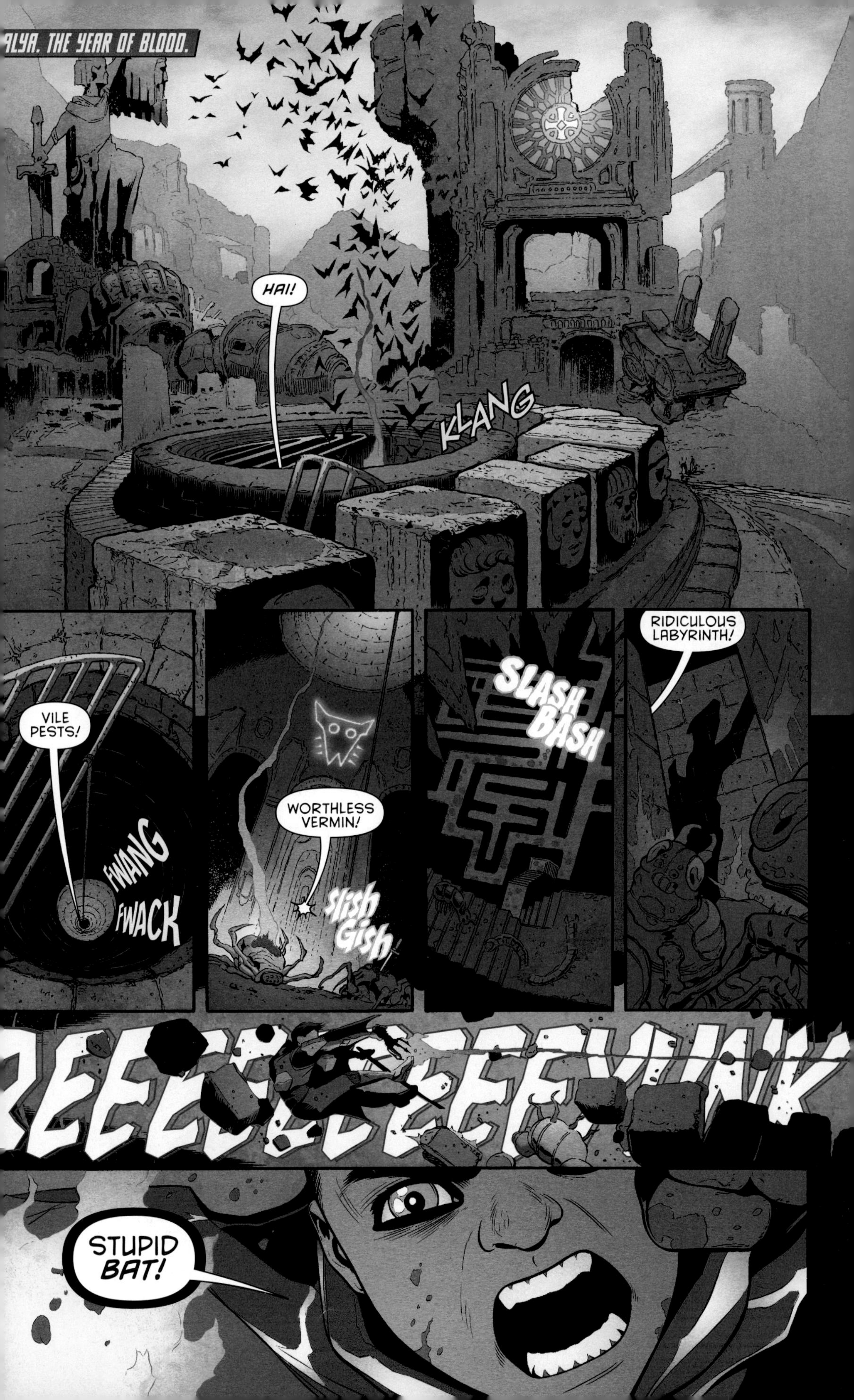
ALYA. THE YEAR OF BLOOD.
HAI!
KLANG
VILE PESTS!
FWANG
FWACK
WORTHLESS VERMIN!
SLISH
GISH
SLASH
BASH
RIDICULOUS LABYRINTH!
STUPID BAT!

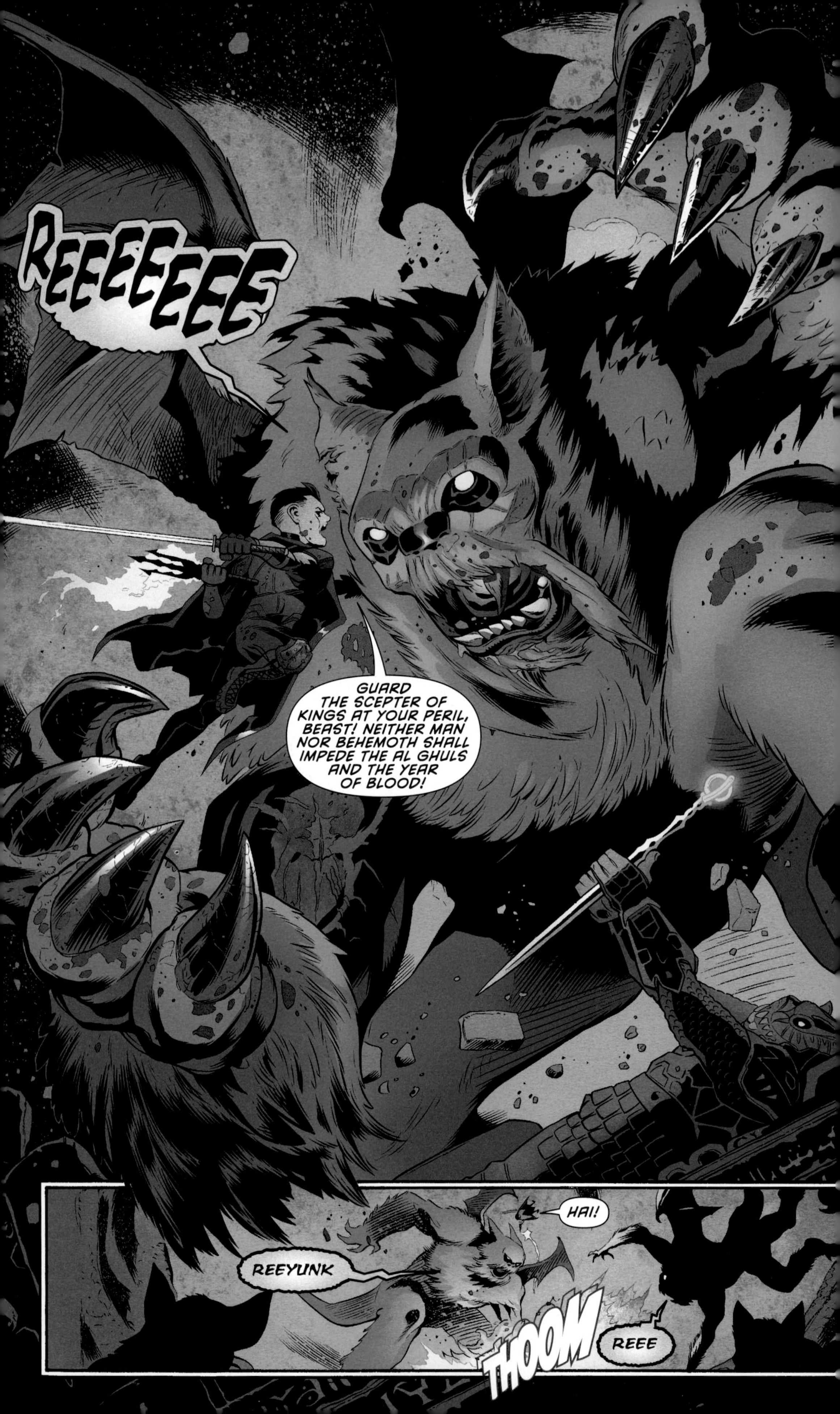
REEEEEEEE
GUARD THE SCEPTER OF KINGS AT YOUR PERIL, BEAST! NEITHER MAN NOR BEHEMOTH SHALL IMPEDE THE AL GHULS AND THE YEAR OF BLOOD!
HAI!
REEYUNK
THOOM
REEE

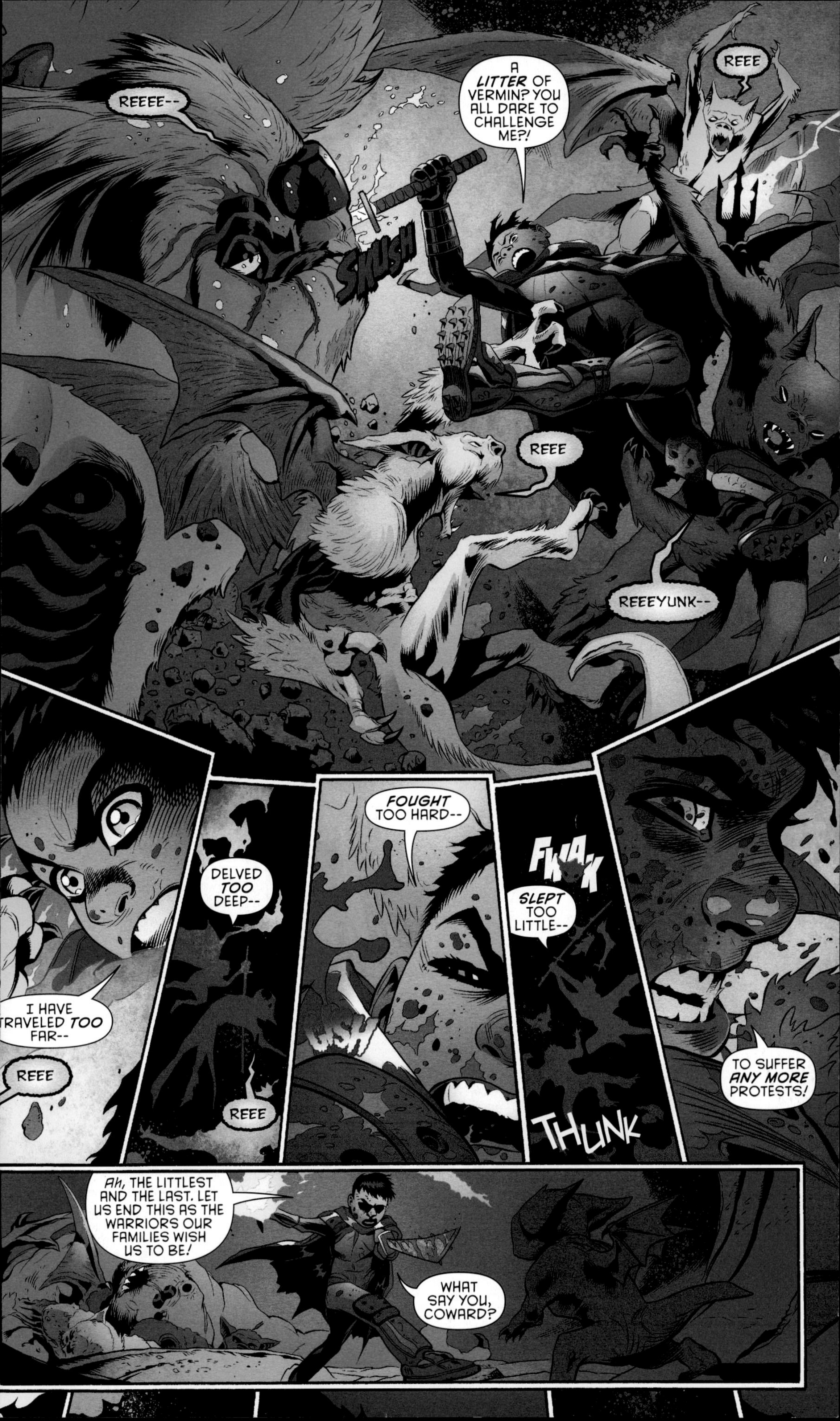
REEEE--
A *LITTER* OF VERMIN? YOU ALL DARE TO CHALLENGE ME?!
REEE
SKUSH
REEE
REEEYUNK--
I HAVE TRAVELED *TOO* FAR--
REEE
DELVED *TOO* DEEP--
REEE
FOUGHT TOO HARD--
FWAK
SLEPT TOO LITTLE--
THUNK
TO SUFFER *ANY MORE* PROTESTS!
Ah, THE LITTLEST AND THE LAST. LET US END THIS AS THE WARRIORS OUR FAMILIES WISH US TO BE!
WHAT SAY YOU, COWARD?

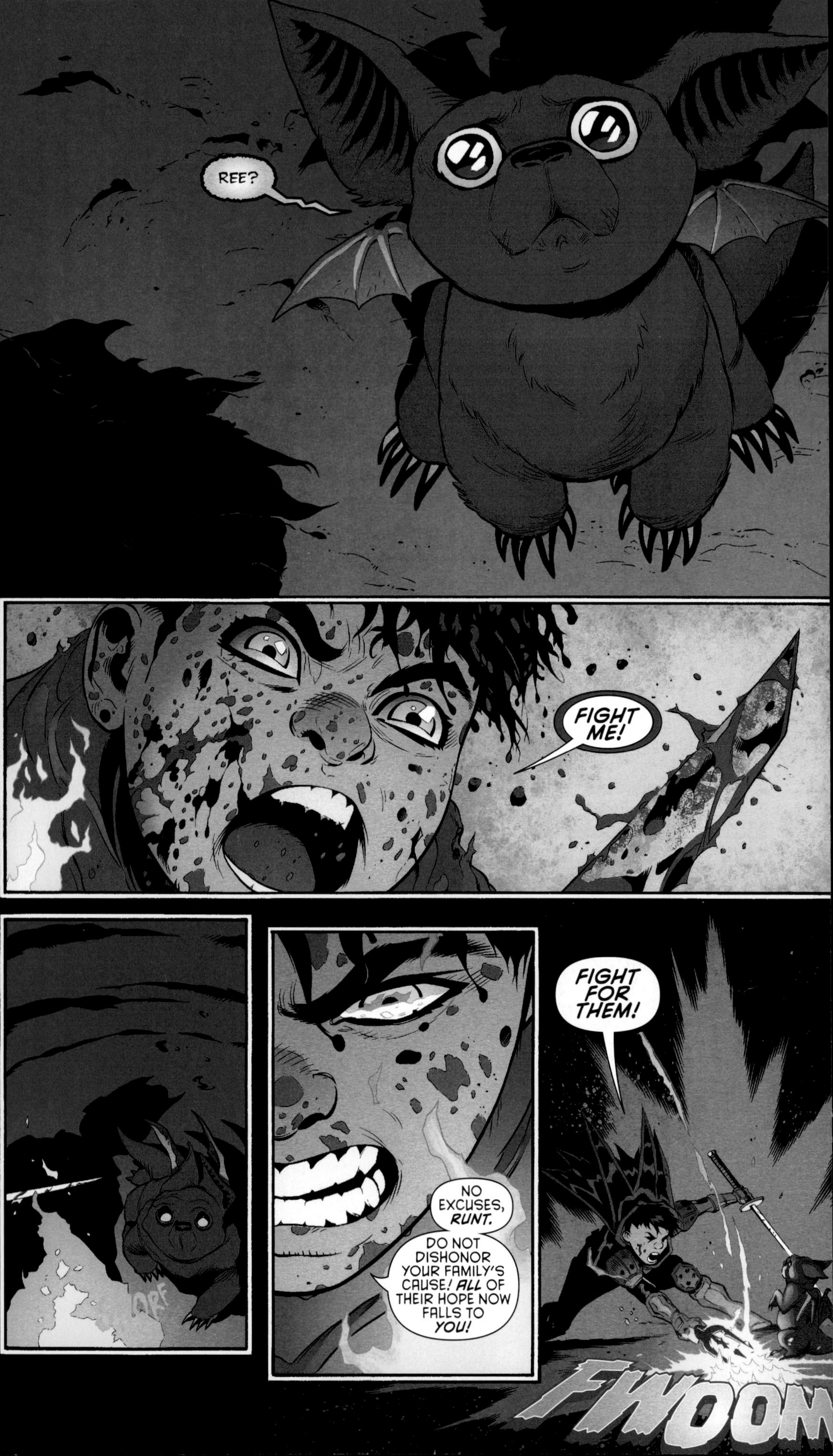
REE?
FIGHT ME!
NO EXCUSES, RUNT.
DO NOT DISHONOR YOUR FAMILY'S CAUSE! ALL OF THEIR HOPE NOW FALLS TO YOU!
FIGHT FOR THEM!
FWOOM

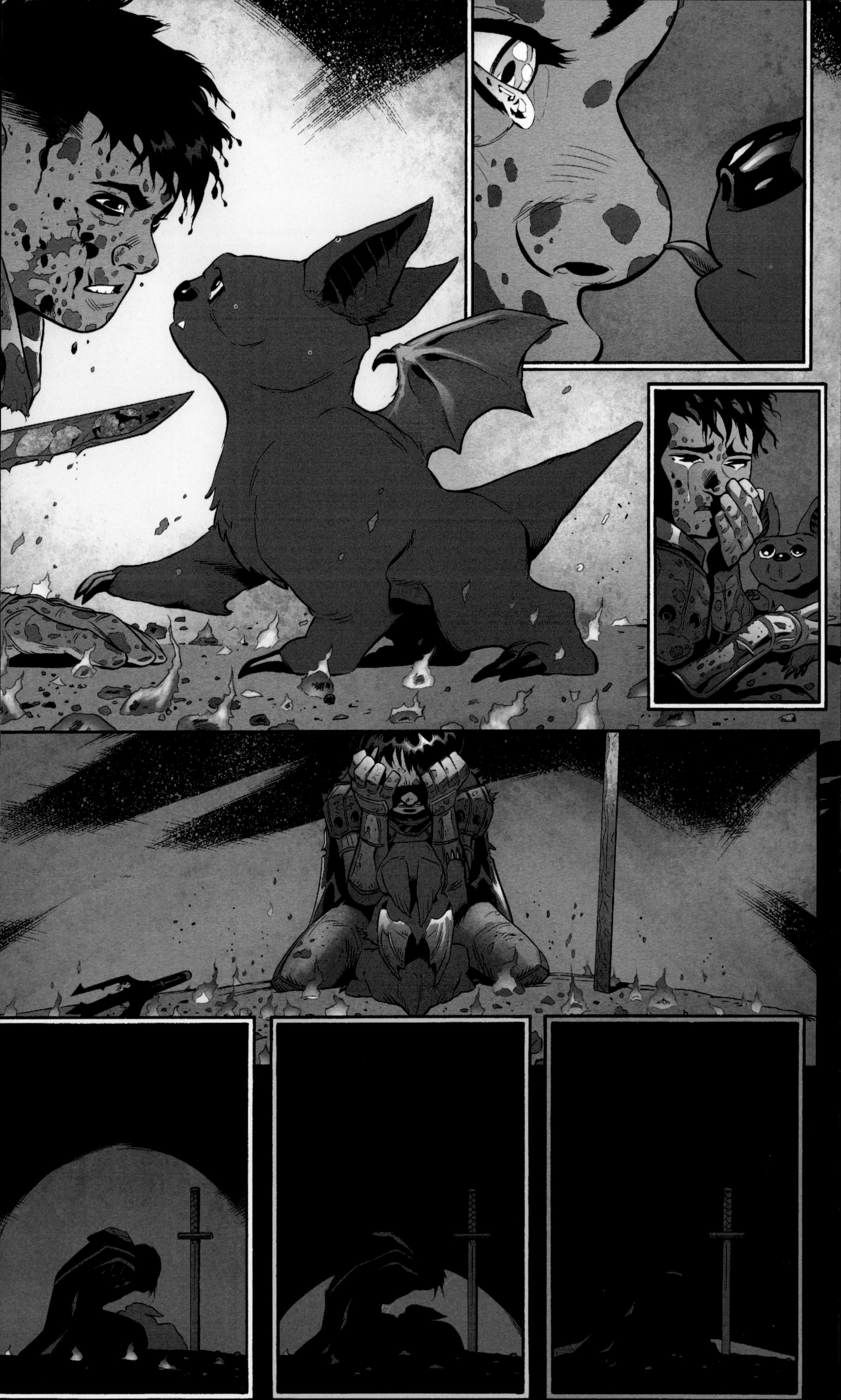

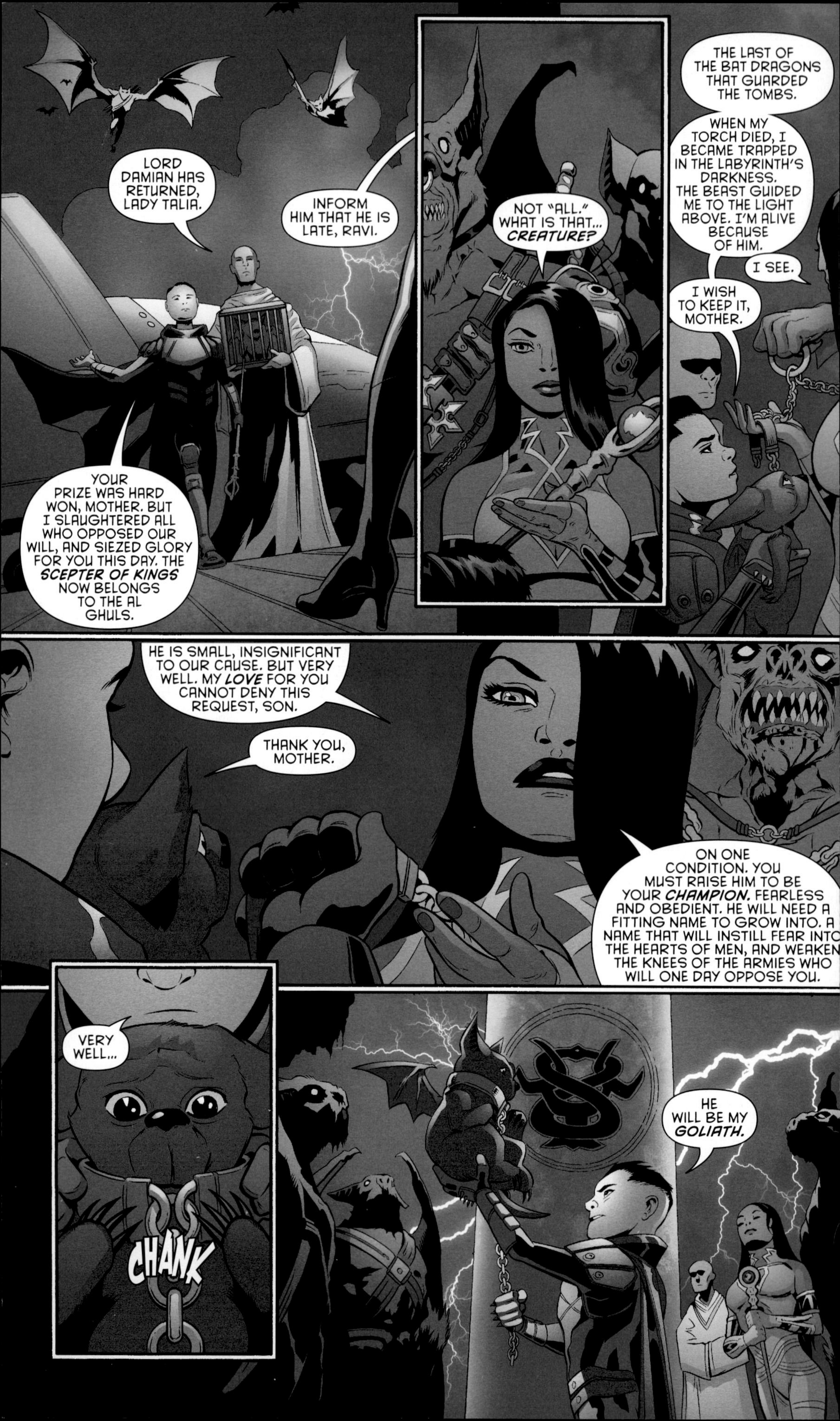
LORD DAMIAN HAS RETURNED, LADY TALIA.
INFORM HIM THAT HE IS LATE, RAVI.
YOUR PRIZE WAS HARD WON, MOTHER. BUT I SLAUGHTERED ALL WHO OPPOSED OUR WILL, AND SIEZED GLORY FOR YOU THIS DAY. THE SCEPTER OF KINGS NOW BELONGS TO THE AL GHULS.
NOT "ALL." WHAT IS THAT... CREATURE?
THE LAST OF THE BAT DRAGONS THAT GUARDED THE TOMBS.
WHEN MY TORCH DIED, I BECAME TRAPPED IN THE LABYRINTH'S DARKNESS. THE BEAST GUIDED ME TO THE LIGHT ABOVE. I'M ALIVE BECAUSE OF HIM.
I SEE.
I WISH TO KEEP IT, MOTHER.
HE IS SMALL, INSIGNIFICANT TO OUR CAUSE. BUT VERY WELL. MY LOVE FOR YOU CANNOT DENY THIS REQUEST, SON.
THANK YOU, MOTHER.
ON ONE CONDITION. YOU MUST RAISE HIM TO BE YOUR CHAMPION. FEARLESS AND OBEDIENT. HE WILL NEED A FITTING NAME TO GROW INTO. A NAME THAT WILL INSTILL FEAR INTO THE HEARTS OF MEN, AND WEAKEN THE KNEES OF THE ARMIES WHO WILL ONE DAY OPPOSE YOU.
VERY WELL...
CHANK
HE WILL BE MY GOLIATH.

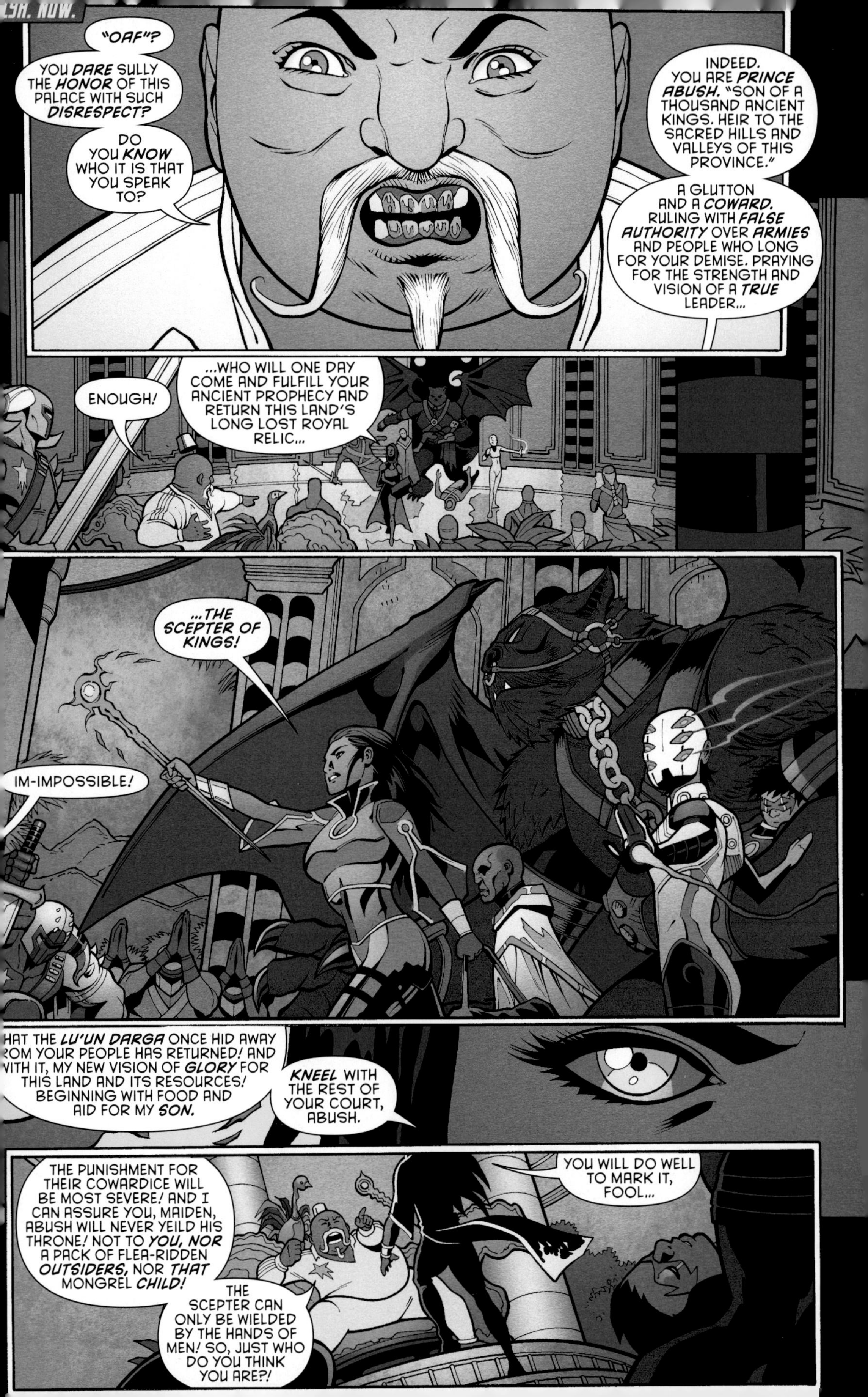

...SH. NOW.
"OAF"?
YOU DARE SULLY THE HONOR OF THIS PALACE WITH SUCH DISRESPECT?
DO YOU KNOW WHO IT IS THAT YOU SPEAK TO?
INDEED. YOU ARE PRINCE ABUSH. "SON OF A THOUSAND ANCIENT KINGS. HEIR TO THE SACRED HILLS AND VALLEYS OF THIS PROVINCE."
A GLUTTON AND A COWARD. RULING WITH FALSE AUTHORITY OVER ARMIES AND PEOPLE WHO LONG FOR YOUR DEMISE. PRAYING FOR THE STRENGTH AND VISION OF A TRUE LEADER...
ENOUGH!
...WHO WILL ONE DAY COME AND FULFILL YOUR ANCIENT PROPHECY AND RETURN THIS LAND'S LONG LOST ROYAL RELIC...
...THE SCEPTER OF KINGS!
IM-IMPOSSIBLE!
HAT THE LU'UN DARGA ONCE HID AWAY ROM YOUR PEOPLE HAS RETURNED! AND WITH IT, MY NEW VISION OF GLORY FOR THIS LAND AND ITS RESOURCES! BEGINNING WITH FOOD AND AID FOR MY SON.
KNEEL WITH THE REST OF YOUR COURT, ABUSH.
THE PUNISHMENT FOR THEIR COWARDICE WILL BE MOST SEVERE! AND I CAN ASSURE YOU, MAIDEN, ABUSH WILL NEVER YEILD HIS THRONE! NOT TO YOU, NOR A PACK OF FLEA-RIDDEN OUTSIDERS, NOR THAT MONGREL CHILD!
THE SCEPTER CAN ONLY BE WIELDED BY THE HANDS OF MEN! SO, JUST WHO DO YOU THINK YOU ARE?!
YOU WILL DO WELL TO MARK IT, FOOL...

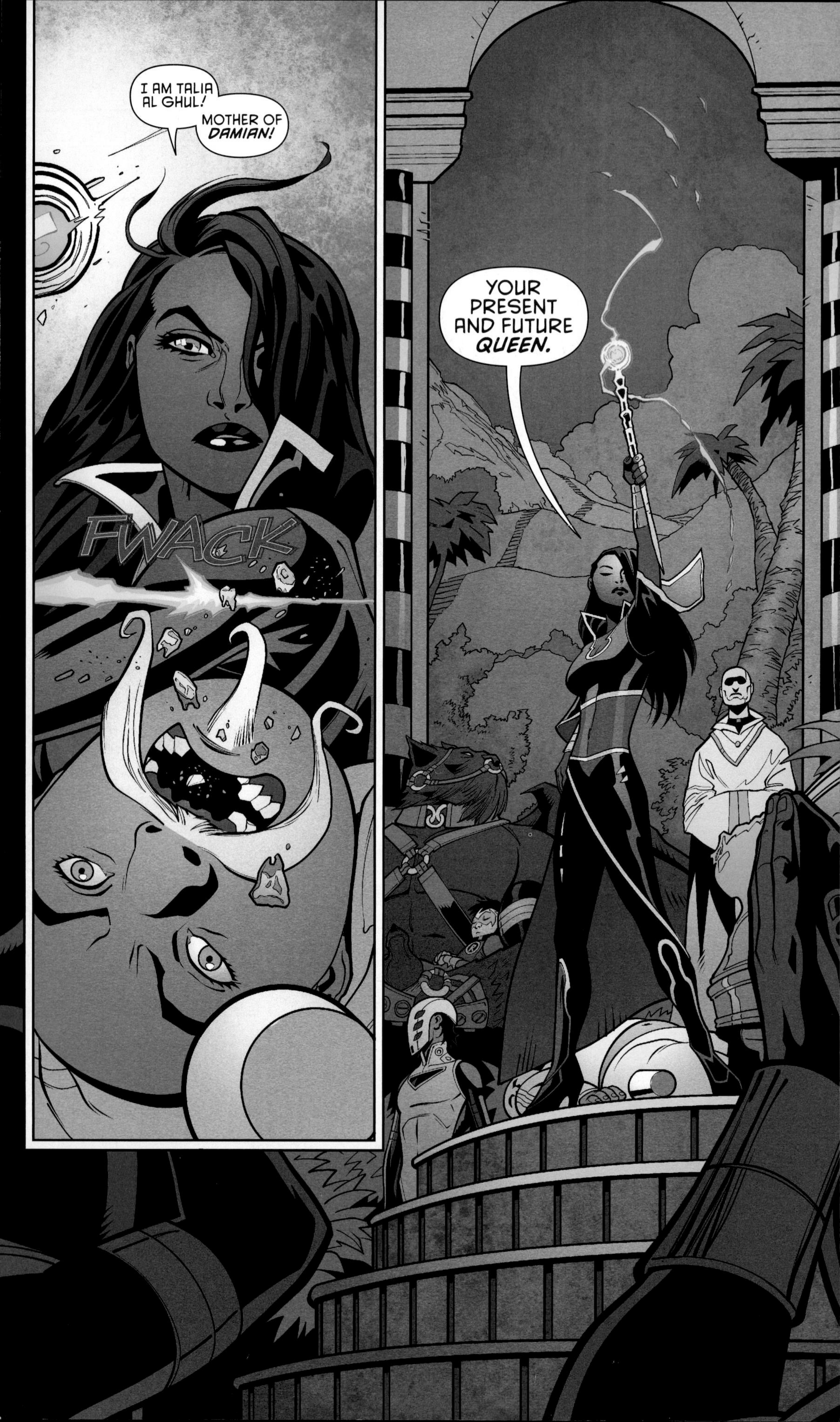
I AM TALIA AL GHUL!
MOTHER OF DAMIAN!
FWACK
YOUR PRESENT AND FUTURE QUEEN.

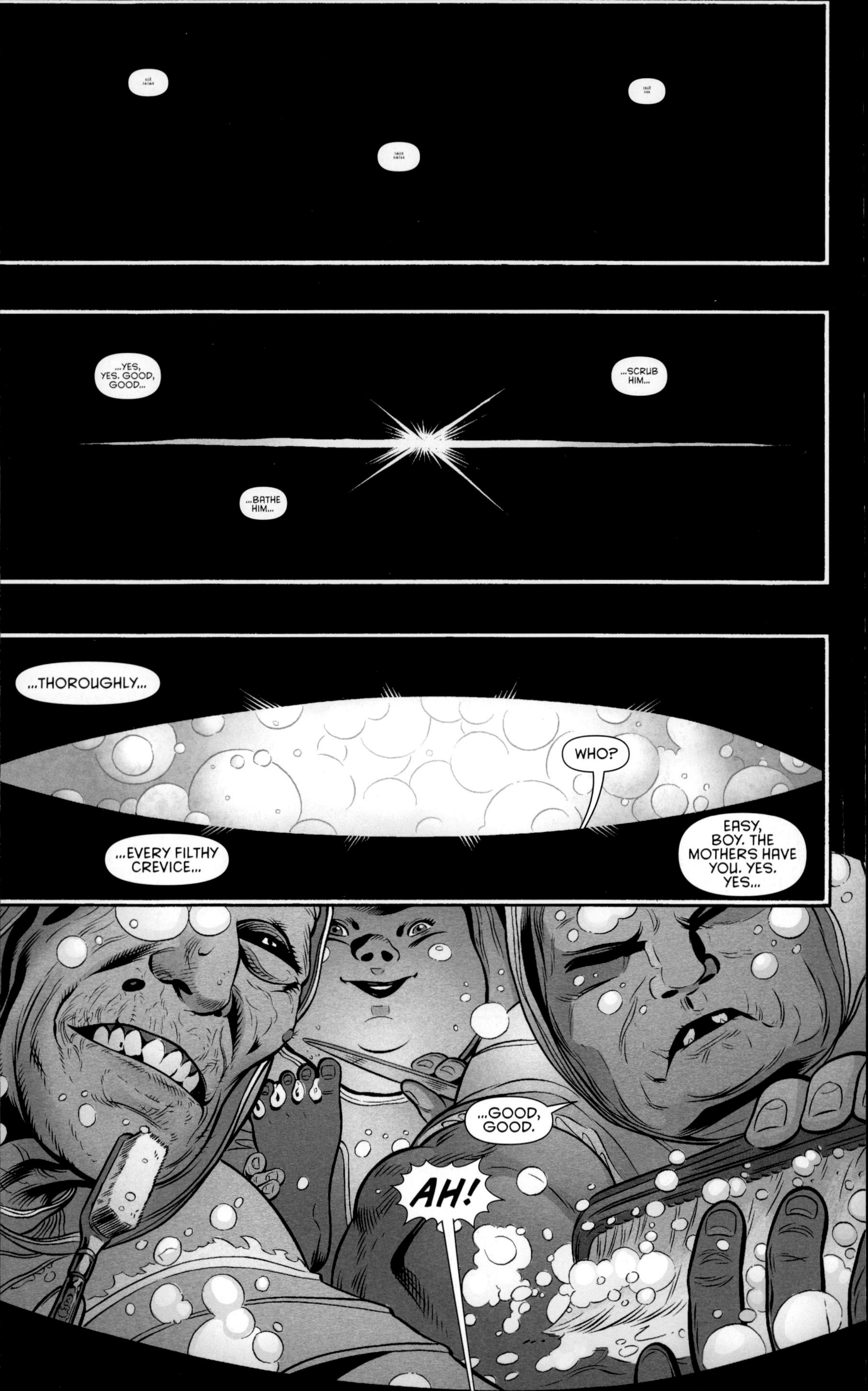
...YES, YES. GOOD, GOOD...
...SCRUB HIM...
...BATHE HIM...
...THOROUGHLY...
WHO?
...EVERY FILTHY CREVICE...
EASY, BOY. THE MOTHERS HAVE YOU. YES. YES...
...GOOD, GOOD.
AH!

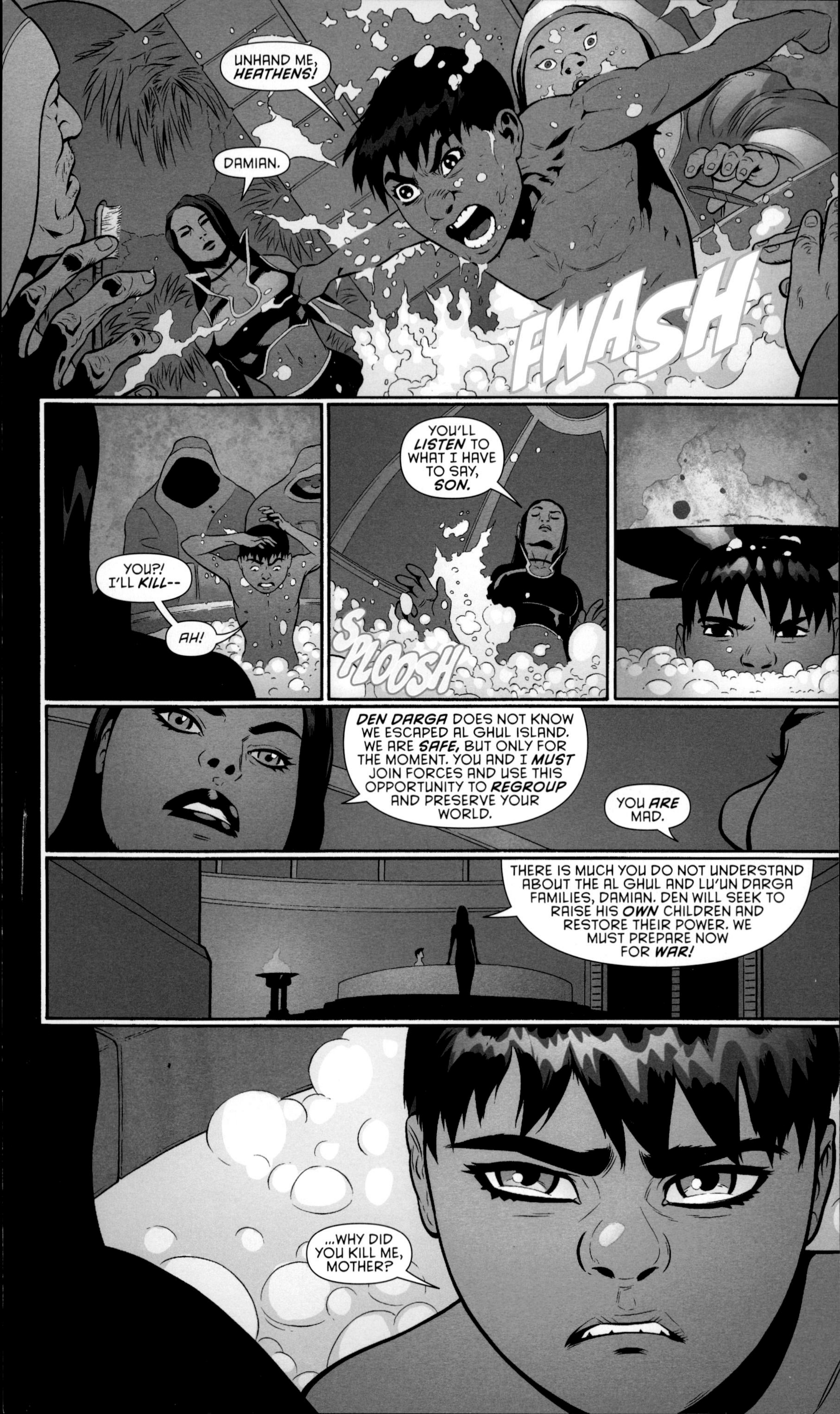
UNHAND ME, HEATHENS!
DAMIAN.
FWASH
YOU?! I'LL KILL--
AH!
YOU'LL LISTEN TO WHAT I HAVE TO SAY, SON.
SPLOOSH
DEN DARGA DOES NOT KNOW WE ESCAPED AL GHUL ISLAND. WE ARE SAFE, BUT ONLY FOR THE MOMENT. YOU AND I MUST JOIN FORCES AND USE THIS OPPORTUNITY TO REGROUP AND PRESERVE YOUR WORLD.
YOU ARE MAD.
THERE IS MUCH YOU DO NOT UNDERSTAND ABOUT THE AL GHUL AND LU'UN DARGA FAMILIES, DAMIAN. DEN WILL SEEK TO RAISE HIS OWN CHILDREN AND RESTORE THEIR POWER. WE MUST PREPARE NOW FOR WAR!
...WHY DID YOU KILL ME, MOTHER?

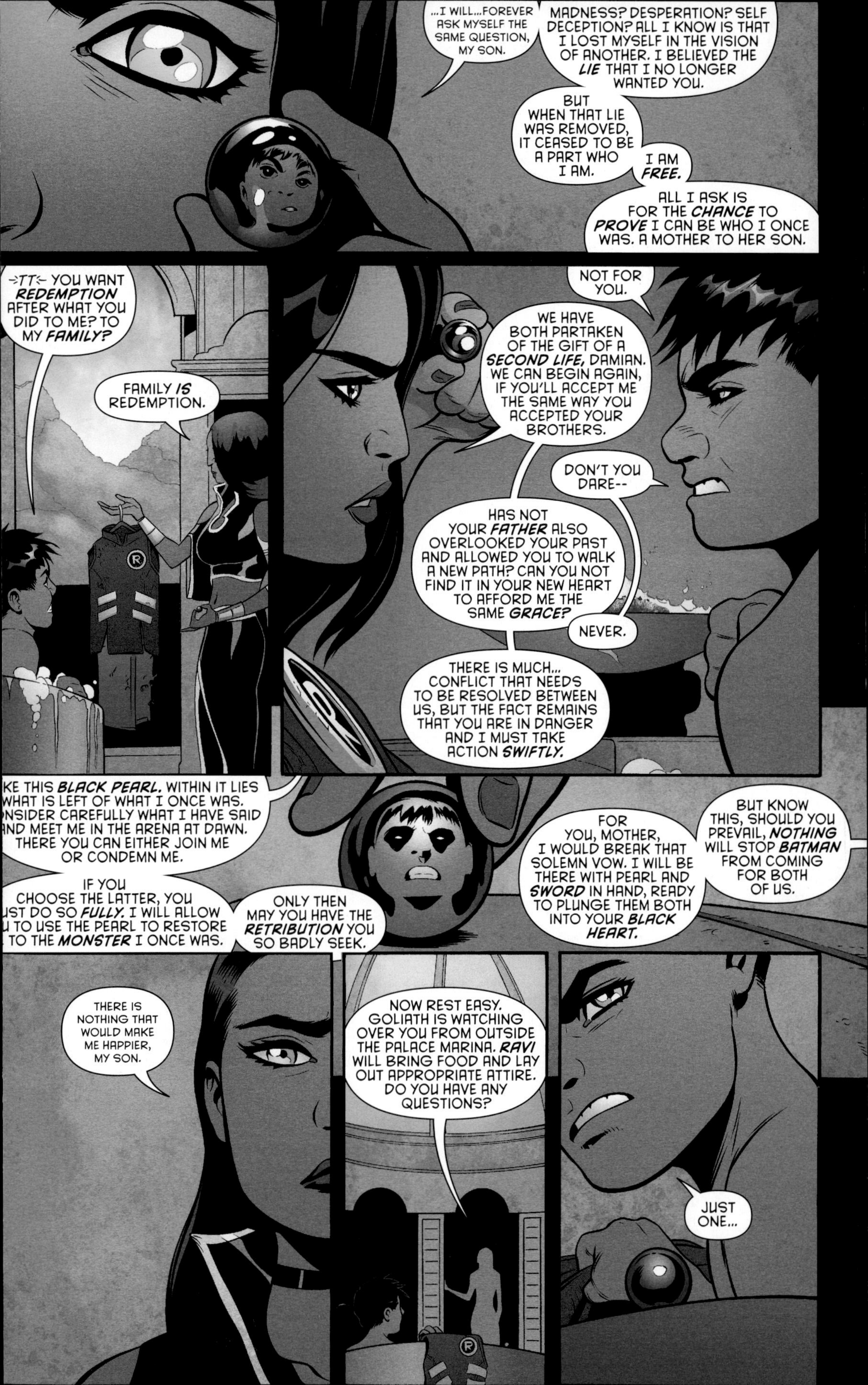
...I WILL...FOREVER ASK MYSELF THE SAME QUESTION, MY SON.
MADNESS? DESPERATION? SELF DECEPTION? ALL I KNOW IS THAT I LOST MYSELF IN THE VISION OF ANOTHER. I BELIEVED THE LIE THAT I NO LONGER WANTED YOU.
BUT WHEN THAT LIE WAS REMOVED, IT CEASED TO BE A PART WHO I AM.
I AM FREE.
ALL I ASK IS FOR THE CHANCE TO PROVE I CAN BE WHO I ONCE WAS. A MOTHER TO HER SON.
-TT- YOU WANT REDEMPTION AFTER WHAT YOU DID TO ME? TO MY FAMILY?
FAMILY IS REDEMPTION.
NOT FOR YOU.
WE HAVE BOTH PARTAKEN OF THE GIFT OF A SECOND LIFE, DAMIAN. WE CAN BEGIN AGAIN, IF YOU'LL ACCEPT ME THE SAME WAY YOU ACCEPTED YOUR BROTHERS.
DON'T YOU DARE--
HAS NOT YOUR FATHER ALSO OVERLOOKED YOUR PAST AND ALLOWED YOU TO WALK A NEW PATH? CAN YOU NOT FIND IT IN YOUR NEW HEART TO AFFORD ME THE SAME GRACE?
NEVER.
THERE IS MUCH... CONFLICT THAT NEEDS TO BE RESOLVED BETWEEN US, BUT THE FACT REMAINS THAT YOU ARE IN DANGER AND I MUST TAKE ACTION SWIFTLY.
KE THIS BLACK PEARL. WITHIN IT LIES WHAT IS LEFT OF WHAT I ONCE WAS. NSIDER CAREFULLY WHAT I HAVE SAID AND MEET ME IN THE ARENA AT DAWN. THERE YOU CAN EITHER JOIN ME OR CONDEMN ME.
IF YOU CHOOSE THE LATTER, YOU UST DO SO FULLY. I WILL ALLOW U TO USE THE PEARL TO RESTORE TO THE MONSTER I ONCE WAS.
ONLY THEN MAY YOU HAVE THE RETRIBUTION YOU SO BADLY SEEK.
FOR YOU, MOTHER, I WOULD BREAK THAT SOLEMN VOW. I WILL BE THERE WITH PEARL AND SWORD IN HAND, READY TO PLUNGE THEM BOTH INTO YOUR BLACK HEART.
BUT KNOW THIS, SHOULD YOU PREVAIL, NOTHING WILL STOP BATMAN FROM COMING FOR BOTH OF US.
THERE IS NOTHING THAT WOULD MAKE ME HAPPIER, MY SON.
NOW REST EASY. GOLIATH IS WATCHING OVER YOU FROM OUTSIDE THE PALACE MARINA. RAVI WILL BRING FOOD AND LAY OUT APPROPRIATE ATTIRE. DO YOU HAVE ANY QUESTIONS?
JUST ONE...

"...WHERE'S THE *GIRL?*"

BATMAN IS *DEAD?!* HE CAN'T REALLY BE--

NO. HE CAN'T. AND HE'S *NOT.* NO WAY. BATMAN WILL NEVER DIE.

ROBIN! YEAH... BUT--

WHAT DO YOU EXPECT? TEARS? AFTER ALL, I CAME BACK, MY MOTHER CAME BACK.

WHY WOULDN'T *HE?* DEATH IS BECOMING MORE AND MORE OF A GREY AREA THESE DAYS.

ALTHOUGH, I DO SUPPOSE THE OTHER CHILDREN IN GOTHAM WILL PANIC AND NEED TO BE ATTENDED TO...

ARE YOU... STILL IN SHOCK OR SOMETHING? ARE YOU FEELING *OKAY?*

NO.

ALL THE WORK IN THIS YEAR OF ATONEMENT HAS ONLY LEFT THINGS IN ASHES. SO GLOAT ALL YOU WANT, *CHICA.*

I KNOW NOW I CAN'T UNDO THE THINGS I'VE DONE. THE ONLY THING THIS STUPID "R" STANDS FOR IS "RUIN."

YOUR BROTHERS DIDN'T THINK SO.

SHUT THAT OFF.

MONSTERS TURNED HEROES. *ROBIN* INSPIRED THAT.

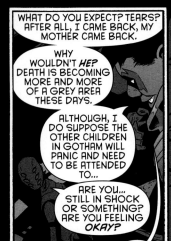

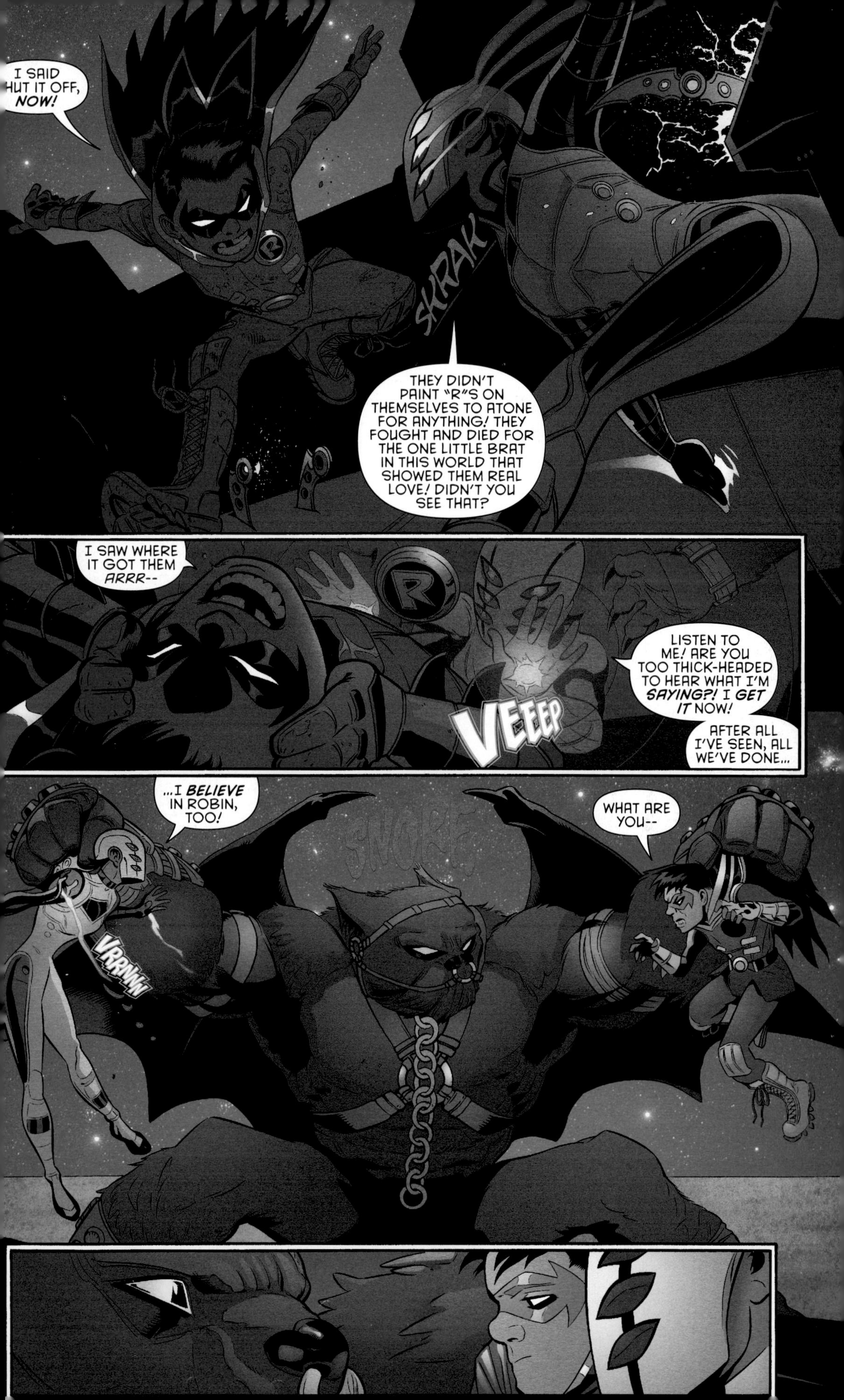

I SAID HUT IT OFF, *NOW!*
SKRAK
THEY DIDN'T PAINT "R"S ON THEMSELVES TO ATONE FOR ANYTHING! THEY FOUGHT AND DIED FOR THE ONE LITTLE BRAT IN THIS WORLD THAT SHOWED THEM REAL LOVE! DIDN'T YOU SEE THAT?
I SAW WHERE IT GOT THEM *ARRR--*
VEEEP
LISTEN TO ME! ARE YOU TOO THICK-HEADED TO HEAR WHAT I'M *SAYING?!* I *GET IT* NOW!
AFTER ALL I'VE SEEN, ALL WE'VE DONE...
...I *BELIEVE* IN ROBIN, TOO!
VRRNNN
WHAT ARE YOU--

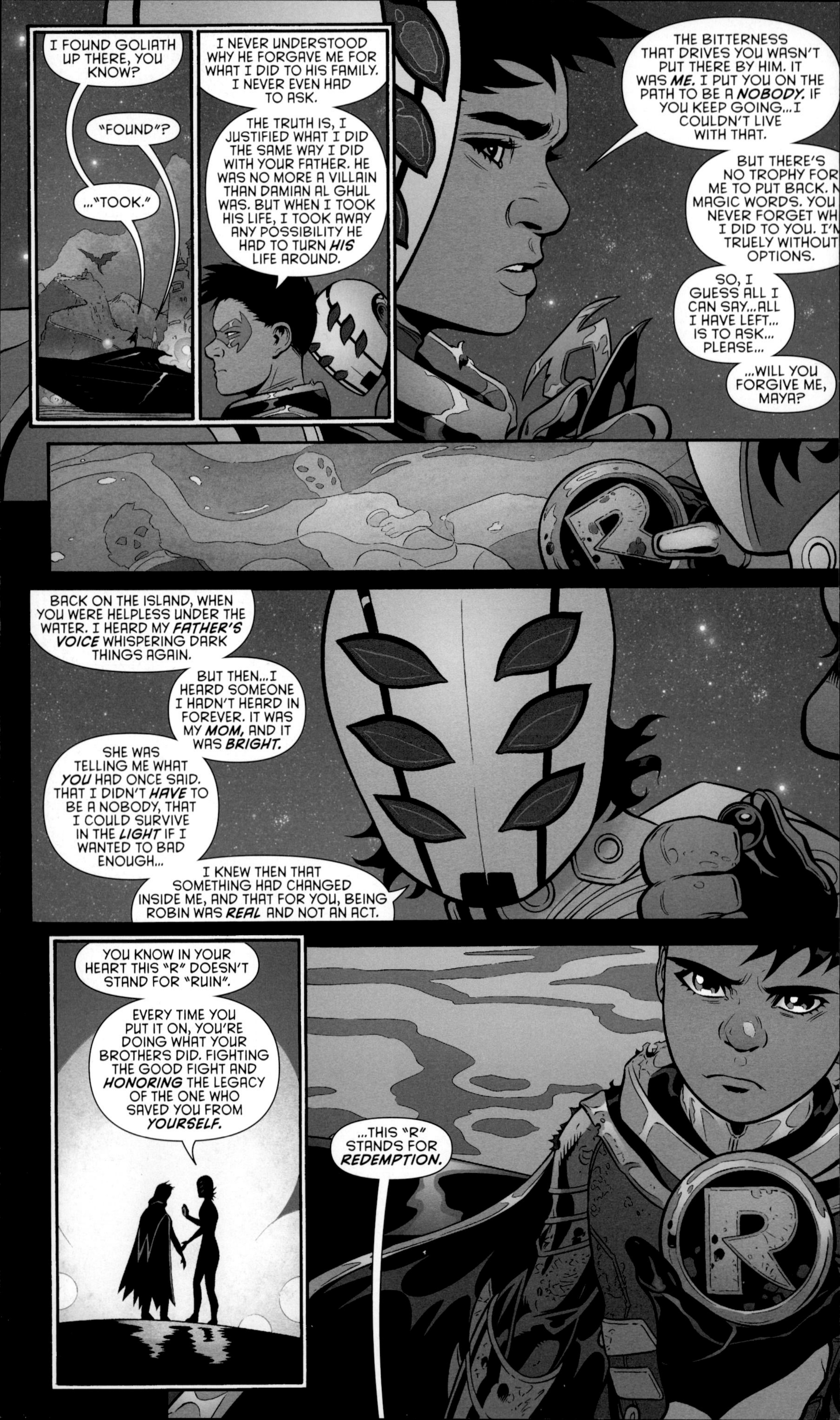
I FOUND GOLIATH UP THERE, YOU KNOW?
"FOUND"?
..."TOOK."
I NEVER UNDERSTOOD WHY HE FORGAVE ME FOR WHAT I DID TO HIS FAMILY. I NEVER EVEN HAD TO ASK.
THE TRUTH IS, I JUSTIFIED WHAT I DID THE SAME WAY I DID WITH YOUR FATHER. HE WAS NO MORE A VILLAIN THAN DAMIAN AL GHUL WAS. BUT WHEN I TOOK HIS LIFE, I TOOK AWAY ANY POSSIBILITY HE HAD TO TURN HIS LIFE AROUND.
THE BITTERNESS THAT DRIVES YOU WASN'T PUT THERE BY HIM. IT WAS ME. I PUT YOU ON THE PATH TO BE A NOBODY. IF YOU KEEP GOING...I COULDN'T LIVE WITH THAT.
SO, I GUESS ALL I CAN SAY...ALL I HAVE LEFT... IS TO ASK... PLEASE...
...WILL YOU FORGIVE ME, MAYA?
BACK ON THE ISLAND, WHEN YOU WERE HELPLESS UNDER THE WATER. I HEARD MY FATHER'S VOICE WHISPERING DARK THINGS AGAIN.
BUT THEN...I HEARD SOMEONE I HADN'T HEARD IN FOREVER. IT WAS MY MOM, AND IT WAS BRIGHT.
SHE WAS TELLING ME WHAT YOU HAD ONCE SAID. THAT I DIDN'T HAVE TO BE A NOBODY, THAT I COULD SURVIVE IN THE LIGHT IF I WANTED TO BAD ENOUGH...
I KNEW THEN THAT SOMETHING HAD CHANGED INSIDE ME, AND THAT FOR YOU, BEING ROBIN WAS REAL AND NOT AN ACT.
YOU KNOW IN YOUR HEART THIS "R" DOESN'T STAND FOR "RUIN".
EVERY TIME YOU PUT IT ON, YOU'RE DOING WHAT YOUR BROTHERS DID. FIGHTING THE GOOD FIGHT AND HONORING THE LEGACY OF THE ONE WHO SAVED YOU FROM YOURSELF.
...THIS "R" STANDS FOR REDEMPTION.

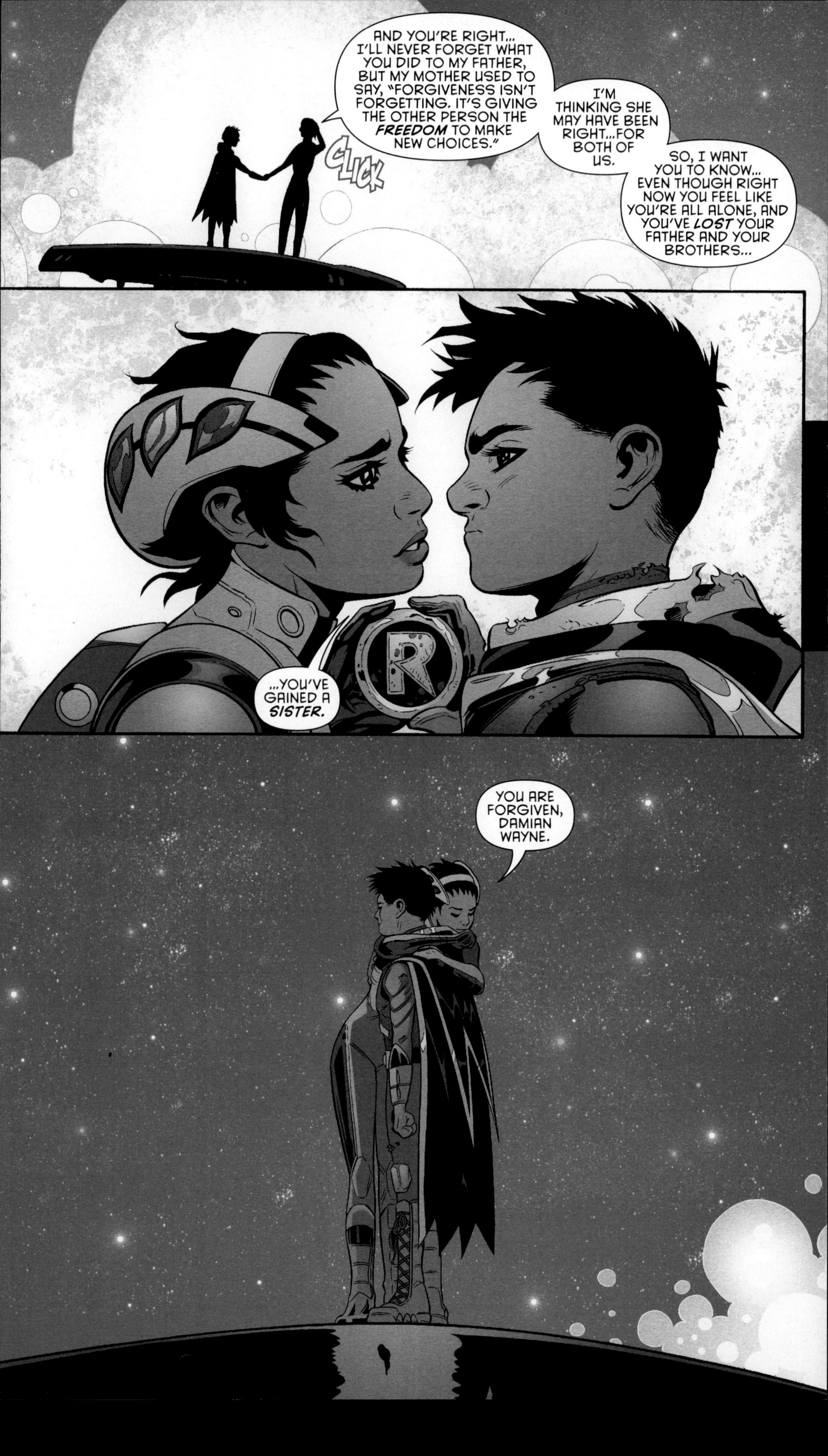
AND YOU'RE RIGHT... I'LL NEVER FORGET WHAT YOU DID TO MY FATHER, BUT MY MOTHER USED TO SAY, "FORGIVENESS ISN'T FORGETTING. IT'S GIVING THE OTHER PERSON THE *FREEDOM* TO MAKE NEW CHOICES."
CLICK
I'M THINKING SHE MAY HAVE BEEN RIGHT...FOR BOTH OF US.
SO, I WANT YOU TO KNOW... EVEN THOUGH RIGHT NOW YOU FEEL LIKE YOU'RE ALL ALONE, AND YOU'VE *LOST* YOUR FATHER AND YOUR BROTHERS...
...YOU'VE GAINED A *SISTER.*
YOU ARE FORGIVEN, DAMIAN WAYNE.

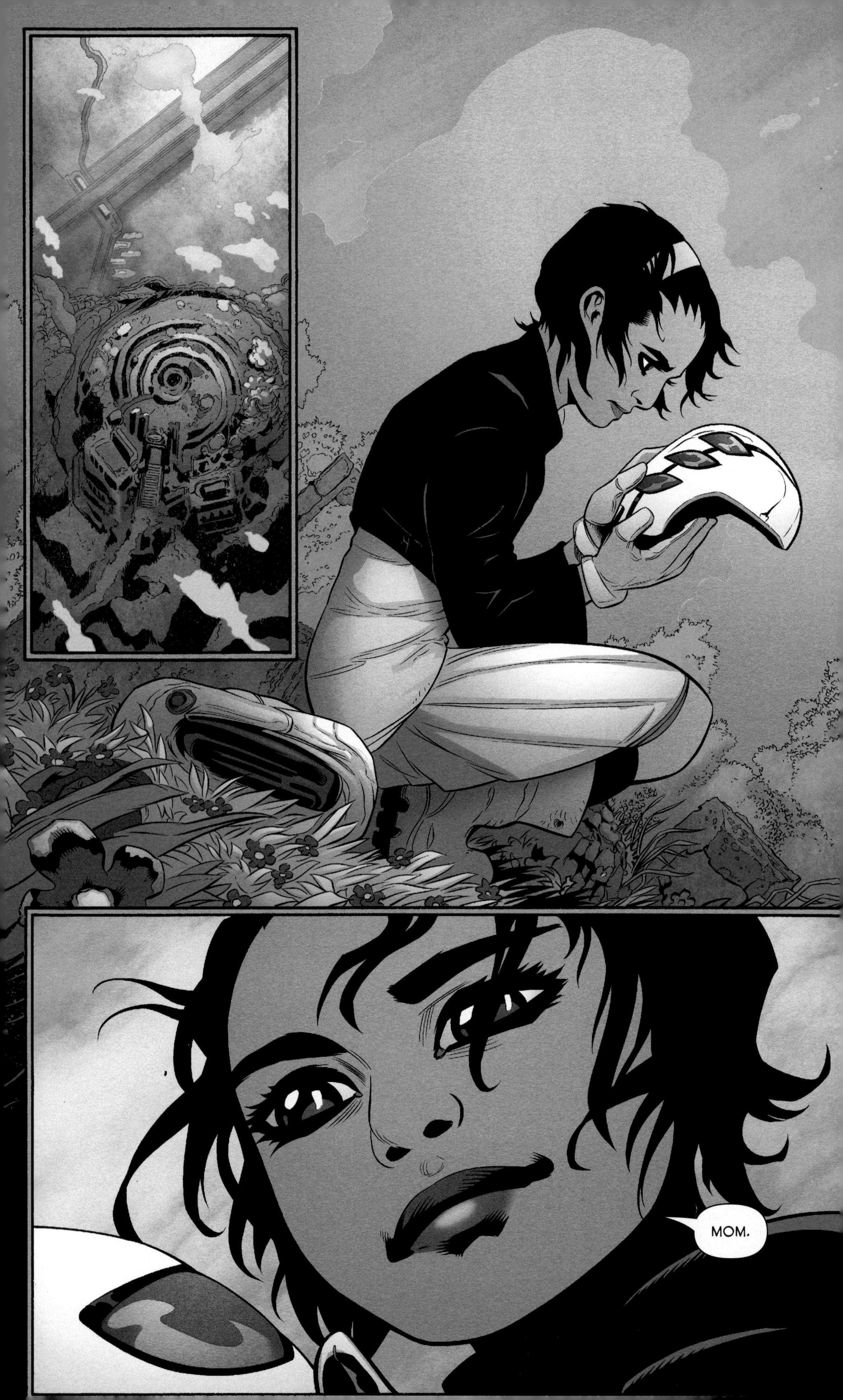
MOM.

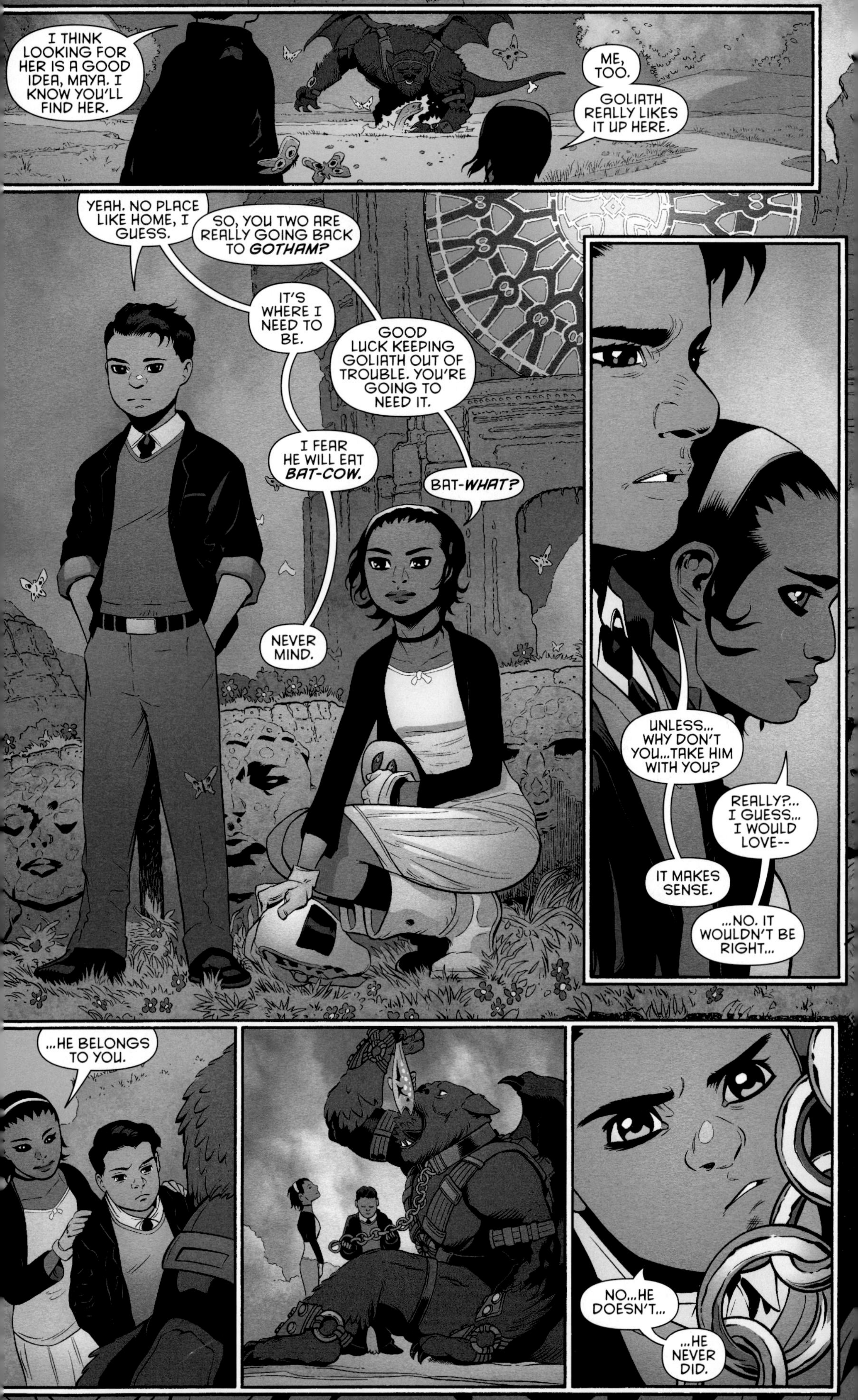
I THINK LOOKING FOR HER IS A GOOD IDEA, MAYA. I KNOW YOU'LL FIND HER.
ME, TOO.
GOLIATH REALLY LIKES IT UP HERE.
YEAH. NO PLACE LIKE HOME, I GUESS.
SO, YOU TWO ARE REALLY GOING BACK TO GOTHAM?
IT'S WHERE I NEED TO BE.
GOOD LUCK KEEPING GOLIATH OUT OF TROUBLE. YOU'RE GOING TO NEED IT.
I FEAR HE WILL EAT BAT-COW.
BAT-WHAT?
NEVER MIND.
UNLESS... WHY DON'T YOU...TAKE HIM WITH YOU?
REALLY?... I GUESS... I WOULD LOVE--
IT MAKES SENSE.
...NO. IT WOULDN'T BE RIGHT...
...HE BELONGS TO YOU.
NO...HE DOESN'T...
...HE NEVER DID.

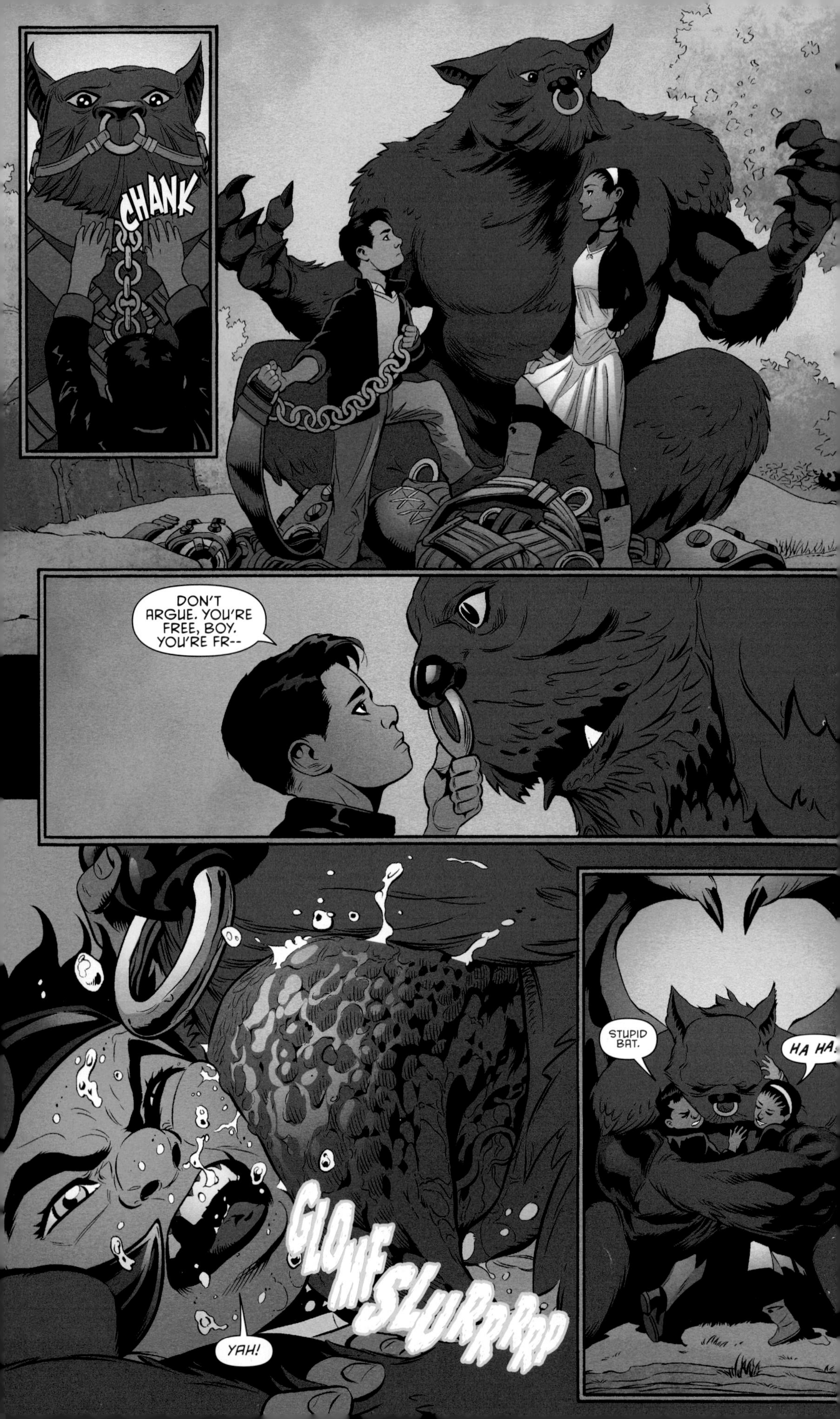
CHANK
DON'T ARGUE. YOU'RE FREE, BOY. YOU'RE FR--
YAH!
GLOMF SLURRRRRP
STUPID BAT.
HA HA

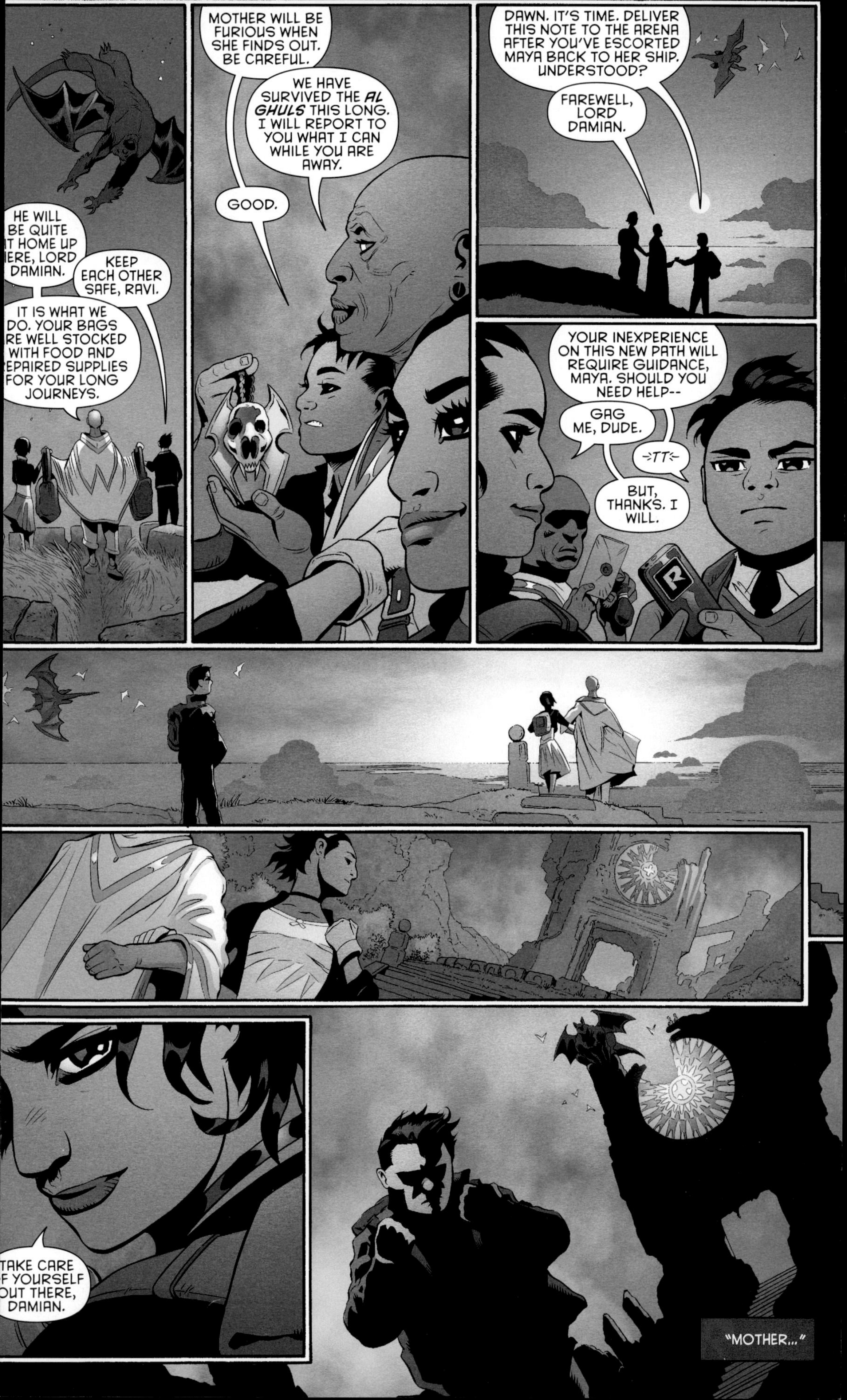
HE WILL BE QUITE AT HOME UP HERE, LORD DAMIAN.
KEEP EACH OTHER SAFE, RAVI.
IT IS WHAT WE DO. YOUR BAGS ARE WELL STOCKED WITH FOOD AND REPAIRED SUPPLIES FOR YOUR LONG JOURNEYS.
MOTHER WILL BE FURIOUS WHEN SHE FINDS OUT. BE CAREFUL.
WE HAVE SURVIVED THE AL GHULS THIS LONG. I WILL REPORT TO YOU WHAT I CAN WHILE YOU ARE AWAY.
GOOD.
DAWN. IT'S TIME. DELIVER THIS NOTE TO THE ARENA AFTER YOU'VE ESCORTED MAYA BACK TO HER SHIP. UNDERSTOOD?
FAREWELL, LORD DAMIAN.
YOUR INEXPERIENCE ON THIS NEW PATH WILL REQUIRE GUIDANCE, MAYA. SHOULD YOU NEED HELP--
GAG ME, DUDE.
TT
BUT, THANKS. I WILL.
TAKE CARE OF YOURSELF OUT THERE, DAMIAN.
"MOTHER..."

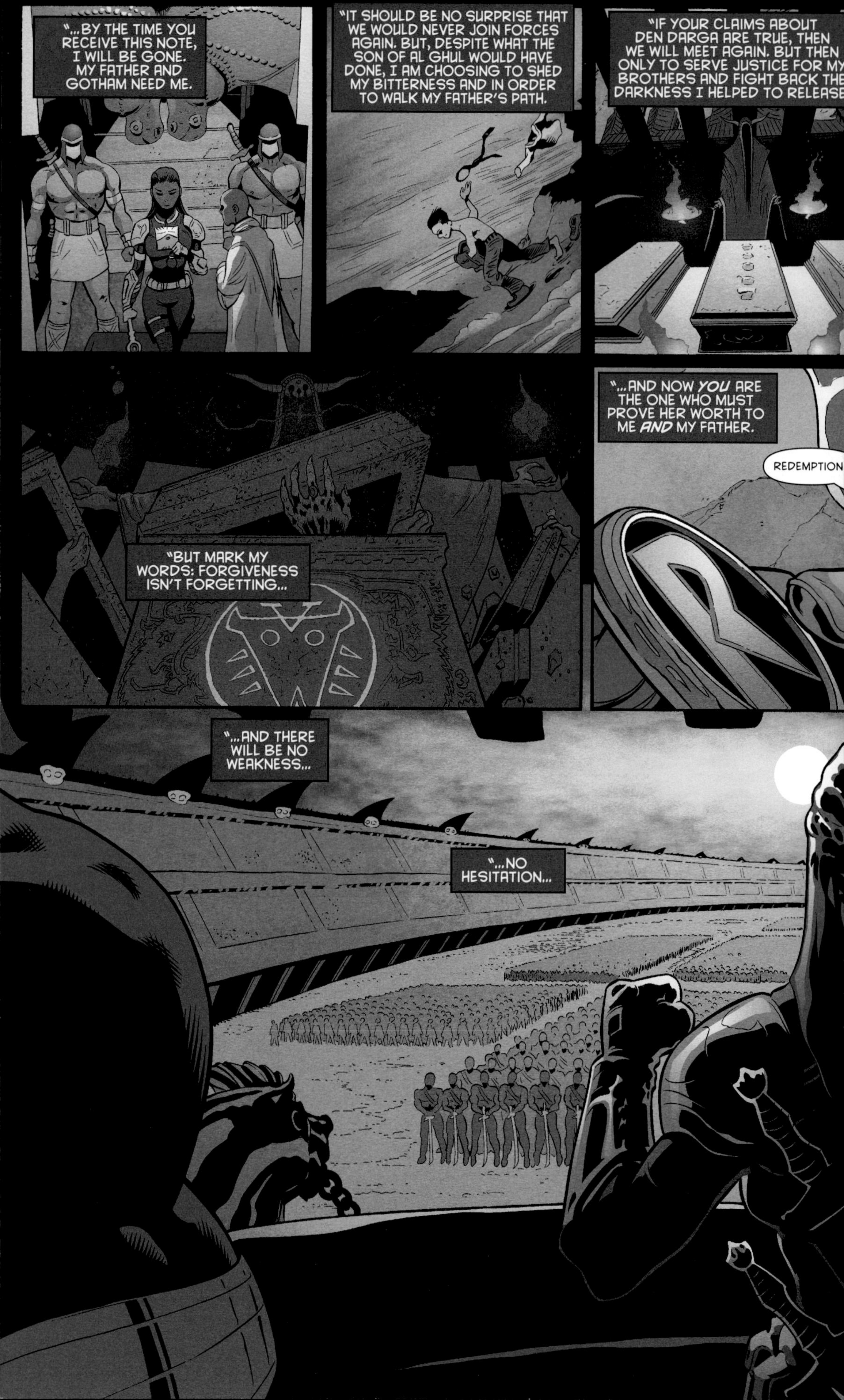
"...BY THE TIME YOU RECEIVE THIS NOTE, I WILL BE GONE. MY FATHER AND GOTHAM NEED ME.
"IT SHOULD BE NO SURPRISE THAT WE WOULD NEVER JOIN FORCES AGAIN. BUT, DESPITE WHAT THE SON OF AL GHUL WOULD HAVE DONE, I AM CHOOSING TO SHED MY BITTERNESS AND IN ORDER TO WALK MY FATHER'S PATH.
"IF YOUR CLAIMS ABOUT DEN DARGA ARE TRUE, THEN WE WILL MEET AGAIN. BUT THEN ONLY TO SERVE JUSTICE FOR MY BROTHERS AND FIGHT BACK THE DARKNESS I HELPED TO RELEASE.
"BUT MARK MY WORDS: FORGIVENESS ISN'T FORGETTING...
"...AND NOW YOU ARE THE ONE WHO MUST PROVE HER WORTH TO ME AND MY FATHER.
REDEMPTION
"...AND THERE WILL BE NO WEAKNESS...
"...NO HESITATION...

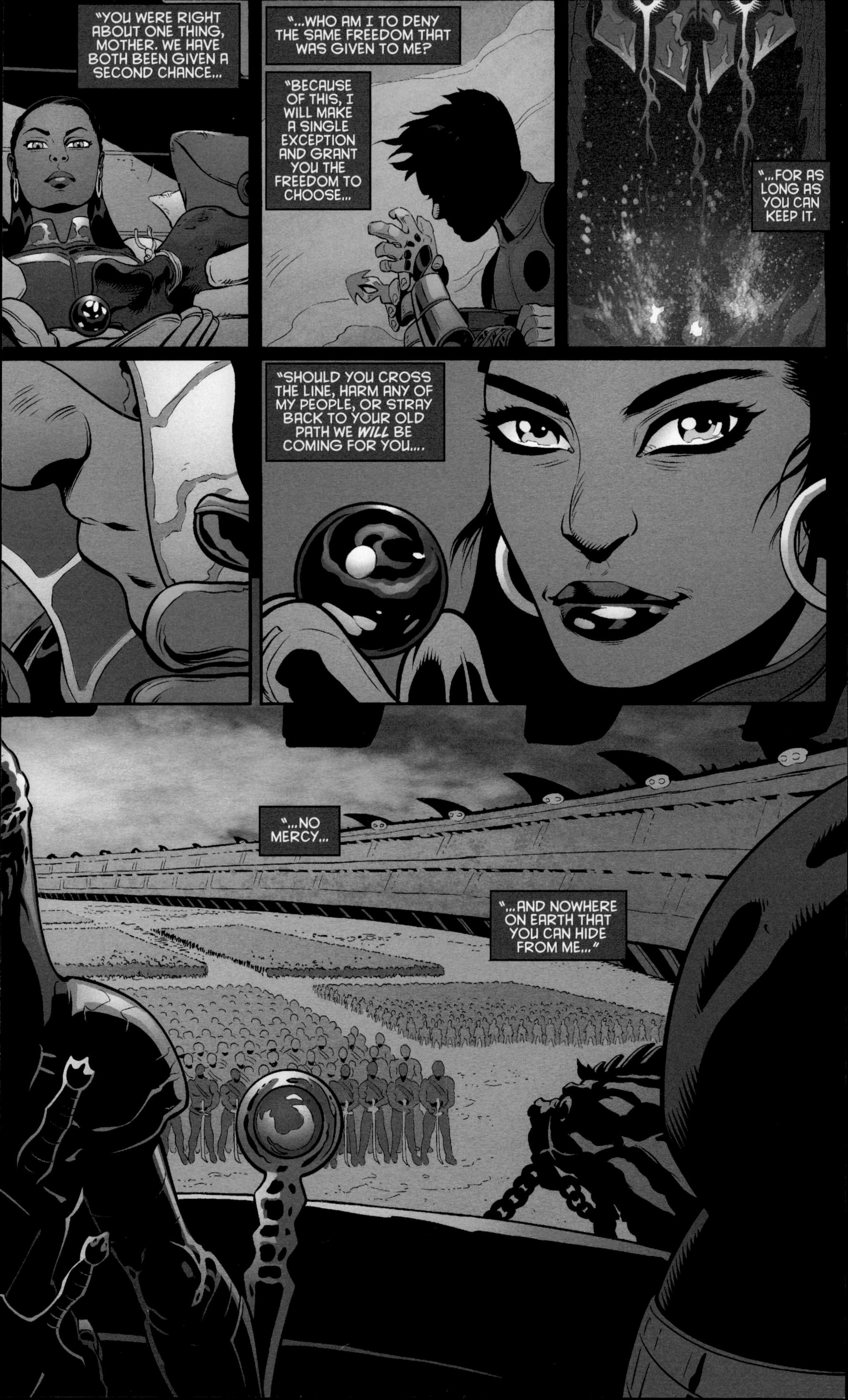
"YOU WERE RIGHT ABOUT ONE THING, MOTHER. WE HAVE BOTH BEEN GIVEN A SECOND CHANCE...
"...WHO AM I TO DENY THE SAME FREEDOM THAT WAS GIVEN TO ME?
"BECAUSE OF THIS, I WILL MAKE A SINGLE EXCEPTION AND GRANT YOU THE FREEDOM TO CHOOSE...
"...FOR AS LONG AS YOU CAN KEEP IT.
"SHOULD YOU CROSS THE LINE, HARM ANY OF MY PEOPLE, OR STRAY BACK TO YOUR OLD PATH WE *WILL* BE COMING FOR YOU....
"...NO MERCY...
"...AND NOWHERE ON EARTH THAT YOU CAN HIDE FROM ME..."

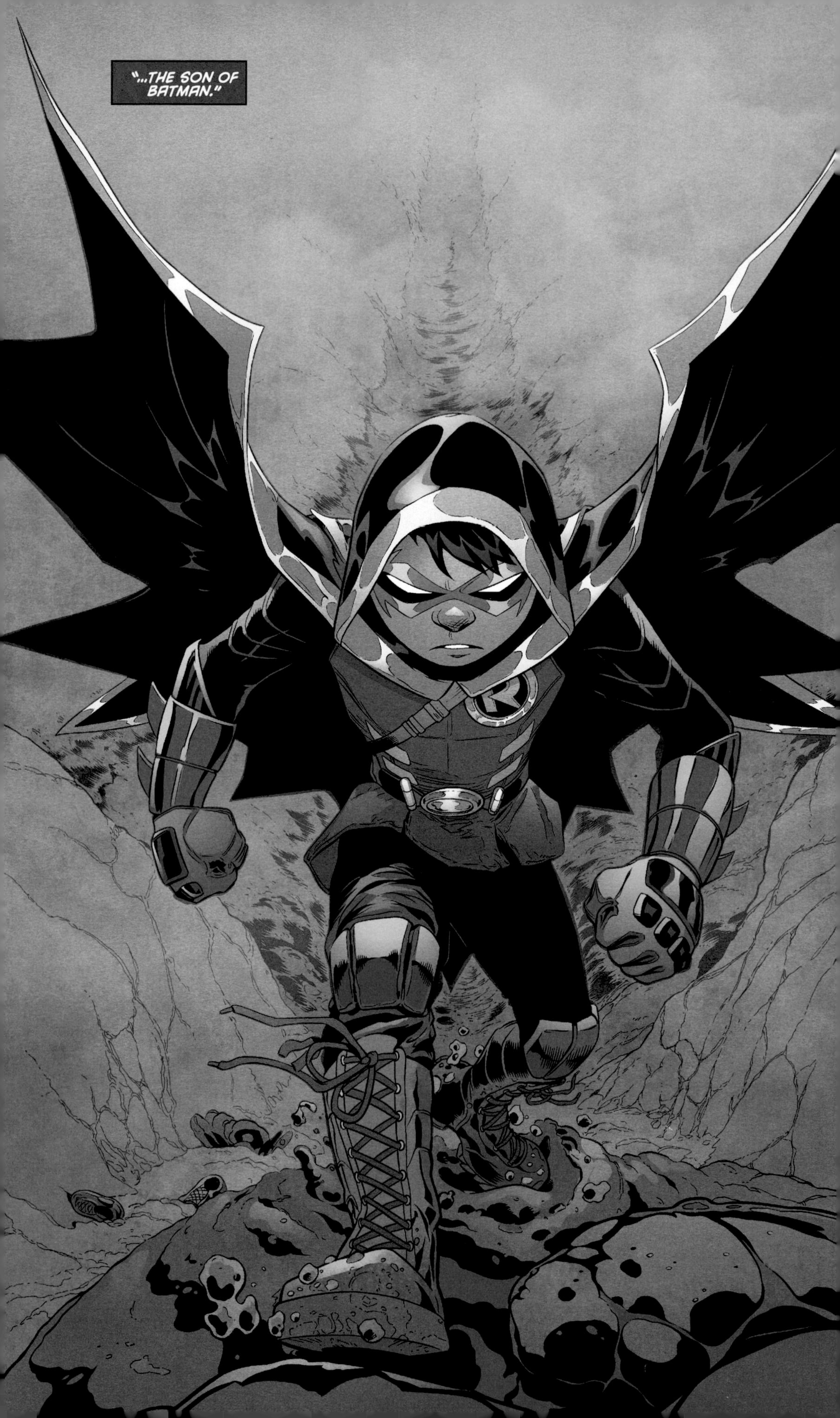
"...THE SON OF BATMAN."

VARIANT COVER GALLERY

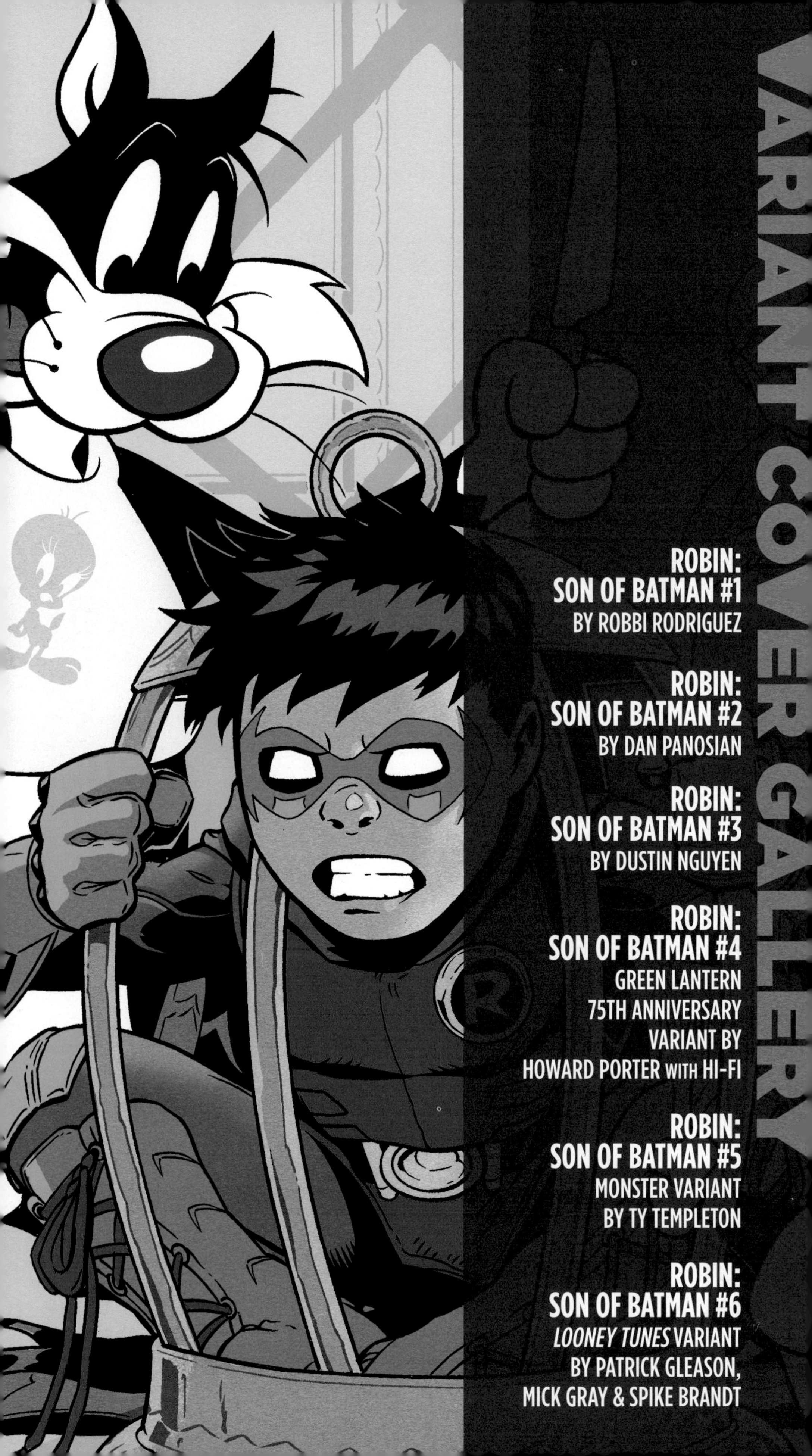

ROBIN: SON OF BATMAN #1
BY ROBBI RODRIGUEZ

ROBIN: SON OF BATMAN #2
BY DAN PANOSIAN

ROBIN: SON OF BATMAN #3
BY DUSTIN NGUYEN

ROBIN: SON OF BATMAN #4
GREEN LANTERN 75TH ANNIVERSARY VARIANT BY HOWARD PORTER WITH HI-FI

ROBIN: SON OF BATMAN #5
MONSTER VARIANT BY TY TEMPLETON

ROBIN: SON OF BATMAN #6
LOONEY TUNES VARIANT BY PATRICK GLEASON, MICK GRAY & SPIKE BRANDT

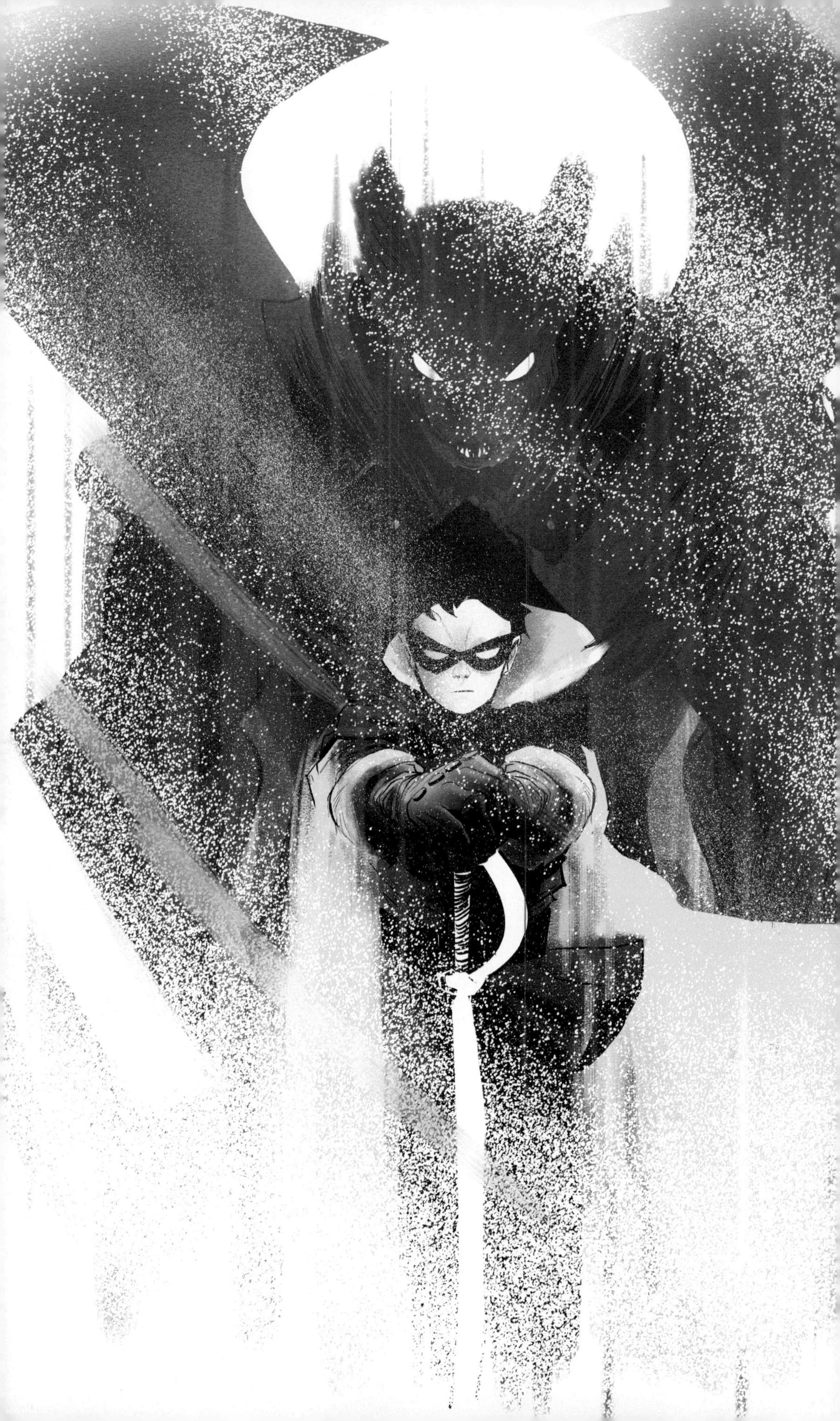

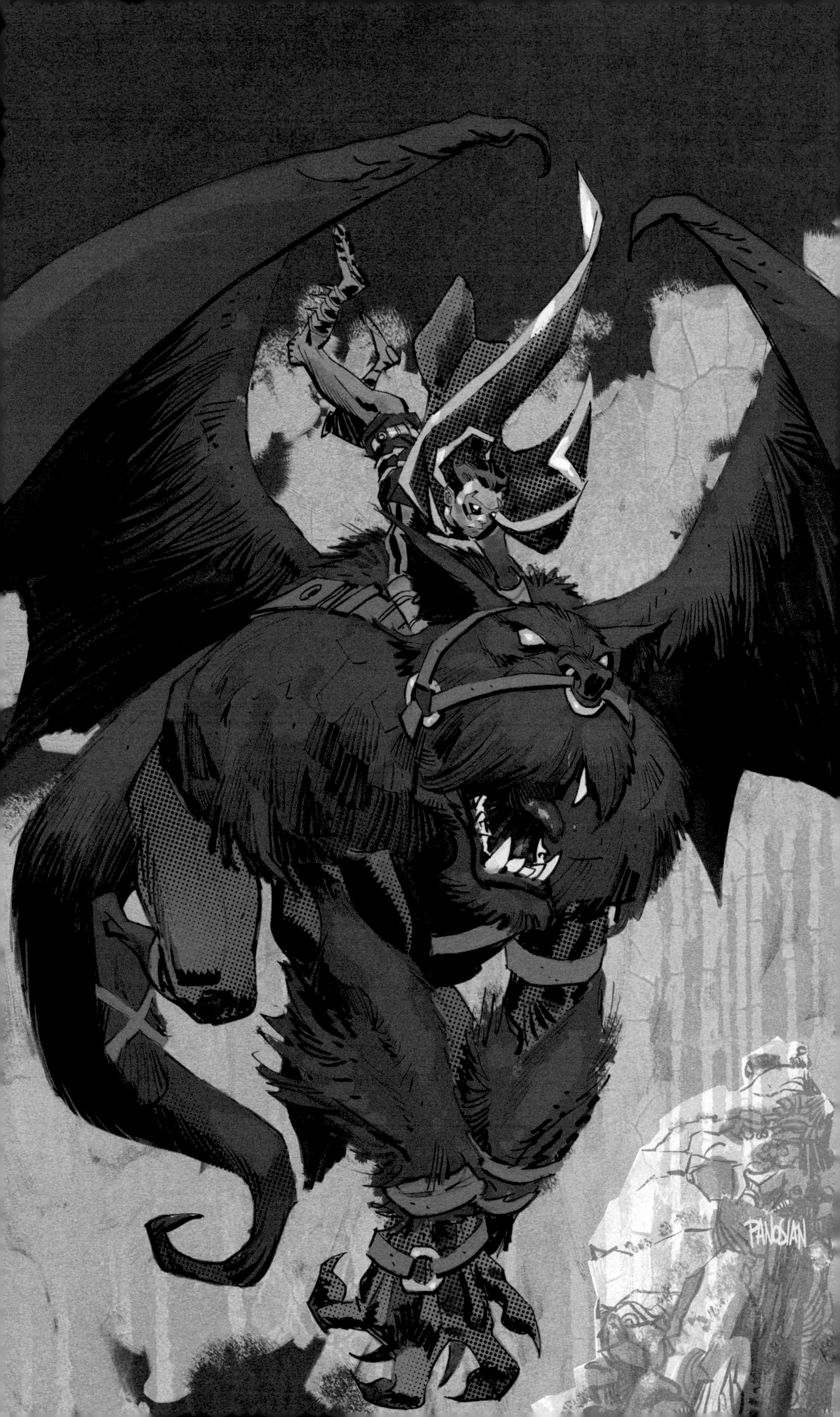
PANOSIAN

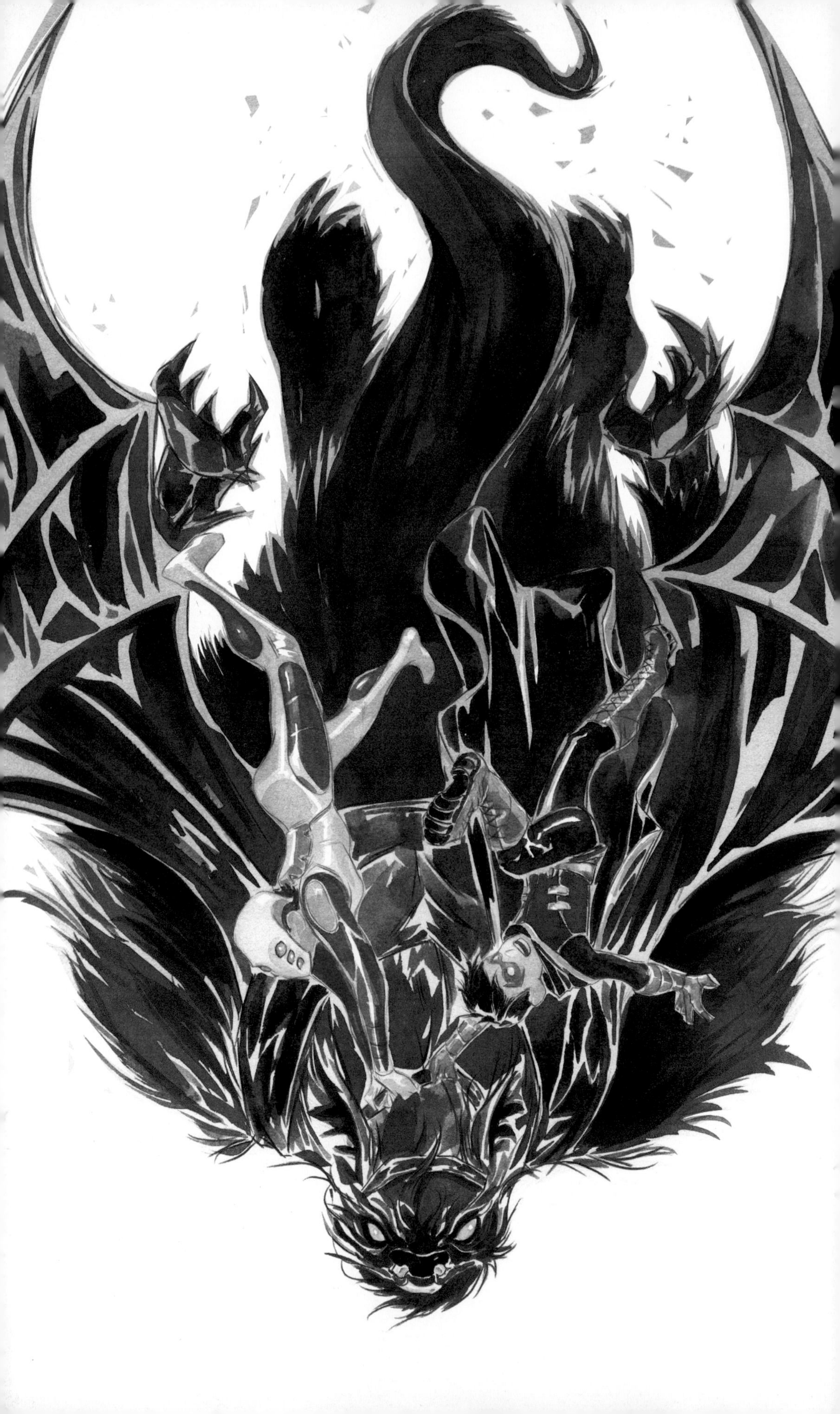

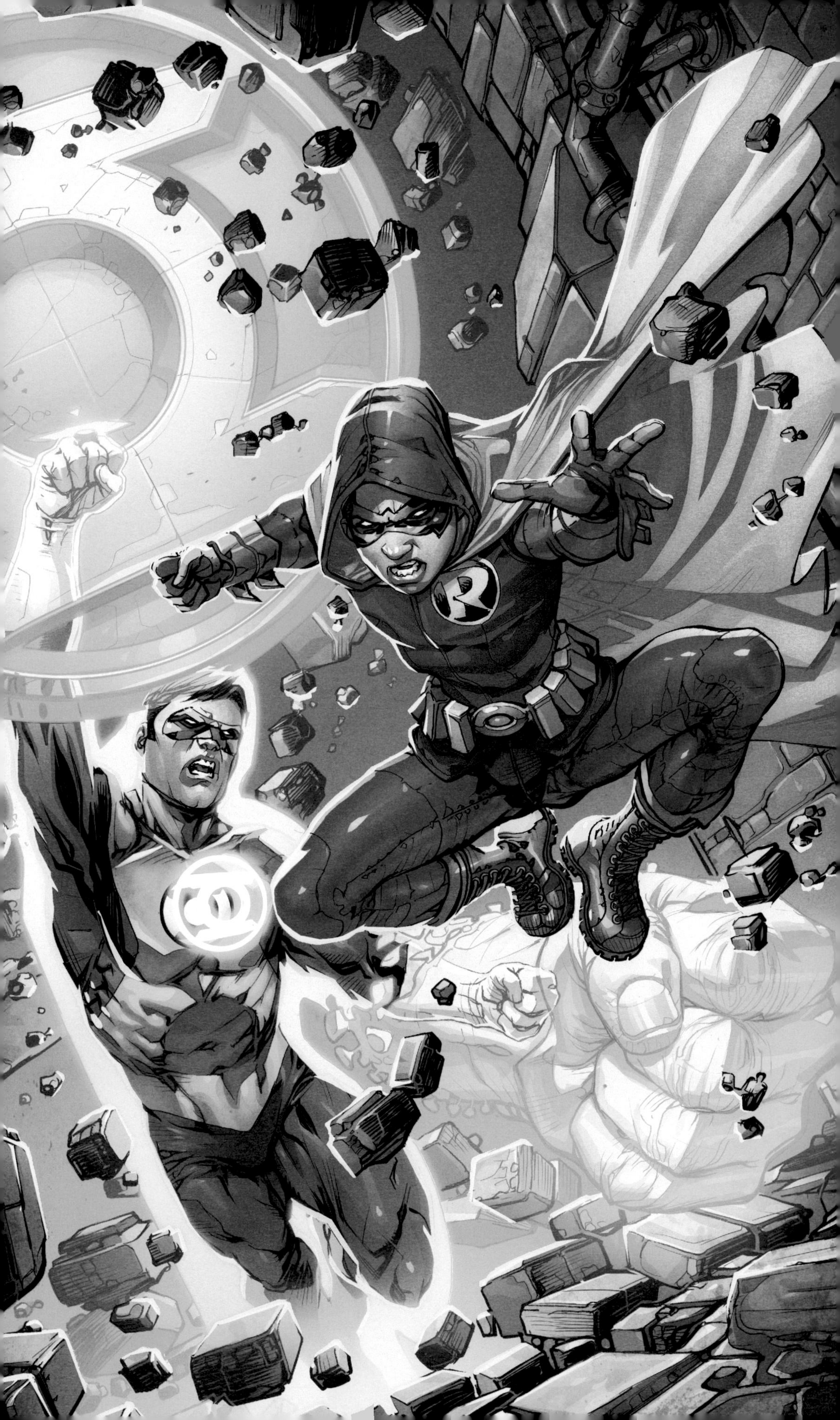

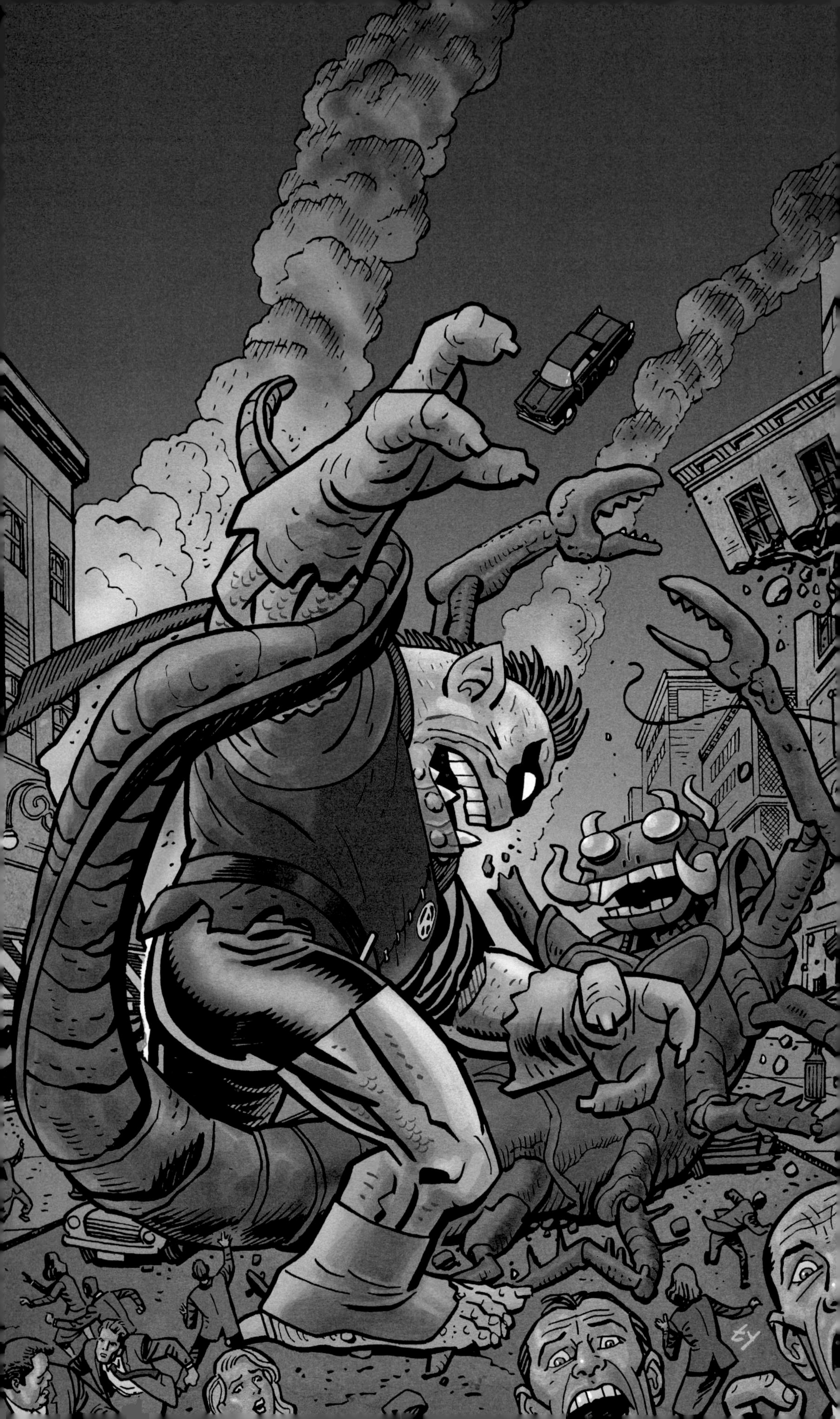

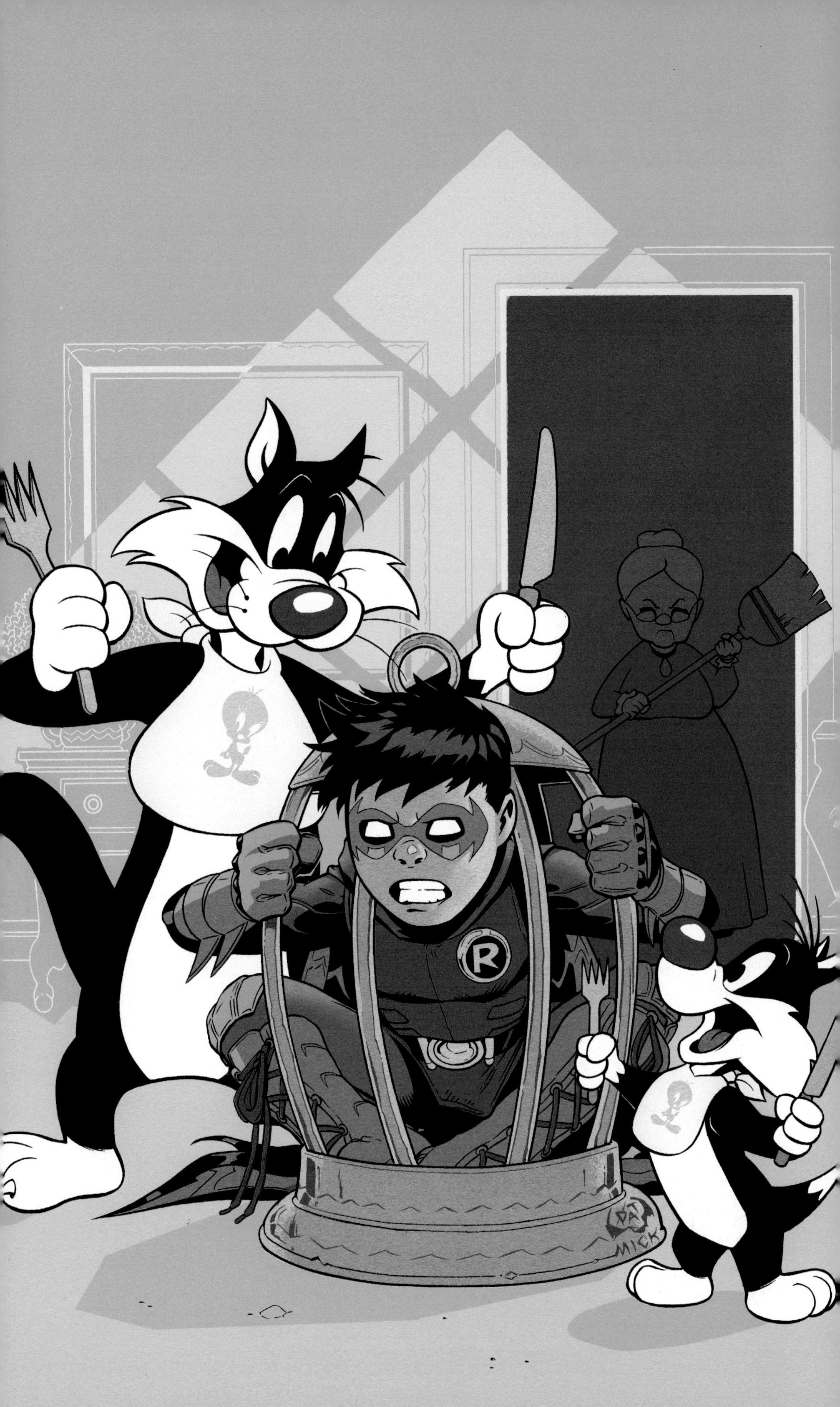

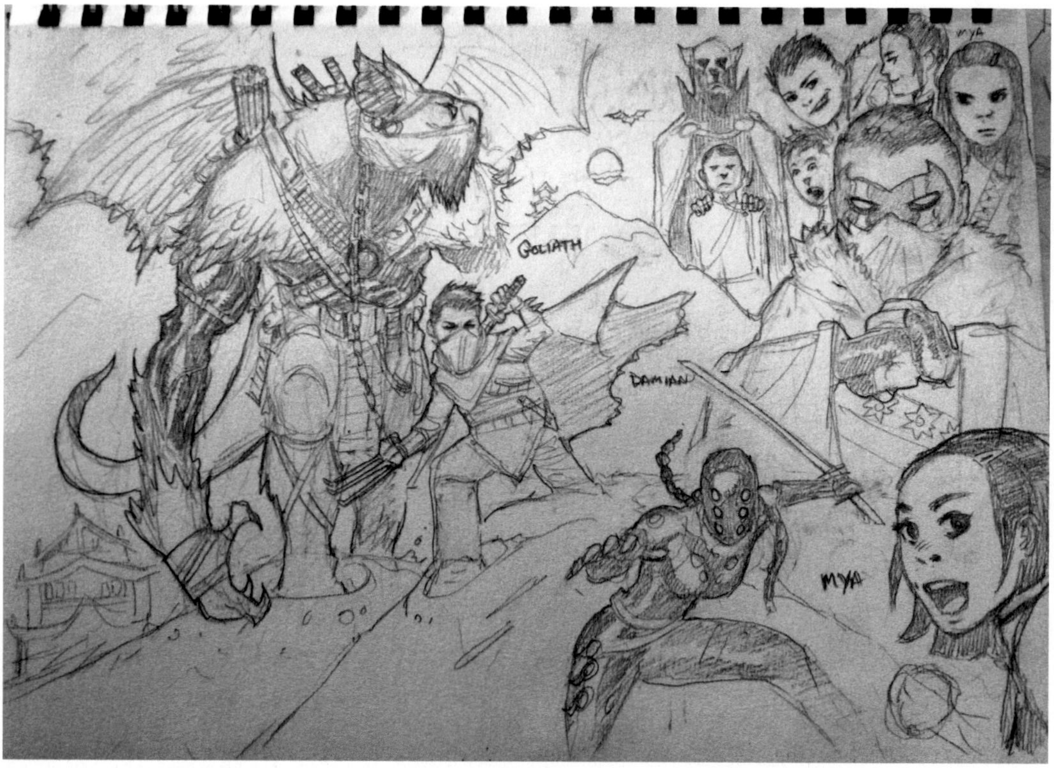
MYA
GOLIATH
DAMIAN
MYA

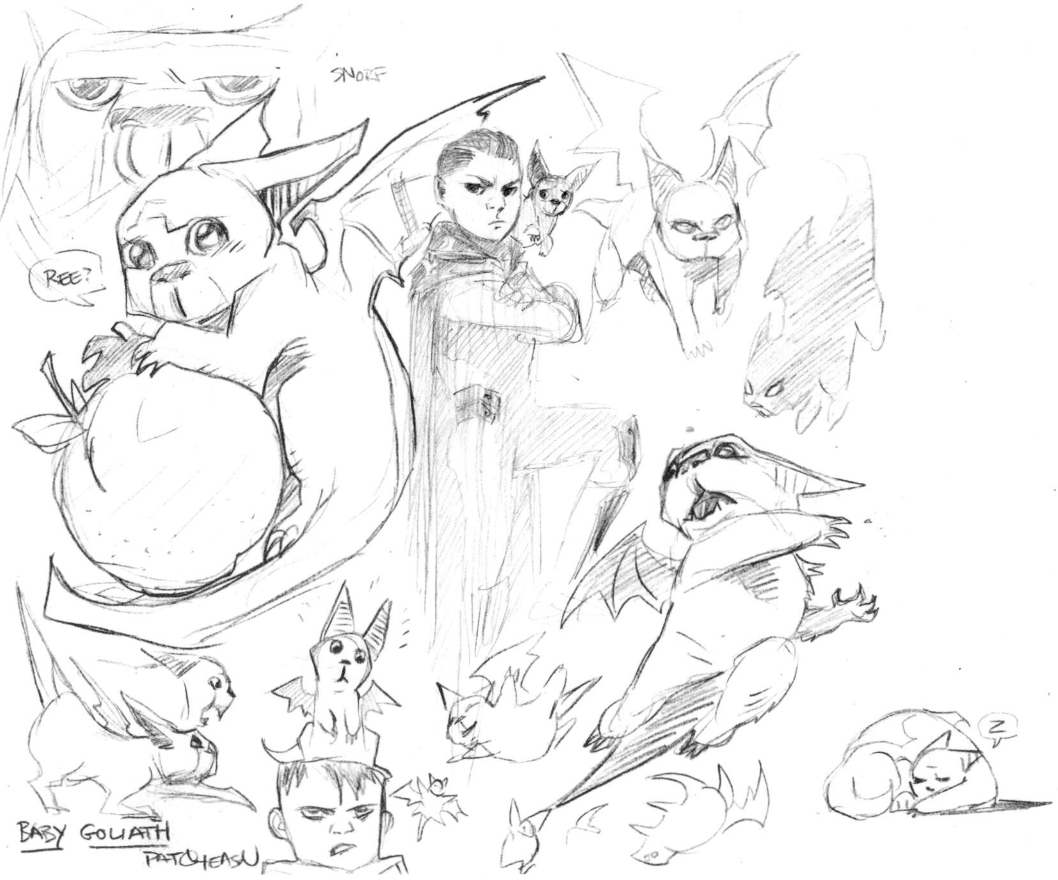
SNORF
REE?
BABY GOLIATH
PATCHEASN

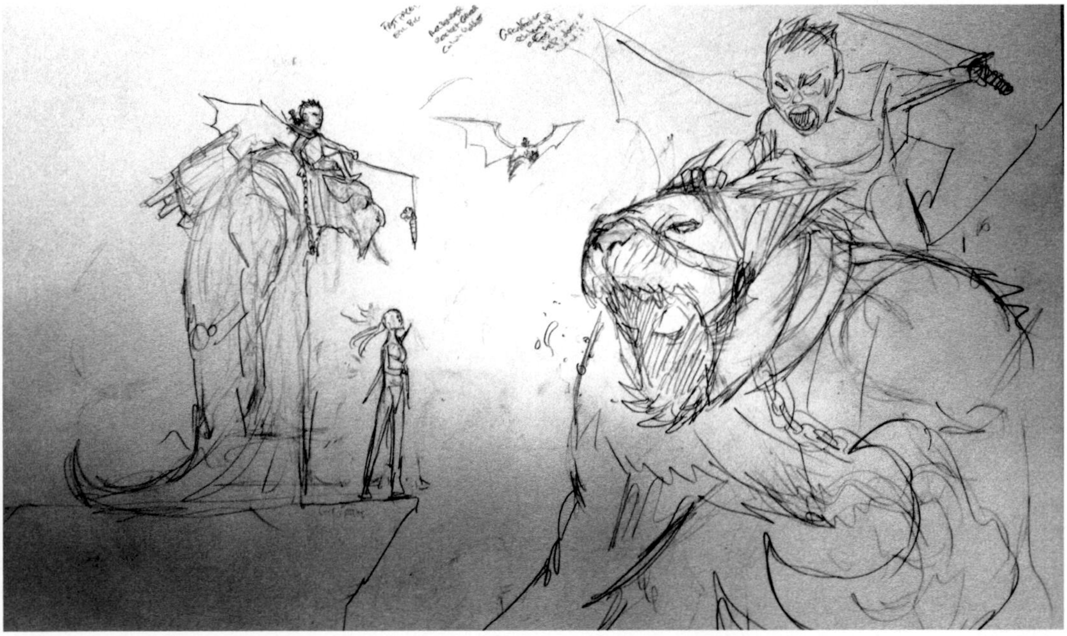

DAMIAN & GOLIATH

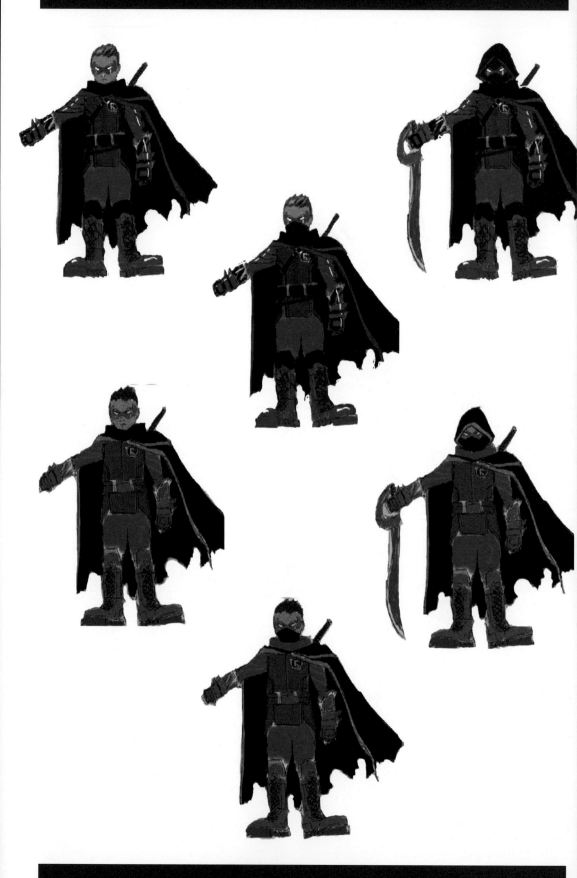

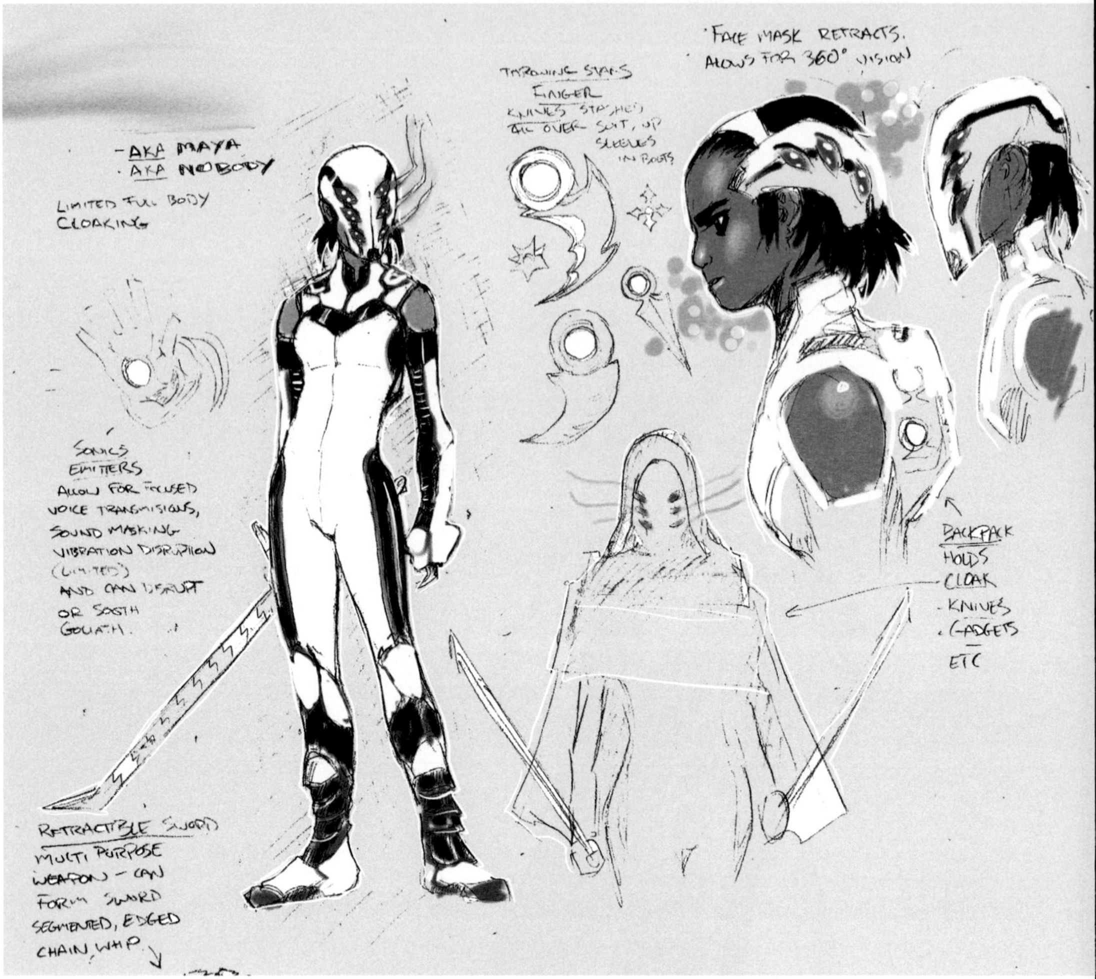

-AKA MAYA
-AKA NOBODY
LIMITED FULL BODY CLOAKING
SONICS EMITTERS ALLOW FOR FOCUSED VOICE TRANSMISIONS, SOUND MASKING VIBRATION DISRUPTION (LIMITED) AND CAN DISRUPT OR SOOTH GOLIATH.
RETRACTIBLE SWORD MULTI PURPOSE WEAPON - CAN FORM SWORD SEGMENTED, EDGED CHAIN, WHIP.
THROWING STARS FINGER KNIVES STASHED ALL OVER SUIT, UP SLEEVES IN BOOTS
FACE MASK RETRACTS. ALLOWS FOR 360° VISION
BACKPACK HOLDS
- CLOAK
- KNIVES
- GADGETS
- ETC

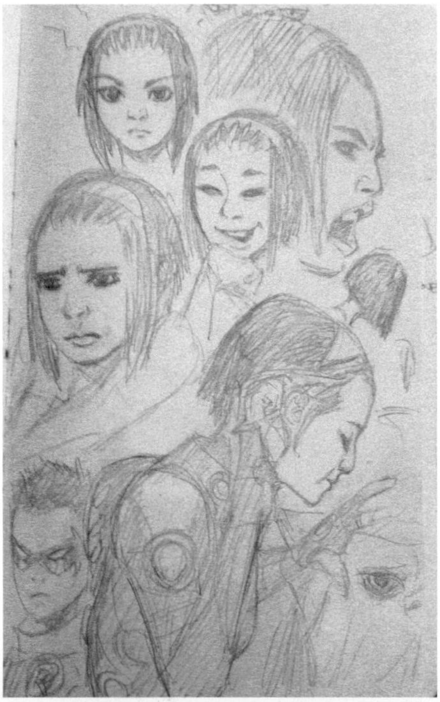

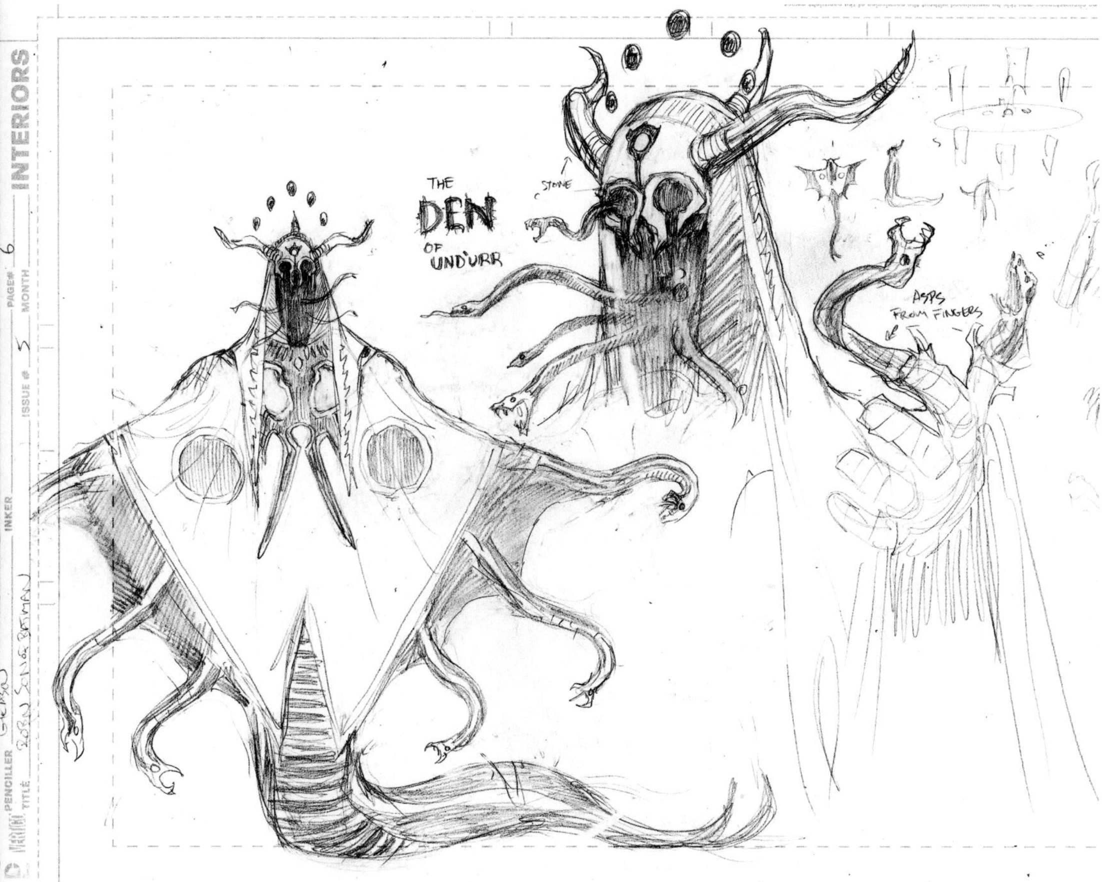
INTERIORS
PAGE# 6
ISSUE# 5
PENCILLER
INKER
MONTH
TITLE ROBIN SON OF BATMAN
THE
DEN
OF
UND'URR
STONE
ASPS
FROM FINGERS

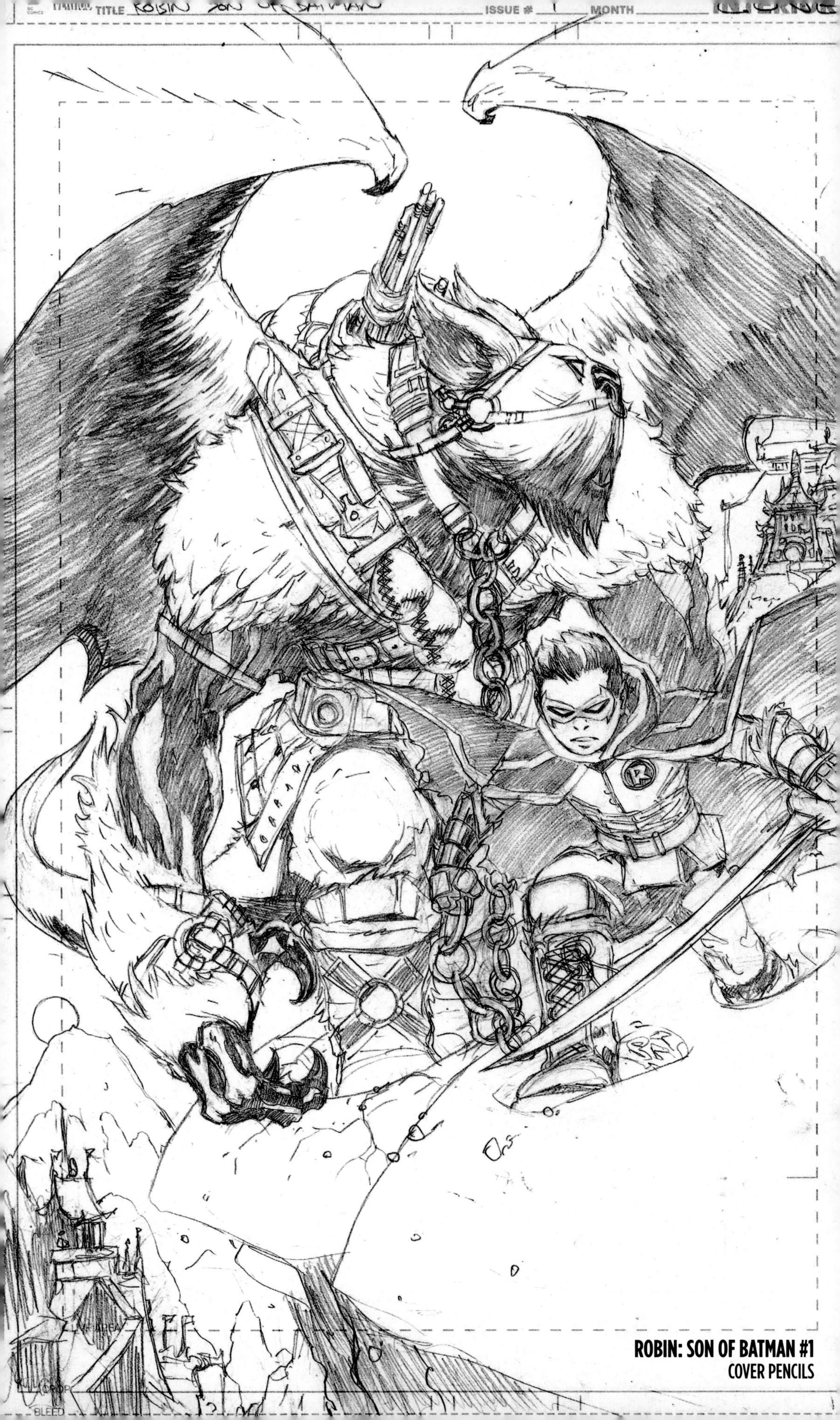
TITLE
ISSUE #
MONTH
BLEED

ROBIN: SON OF BATMAN #1
COVER PENCILS

ROBIN: SON OF BATMAN #6
UNUSED COVER SKETCH

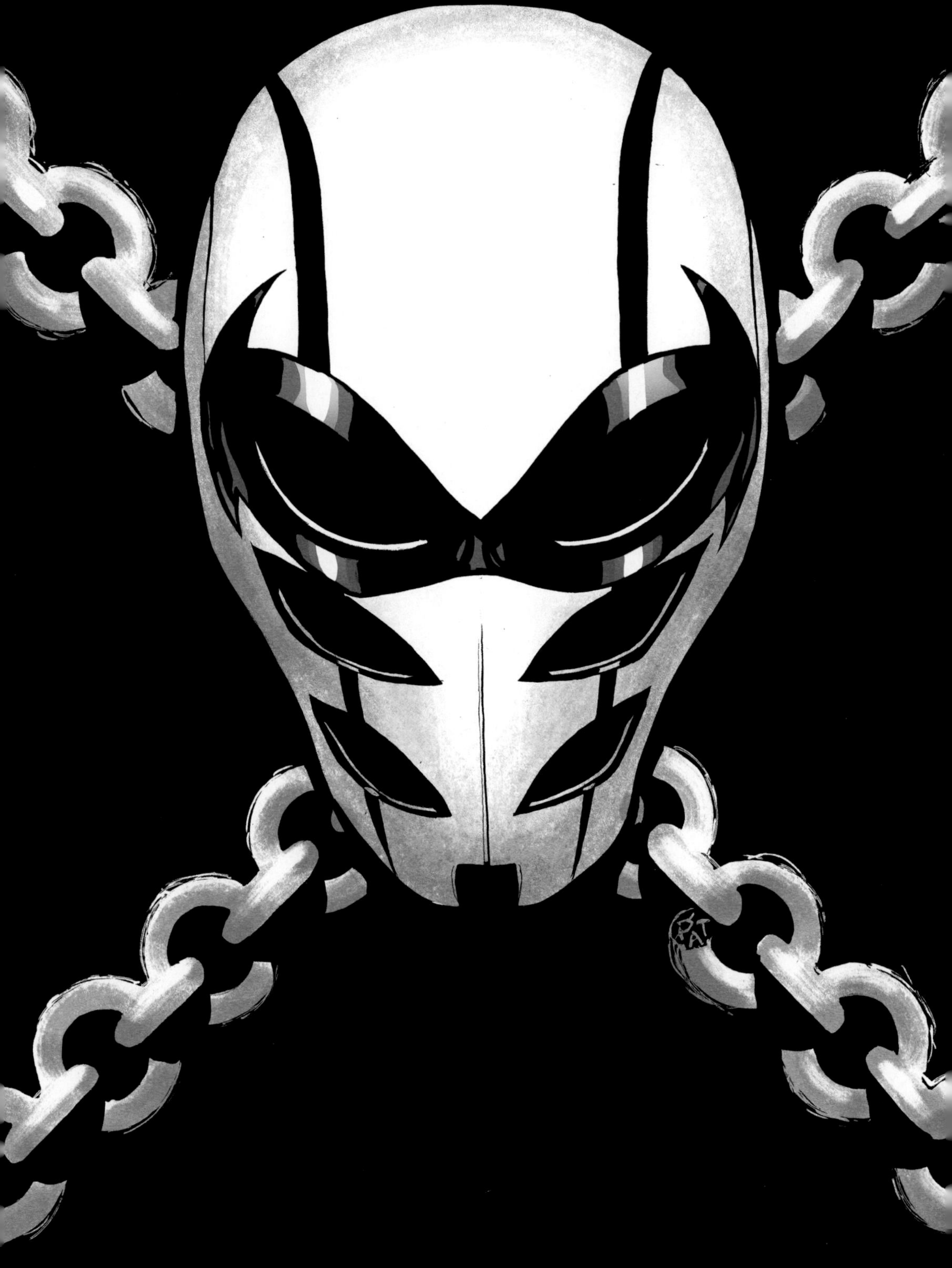
PAT

ROBIN: SON OF BATMAN #3
PAGE 10 PENCILS

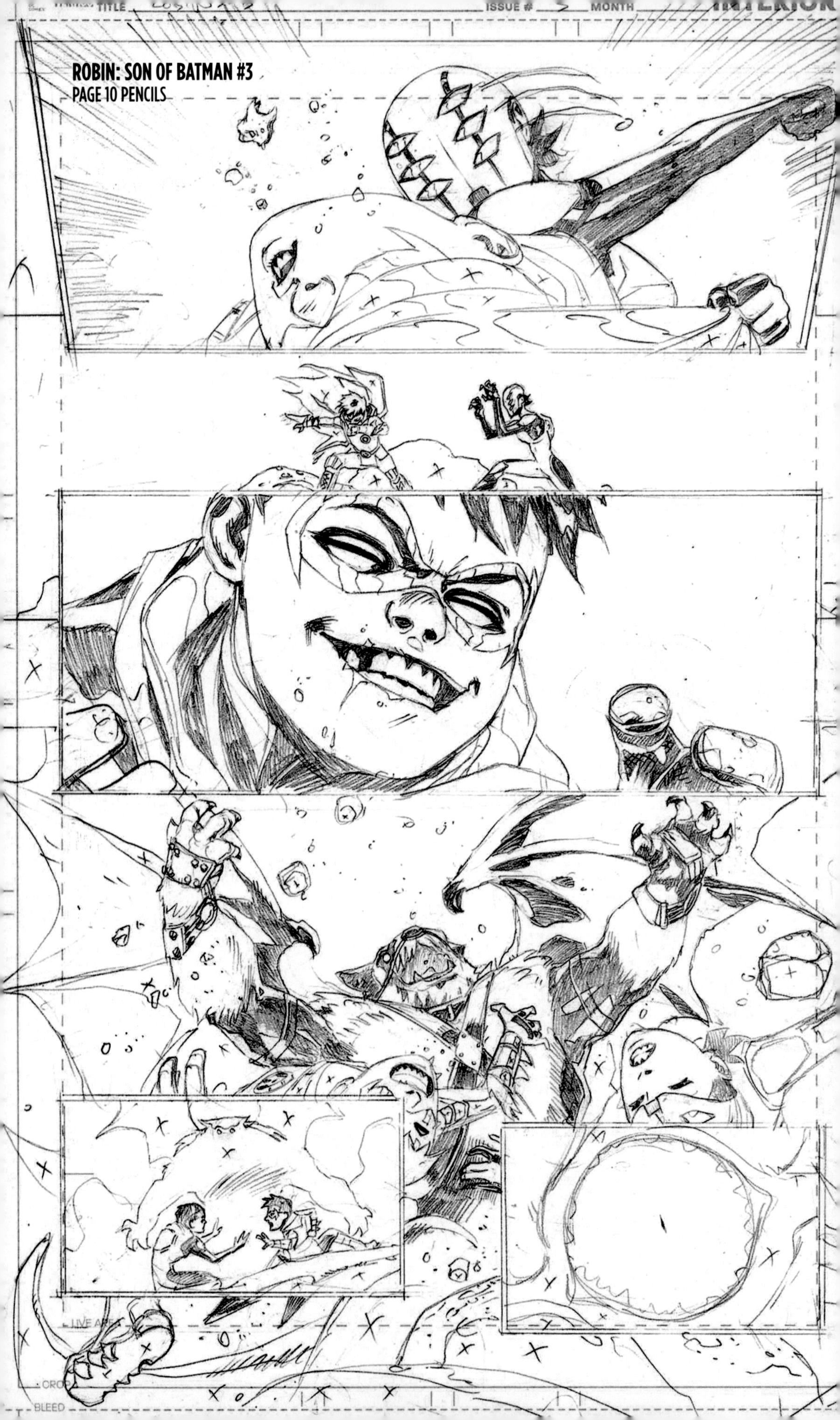
TITLE
ISSUE #
MONTH
CROP
BLEED

ROBIN: SON OF BATMAN #4
PAGE 15 PENCILS

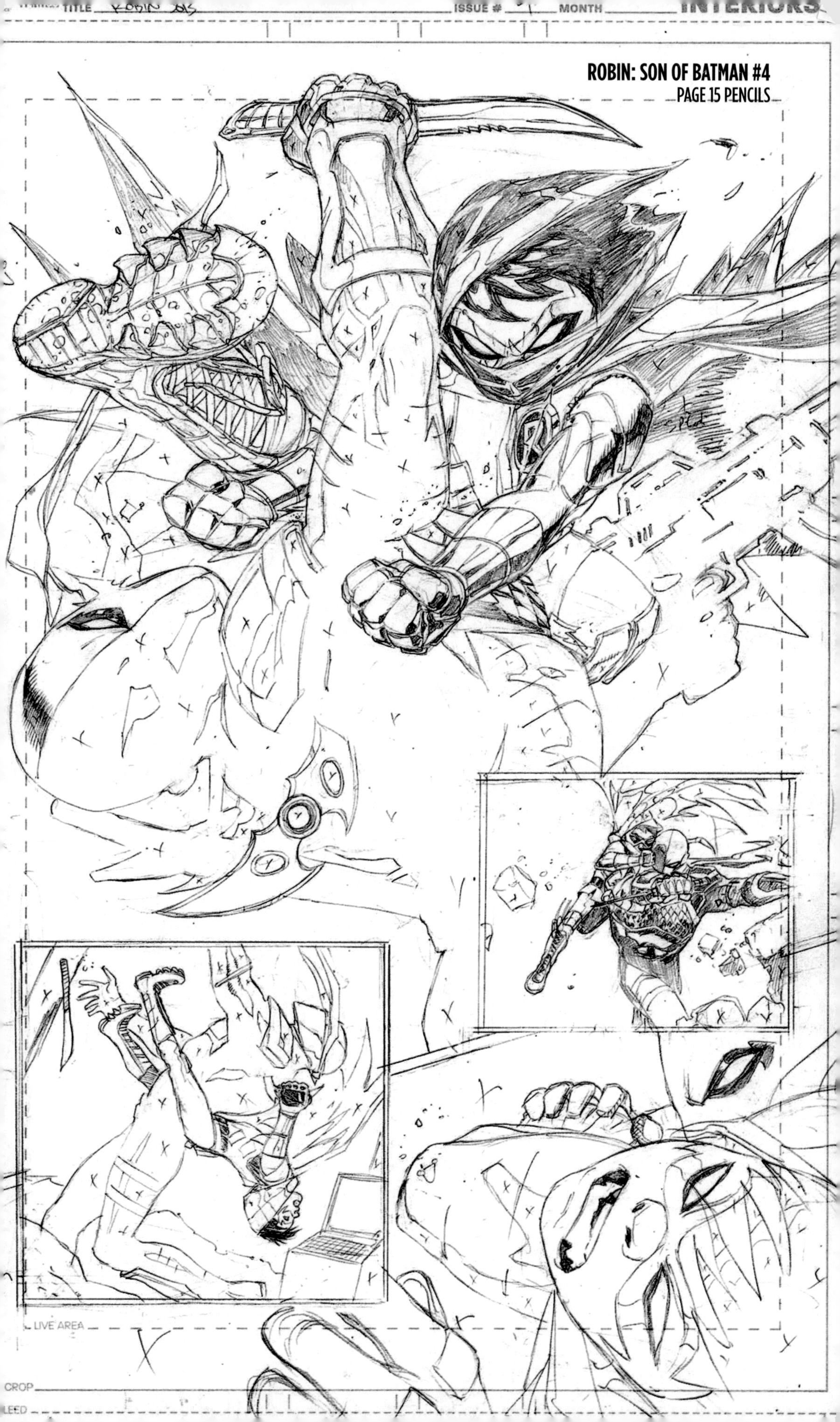

ROBIN: SON OF BATMAN #5
PAGE 16 PENCILS

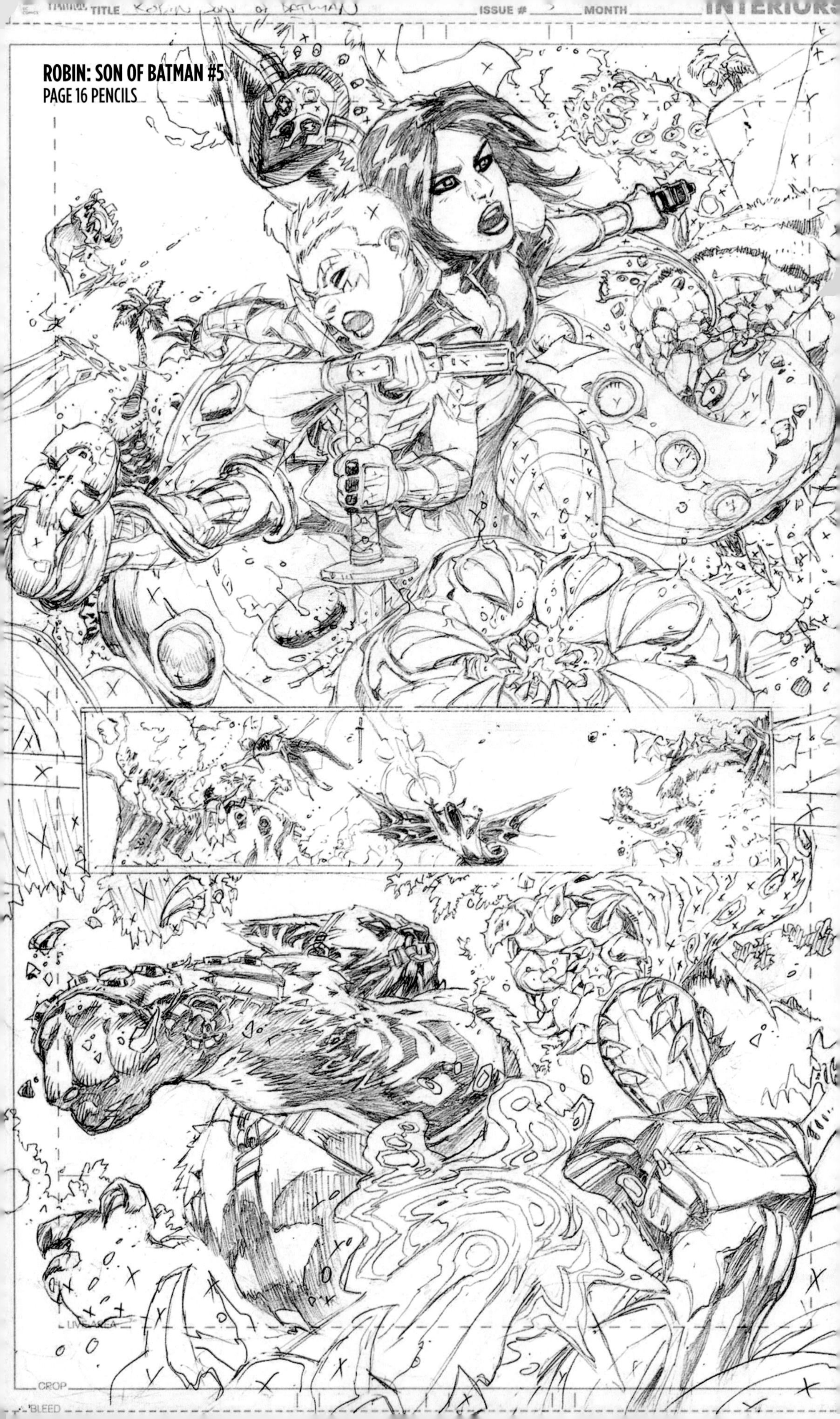
TITLE
ISSUE #
MONTH
INTERIORS
LIVE AREA
CROP
BLEED

TITLE Robin Son of Batman ISSUE # 6 MONTH INTERIORS

ROBIN: SON OF BATMAN #6
PAGE 15 PENCILS

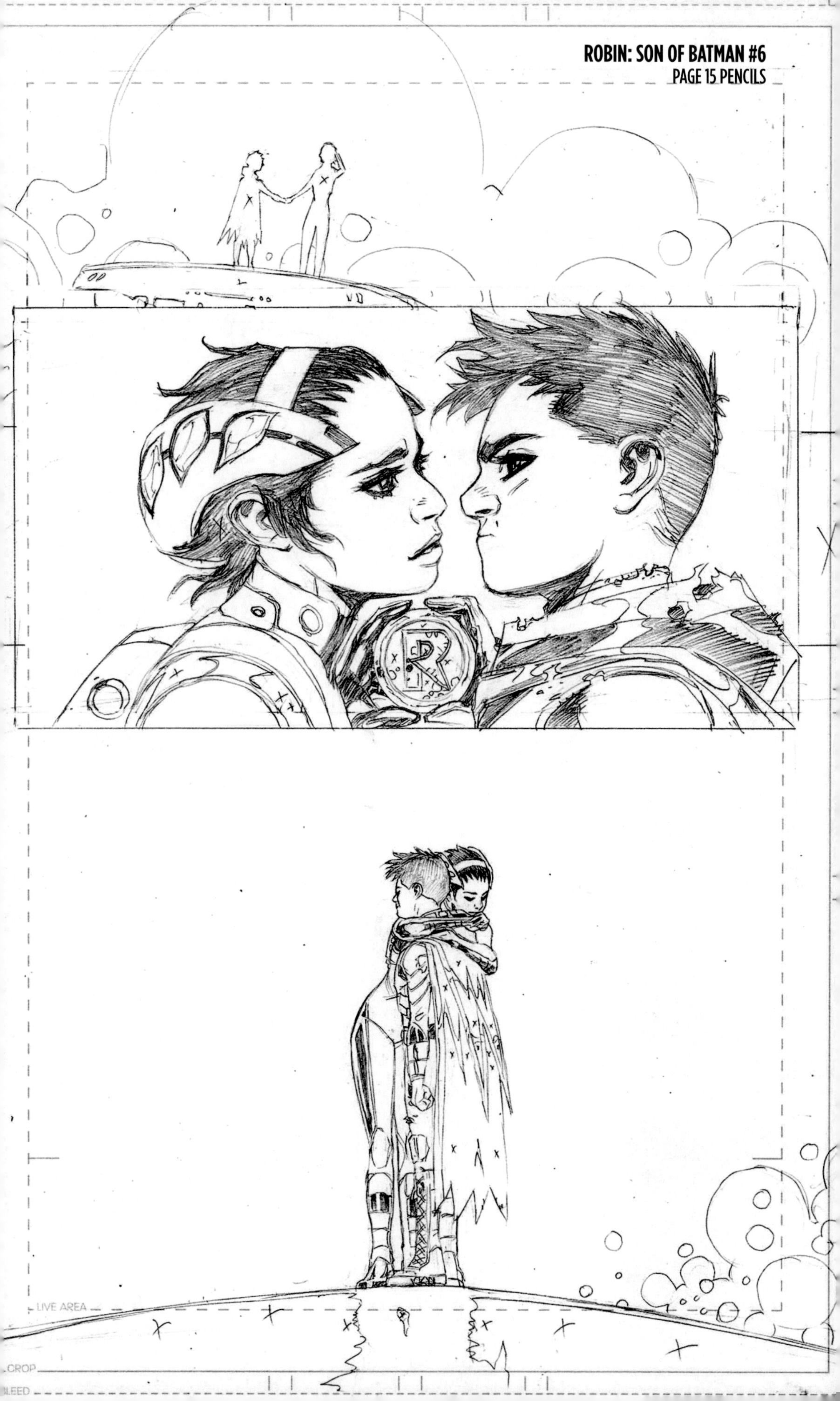
LIVE AREA
CROP
BLEED

"Brilliantly executed.
—IG[

"Morrison and Quitely have the magic touc
that makes any book they collaborate on stan
out from the rest." —MTV's Splash Pag[

"Thrilling and invigorating....Gotham City that ha
never looked this good, felt this strange, or bee
this deadly." —COMIC BOOK RESOURCE[

GRANT MORRISON
with FRANK QUITELY & PHILIP TAN

VOL. 2:
BATMAN VS. ROBIN

VOL. 3: BATMAN &
ROBIN MUST DIE!

DARK KNIGHT VS.
WHITE KNIGHT

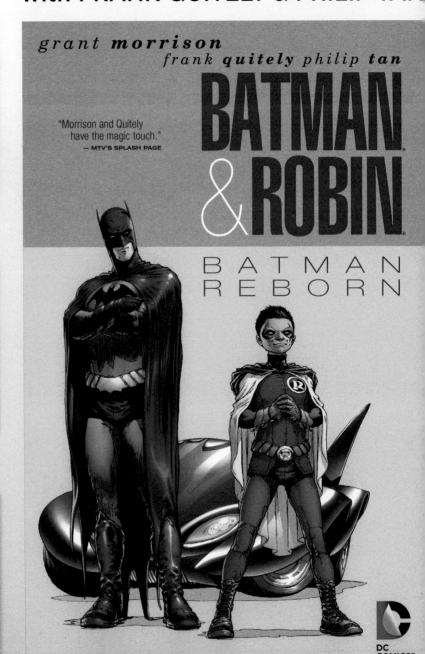

grant morrison
frank quitely philip tan

BATMAN & ROBIN

BATMAN REBORN

"Morrison and Quitely
have the magic touch."
— MTV'S SPLASH PAGE